MARKING A TRAIL

A History of the Texas Woman's University

By Joyce Thompson
Design by Jennifer H. Collins

Texas Woman's University Press
Denton, Texas

First published by TWU Press 1982
First printing

Copyright © 1982
Library of Congress Cataloging in Publication Data

Thompson, Joyce, 1943-
  Marking a trail.

  Includes bibliographical references and index.
    1. Texas Woman's University—History.
I. Title.
LD7251.D44T47   378.764'555   81-23391
ISBN 0-9607488-0-6   AACR2
ISBN 0-9607488-1-4 (pbk.)

for all the girls

    and women

        in the

            long chambray line

Acknowledgments

My very special thanks go to President Mary Evelyn Blagg Huey, who gave the initial impetus to the history-writing project and who has supported the work since its beginning with warm enthusiasm.

Others who have worked steadily with me include Phyllis Bridges, who offered daily encouragement and help; Mary Ann McDuff, who provided major assistance with the research; and Charles Bruce, Dorothy DeMoss, Martha Mitchell, Kitty Magee, and Elizabeth Snapp, who read the chapters as they developed and provided helpful suggestions regarding style and content. Other readers and advisers included Toni LaSelle, Brooke Sheldon, Betty Alford, Catherine Cloud Edwards, Vada Frances Hale, Janie Foster Fletcher, and Elizabeth Lomax. I am deeply grateful for the interest and assistance of each of these people.

The staff of the TWU Library has been unfailingly helpful in checking details and making the resources of the Library available in a most generous manner. My thanks go to Donna Dean, Mickey Dudley, Martha Parks, Angela Alford, Jim Galloway, Alice Johnson, Jean Glasgow, John Hepner, Margaret Macdougall, Kathy Lozano, Oleta Ash, William Wan, and again Elizabeth Snapp.

Others to whom I owe a debt for their help in the preparation of the manuscript and in the production of the book include Florence Langford, Jimmie Willis, Kay Rogers, Pat Ahearn, Donna Dean, Sheila Strickland, Pam Reding, Donna Ryan, Bill Benson, Betty Hood, Charlsa Kern, Kathy Fretwell, Su Hulgus, Weldon Church, Kenneth Presley, Bill Harkins, David Reeves, Janet Howe, Sean McCleneghan, Josie Cantu-Weber, Susan Brown, Jennifer Collins, and the families of Presidents Work, Bralley, Blayney, Hubbard, and Huey.

All photographs and illustrations in the book are from the archives and files of the Texas Woman's University unless otherwise identified. The TWU Library, Office of Information, Department of Journalism and Broadcasting, and Alumnae Association have been rich resources. The Carruth Collection was contributed to the Library Special Collections by Mrs. Beth P. Carruth. Others who contributed photographs and other materials to the University's permanent collection in conjunction with this project are Zelma Millar, W.F. and Janiece Harkins, Kitty Magee, Mary Lou Brown, Wallace Woolsey, Audrey Caughey Tittle, Catherine Cloud Edwards, Mabel Saunders, and Lenore Waldrop.

After all, I am keenly aware of dozens of other "unsung saints" who have helped to make this book a reality.

Contents

Before the Beginning

I

In the thirty-six years between the end of the American Civil War and the beginning of a new college for women in Texas, a number of social and economic forces combined to create an environment in which the college could develop. A new emphasis on practicality and on a scientific approach to all of life accompanied the nation's transition from agrarianism to industrialism. Re-evaluating their curricula, established colleges expanded them to encompass new fields of study and revised them to accommodate new needs of society.

New state colleges, made possible by the Morrill Act of 1862, emphasized practical training, especially in agriculture and engineering. Educational opportunities for women grew with the establishment of a number of the private women's colleges in the East and with the admission of women to many of the new state colleges opening in the West.

Industrialization brought both new problems and new hopes for the improvement of the human condition, and reform groups emerged to combat the problems and champion the hopes. Two of these groups in Texas worked a dozen years to secure legislative approval and support for a state industrial college for women, and others joined their struggle.

The State Grange and Patrons of Husbandry led the campaign. At the annual meeting of the Grange in 1889, A.J. Rose, Worthy Master of the organization, recommended the establishment of the college, a recommendation that the group adopted unanimously.

Pointing to the success of Texas A&M in which the first students had enrolled in 1876, Rose pled,

> "Do [girls] not need an industrial college, too, where they can receive a practical education which will prepare them for some vocation in life, in order that they may not work in the cotton fields from necessity. Certainly the State will not do less for her girls than her boys when appealed to. Let the State Grange stretch forth its strong arm in woman's behalf to the next Legislature and ask that an industrial college be provided for girls."

Rose repeated his request in 1890 and 1891, and in 1891 Representative A.J. Baker of San Angelo and Senator A.M. Carter of Fort Worth introduced similar bills to establish a college for women. Baker's bill passed the Senate but failed in the House.[1] The Texas Women's Christian Temperance Union

The College began classes in one building, Old Main.

1

Helen Stoddard, President of the Texas WCTU, led in petitioning the Legislature for a college for women.

(WCTU) joined the campaign in 1893, petitioned the State Legislature to establish a state college of industrial arts for women and repeating its petition each year until the college became a reality.[2] Helen M. Stoddard, President of the State WCTU, outlined some of the reasons for the organization's support in the college bulletin of March, 1907: "It appeared sane and reasonable that a practical knowledge of doing some definite thing well would be the best protection that a parent could give his daughter. . . . A most generous opportunity must be given all worthy young women to acquire a college education. . . ." The group urged the establishment of a state college, she continued, "to make it of the widest possible opportunity and dignity, . . . that the seal of a great commonwealth should be placed upon the sanc[t]ity and dignity of labor." The group envisioned "an institution of broad culture and wide opportunities" that would "attract the wealthy and noble as well as those of the humbler walks, and it must be open only to those young women whose lives are pure and blameless."

Feeling that the legislation already introduced was too narrow in its scope, Mrs. Stoddard redrafted Baker's bill and supplied a copy of her work to Judge V.W. Grubbs, from Greenville, who introduced the bill in the House in 1899.[3] Both houses rejected the new bill, which contained the outline of a curriculum that would include dressmaking, scientific and practical cooking (including a chemical study of food), practical housekeeping, trained nursing (caring for the sick), and a knowledge of the "care and culture of children." These studies, which went beyond the usual industrial requirements, would make the college unique.

In 1900, upon the urging of Grubbs and others, the Democratic Party adopted a plank favoring the establishment of a girls' college, and the following year Representatives O.C. Mulkey and William Pearson and Senators E.W. Harris and Barry Miller successfully introduced a bill much like the 1899 version. The passage of the bill was the narrowest possible victory, however. Both houses cast tie votes, leaving the deciding affirmative vote to come from the presiding officer of each body. Governor Joseph D. Sayers signed the bill into law on April 6, 1901, creating the "Texas Industrial Institute and College for the Education of the White Girls of the State of Texas in Arts and Sciences."

With the College authorized and funds appropriated, the Governor appointed a commission to visit towns and cities throughout the state to select a location for the new institution.[4] In October the group met to organize. Then in January the commission visited San Antonio, Austin, Taylor, College Station, Waco, Walnut Springs, Dublin, Hillsboro, Denton, Amarillo, Greenville, Terrell, Jefferson, and Huntsville. A.P. Wooldridge,

The locating commission which selected Denton as the site of the College consisted of Rosser Thomas, J. H. Rowell, Dr. J. B. Roberts, George H. Pfeuffer, W. L. Radney (back row, left to right) and J. E. Hooper, E. A. Atlee, W. D. Cleveland, R. T. Milner, Helen M. Stoddard, A. P. Wooldridge, O. B. Colquitt, and J. M. Moore, who is not pictured. Photo courtesy Lenore Waldrop, who received it from the daughter of J. E. Hooper.

vice-president of the commission, later related how the group "went up and down throughout Texas, spying out the land and discriminating the ultimate choice." After making a number of visits, the commission arrived in Denton in a fierce and demoralizing sand and windstorm, which residents assured the group was "absolutely phenomenal." Mrs. W.A. Ponder, President of the Woman's Shakespeare Club of Denton, received the commission in her home. The club depleted its treasury and assessed an additional charge of fifteen cents per member to finance the reception. The local entertainment of the committee was sober, however, because the local citizens were sure the storm had doomed their chances of securing the College.

On February 3, following much debate and seventy-six votes, the commission chose Denton. Denton citizens had promised a tract of about seventy acres of choice land and a cash bonus of $16,500 raised by individual subscription among interested citizens of Denton.[5] They also agreed to dig a six-inch artesian well on the grounds to guarantee an abundant water supply. Nevertheless, Wooldridge said matters of convenience and healthfulness were more important to the decision than were the bonuses.[6]

Early college bulletins describe some of the conditions which made Denton a desirable location. The situation of the town "in a healthful, prosperous, agricultural region" made it attractive; and about five thousand people lived in the "city of good homes, intelligent people, and an elevating moral and social atmosphere." In addition to noting that "good drainage" made the town "one of the most healthful locations in Texas," college bulletins praised Denton as "a clean town morally. There are no saloons here. It is a place of Christian homes, churches, fine social atmosphere, and is permeated with a progressive educational spirit." It was also a point of pride that Andrew Carnegie had recently given $10,000 for a public town library, one of the thousands of free circulating libraries the philanthropist helped establish.

In the northeast part of Denton, lay the land which would become the campus of the new college, a tract described in the first annual report of the Board of Regents to Governor Sayers as

> beautifully situated, gently rolling to the south and west, and commanding an exceptionally fine view of the town and surrounding country. Most of the soil is fertile, and the larger portion of the tract is in excellent state of cultivation, and there are valuable permanent improvements upon the grounds. . . . The northeastern portion of the tract is beautifully wooded.

With the site chosen, Governor Sayers appointed the first Board of Regents in early April.[7] At its first meeting, the Board elected A.P. Wooldridge of Austin, president; Mary Eleanor Brackenridge of San Antonio, vice-president; Helen M. Stoddard of Fort Worth, secretary; and John A. Hann of Denton, treasurer. Other original members of the Board were Mrs. Cone Johnson of Tyler, Rosser Thomas of Bonham, and Clarence Ousley of Fort Worth. The San Antonio *Daily Express* noted on June 12, 1904, that the women were the first women to be appointed regents of a Texas institution and praised them for accepting the responsibility "with no other object than to benefit the girls of Texas."

Moving quickly, the Board invited architects to furnish plans and specifications for a college building which could be occupied immediately upon completion but which could be expanded to accommodate growing needs. The Board selected the plans of Dodson and Scott of Waco on

Judge V. W. Grubbs urged the Democratic Party to adopt a platform in 1900 which favored the establishment of a girls' college.

3

July 1. The plan specified a "neat, substantial" three-story building of pressed brick, trimmed with white limestone. Designed to allow additions to the east and west ends as growth demanded, the original building would have sixteen large rooms plus several smaller rooms, boiler rooms, and miscellaneous spaces. In early August the Regents accepted the low bid ($45,462) of Dennis Mahoney of Waxahachie for the construction of the building, stipulating completion in eight months.

By late November the Board had elected the first President of the College, Cree T. Work, who began his duties January 1, 1903.[8] On January 10, he addressed five thousand people who gathered on a rainy day for the ceremonial laying of the cornerstone of the first building of the College. Setting forth the highest aims and values of America and education in general and establishing high ideals for the "Girls Industrial College of Texas" in particular, Work voiced his desire that "the Author of wisdom guide all our efforts to make his institution a blessing to humanity."

Establishing his philosophy for guiding the new College, Work noted the increased value which was being attached to practical education as a complement to the "purely intellectual, abstract, inactive quality" which had previously characterized formal study:

> In America we stand face to face with the problem of providing a higher education for the common people which will afford culture and practical preparation for common duties at the same time. . . . There is a loud and emphatic call for our educational institutions to cultivate the executive quality in our young men and young women and to prepare them for immediate, well-directed action in the practical affairs of life.

He also emphasized that education designed for men was not necessarily appropriate for women although he was strong in his statement that "woman's sphere" was equally as large as "man's sphere," and that "woman's rights" were "as great as man's."

Lest anyone think that practicality would dominate the curriculum at the expense of scholarship, Work assured his listeners,

Cree T. Work, first President of the College, also taught psychology and ethics and, according to the 1907 yearbook, specialized in "chapel talks and sermonettes."

> The Girls Industrial College of Texas will aim to give culture of the highest order, scholarship of the most efficient kind, and domestic and industrial training of the most modern and practical type. . . . In short, we want to meet the need of our times in training women who will be competent, intelligent and refined; well fitted for self-support if this should be necessary; thoroughly prepared for woman's work in the industrial and commercial world if they so choose to labor; well trained for companionship with worthy manhood and for motherhood, when this is desired.

A month later, addressing the State Farmers' Congress of Texas in the state capitol, Work outlined the values of home and domestic education and of industrial education and upheld practical education for its contributions to intellectual development as well as for its utilitarian and financial results.

He noted that "the mass" of the girls in the state would ultimately be homekeepers or home managers and, thus, should be prepared to conduct the affairs of the home according to sound, efficient scientific principles. He also forcefully defended the rights of young women "to enter other suitable occupations if they so desire." Noting, "The cry has been raised that women are encroaching upon the occupations of men, taking their places and causing reduced wages," Work replied, "While this is probably the fact in many instances, may it not be asked on the other hand, 'Who gave the male sex the monopoly of all industry outside the home?' and 'Why should women not be permitted to do that which is suited to their nature and which they can do well?'

"The answer to the first question," he continued, "seems to be that 'Man *assumed* the monopoly'; and the reply to the second, 'Because he still *claims* the monopoly of such occupations.' " Voicing the sentiment which was to become the motto of the College, Work emphasized, "The spirit of the need of the times demands ability to do, and 'We learn to do by doing.' "9

To illustrate the current conflict between old and new emphases in education, Work described "the voice of a pupil in another part of the house, as he endeavors to recite perfectly his Latin lesson. He is conjugating 'vocare.' It sounds like the voice of past ages. . . ." Turning from the voice in his own house to look out his window at the Austin High School, which contained the Allan Manual Training School, Work realized that "While this pupil repeats his language in the classical department of the school, others will be driving the plane, drawing the fine curve or swinging the hammer in the manual training department."

Never failing to take up the case of practical education for girls, Work interjected his hope that "the girls may soon have equivalent opportunities with the boys, and that ere long cooking, sewing and other industrial work may find a place in the public schools of Austin." Throughout his tenure as President, Work remained a frequent and forceful speaker, spreading the good news about industrial education and about the College for women in Texas.

During the spring and summer of 1903, with the construction of the building provided for and the President selected and at work, the Board of Regents turned its attention to the selection of a faculty, the selection and purchase of equipment, and the development of the curriculum.

In an address to the student body on the occasion of the tenth anniversary of the College in 1913, A.P. Wooldridge, the Board's first president, recounted some of the deliberations of the group in choosing the initial faculty:

> We went all over the land trying to get the best qualified men and women we could for the faculty. We got testimonials from everywhere, had personal interviews with numbers, talked with friends, and finally made choice of . . . as good, capable, and efficient men and women as we could find in the whole country. . . . We took the greatest care in choosing the faculty. I think we were nearly a week upon it, day and night, and I have a very distinct recollection that at the end of the week we worked Saturday night. We worked all that week, reading testimonials, comparing opinions, working out conclusions, and our last session closed between four and five o'clock at Mr. Hann's house on Sunday morning.

The Regents selected fourteen faculty members. In addition to examining their educational qualifications, the Board and Work judged the faculty's moral character, culture, tact, general disposition, habits, social qualities, and special fitness for teaching girls.

A review of the first faculty and their previous places of employment suggests the breadth and thoroughness of the Board's search:

Among original faculty members who served the College for many years were Charles Noble Adkisson (top), photographer and instructor in chemistry and physics, and Aubrey Leonard Banks, instructor in mathematics and later Dean of the College.

Cree T. Work, *President*
Supervisor of Manual Training for the City of San Francisco

Lucy E. Fay, *English Language and Literature*
Teacher, Whitis School, Austin

Jessie H. Humphries, *History and Economics*
Teacher, Dallas High School

Mrs. Gessner T. Smith, *Modern Languages and Latin*
Mistress of Modern Languages and Instructor in Latin, Industrial Institute and College of Mississippi

Aubrey Leonard Banks, *Mathematics*
Associate Professor of Mathematics, Texas A&M College

Charles Noble Adkisson, *Physical Science*
Instructor in Chemistry and Physics, Colorado Chautauqua

Harriet V. Whitten, *Biological Science and Geology*
Instructor in Geology, University of Texas

Helen B. Brooks, *Domestic Art—Sewing, Dressmaking, Millinery*
Assistant Instructor, Pratt Institute

Rebecca M. Evans, M.D., *Physician and Lecturer on Physiology and Hygiene*
Interne, New England Hospital for Women and Children, Boston

Elma B. Perry, *Domestic Science—Cookery*
Director, Department of Domestic Economy, Stout Manual Training School, Menomonie, Wisconsin

Mary Louise Tuttle, *Domestic Science—Dairying, Laundering*
Tutor in Domestic Science, Teachers College, Columbia University, 1902-1903; Student, Connecticut Agricultural College, 1903

Amelia B. Sprague, *Fine and Industrial Arts*
Instructor in Art and Handwork, Ohio State Normal School, Miami University

Jessie McClymonds, *Elocution, Physical Culture, Vocal Music*
Post Graduate Course, Emerson College of Oratory; American Institute of Normal Methods (Music), Boston

Harry Gordon Allen, *Commercial Art*
Director, Commercial Department, High School, Dubuque, Iowa

The four male faculty members held bachelor's degrees, and Banks and Work held master's degrees also. Six of the ten female faculty members held bachelor's degrees, and three of these women also held master's degrees. In addition to the faculty, the first staff members were Wade H. Brymer, secretary; A.J. Seiders, landscape gardener; and C.S. Ferguson, engineer.

Closely allied to the selection of the faculty was the development of the curriculum, a task which the Board also undertook with the greatest seriousness. House Bill Number 35, which created the new College, set forth, both specifically and generally, the kind of education which the institution was to provide:

a literary education, together with a knowledge of kindergarten instruction;

. . . telegraphy, stenography, and photography;

. . . drawing, painting, designing and engraving, in their industrial application;

. . . general needle-work, including dressmaking;

. . . bookkeeping;

. . . scientific and practical cooking, including a chemical study of food;

. . . practical housekeeping;

trained nursing, caring for the sick;

the care and culture of children;

with such other practical industries as from time to time may be suggested by experience, or tend to promote the general object of said institute and college, towit: fitting and preparing . . . girls for the practical industries of the age.

Jessie H. Humphries, original instructor in history and economics, remained a valued member of the faculty for more than forty years.

Because neither faculty, facilities, nor financial resources were sufficient to accommodate all of the subjects specified in the founding legislation, the College began with the subjects which the Regents and President felt would best meet "the most urgent present demand." Guided by the belief that it was "manifestly the spirit of the law" that the new College should include a thorough practical training, the Regents deliberated long and carefully the best way to insure that the new school would become the "first class industrial institute and college" called for in the founding legislation. Fearing that making the institution a "trade school" to prepare working women would stamp the College as "a working girl's institution" and make it uninviting to young women seeking a cultural education, the Board chose to join "real culture" and "practical instruction in the domestic arts and the useful employments adapted to women."

At the celebration of the College's tenth anniversary, Wooldridge recalled some of the factors that influenced the Regents' decisions:

> I grew up in the classical days of education when we were taught principally Greek and Latin and mathematics. The significance of science and the beauty and value of the English language and its noble literature were just beginning to be studied about that time. . . . We were imbued with that sort of an idea for a curriculum—very much on the old models, a good deal of language and a large sprinkling of the ancient languages. . . . I wanted a broad curriculum, and for those who wanted to study those things it was well and good. . . .

The first bulletin of the College, issued February 20, 1903, projected the establishment of six departments to receive students the following September—English-science, domestic arts, rural arts, fine arts, industrial arts, and commerical arts. In the second bulletin, dated June, 1903, rural arts had been eliminated as a separate department with most of its subjects included under domestic arts. The third bulletin, issued in August before classes began in September, set forth the four departments (fine and industrial arts were combined into one department) which would serve as the original academic organization of the College.

The school was at first essentially a junior college. The preliminary announcement advised that three-year courses in each department would lead to graduation. The first or preparatory year was the same in all departments, and graduates of "reputable high schools" could go directly

Students who attended the first classes would find them equipped to help them learn by doing.

into the junior class where concentrated studies in the student's major field of interest began. All courses of study, however, included "thorough training in English, and a certain amount of history, mathematics, science, drawing, cooking, sewing, practical economics, music and physical culture." The August bulletin, which actually guided the opening of the College, included a second preparatory year of uniform study for all students preliminary to their junior year. The first and second preparatory years were equivalent to the tenth and eleventh grades of high school. The junior year offered college courses.

While the curriculum committee of the Board worked out courses of study and announced the intended opening of the College in the fall, the building committee "put in much time and labor in selecting and purchasing equipment for the College." The June, 1904, bulletin boasted, "The equipment of the College is the best that could be obtained, the policy of the Board being that the best is none too good for Texas girls, and that it is poor economy to get second-class equipment."

A partial list of the equipment suggests both the diversity of instruction and the practical applications which awaited the first students. Churns, a butter worker, cream testers, a bottling apparatus, a washer and extractor, wringers, ironing boards and machines, a starcher, benches and tools for light construction work and for wood, iron, and cardboard work, a lathe, a scroll saw, individual drawing tables, oak and cane-bottomed chairs with tablet arms, typewriters, compound microscopes, photographic equipment, a china kiln, a sunlight picture apparatus, an electric stereopticon, X-ray equipment, twenty-two two-place gas stoves and twenty-two roll front cupboards with pots and pans, a large gas range, a coal and wood range, a dozen sewing machines, and a piano were gathered with other equipment, both mundane and exotic, into the three-story building which was to house the College.

As September 23, 1903, approached, the equipment was arranged throughout the new building. The basement contained the creamery, the laundry, a science lecture room for theoretical work in laundering and dairying, the manual training laboratory, the boiler room, and an apartment fitted up as a lunch room and cloak room.

The President, secretary, and physician made ready their offices on the second floor, which housed the art, mathematics, languages, and English rooms, and the library. The second floor also included the commercial room, the rooms for biological sciences—a lecture room and a laboratory—the large physical laboratory adjoined by the instructor's private laboratory, an apparatus room, a chemical store room, and a photographic dark room. The domestic science laboratory, the domestic arts laboratory, and the auditorium on the third floor completed the facility.

The physical plant that awaited the arrival of the first students consisted of a small greenhouse and this one building where, according to E.F. Bates, "The sounds of the carpenters' saws and hammers continued for more than half a year." What others might have regarded as insurmountable obstacles, however, were, Bates continues, "incentives to greater effort" to the "pioneer spirits" who were making a dream a reality. From a perspective of fewer than twenty years later, Bates reported, "The strong bonds of love and loyalty forged from the common endurance of, and common victory over, such hardships created a wonderful force in the outgoing alumnae group, whose influence was one of the most potent elements in the subsequent growth of the College."[10]

CHAPTER I—NOTES

[1]A Mississippian and a distinguished Confederate soldier, Baker was thought to have used the Industrial Institute and College for the Girls of Mississippi as a model for the proposed college. Established March 12, 1884, the Mississippi institution was the first state college in the United States established exclusively for the education of women.

[2]In 1897 Senator William J. Bailey of Tarrant County reintroduced Baker's bill. As in 1891, the bill passed in the Senate and failed in the House, partly because of cries for economy and partly because of philosophical opposition. Other organizations which worked toward securing approval for the College were the Texas Federation of Women's Clubs, organized in Waco in 1897, and the Texas Woman's Press Association. In 1901 Elizabeth Fitzsimmons Ring, later a Regent of the College, presented a petition from the Federation to the Legislature requesting an appropriation to establish an industrial college for girls.

[3]The Twenty-sixth Legislature approved two new normal colleges (at Denton and San Marcos) in 1899, and supporters of the University of Texas and of Texas A&M each sought the establishment of an industrial school for girls connected with their institutions. The Senate voted 11-10 in favor of a College Station location, but the bill failed to pass the House.

[4]The commission consisted of one member from each of the state's congressional districts. Representing districts one through thirteen, respectively, were W.D. Cleveland of Houston, J.B. Roberts of Woodville, R.T. Milner of Rusk, J.H. Rowell, Sr., of Jefferson, Rosser Thomas of Bonham, O.B. Colquitt of Terrell (chairman of the commission and Governor of Texas, 1911-1915), W.L. Radney of Waco, Helen M. Stoddard of Fort Worth, A.P. Wooldridge of Austin, John M. Moore of Richmond, E.A. Atlee of Laredo, George H. Pfeuffer of San Antonio, and J.E. Hooper of Colorado (Texas).

[5]Following a mass meeting of citizens interested in securing the new College, twenty-one citizens of Denton were organized to work on the project: C.F. Witherspoon, president; J.C. Coit, secretary and treasurer; C.C. Bell; G.H. Blewett; J.P. Blount; T.J. Bottorff; Robert Craig; A.E. Graham; John A. Hann; W.F. Jarrell; W.B. McClurkan; A.C. Ousley; W.A. Ponder; R.L. Ragsdale; J.N. Rayzor; J.B. Schmitz; H.F. Schweer; E.C. Smith; M.S. Stout; C.A. Williams; and R.J. Wilson.

[6]Among inducements offered by locations hoping to attract the new school was a special 1901 summer session at Texas A&M which was open to women. It was the first and only summer session of the College before 1909.

[7]The first Regents served two-year terms.

[8]Recommending Work for another position in 1910, A.P. Wooldridge noted that Work did not apply for the Presidency of the College. Recommended by Columbia University when Wooldridge wrote, seeking the name of "an exceptionally well qualified man," Work was chosen from a number of applicants throughout the nation.

[9]Suggested by Mrs. Stoddard as the motto for the College, Comenius' phrase, "We learn to do by doing," was engraved on a pillar of the College's first building.

[10]*History and Reminiscences of Denton County* (Denton, Texas: McNitzky Printing Company, 1918), p. 246.

The central rotunda and the nearby auditorium of Old Main became centers of student activities.

9

A Great Work Now Fairly Entered Upon

II

The first years of an institution may be as critical as the early years in the life of a human being in determining character. In the formative years a slight limp may be corrected with minimal care or left unattended to become crippling. A spark of talent may be nurtured to full flame or snuffed out. Initial imagination and boldness may lead to eminence. Timidity may doom to obscurity.

The new Girls Industrial College was fortunate to have women and men of wisdom and vision to form its character. President Cree Telford Work had a clear idea of the purpose of education—to develop "a clever constructive hand, a clear capable head, a clean Christian heart."[1] He directed his energies toward building an institution that would encourage these qualities in its students. His task was no easy one; but he faced it with energy, enthusiasm, and wisdom.

When his successor, W. B. Bizzell, made his first report to the Board of Regents on November 16, 1910, he acknowledged Work's contributions: "Whatever the future of the College may be, and whatever useful purpose it may serve, it will be largely the result of the wise foundation laid by the retiring President." In April, 1913, when the College celebrated its tenth anniversary with special homecoming ceremonies, Bizzell again paid tribute to the former President: "The longer I stay here and the more I work on the problems of this institution, the greater my admiration grows for the man who headed the institution in the early days of the College work. He was a wise worker, a thoughtful man, a man who knew the problems of the educational world, and knew them as few men who have studied them do."

The problems of the young institution were many, and they surfaced quickly. Although the new College had many champions, it also had detractors. For everyone who thought a woman should prepare to take her place in business or in a profession, another thought that woman's only true place was in the home. For every supporter of scientific practical education for homemakers, a detractor said maintaining home and family was a natural talent of women that required no study. Controversy raged throughout the country over the relative merits of instruction in the new "practical" subjects and in the firmly established "classical" studies. For every person who looked to industrial education as the salvation for the future there was a critic who thought only the traditional subjects of the past merited study.

The founding legislation charged the College with bridging the gap between these two extremes by providing young women a "literary

"Floriculture" was among the first subjects of the new College.

11

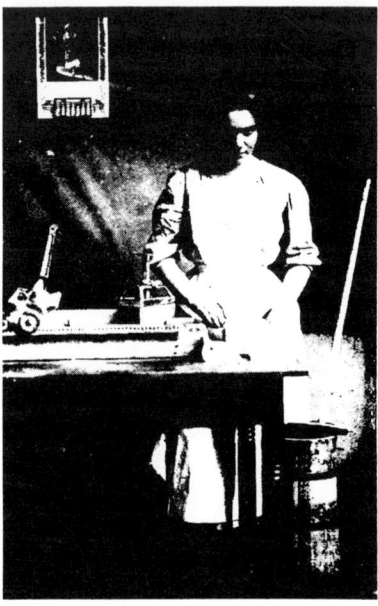

The earliest curriculum included such "literary" and "practical" subjects as botany and dairying.

education" *and* preparing them for "the practical industries of the age." In designing the first curricula, President Work and the Regents carefully combined an emphasis on literary education in the first two (preparatory) years of study with a shift to "manual work" and the development and application of practical skills in the junior and senior (college) classes.

Every graduate of the College completed courses in cooking, sewing, dressmaking, millinery, manual training, laundering, dairying, horticulture, drawing, and household accounts. She also completed studies in a wide range of traditional subjects. In addition to grammar, composition, mathematics, science, and Latin during the preparatory years, all juniors took English, history, and chemistry; and most took zoology or botany and Latin or a modern language. All seniors took history, and most curricula called for English, Latin or a modern language, and physics at the senior level. The college bulletin of January 6, 1904, advised, "Let no student come to the College with the idea that books are here laid aside. Books are among the tools of all the departments of the Girls Industrial College of Texas."

Some critics, nevertheless, felt that the "industrial" College should eliminate literary and scientific studies. In response to this criticism, the Fort Worth *Record* editorialized on March 1, 1905, "The design of an industrial college is not merely to turn out skilled cooks, dressmakers and dairymaids."

Supporters of the College were determined that it should offer more than technical skills and more than a few refined skills in music and embroidery, a vague memory of dates and maps, and a casual acquaintance with foreign language and literature. Advocates of the College saw in it both an opportunity to dignify the work of maintaining a home and family (work conceded to be the responsibility of women) and an occasion to expand women's opportunities outside the home.

Proponents of the new scientific approach to homemaking had high expectations for its results. Mary Eleanor Brackenridge, a member of the first Board of Regents, cited confidence in the value of the scientific approach to home life in the Fort Worth *Record* of March 10, 1907: "The proper nourishment of [a woman's] family will save her husband from the saloon. With proper care, which she will give to her children, we are sure there will be no further need for wings to the asylums. Asylums are not recruited from the homes of trained women." A proper diet was touted as a cure for most of the woes of humanity—from the "purposeless destruction of the Parisian Communists" cited by Martha T. Bell in a "Friday Lecture" at the College on December 8, 1905, to the intemperate use of alcohol and tobacco.

Although these ideals were decidedly unrealistic, there were very real benefits to be gained from practical courses in homemaking, and faculty members carried the good news through the state. Mary Louise Tuttle demonstrated the value of the new courses in helping women run their homes with increased efficiency and economy when she told the district convention of the State Federation of Women's Clubs on May 23, 1905, "An equal amount of nourishment can be purchased in a shoulder roast at 8 cents per pound as in a porterhouse at 12½."

Although domestic arts comprised an important part of the curricula of the College, however, the President, Regents, and faculty members never attempted to confine their students to homemaking. Miss Tuttle advised the members of the Women's Clubs, "The home of today is not woman's refuge but her choice. Many avenues are open to her, and we find her in most of the paths of industrial life." The college bulletin of August, 1906, promised help for women of ambition whether those ambitions were "to be among women, to be independent as workers, to direct the home, or to render philanthropic social service to the race."

In order to make its opportunities widely available to young women, the institution employed liberal admissions policies and carefully controlled expenses. On February 20, 1903, the first bulletin of the College announced that enrollment in the Girls Industrial College of Texas was open to "all white girls of good moral character who have attained to the age of sixteen and demonstrated their abilities and their good attitudes." Applicants who performed satisfactorily on an entrance examination prescribed by the faculty and who met other entrance requirements were admitted to the College for the opening of the first term on September 23.[2] Adults who did not wish to pursue a full course of study could be admitted as "special students" in courses not leading to a diploma.

Tuition was free. Students paid only a one-time matriculation fee of five dollars at their initial registration and an incidental fee of five dollars each term. The school year consisted of three terms.[3] Other school expenses included the rental of textbooks at a cost of approximately ten dollars per year; and early bulletins estimated the cost of room and board at twelve to fourteen dollars per month, "including light and fuel."[4]

One hundred seventy-three students, representing three states and sixty-six counties, attended the first term of the College. The number grew to 186 students representing eighty-eight counties by the end of the first year, June 8, 1904.

The student body reflected the rural make-up of the state. Only thirteen of the original students lived in the city; ninety lived in towns or small cities; seventy-five lived in the country. Seventy-eight of the students were daughters of farmers or stockmen; twenty-nine, daughters of skilled tradesmen or merchants; and nine, daughters of physicians.

The average age of the students was eighteen years and two months. Most (133) of the students entered on examination. One was enrolled in the senior class; twenty-two, in the junior class; thirty-three, in the second preparatory class; sixty-five in the first preparatory class; and fifty-two special students (adults who did not seek diplomas) were enrolled in the irregular class.

Because the College had no dormitory facilities when it opened, students boarded with private families or in boarding houses. Because there were few homes near the College and no street cars, most students and faculty walked from one-half to two miles to school. Both dormitories and sidewalks became high priorities for the College.

All homes or boarding houses had to be approved by Work, who established strict standards of student conduct and circulated them in a letter to the women with whom the students boarded. The regulations

The first students assembled on the steps of Old Main in 1903.

13

governed everything from students' keeping their rooms neat and clean to their notifying the college physician in case of sickness. Work specified study times from seven to ten o'clock each evening, except Sunday, with the admonition that "Late study should not be permitted—10:30 o'clock p.m. is a reasonable limit." Students could attend evening church services and entertainments of the Lyceum Course, but they were not to go walking or to other evening meetings without direct permission of the faculty.[5] "Exercise should be taken and errands performed in the afternoon between school hours and supper."

Company was restricted to Saturday evenings, "such company to be entertained in the parlor, and not to remain later than 10 o'clock. It is not considered proper for students to entertain their gentlemen friends in their own rooms, on the gallery, or on the streets." Students were not to entertain "regular company" without filing in the President's office the written consent of their parents.

Students were not to go driving with men. Even driving in a "properly chaperoned party" required the special advance permission of the faculty. The college bulletin of June, 1907, advised that "on proper occasions, socials, parties, and picnics are among the forms of pleasure that are heartily entered into by students and members of the faculty. Arrangements for such socials by classes or societies must be made through the Entertainment Committee of the Faculty."

Students had been advised in the second college bulletin that they should "plan to make but one visit home during the year—at the Christmas vacation"; and Work reminded the boarders that they were not to leave town to go home or elsewhere without special permission. The College assumed almost total responsibility for the students during their attendance. They were asked to notify the President or secretary of the College of the day and hour on which they would arrive in Denton so that someone from the College might meet them and escort them to the campus.

A new section on "Discipline" was added to the college bulletin of June, 1906. The section noted that rules were prescribed to lead students to "self-control and reliability" and that "outside interests must not encroach upon the time and duties of students." The main duty was "to learn," and students were to be "ready to receive instruction relative to their conduct as well as in other subjects." Students who were not prepared to comply with the established standards of the College were simply "not desired."

Strict discipline characterized Work's administration. The rules he outlined for the first boarders of the College remained largely intact when dormitories began to house students on the campus. Additions to the rules were forcefully stated: "Midnight visiting and socials among students in their rooms are not tolerated."

The lack of dormitory facilities plagued the College for a number of years, however, before it could offer housing to its students. The college bulletin of June, 1905, noted "general disappointment" that the Legislature had not appropriated money for a dormitory. Lest the writer be thought unduly critical, however, he added, "All realize that it was the lack of funds and not the lack of desire that caused the solons to grant less than the Regents asked. The College has many friends among the Legislators."

Supporters of the institution joined in pleas to the Legislature for help. The State Women's Christian Temperance Union, which had petitioned the Legislature for the establishment and maintenance of the College at each of its annual conventions since 1893, resolved at its convention in Marshall in October, 1906, to ask the Legislature to provide a dormitory "that no girl may be denied the training this College offers because of the lack of boarding facilities."

Students maintained a sense of humor about strict rules.

14

Professor Adkisson's home included the advantages of electricity and the disadvantages of muddy streets without sidewalks, which were typical of the homes in which students boarded.

Work noted in his report to the Regents the following December 28, that the lack of a state dormitory was one of several factors limiting the growth of the enrollment. The college bulletin issued at the same time announced boldly, "It is safe to say that the attendance would have been double at least if the College had its own dormitories." To support this claim, the bulletin cited the dormitory established near the College during the past year by a society of Methodist women: "It has now twenty-six girls, and has had applications for fully as many more who could not be accommodated. These girls who could not be accommodated did not attend the College."

A second alternative to boarding in town was a small residence furnished by Regent Brackenridge where a group of girls did their own housekeeping. The College equipped a similar cottage; and Clarence Ousley, President of the Board of Regents, noted in the bulletin, "In one of these cottages the girls maintained themselves comfortably at the expense of only $8 apiece."

Never hesitant to ask for what the College needed, Work used the bulletin to remind readers that the Legislature had appropriated fifty thousand dollars for the building of a dormitory four years earlier. Tactfully noting that the Governor had withheld that amount, "foreseeing the approaching deficit in the State Treasury," Work emphasized that the need for the dormitory had not disappeared. It had, in fact, increased; and the Board of Regents asked the Legislature for $125,000 to construct the building. Work closed his plea with a statement of the contributions this facility would make to the moral, intellectual, and physical welfare of students and identified matters of economy, convenience, and practicality which should be considered.

Miss Brackenridge once again took the plight of the College to the public through the Fort Worth *Record* on March 10, 1907: "The Democratic platform and the Governor's message both speak favorably of the College of Industrial Arts; however, there is no mention made of our greatest need, the dormitory, nor of any increased facilities for teaching." She continued her case with impassioned rhetoric: "A wing in the Insane Asylum is favorably mentioned. Will the State do more for her hopeless past than for her hopeful future? Will she appropriate funds to take those who are out of harmony, who are disagreeable to their families and place them under roofs, while she leaves to chance protection the flower of the State, the future hope of the State, the innocent, ambitious, lovely, future mothers of our statesmen and our citizens?" In a telling blow, she suggested that women be returned a small part of the taxes they paid: "Women nowhere

Methodist women provided the first dormitory for students.

The first state dormitory was Stoddard Hall, which came to accommodate 150 students; it was located approximately a hundred yards from Old Main.

meet with tax exemptions, and surely women are entitled to tax representation, and we have the right to ask that the womanhood of the State should share in the benefits.''

The college bulletin of June, 1907, humbly reported, "It is gratifying that our lawmakers appropriated $60,000 to build a dormitory." The two-story structure with basement was constructed to the north of the main building of the College. It contained rooms for ninety students and for several teachers, matrons, and servants and apartments for the President and preceptress. A kitchen, large dining room (40' x 70'), parlor, office, recreation room, reading room, girls' kitchen and private dining room, bath rooms, and laundry completed the facility which, the bulletin boasted, would be "heated by steam and lighted by electricity." The bulletin also noted rather proudly, "There is not an undesirable room in the building."

Costs in the dormitory ranged from fifteen dollars per month for a double room to seventeen dollars per month for a large single room. The price for room and board included the laundering of fifteen items per week, provided there were not more than nine pieces of wearing apparel. Visitors (parents and friends) were welcome to stay for a dollar a day and twenty-five cents a meal if room permitted.

Across Bell Avenue to the east of the state dormitory, the Woman's Home Mission Society of the North Texas Conference of the Methodist Episcopal Church, South, was constructing a Methodist dormitory to house fifty students. Both dormitories were to be ready for occupancy by the 1907 fall term, but the state dormitory was not completed until the following April. It was, nevertheless, filled with ninety-six students; and fifteen others placed their names on a waiting list before the fall term began. The Legislature named the new state dormitory "Stoddard Hall" to honor Helen M. Stoddard, an original member of the Board of Regents who was instrumental in founding and locating the College.[6]

Work boasted both of the outstanding construction of the building and of the economy it offered its residents in his report to the Regents on November 15, 1908. One hundred students had found places in the dormitory, living, according to some of their parents, more economically than they could live at home. The College attempted to minimize costs both by carefully buying services and foods for the dormitory and by applying some of the skills it was teaching. Four thousand cans of fruit and vegetables were preserved on the campus for use in the dormitory.

Satisfied only briefly with his victory, Work reported the great benefits to both students and faculty that the new dormitory provided and immediately made a plea for additional dormitory space to house two hundred students in the next two years. He left his post with this new dream unrealized, however. When the Regents submitted their report to the Governor in November, 1910, the dormitory had not been approved; and they noted that the state still provided living accommodations for only one hundred of the two hundred seventy-five students in attendance.

Stoddard Hall and other additions to the grounds rapidly changed the appearance of the campus during Work's administration.[7] Orchards and berry gardens, a dairy barn, poultry yard, and greenhouse all provided raw materials for the use of students in the domestic department.[8] An oak grove to the north of the main building and nearby tennis and basketball courts offered students and faculty rest and recreation.

The annual report which the Board of Regents submitted to Governor Lanham and the Legislature on December 12, 1904, noted other advances: "The southern portion of the grounds has been fenced, graded and otherwise improved. . . . Among the improvements on the grounds are a cottage for the gardener and superintendent of grounds, a system of waterworks, including sewerage for the main building, athletic grounds, etc. . . . The cost of erecting the main building was defrayed by an appropriation made by the Twenty-seventh Legislature. The other improvements mentioned were paid for in large part by the citizens of Denton." The Regents also reported that the local fund had been exhausted so that "it will devolve upon the State to further develop and keep up the College grounds and buildings." The Regents requested that the Legislature provide a thousand dollars a year for labor on the grounds and an additional thousand dollars a year for student labor.

By the summer of 1905, Oakland Avenue along the west side of the campus had become a popular drive; and townspeople were enjoying the grassy slopes and shady knolls of the campus like a park on pleasant Sundays. The community gained a great deal more from the new College than just a happy place to spend Sunday afternoons, however. Work and the faculty members offered the women of the area a chance to share the benefits of scientific homemaking, and the citizens of Denton (primarily the women) organized special programs for the students of the town's two colleges. The Civic Improvement League inaugurated a Lyceum Course to provide first-class entertainments, described in the college bulletin of January, 1904, as the "best platform and musical talent of the land." The College offered a series of free lectures to the women of the Denton area.

Often illustrated with experiments and pictures and always free from technicalities, the lectures ranged from "What Happens in Cooking" to home sanitation and decoration and from "The Care of Milk" to "Care of the Young." The series was highly successful. The eighty-seat lecture room overflowed with women by the second lecture so that the series had to be completed in the auditorium.

During the 1905 fall term, senior students worked with faculty members to organize a lecture and entertainment series. Continuing lectures on domestic subjects, the series added cultural entertainment. Distinguished actor Frederick Warde presented the first lecture on "Shakespeare and His Plays," and subsequent lectures covered topics from "Education in Japan" to "The Growth of Plants." Free to the general public and to students and often accompanied by stereopticon slides, the popular series became a regular feature of the fall and winter terms. In addition to the Friday lectures and the Lyceum Courses, a wealth of other activities, both on and off campus, contributed to the social, cultural, and moral development of students and offered them almost unlimited opportunities to "learn to do by doing."

In June, before the College opened in September, the second college bulletin announced that "Proper student organizations within the College will be encouraged."[9] By the beginning of the second term (January, 1904), a chorus had been organized "for the purpose of securing unity in singing and to cultivate an appreciation for classic music." At the end of the second school year the chorus of sixty voices had "mastered some difficult productions from the best musical composers."

By August, 1905, a glee club with thirty members was furnishing music for the Friday afternoon lectures. Trimmed down to twenty members, the group made its first formal appearance before a capacity crowd in the college auditorium on April 2, 1906. The college bulletin of June, 1908, announced "a new organization, which has evoked much enthusiasm," the CIA Orchestra. The bulletin characterized the orchestra, which the girls had formed with no outside leader, as "immensely popular with the students and the public." The May bulletin of the following year encouraged students "who play instruments of any kind . . . to bring them along and to join the orchestra."

Two literary societies were also organized during the first term of the College. They were "ready for earnest work" by January, 1904. Every student was urged to join either the Athene or the Georgic, which met

The greenhouse by the tennis courts reminded members of a 1907 tennis club that study and work were not far away.

every two weeks for programs of music, recitations, and papers. By March, 1905, the two groups had consolidated under a new name, Chaparral Literary Society.[10] In February of the following year, the society inaugurated *The Chaparral Monthly,* a sixteen-page paper, with College news, class notes, contributed articles, and other materials. The yearly subscription rate for the paper, which was credited with fostering "the College spirit," was seventy-five cents. By February, 1908, students who felt that the Chaparral Literary Society had grown too large to serve the individual needs of its members organized the M. Eleanor Brackenridge (M.E.B.) Literary Society to promote a "healthful rivalry." By May, 1909, students were managing and issuing a twenty-four page paper, *The Daedalian.* The senior class issued the first college annual, *The Chaparral,* in June, 1906. Students paid $1.50 for the volume with its history, class songs, original poems, humorous and satirical "hits," class rolls, and other "vital" information.

By March, 1906, the second preparatory class had organized a tennis club and a new literary club, the Elizabeth Browning Society. In addition, the list of student organizations in the college bulletin included the Reading Circle, Allen Reading Club, Deutsche Gesellschaft, Young Woman's Christian Association, Domestic Arts Club, Brush and Pencil, junior and senior basketball teams, and class organizations. By December of that year the college bulletin noted, "Much interest is also being taken in athletics, several tennis and basketball teams having been formed, with Miss Toeppen, the instructor in Rural Arts, as coach." Within two years, interest in athletics had grown enough to support an Athletic Association with three departments—basketball, tennis, and golf—and a teacher to head each section.

Activities built toward a climax at the end of each spring term. The college bulletin of June, 1906, recorded "the most charming social event of the school year," a party given by the junior class to honor the graduates. The students elaborately decorated the college building with senior colors (yellow and white) and the senior flower (the daisy). A music contest and fishing pond provided entertainment. The following year the Chaparral Literary Society and the second preparatory class gave a May party complete with Maypole dances and the crowning of a May Queen. A week later the junior reception for seniors included the wearing of Greek costumes by the juniors and the playing of games "in the manner of the ancients." The college bulletin of June, 1907, called it "the most beautiful

The yearbook staff of 1907 published the second college annual, The Chaparral.

entertainment ever given at the College.''[11]

Commencement, the real highlight of each year, offered the students an opportunity to demonstrate their accomplishments. Every department displayed the products of its students' efforts. Social functions allowed students to practice their skills as hostesses, and traditional ceremonies of friendship bound the students to their alma mater and to each other.

Although only one student graduated at the first commencement exercise,[12] the San Antonio *Daily Express* of June 12, 1904, gave a glowing account of the ''BRILLIANT CLOSING OF A SUCCESSFUL YEAR'S WORK.'' The exercises of the week were ''most entertaining, and were largely attended'' according to the newspaper. Among the entertainments of the week, the paper reported a ''display of millinery, dressmaking and fine arts [which] rivaled anything which might be produced in fashionable centers.'' Garments ranged from plain underwear to ''stylish and elegant'' gowns; and the hats included ''walking hats, dress hats, beautiful chiffon creations and sailors.'' The second preparatory class in cooking prepared a dinner for the Regents, and President and Mrs. Work honored the first graduate with a dinner.

The following year, commencement week began with senior class exercises on Monday.[13] The ceremonies included burying the hatchet on the campus and planting ivy. In the evening, the main building, according to the college bulletin of June, 1905, was ''lighted from dome to basement and elaborately decorated, the College greenhouse and grounds affording great facilities in this line.'' With an orchestra furnishing accompanying music, the faculty entertained students and more than two hundred guests at a reception. The classes demonstrated their spirit at the end of the reception, displaying class colors, singing their class songs, and filling the air with class yells.

Commencement week in 1906 began with the ''ceremony of planting the chaparral.''[14] Promptly at ten in the morning the students gathered to march from the gate on the edge of campus to the top of the hill on which the College building stood. Each class surrounded itself with chains of its class flower or of cedar interspersed with flowers and carried class banners and emblems. After the seniors buried the hatchet and sang their class song, the students proceeded to the auditorium for other exercises, including the delivery of the class prophecy with stereopticon illustrations.[15]

Class day in 1907 was much like that of the previous year except that the students again planted the traditional ivy instead of chaparral. Also, their procession marched to the site of the recently approved state dormitory for ground-breaking ceremonies, and the six members of the senior class who had attended the College from its beginning were crowned with wreaths of flowers. The class dedicated itself to the service of its alma mater; and the college bulletin of June, 1907, notes, ''The girls lingered long to sing their class songs and give the class yells.'' The President hosted a reception for the graduates at which he awarded a gold thimble for the best work in sewing and a gold medal for the best work in cooking.[16]

Alumnae of the College welcomed the new graduates to their ranks with the first annual banquet of the Alumnae Association on June 6, 1907.[17] Following refreshments at a ''down-town purveyor's,'' alumnae and students returned to the campus for a business and social meeting which ended with an informal dance.

Commencement week in 1908 began with the baccalaureate sermon on Sunday, followed by student programs on Monday evening. The auditorium was full (one hundred people were turned away for lack of space) to see the performance of the college orchestra, glee club, and double quartette, and of student actresses in six scenes from Shakespeare's *Merchant of Venice.*

The first graduate of the College was Beulah Kincaid in 1904.

19

On Tuesday, class day exercises included the traditional processions and the burying (by nine "pioneer" seniors who attended all four years at the College) of the class record at the foot of the tree planted by the previous senior class. The 1908 ceremony included the presentation of a statue of the "Winged Victory"[18] to the College by the seniors. On Tuesday evening, the College building served as a reception area where the faculty, assisted by members of the junior class, entertained students, visiting relatives and friends, and more than a hundred townspeople.

On Wednesday, Demonstration Day, hundreds of visitors toured the campus, visiting each department to receive detailed instructions from students about the work they did there or to view the work in progress. The Denton *Record and Chronicle* of June 11 described "a corps of students . . . busy handling milk in all forms, making butter, separating cream, etc." The products of manual training on display ranged from match scratchers to elaborate furniture such as a Morris chair of weathered oak, which, the paper reported, was "of sufficient beauty to grace any home in the land."

Materials from the simplest linens to dainty laces and "gorgeous creations that delight the feminine heart" were on display along with notebooks to explain the laundering procedures that had preserved the beauty of these handiworks. The literary departments displayed notebooks. Leatherwork, metalwork, baskets, painted china, sketches, and other creations represented the work in the arts classes. Millinery in various stages of development and dresses, including the graduation gowns which students were required to make, were on display. In the room where the domestic arts were displayed, young ladies served "delicious morsels" to the visitors who came to see how to plan a nutritious meal, how to serve it attractively, and how to plan kitchens and even entire homes.

On Wednesday, the President hosted about one hundred fifty guests in Stoddard Hall in his annual reception for the graduating class, their relatives and visiting friends, Regents, and members of the faculty. On Thursday, Wooldridge, former President of the Board of Regents, delivered a commencement address full of "thoughful and fatherly advice"; and thirty-seven graduates received diplomas from Clarence Ousley, President of the Board of Regents. Miss Brackenridge, vice president of the Board, presented teacher's certificates to thirty-three students.

Needlework, plain and fancy, was a part of the studies of all students. These sewing projects were exhibited in 1917.

On Thursday afternoon, the Alumnae Association met. Among the items of business was the establishment of a memorial fund, which would be invested to earn interest to support an alumnae scholarship. The original scholarship amounted to three to five dollars a year. The annual social meeting and banquet on Thursday evening in Stoddard Hall celebrated the fulfillment of the dream of not just one dormitory but two.

While students pursued their entertainments and their studies, Work labored to protect the integrity of the institution, to defend and promote its purpose, to win support for its most basic needs, and to expand the original course offerings in accord with the broad scope of educational programs set forth in the creating legislation. None of the President's jobs was easy.

The very name of the College created problems. The press and the public often called the College an industrial school, a name which many people associated with the score or more of reformatories around the country which were known as industrial schools. To eliminate the confusion the Board of Regents changed the name from Girls Industrial College to College of Industrial Arts (CIA) early in 1905. The name change did not immediately solve all problems, however; and for several years college bulletins included rather defensive statements about the nature of the College. In August, 1905, the bulletin, which was distributed widely to the press, proclaimed, "This is not an orphanage, a hospital, an asylum nor a reformatory. It is a high class school for rich and poor alike, if they desire to attend it and can meet the conditions for entrance."[19]

Work had strong supporters to aid him in his campaign to make a place for the College of Industrial Arts. Mrs. Cone Johnson, one of the original Regents of the College and President of the Texas Federation of Women's Clubs from 1905 to 1907, delivered an address on April 28, 1905, in which she called on the women of Texas to continue their support of the College. "We see in it the promise of the uplifting of the womanhood of Texas," she assured her listeners. At its annual meeting the following November, the organization unanimously endorsed the work of the College and commended the institution to "the favor, patronage and support of the people of Texas."[20]

At the same time the group endorsed another project which was important to Work and to the future of the College. The resolution it adopted asking the Legislature to approve the issuance of teacher's certificates to graduates was reinforced by a similar resolution adopted by the Texas Farmer's Congress at College Station on July 13, 1906. The 1906 platform of the state Democratic Party also supported the proposal, and in the following legislative session the lawmakers validated the diploma of students of CIA who satisfactorily completed a course in pedagogy along with their other studies as a first-grade teacher's certificate. The College could begin preparing teachers of industrial arts for the public schools.

The legislative session also brought other triumphs for the College. The $60,000 appropriation for the building of Stoddard Hall combined with a $6,000 appropriation for a hospital and home nursing department to improve considerably the living conditions for students.[21] In addition, the Legislature passed the free kindergarten law (the founding legislation for the College charged that it provide students a knowledge of kindergarten education), and the Blanton pure food law located the office of the Food and Dairy Commissioner at the College.

The gains were significant; but, as usual, Work saw the need for even more support for the programs of CIA. For the rest of his administration, which lasted until the beginning of the fall term in 1910, he presented an ever-growing list of needs to the Regents, who forwarded them to the Governor and Legislators. Using every forum, the President added a section on "Needs of the College" to the college bulletin of November,

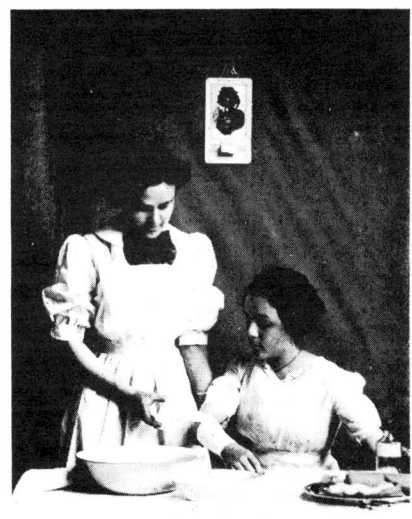

The Legislature approved funds for a campus hospital and for a home nursing department in 1907.

By 1914 the library had expanded beyond its original small room, but it remained crowded.

Facilities for photography also expanded and improved before this photograph appeared in the 1913 yearbook.

1907. Taking its place along with information about courses and costs, triumphs and endorsements, the section identified two top priorities. First, Work emphasized the need for a trades school and for broadening and strengthening the courses already offered. The necessary additional facilities and faculty to meet this need were not forthcoming.

Work's second concern was the development of a funding system which would insure adequate support not only for CIA but also for all of the state's institutions of higher learning.[22] He found the biennial plea to the Legislature for operating funds particularly onerous because, as he stated in the bulletin of November, 1907, the appropriations were irregular and uncertain, and appearing before the Legislature to "beg" for funds to supply the institution's daily needs was a "political annoyance." Among the possible solutions he suggested was an inheritance tax or a property tax which would be distributed equitably among the state's colleges.

Even a casual review of some of the growing pains of the College reveals the validity of the President's concerns. For example, the Thirtieth Legislature approved the issuance of state teacher's certificates to graduates who completed the necessary course of study in pedagogy but made no financial provision for the addition of faculty or facilities to handle this addition to the curriculum.[23] Also, even the modest growth in the number of students enrolled and in the kinds of courses offered had quickly overloaded CIA's one building and its faculty.

In his report to the Regents on November 15, 1908, Work carefully detailed the crowded conditions that called for new instructional facilities. Several kinds of art studies requiring different equipment and processes were crowded into one room. The library was in a fourteen-foot-square room. The classes in pedagogy had to float from room to room as space was available. The photography class had outgrown the closet originally set aside as a darkroom *and* the chemical storeroom which was subsequently designed for it. Courses in physical culture, expression, and vocal music were conducted in the auditorium. Instrumental music students were studying in the home of a teacher in town and practicing wherever they could find instruments in the neighborhood. Work lamented, "The dark closet which we have been compelled to use for the book store is so crowded that there is scarcely room for the proper storage and care of the books belonging to the school." There was no rest room for the teachers, and several departments had no office for their faculty.

Some departments had outgrown their space and were relying on closets or other space for additional room. Still others were at the bursting point with no room for growth, and the College had no spare room for the addition of courses in trades and kindergarten education which Work proposed. He recommended the addition of twenty-one or twenty-two new rooms either in a separate building or in a wing to be added to the original building.

The need for equipment was as critical as the need for additional space. Work cited the fact that the College owned only one camera to be used by twelve photography students as an example of shortages which confronted the institution. He also proposed the addition of equipment which would make possible the study of engraving and illustrating in the art department. One or two small presses plus typesetting equipment in a small room would serve the needs of the art department and enable students to print their own monthly paper, he noted. Drawing tables, typewriters, blackboards, pianos, dumbbells, and microscopes were only a few of the badly needed materials Work identified. He also decried the lack of money for "stationery, postage, library additions, materials and supplies, light, and heating . . . summer school, . . . inside improvements, . . . [and] improvement of grounds, outhouses, etc."

In addition, pleading for funds to care for the aesthetic needs of the College, he noted, "Our attempts at teaching art are but mocked by the State, when appropriations made are so meager that it is impossible to provide [an] attractive and esthetically wholesome environment for students of the College of Industrial Arts." To support his claim, he pointed out that girls who were educated in an unattractive setting could not be expected to establish attractive homes. Although the campus had many naturally pleasing features, Work continued, visitors had criticized the "neglected and undeveloped condition" of the property. The condition could not be corrected, he insisted, without the addition of three or four men besides the superintendent and his assistant.

Work also petitioned for the building of sidewalks so that the College could enjoy free mail delivery: "The delivery of mail at the College and dormitories is of such vital importance to the interests of the school that for two or three years past we have felt the necessity of taking a portion of the time of our janitor (although he really ought not to spare the time from his work) to bring the mail to the College."

Rural students could feel much at home on the campus which Professor Adkisson captured in his 1903 photograph.

Perhaps the janitor preferred his role as mailman to that of custodian of the College building, for Work also noted in his report, "The College has one janitor, to whom it pays $30 per month. It is a fact patent to all . . . observant people that the condition of our College building, so far as janitor work is concerned, is little less than a disgrace. Yet we are paying all that the State of Texas has allowed for this purpose." The janitor at Denton High School received fifty dollars a month, Work reported; and he cited other positions on campus, such as that of the dairyman, for which salaries fell far below amounts required to employ competent people.

Work decried the less than generous support which had been provided for CIA: "Within recent years, several cities throughout the United States, as well as other State governments, have done more by way of providing facilities for industrial education for their young women than the State of Texas has done at the College of Industrial Arts." Cleveland, St. Louis, Kansas City, and Los Angeles were among the cities he cited for their generous support of industrial education. The College of Industrial Arts, Work pointed out, was established for only a fraction of the money that these cities had provided for their schools, and it was maintained for between a third and a fourth of their annual budgets.

President Work offered his proposed solution to the funding problem in a request that the Board of Regents join with other boards throughout the state to petition the Legislature for a system of automatic support for the state's institutions of higher education. He made both his criticisms and his suggestions for improvement widely available by reprinting his report to the Board in the College bulletin of November, 1908.

As the college president with the longest tenure in Texas, Work took the lead in proposing legislation that would make the long-discussed system of a state education fund a reality. Calling once again on the Texas Federation of Women's Clubs for support and on the Daughters of the Confederacy and the State Teachers' Association, Work presented his case to the Thirty-first Legislature. The State Commissioner, L. T. Dashiell, recommended it strongly to the Governor and the Legislature. The organizations mentioned above adopted resolutions in support of it. And Work contacted the presidents of Texas A&M, the University of Texas, and the state's three normal schools to seek their support of the bill he drafted. Assistant Attorney General W. E. Hawkins and State Tax Commissioner T. B. Love helped Work redraft and perfect the bill, which was introduced unsuccessfully in the Senate.

In December, 1909, Work carefully outlined the work which had gone into preparing the bill and cited the "ox-cart economy" which the Governor had employed in vetoing certain important items in the appropriations bill which provided for some of the most critical needs of certain schools:[24] "Had the needs of the institutions been provided for by an annual tax, the schools and their friends would have been saved the humiliating and arduous experience of begging maintenance funds from the Legislature, and the Chief Executive would hardly have been in a position to cripple the work of the people's institutions of learning."

Work did not realize his dream of a fund to support the state's colleges, and he left his office in 1910 with other dreams unrealized as well. Nevertheless, his contributions to the development of a solid academic, physical, and administrative foundation for the College of Industrial Arts were significant. He established a system of committees among the faculty to make recommendations on such matters as the curriculum, classification of students, graduation, literary societies, exhibitions and entertainment, athletics, boarding, and the press. Based on the recommendations of the faculty during his administration, the Board of Regents raised the academic standards of the College and added a third year of college-level study. A "middle" year between the junior and senior years offered the studies previously taken in the senior year, and additional advanced work was offered in the new senior year. The curriculum encouraged a new thoroughness and strengthened the attention given to practical studies.

In assessing the accomplishments of his administration, Work could identify both triumphs and disappointments. Perhaps the best evaluation of the state of the College at the end of his administration lies in his own words in the college bulletin of May, 1910: "The College is yet in its infancy, and although splendid progress has been made, it may all be counted as but the beginning of a great work now fairly entered upon."

CHAPTER II—NOTES

[1]Address to State Farmers' Congress of Texas, Austin, February 12, 1903. According to his son Telford, President Work acquired his philosophy of education as a student at Columbia University. His professor recommended Work for a position in the schools of San Francisco where he introduced manual training before moving to Denton. From Denton he became the first principal of the Venice (California) Union Polytechnic High School where he patterned the curriculum after that of the College of Industrial Arts, adding studies in motion pictures and printing. Telford Work also credits his father with persuading California State Assemblyman Charlie Lyon to introduce the legislation which led to the establishment of the branches of the University of California (personal letter to Mary Evelyn Blagg Huey, February 5, 1979).

[2]The examination covered orthography, reading, arithmetic, English grammar, composition, geography, physiology and hygiene, the history of Texas and the United States, and civil government. Students who had completed the tenth grade (sometimes the ninth) were usually prepared to enter the first preparatory class, and high school graduates could enter the junior class without examination. Beginning with the 1908-09 school year, the College added another year of high school studies to the requirements for admission to the first preparatory class.

[3]Although tuition remained free throughout Work's administration and incidental fees remained fixed at five dollars per term, two additional fees were added during Work's tenure. The college bulletin of June, 1905, noted, "On account of the fact that the Legislature failed to appropriate enough money for the purchase of materials and departmental supplies, the Regents have been compelled to charge a material fee of $2.50 per term." The college bulletin of June, 1908, announced the addition of a $2.50 hospital fee each year to cover medical expenses.

[4]By the end of the second school year, the College had determined total costs. The college bulletin announced, "Two hundred and fifty dollars will cover all essential expenses for a student in the College of Industrial Arts for the year; some spend more than this, others less." A letter from President Work to newspapers throughout the state in August, 1905, noted, "Itemized reports from eighteen students show their average expenditure, for all purposes, for the school year closing June 7 to have been $216 per student."

The itemized reports to which he refers are the account books which each student was required to keep. Under the supervision of the head of the Commerical Department, each student carefully recorded her receipts and expenditures. At the end of each term, or at such other time as he might request it, the President received the reports. From time to time he published sample accounts in college bulletins. One such report included every expense

The required blue serge uniform and mortar board made every day seem like commencement.

Students wore uniforms in the classrooms and in the college gardens, which they tilled as part of the educational program designed to free them from the necessity of working the cotton fields.

which a student incurred from September 24, 1906, to June 6, 1907—everything from room and board for 8 1/2 months ($106.25) to expenses for "telephone, telegraph, etc." ($.05).

[5]Students were expected to attend church, and the College offered daily chapel services under the direction of the faculty. The college bulletin of June, 1907, admonished, "Excursions, picnics, and other purely social gatherings of students are forbidden on the Sabbath because this is the day of quiet rest and worship and should be so observed."

[6]Mrs. Stoddard was born July 27, 1850, in Wisconsin. She was valedictorian of her class in the Genessee Wesleyan Seminary in New York in 1870. In 1875 she married a former classmate, R.D. Stoddard, who died five years later. Soon after her husband's death she moved with her young son Robert to Texas where she taught until she accepted the presidency of the Women's Christian Temperance Union in 1891. In 1907 ill health forced her to move to California. She returned to Texas following the death of her son, with whom she had been living; and on January 1, 1941, she died in a Dallas hospital. In addition to her work on behalf of CIA, Mrs. Stoddard was nationally known for her temperance work, using her influence to secure the passage of the so-called "scientific temperance instruction law" for teaching the effects of alcohol; and she helped secure passage in Texas of a law raising the age of protection for girls.

[7]Of the buildings and other facilities erected during this time, however, only the original main building of the College still exists.

[8]In addition to the original orchard, the College planted six hundred peach, pear, plum, and apple trees during the winter of 1904-05.

[9]All organizations required the approval of the President.

[10]The Chaparral Literary-Social Club is still active.

[11]The junior entertainment of the seniors in the spring is a continuing tradition.

[12]Beaulah Kincaid (who later married D.H. Fry) was the first graduate of the College, completing the equivalent of a junior college course of study in commerical arts. The College did not award degrees for the completion of four years of work until 1915.

[13]Nine students graduated in 1905.

[14]That year students selected the little evergreen bush, a native of Texas and Mexico, as more representative of the College than the traditional ivy. Both the yearbook and the monthly newspaper which were initiated in 1906 and a thriving literary society formed in 1905 bore the name of the plant.

[15]Twenty-nine students graduated in 1906.

[16]Mrs. J.H. Hann of Denton, whose husband was a member of the Board of Regents from 1902 to 1907, contributed the prizes.

[17]Beulah Kincaid Fry, the first alumna, organized the Alumnae Association in 1905 and served as its first president. It originally had ten members, Mrs. Fry of the class of 1904 and the nine graduates of 1905.

[18]Much weathered, the statue now stands before the main entrance to the original College building (now called "Old Main").

[19]The bulletin also identified the College as the "Texas State College for young women," a title which was to be adopted with slight modifications some years later as the official name.

[20]The Methodist women of Texas demonstrated their endorsement very concretely with the construction of a dormitory near the College. Girls preparing for mission work could combine the cultural and industrial offerings of the College with religious training provided in the dormitory.

[21]From the first school term, a college physician looked after the health needs of students. The college bulletin of January, 1904, notes that the doctor advised simple home remedies as often as possible for the sake of economy and for the instruction of the students who were taught to see causes so that they could learn prevention as well as cure. The students sought the advice of the physician readily. The bulletin notes that the physician made more than a hundred calls on out-patients during the first month of school. Apparently the illnesses were not serious for the most part. The bulletin adds, "As the work progresses and the College enthusiasm increases, we are glad to see the worst cases of nostalgia rapidly disappearing." The need for a medical facility did not disappear, however; and in his report to the Board of Regents dated December 28, 1906, Work cited the lack of a hospital building as one of the limitations to the growth of the College:"The President has been compelled to give up his private office for the use of the College Physician."

[22]He originally offered his proposal to the Regents in June, 1904.

[23]Another area of great concern involved summer school for students who could not attend regular sessions. The faculty volunteered to give instruction in sewing, dressmaking, millinery, dairy work, cooking, laundering, photography, manual training, and other subjects for the first summer term in 1905. Although the first session was well attended, the Legislature denied the request of the Regents for appropriations to continue summer studies. Not until Miss Brackenridge contributed a thousand dollars for a summer session in 1907 did the Legislature agree to appropriate a thousand dollars a year for summer terms in 1908 and 1909.

[24]One of the items the Governor vetoed was a $50,000 appropriation for a second college building at CIA where vocational or trades courses could be taught. Even without the new building, however, Work developed plans for the introduction of these courses in the 1910 fall term.

Growing in Favor

III

When young William Bennett Bizzell left the superintendency of the Navasota schools to succeed Cree T. Work as President of the College of Industrial Arts on September 1, 1910, he had placed in his care a young institution which had survived the threats of a rather perilous infancy. Because the College was unusual, it had attracted a great deal of attention, not all of it favorable. Nevertheless, its natural strength, aided by the fiercely protective posture of President Work, members of the Board of Regents, and outstanding women of Texas, had enabled it to take its place among Texas' growing family of educational institutions. Mrs. Chalmers W. Hutchison, President of the Texas Mothers' Congress, described the College in an address at the 1913 homecoming celebration: "There had not been a daughter in this family before, and while she was an innovation, she was truly a beautiful child, unusually strong and forceful in her constitution, in full possession of her innate powers of growth."

Like a child outgrowing her clothes faster than parents can provide new ones, the young College continually demanded larger facilities. Its growth during Bizzell's four-year administration was not simply unexpected; it was unprecedented in the history of higher education in Texas. At the beginning of his third year in office, Bizzell reported that the number of students had almost doubled since he made his first report to the Regents in November, 1910.[1] The report also noted that in its tenth year the College had a student body more than twice as large as that of Texas A&M in its tenth year. Attendance at CIA exceeded that of the "State University" in its tenth year by one hundred twelve students. The Regents' report to Governor Colquitt and the Thirty-fourth Legislature (November 16, 1914) noted, "No other college or university in Texas began the session of 1914-1915, as did the College of Industrial Arts, with a larger attendance than the total enrollment for the last session."

Bizzell enthusiastically assumed the task of guiding the young College and seeing that it received the encouragement required for healthy growth. Working with an affable style somewhat less fiery than that of his predecessor, he was no less forceful than Work in seeking the support necessary for the full development of the College. Quickly acknowledging the validity of the needs identified by Work, Bizzell established himself as a tireless worker in securing necessary legislative support. He spent so much time working with State Senators and Representatives that he sometimes described himself as a member of the third house of the Legislature.

Although the College was still plagued by many of the financial and physical problems of Work's administration, Bizzell found one battle

In 1910 William Bennett Bizzell became the second President of CIA.

29

already fought and won. Work had waged a successful campaign to insure the survival of industrial education and of the College of Industrial Arts in Texas. The Regents' report to Governor T. M. Campbell (November 23, 1910) noted that the College had passed through "a stage of experimentation and demonstration" during which it had proved itself to its students and to the people of Texas. Clarence Ousley, President of the Board of Regents, concluded,

> It is gratifying to observe that the merits of the system have been abundantly established, and the College is growing in favor as a place where a young woman may receive not only a cultural education but practical equipment for earning a livelihood. . . . Its graduates are in great demand as teachers of domestic art and science in the public schools; or those who do not care to teach find ready employment in the practical industries for which they are equipped; or they take their places as intelligent and cultured home-makers.

A week earlier, in his report to the Regents, Bizzell had jubilantly predicted "Nothing can prevent its [CIA's] unprecedented growth except meagre appropriations and hostile legislation."

In spite of his optimistic outlook, Bizzell was not blind to the limitations of the College. Quickly acknowledging the soundness of many of Work's requests, Bizzell adopted them as his own. In his initial report to the Regents (November 16, 1910) he noted, "The needs of the College are many, some are pressing and imperative, others can wait for a time." Among the most pressing needs he identified was that for additional space, a need which grew progressively worse for some departments even though the Thirty-second Legislature appropriated $75,000 for a new Household Arts and Science Building. The building (144' x 177') consisted of two stories and a basement located just west of the main building. Described by college bulletins as "one of the most modern and best equipped buildings of the kind in the country," it brought together the work of the various industrial departments. It included rooms for woodworking, metalworking, mechanical drawing, pottery, clay modeling, china painting, textile chemistry, dyeing, and dry cleaning.

The first floor contained offices for the President and secretary of the College, the book and supply room, and a laboratory and classrooms for drawing and design, interior decoration, water color, and still life painting. The second floor offered extensive laboratory, office, lecture, and storage space for domestic art and domestic science courses. The most

The Legislature appropriated money for a second major instructional facility, the Household Arts Building, in 1911.

30

modern cooking equipment, including gas and electric ranges and an "electric fireless cooker," was available in the east wing for students in domestic science. The wing also included a "beautifully decorated and elegantly furnished" dining room where students could learn the art of serving. The west wing accommodated studies in the domestic arts with space and equipment to study textiles and dress fitting.

The building also contained an auditorium with "beautiful scenery" and four dressing rooms. Having quickly outgrown the auditorium in its original building, the College welcomed the new facility which could seat 1,114 people in the oak opera chairs in its main floor and balcony. Two "main" buildings now on campus necessitated the designation of the original building as the Academic Arts Building.

Even the construction of this second major instructional building and the addition of several smaller facilities, however, proved inadequate to meet the needs of a growing student body and expanding curriculum. Bizzell sounded the call for a library, a gymnasium, and a new laundry; and he sought approval for the addition of the wings which were specified in the plans for the original college building. The Thirty-third Legislature appropriated $12,000 for a laundry building, $18,000 for a second demonstration cottage,[2] and funds for a gymnasium. The laundry and gymnasium were completed during the spring of 1914. The gymnasium was a frame building (40' x 82') located just north of Stoddard Hall.

Although appropriations to complete the Academic Arts Building had twice received legislative approval, the Governor had twice vetoed the appropriations. Thus, when the Board of Regents submitted its report to the Governor and the Legislature in November, 1914, it included a third request for funds to complete the building and fireproof it. In addition, the small, recently completed gymnasium was proving entirely inadequate to meet the needs of the Department of Physical Training; thus, the Regents petitioned the Thirty-fourth Legislature for "a gymnasium of modern type with all necessary equipment."

The Household Arts Building included a new auditorium to replace the inadequate one in Old Main.

31

Students of the class of 1913 presented The Taming of the Shrew, *April 29, 1912, performing both the men's and women's roles.*

Moderately successful in securing needed space for instruction, Bizzell failed in his attempts to acquire sufficient housing facilities for students. The Regents reported to Governor Colquitt (November 22, 1912) that the increased enrollment of the past two years was "gratifying in the light of the fact that both teaching room and boarding facilities were inadequate, and students were compelled to undergo very trying hardships to attend the College at all." Although there were diverse opinions throughout the nation about whether state universities should provide housing, the Regents reported that all southern states and many northern states provided dormitories; and "in every case where dormitories were not provided the authorities declared that boarding conditions were unsatisfactory."

To illustrate the problem, the report cited the deficiencies, in both number and quality, of boarding facilities in Denton. Even when students who could not find space in the dormitory found lodging in town, the report continued, "Students in town use kerosene lamps, make their own fires, and go considerable distances for their meals and pay $16.50 to $18 per month." By contrast, students in the dormitory had "electric lights, steam heat, and sewerage for $15 per month." Concerned for the health, safety, and general welfare of the students who lived in town, the President, preceptress, and college physician visited the boarding houses frequently; and, according to the college bulletin of May, 1914, a faculty advisor was assigned to each boarding house to "assist the lady in charge of the home in securing the observance of study hours, regulating the use of the telephone, and observing the conditions of the rooms of the students." The College would not approve boarding houses which required a student to pass through the business section of Denton on her way to school.[3]

Although the Thirty-second Legislature appropriated $75,000 for a dormitory, the Governor vetoed the item, an action which the Regents decried in their report (November 22, 1912) as "nothing less than a calamity." Two hundred students had been denied admission to CIA because of insufficient boarding facilities. Twice as many girls applied for space in the Methodist dormitory as could be accommodated. Parents often made reservations six to twelve months ahead for space in Stoddard Hall, which was crowded beyond capacity. Curtains had been used to cut off the ends of hallways and corners in the state dormitory to improvise rooms so that one hundred forty-five students were crowded into space built to accommodate one hundred.

Coupled with the shortage of instructional and residential space was the shortage of faculty. Bizzell's first report to the Regents on November 16,

1910, expressed dismay that as many as fifty students might be taught in one English class. In addition, the dean of the College taught all mathematics courses; and one teacher provided all of the instruction in chemistry, physics, and photography. In his 1912 report to the Regents, Bizzell stated that the size of the faculty had grown by three during the last two years (to twenty-seven) while the student body had almost doubled in number. Two years later in their report to the Governor, the Regents noted, "The College at present has fewer teachers per one hundred students than has any other state institution of higher learning in Texas."

In spite of the constraints imposed by space and funds and faculty, however, Bizzell perpetuated and even transcended many of Work's dreams for improving the educational program of the College. Bizzell strengthened admission requirements and, in his last year in office, secured approval for the addition of a fourth year to the curriculum. He also obtained legislative approval for validation of the CIA diploma as a first-grade state teachers' certificate issued by the state Department of Education. The CIA certificate enjoyed the same stature as did the certificates issued by the state's normal colleges. The addition of the fourth year to the curriculum established CIA as a degree-granting institution and spurred the state's normal colleges to seek the same status.

The courses of study remained essentially the same during Bizzell's tenure as they had been during Work's administration, but a solid academic organization emerged. The report of the Regents to Governor Colquitt in 1914 identified eighteen departments: Domestic Science, Domestic Art, Rural Arts and Science, History and Social Science, Mathematics, Commercial Arts, English, Manual Arts, Languages, Fine and Applied Art, Philosophy and Education, Physical Science, Biology, Physical Training, Expression, Hygiene and Home Nursing, and Music.

Within each department a variety of courses was available; but the College took special pride in its music department. Although the College had offered instruction in vocal music from its beginning, it had not been able to secure adequate room, pianos, and teachers to meet the demands for piano instruction. In 1910 the College became the first institution of higher learning in Texas to develop and maintain a Department of Music. In 1911 the department added an instructor in piano, one in voice, and one in violin; and in 1912 it added another instructor in piano. The college bulletin of November, 1913 (a special issue devoted solely to music), claimed, "At the present time there is probably no institution in this

The Glee Club of 1912-13 was one of many musical groups which developed after CIA established the first Department of Music in a Texas college in 1910.

Typical of the inadequate facilities which plagued CIA was this building, sometimes called the "music conservatory" and sometimes called one of the "shacks."

section of the country that can boast of a stronger department of fine arts than that maintained at this institution."

If the faculty were outstanding, however,[4] the instructional facilities were appalling. Voice lessons were moved from the Stoddard Hall parlor to the demonstration cottage dining room, to the cottage hall, to the damp basement, then to the auditorium and dressing room in the Academic Arts Building, to a teachers' sitting room, and finally to the third floor of the Academic Arts Building. Meeting equally difficult problems, piano students had to practice in a small outdoor room where the piano was not even protected from rain. In their 1914 report to the Governor, the Regents proposed an addition to the Household Arts Building to help relieve the unsatisfactory conditions in the department.

In addition to its academic departments, the College also maintained an extension program. Strongly advocated by Work, the program began with the employment of Harriet Odell as Extension Demonstrator of Home Economics on September 1, 1911. The program concentrated on promoting the College and on fostering the welfare of rural women in their farm homes. Serving until late summer, 1912, Mrs. Odell visited the Dallas fair and a number of county fairs, women's clubs, and other organizations. Bizzell and the Regents advocated the expansion of the scope of extension work to include demonstrations, lectures, advice to public schools which were planning related studies, and correspondence study so that rural women might have the same assistance as that provided to farmers through extension work offered by Texas A&M. The leaders of CIA requested that the College receive exclusive authorization to develop an extension program designed to improve farm homes.

In January, 1913, Clarence A. Tripp was employed as director of the extension department. The following April, addressing the tenth anniversary homecoming of the College, Bizzell proudly reported that even with "meager and insufficient" funds the College had already equipped a railway car which "traversed the entire T&P and I&GN Railway systems, in connection with the agricultural train of A&M College." It was his hope that several trains could be equipped, for he exulted, "We have no less a vision than that of carrying the gospel of good housekeeping to every home in Texas." Already the faculty member who accompanied the exhibit on the train was delivering lectures which reached thousands of women.

Floris Culver was employed in October, 1913, to demonstrate and lecture on home economics. In November, 1914, the Regents reported to the Governor that extension programs had reached approximately 300,000 people outside the College during the 1913-14 school year and requested funds for an ambitious program of domestic education to be taken to the homes of women throughout the state.

Bizzell also shared Work's interest in strengthening and expanding the summer school offerings of the College. Faculty members still taught summer sessions at personal sacrifice, however. Bizzell reported to the Regents in November, 1912,

> Most of the teachers of the summer faculty are members of the regular faculty, and to ask them to work six weeks for about half the monthly salary of the regular session, when the work is more arduous and difficult, is hardly fair. However, I owe it to them to state that most of the members of our teaching force have cheerfully consented to make the sacrifice in the interest of the College and for the good of the State. But our teachers should not be expected to make this sacrifice.[5]

34

The College offered its first summer normal for teachers in connection with the summer school of 1911. Enrollment increased by forty-one over the previous summer's enrollment (from 69 to 110), and attendance more than doubled for the 1912 summer session. The summer session of 1911 was increased from four weeks to six, and Bizzell proposed extending it to ten weeks so that it could be a regular quarter of the academic year and could provide instruction for teachers and other persons who would otherwise have to leave the state to take the courses they needed. The extension was not approved during his administration, however.

Along with his interest in the physical and educational needs of the students, Bizzell also was sensitive to their spiritual needs. Maintaining strict rules and regulations established by Work to govern students' conduct,[6] the preceptress, Harriet V. Whitten,[7] and the President praised the general behavior of the students. In his report to the Regents in November, 1912, Bizzell noted that "discipline is almost unknown at the College at the present time" and quoted Miss Whitten's report to him that "the relation existing between the student body and faculty is most excellent." The report of the Regents to the Governor in November, 1914, affirmed that "problems of discipline of a serious character never arise and only the adjustment of minor differences among students required the attention of the authorities of the College."

Because of his keen interest in the religious life of the students, Bizzell

CIA equipped this railway car and staffed it with a faculty member to "carry the gospel of good housekeeping" to thousands of women in Texas.

was instrumental in the establishment of a YWCA on the campus. Other student organizations and activities remained largely the same as those developed during Work's administration, but students initiated a number of regional clubs during the 1912-13 and 1913-14 sessions: Bachelor Girls, San Antonio Club, East Texas Club, Bell County Club, Smith County Club, Denton County Club, and Collin County Club.

The Student Association continued to conduct the Lyceum program, and the College sponsored outstanding speakers in education from throughout the nation. Denton businessmen secured a Chautauqua course to coincide with the 1914 summer school. Faculty and student recitals were well attended, and the *Daedalian Monthly* and *Daedalian* continued to record campus life.

Maintaining the same delicate balance between industrial and literary studies that had characterized Work's administration and striving against the same fiscal and physical shortages, Bizzell, nevertheless, managed to lead the young College forward. Enrollment grew from 340 during the 1910-11 school year to 866 in the 1914-15 school year. Expanded curricula offered students both a three-year program of study leading to a diploma and a four-year program leading to the Bachelor of Science degree. The addition of the fourth year firmly established the College among the institutions of higher education in Texas, and the demonstrated practicality of its studies won it a place in the affection of the people of the state.[8]

Among numerous regional clubs which developed was the West Texas Club, shown initiating new members in 1913-14.

The President's Home, first occupied by Bizzell in 1912, served as the residence of the College's leaders for almost forty years.

CHAPTER III—NOTES

[1] Enrollment grew from 340 to 562 during this time.

[2] Students in the industrial arts department planned the interior decorations and furnishings for the first demonstration cottage during Work's last year in office. The cottage was a five-room dwelling already on the campus, located near the garden and demonstration plots. The College received contributions for furniture; and beginning with the 1910-11 school year, seniors lived in the cottage, applying the skills they had learned in their domestic arts and sciences courses. Although the College was proud of its unique offering, the building was old and had to be abandoned for ''various causes'' after its second year of operation.

[3] The square was about a mile from the campus.

[4] Among the faculty were tenor Albert, G. Pfaff, a student of Seagle in Paris, and violinist Lucy Ault, a graduate of Conservatorium der Musik of Cologne.

[5] No appropriation had been made to compensate additional teachers needed for summer school.

[6] The college bulletin of May, 1912, advised students that they were to be in their own rooms when not at school. Visiting—even among fellow students—was forbidden without specific permission for each visit from the director of the dormitory or the student's faculty advisor.

[7] She had been a member of the faculty since 1903.

[8] From CIA, Bizzell moved to Texas A&M where he was President from 1914 to 1925. Under his leadership A&M received large appropriations for buildings and established a solid academic reputation. While at A&M, Bizzell also served on the locating board which chose Lubbock as the site for Texas Tech University (originally Texas Technological College), and he was instrumental in the development of the University of Texas at Arlington (originally Grubbs Vocational School) and Tarleton State University (originally John Tarleton Agricultural College). From Texas A&M, Bizzell went to the University of Oklahoma, which he served as an able President until his retirement at age sixty-five in 1941.

MAUDE HOLT
The Most Popular Girl

The Law Has   IV
Been Met

Francis Marion Bralley, who assumed the Presidency of the College of Industrial Arts on September 1, 1914, quickly directed his energies toward three major areas: classroom and laboratory instruction, research, and extension services. Although his educational experience did not include college work, he was widely known and admired in the state as a progressive educator and an able administrator. He was, according to E.V. White, "a great organizer, a wise counsellor, an eloquent speaker, an outstanding figure in any group of men assembled."[1]

Bralley was no stranger to either practical education or CIA. His most recent experience before coming to Denton had been as Director of the Department of Extension of the University of Texas; and he brought with him a strong commitment to the value of extension service and a firm belief that CIA was better suited than any other institution to improve the homes of the state through extension programs.

He had visited the campus during the tenth anniversary homecoming celebration in April, 1913, and may have heard President Bizzell outline his goals for the College: establishing an efficient extension department, enlarging the faculty and school plant, extending the courses of study, and developing the religious life of the individual students. Whether Bralley heard Bizzell or not, the program he undertook less than a year and half later corresponded closely with Bizzell's ideas.

The second decade of the College was a period of both a phenomenal growth in enrollment and an accompanying growth in physical facilities, faculty, and courses of study. Enrollment almost tripled during the decade,[2] and Bralley's success in securing classroom and residential buildings far surpassed that of either of his predecessors. In addition, he was able to acquire legislative funding to enlarge the extension program, carrying both practical and literary instruction far beyond the walls of the College.

During Bralley's first year in office, the College initiated four-year college-level curricula, awarding its first three degrees in 1915. Although the new academic plan lacked clear direction (White describes it in his *Historical Record* as "a sort of educational dessert" with a heavy emphasis on industrial courses), a curriculum committee of faculty members, chaired by C.N. Adkisson and led, in addition, by White, reevaluated and rewrote the courses and developed standard degree requirements during the 1915-16 school year to be implemented in the 1916-17 session. The schedule of classes changed from a typical high school schedule, with

A page from the 1921 Daedalian *suggests qualities which students admired in their friends.*

President F. M. Bralley assumed his post in September, 1914.

students taking from nine to twelve subjects in forty-five-minute recitation periods five days a week, to a college schedule, with students normally taking five standard subjects in sixty-minute class periods three days a week (Monday, Wednesday, and Friday or Tuesday, Thursday, and Saturday).

In his autobiography, White reports that the changes were not universally welcomed among the faculty. Describing the work of revision as "long and tedious" and the work of the committee as a "vitriolic fight," he notes, "Old members of the committee fought the changes bitterly, and for a while it looked like they might out-vote us. Bralley solved this situation by enlarging the committee and appointing only those who would be favorable to the proposed change."

As a result of the major revisions, the State Department of Education recognized CIA in 1916 as "a college of the first class," the designation toward which the institution had been working since the founding legislation gave it its charge. This recognition meant that the bachelor's degrees of CIA would carry equal recognition with the bachelor's degrees of any other college or university and that CIA had the same privilege as that accorded the University of Texas in issuing teacher's certificates; i.e., graduates were entitled to receive teacher's certificates based on college courses.[3]

The designation of first-class status was a major triumph for the College and for Bralley, who often electrified the students by vehemently saying, "As long as I have anything to do with it, the College of Industrial Arts will never be the tail of the educational kite of any other educational organization in Texas!" Like his predecessors, he was determined that CIA should be considered on an equal standing with the University of Texas and with Texas A&M, subservient to neither, and with a student body, new buildings, and a salary schedule comparable with those of the other two institutions.[4]

Accompanying the revised curricula and scheduling were the classification and strengthening of academic standards, the raising of admission requirements, and the formal statement of stringent attendance regulations, which applied to classes and to chapel exercises held every Tuesday, Thursday, and Saturday.[5] The College also developed a complicated system for honoring students who excelled in their studies and maintained exemplary conduct.[6]

By the fall of 1923, the College had firmly established academic standards which qualified it for membership in the Southern Association of Colleges and Secondary Schools. When E.V. White, who had carried the application to Richmond, Virginia, wired news of the acceptance back to Denton, Bralley assembled the students and ordered a holiday. Acceptance by the Association established the institution as a liberal arts college although technical and industrial subjects remained a major part of the curricula.

Students pictured the faculty in the 1915 Daedalian *with the plea, "O wad some power the giftie gie us,/To be at this where they can't see us!"*

The college bulletin issued February 1, 1924, contained a large section entitled ''The Law Has Been Met,'' which discussed the full compliance of the College with all the requirements established in its founding legislation. In accord with the instruction to provide a literary education, forty teachers were devoting full time to teaching literary and science courses. Sixty-six full-time teachers guided students through modern standardized enriched courses in technical and industrial subjects. The bulletin also noted, ''Every subject named in the act is now a part of the College curricula.'' Bralley had been able to obtain the funds to support kindergarten education, which had eluded Work and Bizzell; and during Bralley's administration, the College added courses in telegraphy. All other subjects were already being offered by 1913.

Thus, the College had met the letter and fulfilled the spirit of the law. Determined to be progressive, it added to the curricula subjects which the law required for ''fitting and preparing . . . girls for the practical industries of the age.'' The *Lass-O* of January 30, 1915, noted, ''The girl who is thrown on her own resources seldom lands in an easy chair. It might be added, however, that being a graduate from the College of Industrial Arts puts a cushion in it.''

Founders of the College might have been amazed at the diversity of careers for which the College was preparing its students twenty years after its beginning. Although the training of teachers had not been a direct charge of the College, its unique offerings in home economics, music, and a number of vocational subjects logically made it a trainer of teachers in those areas.

Approximately half of all students and ninety percent of the women enrolled in Texas colleges in 1924 were taking education courses, and teachers' colleges accommodated less than one-third of them. By 1924, CIA had become one of eleven Texas colleges in which the Department of Education was the largest as the colleges attempted to meet demands for ten thousand new public school teachers each year.[7]

To strengthen its preparation of teachers, CIA organized a Demonstration High School in which faculty members supervised student teachers who instructed students lacking sufficient credits for admission to CIA, enabling them to remove their deficiencies. The College also instituted the first kindergarten at a state college in September, 1917. Occupying the southwest corner of the Household Arts Building, it became the play and work room for thirty children and the laboratory for students engaged in practice teaching and for students involved in the observation of children for courses in household arts.

As the first educational institution in Texas to offer home economics instruction (even the high schools offered no systematic training in household industries in 1903), CIA became the leader in preparing teachers of home economics; and the annual announcement for 1915-16 reported that the College had furnished "more teachers of household arts to the high schools and colleges of Texas than all other institutions of higher learning combined." In 1919, the Regents reported to Governor Hobby that "with only one exception, all of the teachers teaching vocational home economics under the Smith-Hughes law in the day schools of Texas, are graduates of the College of Industrial Arts." Although teaching was often described as "the most desirable of the lucrative professions in Texas open to women," opportunities in business were increasing rapidly; and the College prepared its students for those opportunities as well.

The College also demonstrated a progressive spirit in other ways, one being its approach to extension services. Offered partially to repay the women of Texas for their hard work in securing the establishment of the College and, as noted in the Regents' report of 1916, in response to the "clamoring" of some two thousand women's organizations in the state for information about homemaking, the College was a pioneer in providing extension service in home economics.[8]

Organizing and conducting the first state-supported home economics laboratory in Texas, CIA was the first to carry the work of its laboratories into homes through lectures and demonstrations. In addition, the College prepared a series of bulletins, educational exhibits, and short, practical courses for distribution; and faculty members answered many questions through direct correspondence with homemakers.

The bulletins varied in scope from the all-inclusive *Home Makers Course,* which the College prepared for distribution by the Texas Congress of Mothers and Parent-Teachers Association (issued July 1, 1915), to such specific topics as "Suggested Clothing for the High School Girl." The homemakers' course offered information on virtually all aspects of the home from house planning and decoration to household sanitation, personal hygiene, and home care of the sick.[9] The second bulletin offered designs and patterns for a suitable wardrobe, designed by senior CIA students in the domestic art classes.[10]

Among the major goals of the extension programs were increased efficiency and the application of scientific principles to homemaking. Ac-

Students and homemakers throughout the state could learn to lay a dinner table for home service or for Russian service of many courses, to lay a teawagon for informal tea, or (as pictured here) to lay a table for five o'clock tea.

cording to the college bulletin issued November, 1917, the two million women of Texas spent from eighty-five to ninety percent of the family income of the state;[11] and a major focus of the extension program was on the conservation of resources. Thus, more than sixty years ago, the college bulletin reported "Conservation work is not a new thing with the College of Industrial Arts." Lectures offered practical advice on "The Preparation of Tough and Tender Meats" and the use of meat substitutes for economy; and women learned to repair and recycle clothes and to launder and clean them in ways that would assure their long life. One lecture offered tips on "Cutting the Hatbill in Half."

World War I made new demands on the resources of the homemaker, and CIA offered a variety of bulletins to help women cope with their new problems. Responding to an anticipated shortage of wheat, "Breadmaking with Wheat Flour and Wheat Flour Substitutes" (August, 1917) recommended rye, barley, and rice flour; cornmeal and buckwheat; and less well-known grains such as millet, kafir, feterita, and milo as substitutes.[12] The bulletin provided reassurances concerning the nutritional value of the substitutes and offered recipes adapted to their use.

"AN OPEN LETTER TO HOUSEKEEPERS" (December 15, 1917) emphasized the need for "keeping up with the times" both to deal with the emergencies of the war and to benefit fully from new information developed at colleges. An undated brochure, probably issued about the same time, offered help to "Kitchen Soldiers" bombarded with war recipes of questionable worth. The booklet included carefully tested recipes to help people until they could turn "back to the flesh pots of Egypt [with] meat, wheat, and sugar in abundance" at the end of the war. The brochure also offered such suggestions as, "Do not embarrass your company by serving them foods we are asked to save; it is a reflection on their patriotism."

The war brought women out of their homes, and the Nineteenth Amendment gave them a direct voice in government and in the solution of social problems. Continuing to offer practical help for homemakers, the CIA extension program also began to address the new concerns of women. The college bulletin of November 1, 1921, assigned moral and social responsibilities to women for "the three D's—dependents, defectives, and delinquents"; and bulletins and lecturers campaigned for many reforms.

The extension service offered help in organizing infant welfare centers, free children's clinics, and community nurses. The bulletin of May 1, 1921, advocated a pure textile law similar to the pure food law so that consumers would not be at the mercy of "ignorant clerks." The bulletin of January 1, 1921, discussed all aspects of the school lunch program from its history to its financing and expected results, including even such concerns as table setting and leftovers. Bulletins advocated a millage tax to support higher education "so that it might be removed from politics."[13]

The bulletin of November 1, 1921, offered advice and encouragement to new women voters. The history, provisions, and significance of the Nineteenth Amendment were included along with recommendations that women develop skills in such areas as parliamentary law and constitution-making. In addition, the bulletin encouraged women to learn about finances and state institutions and recommended laws dealing with compulsory education, labor, liquor, divorce, public health, morals, and safety as special areas of concern for women. Suggestions for civic improvement ranged from anti-loafing and anti-spitting ordinances to the regulation of unsanitary buildings and firetraps. The bulletin encouraged close scrutiny of local and state laws dealing with redistricting, marriage and divorce, public utilities, and educational appropriations; and it recommended examination of international concerns such as disarma-

Students performed their domestic chores with good humor and soldierly steadfastness. The 1916 Daedalian *pictured "Lieutenant Murrey" guarding "Ft. Demonstration" against dust and germs.*

This 1917 metal work exhibit demonstrates one area of students' accomplishments.

ment, the League of Nations, the Far East, and South American relations.

In addition to providing information related to homemaking and to the new concerns of women, the College also addressed "less tangible, but no less powerful spiritual and cultural phases of human life" in courses in music and in fine and liberal arts. Convinced that it was a critical need of society to have women "who can read as well as they can cook, who can interpret great minds as well as they can sew, who can assimilate the ideals of others as well as they can furnish homes," the extension department offered recitals, lectures, programs of study, and assistance to persons who wished to develop community and public school music. Lectures and programs listed in bulletins in 1921 and 1922 ranged from "The Art of Italy: Sculpture, Architecture, and Painting" to study guides for novels, poetry, drama, and the short story.

Thus, by April, 1922, while still holding to its "original idea and purpose of service by helping to make better homes in Texas," The extension service had expanded its scope to include lectures from "Nine Things Every Child has a Right to Demand" to "The Birds of Texas: Their Habits and Economic Relation" (illustrated with colored lantern slides and Victrola records of bird songs and calls). Persons who dined out could even receive instruction on "Sauces: Aiding in the Interpretation of the Hotel Menu."

Women could meet with faculty members to discuss the cleaning and care of woolen garments or the social ideals in contemporary literature. Interested persons could learn to interpret house plans, write business letters, avoid food poisoning, or deal with accidents at the table. The extension program had expanded greatly from the programs in "practical sewing, cookery, canning and preserving, laundering, gardening, poultry-keeping and dairying, and rural social problems" identified in the bulletin of August, 1916; but it had not abandoned these early programs. The annual announcement of the College for 1915-16 proclaimed a policy "to teach people and life, rather than books"; and the extension department provided itself an able teacher with eager disciples throughout Bralley's tenure.

Also during the decade of Bralley's service, the summer sessions continued to attract students who could not attend the regular quarters. In spite of continued financial problems (the Regents reported to Governor Ferguson on December 1, 1916, that "the funds with which to properly organize and conduct the summer sessions have been utterly inadequate"), summer enrollments grew at the same pace as enrollments for the regular sessions, more than tripling from 249 in 1915 to 729 in 1924.

In spite of a shortage of funds, the offerings of the summer session were rich in their variety. All departments of the College operated during the summer, and the announcement of the 1917 summer session declared the availablity of more than three hundred courses, more than the number offered in any other quarter. In addition to regular courses, the College also offered non-credit courses for housekeepers; and the Summer Normal Institutes attracted many teachers.

Announcements of the Summer Normals emphasized "the competent, progressive, and successful teachers, principals, and superintendents of Texas public schools" who served as instructors and capitalized on the wide acquaintance of Bralley and others who could help "worthy teachers in finding and securing positions." Among the courses for teachers were instruction in playground supervision, library methods, public school music; and industrial and vocational courses in canning and preserving, basketry, leatherwork, millinery, stenography, and typewriting. The announcement for the 1915 summer session emphasized the ability of the College to prepare women for the teaching of home economics, "one of

Not plagued by "artificial means" of keeping cool, students found the south veranda of Stoddard Hall an inviting place to study and work on projects.

the most pleasant and the most remunerative means of a livelihood in which a young woman may engage''; and the announcement of the 1917 summer session identified the fine and applied arts program of the College as "the strongest department of its kind in the Southwest."

The College did everything possible to make its summer offerings attractive. It limited lecture classes to thirty students and laboratories to twenty. It arranged reduced railroad fares for teachers who wished to come to Denton from anywhere in the state. It capitalized on Bralley's wide acquaintance to attract outstanding educators for the Summer Normals. And it stressed the positive when describing the campus.

Instead of bemoaning the shortage of dormitories and instructional buildings, the announcement of the 1915 summer session proclaimed, "Cool, refreshing breezes, unobstructed by other buildings, sweep across the campus and through the buildings which are on the coolest and most pleasant location in the city of Denton." Instead of longing for air conditioning, the announcement pointed scornfully at other campuses where "students and teachers are practically exhausted from the sweltering heat and are forced to resort to artificial means in an effort to be comfortable." The bulletin boasted that "the work on College Hill in the Summer Normal . . . is delightfully refreshing and invigorating." In addition "large commodious dormitories" offered a "high elevation and beautiful location, . . . excellent meal service, and . . . perfect and sanitary care."

The cost of attending the summer sessions was also attractive. The six-week session of 1915 cost $30.00, exclusive of railroad fare—$24.00 for six weeks' room and board in Stoddard Hall, $5.00 for the Teachers' Normal Course, and an incidental fee of $1.00. The cost had risen considerably by 1924 when tuition for each of the six-week summer terms was $10.00 ($17.50 for both terms if paid in advance of the first term). Total expenses—including room, board, laundry, stationery, and in-

Poultry raising was one of several options offered in the rural arts and sciences.

45

Boating on local lakes and swimming in the College's indoor pool were among numerous recreational activities.

cidentals—for the entire summer (three months) "need not exceed" $125.00 reported the college bulletin of February 1, 1924; and Summer Normal Students continued to pay only $5.00 tuition for their entire ten-week session.

In addition to regular classwork the summer sessions also offered lectures by outstanding educators; and the Interdenominational School of Missions, which lasted ten days during the 1915 summer session, attracted notable women to lecture. Social and recreational activities included woodland picnics, receptions, drives, and a Fourth of July Celebration in 1915; and by 1917, the College offered "Victrola concerts, moving pictures, and lectures" on "the large and commodious roof garden of Brackenridge Hall, the beautiful new $140,000 dormitory." Just north of the campus, Taylor's Lake offered boating, swimming, and golfing on CIA

days; and the tennis and basketball courts of the College were open for students' use.

The addition of Brackenridge Hall to the campus was among the first of several major triumphs for the College in securing more nearly adequate facilities during Bralley's term. In 1913, at the tenth anniversary homecoming of CIA, Mrs. Chalmers W. Hutchison, President of the Texas Congress of Mothers, described the College as "a precocious miss of ten years, . . . like all others of her kind, demanding new finery which to adorn herself." On the same occasion President Bizzell indentified not "finery" but basic facilities with the College needed and which it would request from the Legislature in the immediate future—a fine arts building for the music department, a library building, a science building, a trade building, and a gymnasium.

"I hope and pray when you come back here ten years from now they will have been erected upon this campus," he declared; "and my faith in the intelligence and liberality of the people of Texas causes me to believe that they will be erected." He also announced the expected approval of $125,000 by the Thirty-third Legislature for the building of dormitories and approval for the addition of wings to the main building.

Although not all of Bizzell's hoped-for buildings would stand ten years later, the facilities increased remarkably in the next decade as the Legislature responded to the needs of the growing College. The expansion of the main building and the addition of a residence hall, which Bizzell anticipated, were completed in 1916. The addition of the east and west wings to the main building doubled its capacity to seventy-eight classrooms and offices, including the College library, a U.S. post office, the College bank, and a general supplies room.[14]

Other major instructional facilities added in Bralley's administration were the long-sought gymnasium and the auditorium-music hall. A popular CIA student song published in 1922 described the improvements to the tune of "Little Brown Jug":

> Various things which we request,—
> Indeed it seems that we are blest.
> When walls are full up to the brim
> Lo! the Assembly Hall and Gym.

Although it may have seemed to the students that the new auditorium and gymnasium appeared as if by magic, the buildings had long been goals of CIA Presidents. Bizzell described the need for both buildings in his first report to the Regents in 1910; and the small gymnasium approved by the Legislature and completed in the spring of 1914 proved inadequate so quickly that when the Regents submitted their report to the Governor the following November, they petitioned again for a modern gymnasium. In their report to Governor Ferguson in 1916, the Regents described the facilities for physical training as "wretchedly inadequate."

In the same report they requested funds to build a fireproof music hall with studios, practice rooms, and a large auditorium because the existing auditorium was barely large enough to accommodate the student body; and, they said, CIA had "suffered great embarrassment in trying to provide for the instruction of students in music" in facilities that were "disorganized and demoralizing."[15]

The Regents repeated their request to Governor Hobby in 1919. In the meantime, the College rented a ten-room house and acquired rental practice rooms in seven different houses off the campus. The campus facilities for music consisted of a "a temporary wooden structure with thin walls, poor ventilation and heating facilities." Even two of the stage dressing rooms in the Household Arts Building had been forced into service as voice studios, and still the Regents noted, "It is . . . necessary to use the studios as practice rooms at every available hour."

Responding at last to the needs of the College, the Thirty-sixth Legislature appropriated $85,000 for the building of a gymnasium and $150,000 for a music hall and auditorium. The auditorium would seat 600 in its balcony and 1900 on the main floor, and the building included studios for private music lessons. The college bulletin of February 1, 1924, described the building, which was completed in the spring of 1922, as "a model of its kind and the pride not only of the College, but of the community. It is spacious and comfortable, and at the same time elegant and beautiful in its simplicity." By the time the building was completed, however, the temporary buildings required on campus to provide space for instruction and practice in music had grown to three in number.

The Thirty-seventh Legislature added $85,000 to the appropriation of the previous Legislature for the gymnasium, which was completed and ready for use in the fall of 1921. The gymasium included rooms, equipment, and lockers for classes in physical training and facilities for games and lectures. It also contained a swimming pool which was soon providing swimming lessons to a thousand students a year.[16]

Complementing the major permanent additions to the campus during this period were the expansion of the College laundry and major changes in the Household Arts Building. The auditorium was converted to classrooms, and a cafeteria and tearoom were developed as were classrooms and laboratories for the kindergarten training school and for public school and orchestral music. Besides the three temporary buildings which housed music studies, another served as a photography studio, and a fifth relieved crowded classrooms in reading. The popular name for the buildings, "the shacks," suggests their unsuitability for long-term use. In 1918, the College also added a new greenhouse and dairy barn far to the

(Top to bottom) Students overflowed the original auditorium in Old Main, then the auditorium in the Household Arts Building, necessitating the construction of a new auditorium/music hall, which still serves as the main auditorium of TWU.

north of the instructional and residential buildings, and in 1920 it built a one-story rural arts building adjoining the greenhouse.[17]

With more than half of its students coming from rural areas, the College continued to maintain strong rural arts programs. A poultry flock of more than three hundred fowls for feeding and breeding experiments; a seven-acre area set aside for "a truck patch, home garden, small fruits, and orchard"; and a hog farm of fifty or more animals offered direct experience. The construction of two small demonstration cottages during this time re-established an innovative program begun under Work and abandoned under Bizzell for lack of satisfactory facilities.[18] The first cottage, named for Ellen H. Richards, was completed in the summer of 1915;[19] and the second, named for Mary M. Bralley, in 1919.

Along with instructional facilities, additional dormitories remained a high priority. Brackenridge Hall, adjoining Stoddard Hall, was completed

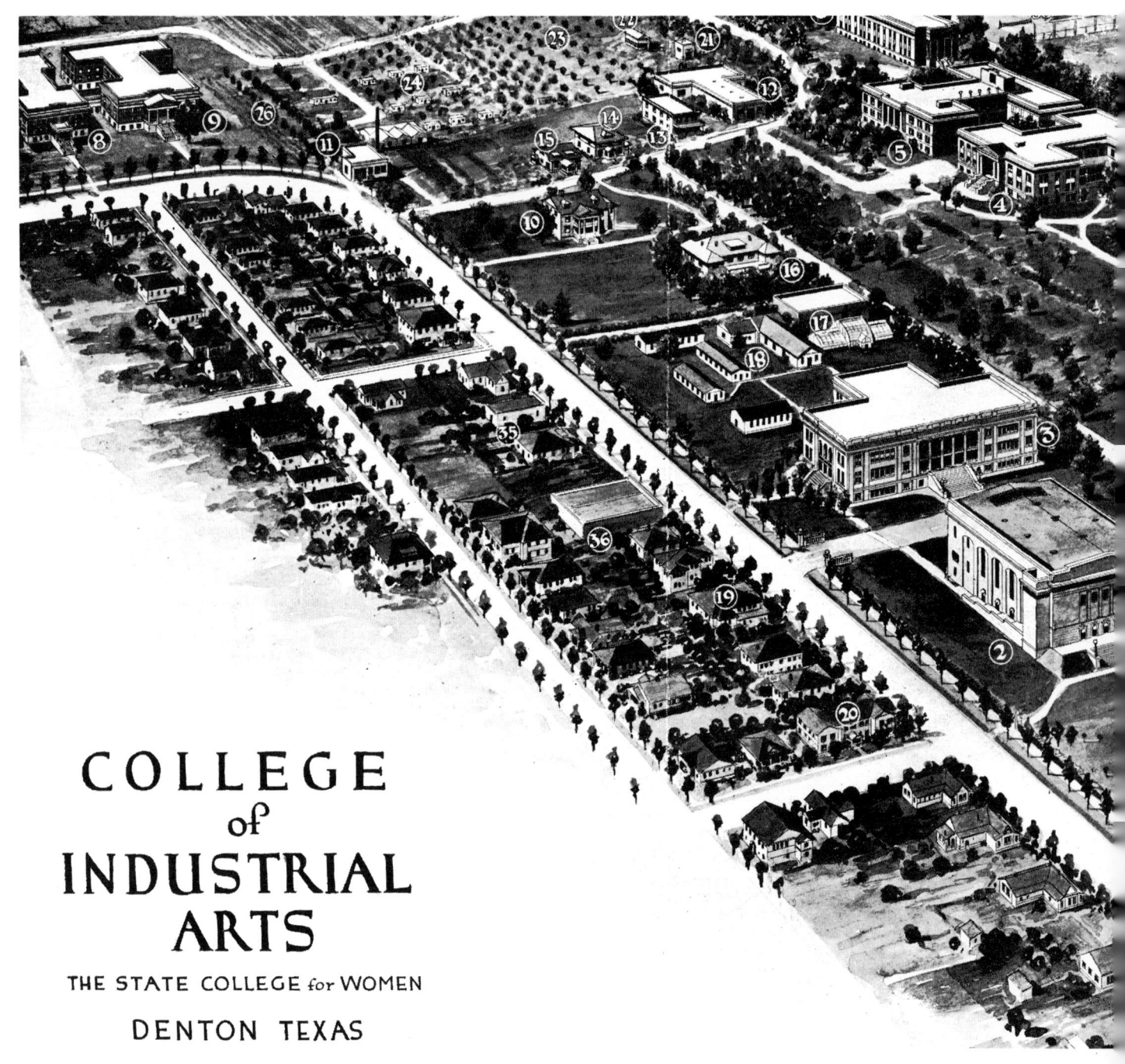

COLLEGE
of
INDUSTRIAL ARTS

THE STATE COLLEGE for WOMEN

DENTON TEXAS

in the fall of 1916.[20] On December 1, 1916, the Regents reported to Governor Ferguson that the College could still accommodate only 425 of its 1038 students in dormitories and requested three new halls with a capacity of 175 to 200 each. The Legislature and Governor approved two additional buildings. Lowry and Capps Halls were added to begin "dormitory row" in the spring of 1918.[21]

Housing facilities still remained inadequate, however; and the Regents' report to Governor Hobby, January 18, 1919, requested three additional dormitories to house from 175 to 200 students each. The *Lass-O* of September 23, 1919, reported about three hundred girls who were forced to leave because of the lack of both dormitory and private housing. The dormitories were not approved during Bralley's tenure, but the College dealt with its housing needs in a positive manner. The bulletin of June 1, 1921, noted that the College had leased six "modern, well built, and

This map of the campus appeared in the 1923 college bulletin.

CAMPUS AND COLLEGE PLANT

The campus of the College of Industrial Arts is well-kept and attractive, and occupies a commanding elevation of seventy-five acres in the northeast part of the city of Denton, and is reached by paved streets from the railway station and the business portion of the city.

The College plant has been developed from the point of view of efficient service, careful consideration having been given to every subdivision and appropriate aspect of college life. The buildings designated by numbers in the accompanying panoramic view are as follows:

(1)—Administration Building.
(2)—Auditorium-Music Hall.
(3)—Household Arts Building.
(4)—Stoddard Hall.
(5)—Brackenridge Hall.
(6)—Gymnasium Building.
(7)—Smith-Carroll Hall.
(8)—Capps Hall.
(9)—Lowry Hall.
(10)—President's Residence.
(11)—Power Plant.
(12)—Steam Laundry.
(13)—Hygeia Hall.
(14)—Mary M. Bralley Cottage.
(15)—Ellen H. Richards Cottage.
(16)—Oakland Hall.
(17)—Greenhouse and Rural Arts Building.
(18)—Temporary Buildings (Shacks) for Music and Reading.
(19)—Los Alamos (senior house).
(20)—Shadow Lawn (senior house).
(21)—Incinerator and Garage.
(22)—Canning Plant.
(23) and (28)—Orchards.
(24)—Poultry Plant.
(25)—Y. W. C. A. Hut in College Park (for picnics and recreation).
(26)—Vineyard.
(27)—Vegetable Garden.
(29)—Dairy Lot and Sheds.
(30)-(31)—Dairy Barns.
(32)—Dairyman's Home.
(33) and (37)—Tennis Courts.

(Top to bottom) Sin Cuidado, Neal House, and Los Alamos were among the private houses where CIA supervised the residence of senior students who had no room in college dormitories.

comfortable residences." The senior students "divide themselves into congenial groups and occupy these houses under College supervision."

President Bralley proved successful in obtaining the appropriations necessary for the continued growth of the College. The value of the campus property grew during his administration from $300,000 to more than $2 million with accompanying increases in the value of equipment. According to Mildred Pearce Holt, who prepared a history of the College in 1926, "The only appropriation of great consequence ever refused him was for a library building. This building was recommended by the Board of Control, and in 1923 only a few months before President Bralley's death, the Legislature made the necessary approrpriations for its construction."

As the growing facilities gave the campus a collegiate appearance and the academic program developed into that of a firstclass college, student life also matured. Although the College continued to assume major responsibility for the well-being of its students and to provide careful supervision of their conduct, it reflected an appreciation for their increased maturity and for the changing world in which they lived.

Student life changed steadily as the institution and the world changed. In 1914, the *Lass-O* cautioned that "very little policing has been done or will be done, but that does not mean that the CIA girls are to run wild." The 1915 *Daedalian,* on the other hand, facetiously recommended that all students should plan at least two months in advance "some unique way of destroying the plastering and breaking the beds down [in the dormitory]."

In 1917 students pledged their help to win World War I. Literary societies canceled their annual dances to contribute to the War Relief Fund. Students pledged and contributed $5,000 to the fund, and 971 students signed cards pledging food conservation through practicing and preaching the "Gospel of the Clean Plate" and avoiding sweets and between-meal snacks. In 1921, the *Lass-O* admonished, "Jazz dancing must go," and "unusually stringent times" forced the cancellation of the annual trip to the state fair.

When the Dean of Women announced the privileges of the Senior Class of 1922, they included the right to "read in the Library in the evening from 7:00 p.m. to 9:00 p.m." and the right to "go to the picture show once a week at night (but never on Saturday night) provided they go in groups of not less than four, wear the senior cap, and make arrangements for going with the Hostess of the Senior House."

Students were still required to live in approved housing and to conform to these strict codes of social conduct, but they were given increased responsibility. Whereas parents had previously been asked to send all money for their daughters directly to the College and students had been forbidden to contract bills with local businesses, the College established, during President Bralley's administration, a bank for the convenience of the students and left the matter of their charge accounts to them and their parents.

Student government became firmly established. The college bulletin of August, 1916, credited the Students' Association and the Students' Council with "contributing much to the social solidarity of the student body and rendering valuable service in the maintenance and promotion of high ethical ideals." The entire student body comprised the Association, with executive power vested in the various "House Councils" and in the Students' Council composed of elected representatives from the different classes. The Dean of Women possessed advisory power in all student activities, and the Students' Council submitted all decisions to the Faculty Council for ratification. The student government was designed not only to give students a voice in campus policies but also to prepare them for active participation in public life.

Among the contributions of the student government were the development of a Students' Loan Fund—financed by an annual sale of articles donated by students, faculty, and alumnae—and a unanimous recommendation that students pay a $5.00 student activities fee at the time of matriculation. The fee provided students access to all student athletic games, subscriptions to the student newspaper and literary quarterly, and admission to all Artists' Course offerings at no additional cost. The fee was a bargain; by the time it was reported in the college bulletin of March 1, 1922, the College had rich offerings in each of these areas.

In 1914, the newly organized Press Club proposed an experimental alternative to the *Daedalian Monthly,* which had been published since 1909.[22] The students would offer a four-page weekly newspaper, the *Lass-O,* with a quarterly literary supplement, the *Daedalian Quarterly.* Both publications were under the supervision of the Department of English as was the college yearbook.

The first *Lass-O,* issued Saturday, November 7, 1914, presented itself as "an experiment to be ceased if it fails."[23] Students could obtain the paper by a $1.00 annual subscription. The paper carried not only campus news but also items of interest from other colleges in the state and reports on the arts from throughout the country. Book reviews and a report on the status of the grand opera season in New York took their place by reports on a new grading system at CIA and a correction of stories in Dallas and Fort Worth papers that proclaimed a small pox epidemic at the College when there had, in fact, been only one mild case.

Among topics of concern to the first *Lass-O* editor, Josephine Ray, and her staff was the lack of enthusiasm for athletics; and articles and editorials chided students for their apathy and for their lack of participation in the Athletic Association through which students worked with faculty to arrange competitions in tennis, basketball, tether tennis, and track and field. To encourage greater participation, the students recommended, and the faculty adopted by January 16, 1915, a proposal which left Thursday, Friday, and Saturday afternoons free for athletics and recreation. Nevertheless, the *Lass-O* of January 28, 1916, decried the "deplorable lack of enthusiasm in athletics at present."

The Department of Physical Training sponsored annual field days with games and competitive track events, and classes competed for pennants awarded at the winter basketball tournament and the tennis tournament. The *Lass-O* of November 21, 1914, reported that high spirits at the invitation of Texas Christian University to play basketball had been dashed when the faculty declined the invitation because "never has it been the

Students joined enthusiastically in what the 1919 Daedalian *described as "the first international holiday" and continued their celebrations for many years with Denton residents. This float represented CIA in the 1927 Armistice Day parade.*

Classes competed for pennants in basketball, tennis, and other sports; but the faculty declined invitations for students to participate in intercollegiate contests.

custom of the College to have intercollegiate basketball." Intercollegiate competition in tennis, however, was a fact by March 13, 1915, when the *Lass-O* reported that CIA had invited Trinity University for a tennis tournament.

If athletics did not spark great enthusiasm, other activities caught the imagination of students in such a way that they have continued in only slightly modified form to the present. The *Lass-O* of February 4, 1916, described the Freshman Follies, "a rather unique vaudeville entertainment"; and it described the Sophomore Stunts as "one of the best entertainments ever given by the students." The stunts ranged from a spoof of the faculty to a Spanish dance and scenes from Sheridan's *School for Scandal*. On March 27, the freshmen performed their original stunt, "Everystudent." Modeled after medieval morality plays, the stunt portrayed a student who learns she can find fame at CIA if she makes work her friend. The original stunts proved so popular that the YWCA adopted the idea for its get acquainted party the following fall, and each YWCA committee and the faculty advisory board performed a stunt to introduce new students to their purposes.[24]

Students also had many opportunities to demonstrate their talents in major productions on the campus. One hundred students participated in the Glee Club Operetta, "Prince Charming," on February 8, 1915. Two hundred fifty students participated in a Shakespearean pageant during the 1915-16 commencement week; and more than two hundred students participated in the three-day Spring Festival in May, 1917. The festival included a series of pastoral dances under the direction of the expression department and a concert by a chorus of more than one hundred altos and sopranos plus three soloists. On the third afternoon the St. Louis Symphony Orchestra, conducted by Max Zach, performed; and in the evening it accompanied the Denton Choral Society and the College Chorus in Joseph Haydn's *The Creation*. More than two hundred students participated the following year when the two choruses combined again to present the oratorio, *Elijah,* with the Russian Symphony Orchestra.

Purely social entertainments ranged from the Chaparral Hallowe'en (reported in the *Lass-O* of November 7, 1914) where "hundreds of spooks fell into line for the grand march" to elaborate dinner dances where students abandoned their uniforms for fancy dresses. The annual dance given by the "middlers" for the seniors in February, 1915, opened with a cotillion led by the class presidents.

Other amusements included excursions and picnics in woodland retreats—Highland Park, "Blue Hole," and Country Club Lake—supplemented by small luncheons and picnics on the campus. Formal and informal tea parties and receptions combined pleasure with the development of social skills. A number of the excursions combined recreation with instruction as "woodland tramps," often accompanied by "picnic lunches and bacon breakfasts," provided first-hand knowledge of native plants and of general biological principles.

Movies became a popular form of entertainment after the junior class presented a moving picture machine to the College in February, 1916, and exhibited the first of a series of movies, *The Carpet from Bagdad*. The bulletin of May, 1917, proudly announced the showing of films "of entertaining character or of educational value . . . notable among these being *The Birth of a Nation.*"

Clubs brought together all kinds of students with common interests. The *Lass-O* of December 12, 1914, reported the organization of twenty-seven city, county, and regional clubs during the previous fall. Students also organized an art club which sponsored exhibits and speakers; and in January, 1915, they organized a tennis club. Other organizations ranged from an active "red-headed club" to a Farm Girls' Council.

New literary societies were organized during the period: the Athenaeum Club in 1917-18; the Aglaian Club by June 1, 1921; and the L'Allegro and Philomathia Clubs by March 1, 1922. Like their predecessors, the M. Eleanor Brackenridge Club and the Chaparral Club, each club was a full member of the Texas Federation of Women's Clubs.[25]

The YWCA continued to be an active force, growing from 350 members in 1916 to 800 in 1919 (approximately two-thirds of the student enrollment). Its activities included welcoming new students, sponsoring weekly inspirational meetings and numerous social activities, cooperating with town churches in Sunday School work and mission study classes, and contributing to the partial support of a YWCA secretary in China.

The annual trip to the state fair in Dallas became a highlight of the year. The first *Lass-O* reported, "Over Four Hundred Strong Left Denton Saturday Morning in a Ten Coach Special to Spend the Day at the Dallas State Fair" for "C.I.A.—A.&M. Day." The following year (October 22, 1915) the paper reported "Yell Practice Every Afternoon this Week" as all chapel periods were devoted to yells so that students could prepare to demonstrate their spirit at the fair. The next year (October 26, 1916) the paper good-naturedly reported the activities of some fifty to sixty "dissidents" who chose to stay at home and form an "ugly club" instead of attending the fair.

Even students who chose to remain constantly on campus, however, did not lack for entertainment. The lecturers, musicians, authors, artists, and entertainers who came to the campus were nationally and internationally renowned.[26] Speaking to a thousand people on the campus on March 17, 1916, former Secretary of State William Jennings Bryan opposed the war in Europe and warned of the dangers of the American preparedness policy. "This war," he noted, "has no parallel in history."

The following fall, the Devereux Company, described in the *Lass-O* of September 12, 1916, as twenty-five of the "best artists on the stage," arrived on the campus with a "car-load of scenery" and forty trunks of costumes. For several years they presented English plays of the renaissance and eighteenth century. Speakers ranged from Dr. Russell H. Cowell who lectured for the Lyceum on "Acres of Diamonds" to Dr. Leonidas Warren Payne, adjunct professor for the University of Texas, who spoke on "Types of Southern Humor." The programs for 1915-16 included Rudolph Ganz, Swiss pianist described in the *Lass-O* of December 12, 1914, during an earlier visit as "Greatest of the World's

Faculty members participated in Stunts in 1919.

53

Pianists,'' Kitty Cheatham, the Zoellner String Quartette, and Metropolitan Opera Company member Giovanni Martinelli, described in the *Lass-O* of September 12, 1916, as ''the second greatest tenor in the world'' sometimes ranked with Caruso.[27]

The visiting artists, the students, the faculty, the administrators, the alumnae, and others who took an interest in the College during its second decade saw it mature in virtually every area. As Mrs. Hutchison had predicted on the tenth anniversary of the College, it developed into ''a strong, healthful, forceful, individual, practical womanhood, filling her station even as well as her brother institutions.''

In summarizing the accomplishments of the College in its bulletin of July 1, 1924, Bralley reported,

> The College is . . . proud of the record it has made in its efforts to serve, broadly and helpfully, the state of Texas. In the homes, in the communities, and in many of the suitable vocations for women, throughout Texas, are thousands of the former students of this College whose vision and leadership are recognized. Their service makes Texas a better and safer place in which to live, and their influence for good will bless the oncoming generations of the State.

The bulletin continued that alumnae may find themselves bewildered by the ''bigness that has taken possession of every phase of the College,'' but ''they soon recognize that the spirit and character of the institution [have] not changed.''

Bralley had undertaken the tasks established by the founding legislation and reaffirmed in the college bulletin of June 1, 1921: ''namely, to keep up with the spirit and progress of the times, by adding 'such other practical industries as from time to time may be suggested by experience,' and to extend the material growth of the College so as to make it a physical possibility to take care of the increasing multitude of students who are to ask for admission at its doors.'' His sudden death left those tasks to his successors.[28]

CHAPTER IV—NOTES

[1]Born March 6, 1867, on a farm near Honey Grove, Texas, Bralley graduated from Carlton College, a Methodist college in Bonham, in 1887. (A classmate was Ela Hockaday, who founded and was the head of Hockaday School in Dallas.) Working on a farm in the summer of 1887, he studied during his rest hours and successfully attempted examinations for a certificate to teach. For the next five years he taught in small one-teacher community schools in Lamar and Fannin Counties. In 1892 he married Mary Melzina Meade, who had been a student at his school at Allen's Chapel in Fannin County.

Also in 1892 he opposed and defeated the Fannin County Superintendent who had held his position for many years. Bralley served as County Superintendent for five years. He also became Superintendent of the Honey Grove public schools, where he served until January, 1905, when he became Chief Clerk of the State Department of Education in Austin.

In 1908 he resigned this position to serve briefly as General Agent for the Conference for Education in Texas. From September 6, 1908, to January 1, 1910, as Superintendent of the State School for the Blind at Austin, he effected substantial improvements.

When the State Superintendent of Public Schools resigned to become President of West Texas State Teachers' College (now West Texas State University), Bralley, encouraged and supported by resolutions from a number of groups in the state, sought and attained the state superintendency, an office which he held until 1913 when he became Director of the Department of Extension of the University of Texas.

Biographical information comes from ''The Biography of Francis Marion Bralley, LL.D.,'' a master's thesis completed in August, 1925, by Ella Ernestine Lunday at the University of Texas and from a personal written recollection prepared by Jewel Rattan-Bralley and mailed to TWU President Mary Evelyn Blagg Huey in August, 1978.

White came from the University of Texas to CIA as Dean of the College on April 1, 1915, after the first Dean, A.L. Banks, resigned to become postmaster at Denton. White served as Dean more than thirty years under three Presidents. His *Historical Record*, published as a college bulletin on December 1, 1948, and his autobiography, *Lengthening Shadows*, both provide helpful information about the College.

[2]The total enrollment for the 1914-15 school year, including summer enrollment, was 866, a number which increased to 2364 in the 1923-24 school year and to 2454 in 1924-25, the year which followed Bralley's sudden death on August 23, 1924. A message from Bralley, printed in the *Lass-O* of January 16, 1915, predicted, ''At its present rate of increase . . . [CIA] will in a short time be second in size of student body only to the University of Texas, and will easily surpass the University in number of young women students.''

[3]Early courses of study led to the Bachelor of Arts (B.A.), Bachelor of Science (B.S.), Bachelor of Business Administration (B.B.A.), Bachelor of Literary Interpretation (B.L.I.), and Bachelor of Music (B.M.) degrees.

By 1924, majors for each degree included English, education, a foreign language (Latin, French, Spanish, or German), history and social science, mathematics, physical science (chemistry or physics), and biological science (bacteriology, botany, physiology, or zoology) for the B.A. degree and general home economics, general home economics for teachers, foods, textiles and clothing, home demonstration, commercial advertising, costume design, applied design, drawing and painting, interior decoration, art education, ceramics, secretarial studies, literary interpretation, piano, violin, voice, public school music, kindergarten, physical education, woodworking, mechanical drawing, crafts, linotyping, rural arts, industrial chemistry, bacteriology, and pathology for the B.S. degree.

The College continued to provide one-, two-, and three- or four-year programs of vocational preparation which led to vocational certificates instead of degrees. According to

May Day celebrations included the selection and crowning of a Queen of the May.

The CIA Orchestra of 1915 included violins, mandolins, a cornet, a cello, and a piano.

55

William Jennings Bryan delivered his "Peace lecture" in the CIA auditorium in 1916.

the college bulletin of July 1, 1924, the programs offered adequate training for dietitians, journalists, social workers, secretaries, institutional managers, interior decorators, home demonstrators, costume designers, linotype operators, industrial chemists, photographers and telegraphers.

All programs continued to include "practical, home-life training"; and the large number of rural students called for continued training for vocations in dairying, farm managing, and poultry raising.

[4]As noted earlier, enrollment almost tripled during Bralley's tenure, and the College developed a national and even international reputation. For the five years preceding the Regents' report to Governor James Ferguson on December 1, 1916, CIA had a greater percent gain in attendance than any other college or university of the first rank (26.2% for the regular session and 28.6% for the two years of Bralley's presidency). Not only was CIA the largest college for women in Texas, it also enrolled more women students than did any other college or university of the first rank in Texas.

By Bralley's last year in office, students were coming to the College from foreign countries. Students from Scotland, Canada, and Mexico attended the 1923-24 session, and other international students had attended earlier sessions. Fifty percent of the students came from more than 100 miles from Denton, and 32% came from more than 200 miles away. As late as 1917, 60% of the students still came from rural areas.

In 1919 the Regents reported a total cumulative enrollment of 10,000; and in 1924, the college bulletin published an extensive list of alumnae, not including the 18,000 students who attended the College for a year or more but did not graduate. The College of Industrial Arts with 2364 students in 1923-24 claimed more than its share of the 22,964 students enrolled in the 51 colleges of Texas.

Bralley's success in acquiring new buildings is detailed in subsequent pages, but an examaination of his progress in upgrading the faculty and their salaries is in order here. Twenty-two (59%) of the thirty-seven faculty members who served during his first year in office had no degree and only eight (22%) held the master's degree. Only one held the doctor's degree. The faculty for 1924-25, which Bralley hired before his death, included 44 of 112 members with master's degrees (30%), three with doctor's degrees, and only twenty (18%) with no degrees. The faculty included twenty professors, thirteen associate professors, thirty-five assistant professors, and forty-four instructors.

Salaries also improved under Bralley, for even the legislative committee which visited the campus before the Regents submitted their report to Governor Hobby in 1919, lamented the low salaries of the teachers. Twelve teachers received less than $1200 per year; six received $2000; and only one received more than $2000. The only teacher to receive a raise in 1917-18 was one who received a $200 raise to $1600 after she had been away for a year studying at her own expense. The Regents' report included the remarks of the legislative committee: "Your committee strenuously opposes extravagance but affirms that the best teachers in the world in their special lines are not too good for Texas girls." At the end of the 1916-17 school year, ten of sixty-seven faculty members left for higher salaries; and twenty of eighty-five left at the end of 1917-18.

By the last year of his administration, Bralley had at least partially realized his goal for teachers' salaries. According to Mildred Pearce Holt, professors at CIA received from $3000 to $3200 compared to $3000 to $3750 at A&M; and associate professors and below received approximately the same at the two colleges. The deans fared somewhat less well at CIA than at A&M. The average salary for deans at CIA was $3000 to $3250 compared to $4500 at A&M. Associate professors at CIA earned from $2000 to $2750; assistant professors, from $2000 to $2500; and instructors and others, from $1750 to $2000. The median salary paid in state colleges in the U.S. was $3500 for professors, $2800 for associate professors, $2400 for assistant professors, and $1840 for instructors.

[5]The college bulletin of May, 1914, specified grades: *Excellent* (95-100%), *Good* (85-95%), *Medium* (75-85%), *Passable* (65-75%), *Unsatisfactory* (50-65%), *Failure* (less than 50%). Students with "unsatisfactory" grades could make up their work, but students who failed were required to repeat the work. The college bulletin of August, 1916, recorded grades *A, B, C, D, E,* and *F* (92-100%, 83-91%, 74-82%, 65-73%, 60-65%, and below 60%, respectively). Again the grade of *E* allowed marginal students to make up unsatisfactory work by examination. In the bulletin of March 15, 1918, the grade of *E* was eliminated and a grade of *F* assigned to work below 65%.

The college catalog issued March 1, 1919, set forth a three-point grading system and a requirement of sixty units and sixty grade points to obtain the bachelor's degree. The present University-wide requirement of the successful completion of 124 semester-hours for graduation was announced in the bulletin of October 1, 1923.

College bulletins issued February 1 and 15, 1919, specified the completion of fifteen units in a standard high school as a requirement for admission: three units in English—one in American and English literature, one in composition, and one in grammar—and twelve elective units. When CIA applied for admission to the Southern Association of Colleges and Secondary Schools in 1920-21, the Association advised that an increased emphasis on literary work would be necessary for classification as a "liberal arts college." Thus, when the College issued its summer session announcement on January 1, 1921, it had identified admission requirements similar to those still in effect: three units of English, two units of algebra, one unit of plane geometry, two units of history, two units of language or natural science, and five units of electives.

The bulletin of October 1, 1923, announced that 429 of the 595 new freshmen (72.1%) who entered in the fall of 1923 offered the fifteen units required for full admission. The remaining 166 students were admitted conditionally with thirteen or fourteen units, the deficiencies to be made up in preparatory classes.

CIA had been accepted as a member of the Association of Texas Colleges in 1918; and, the bulletin announced, in order to maintain its membership, it would require a minimum of fourteen units for admission in the fall of 1924 and fifteen in the fall of 1925.

[6]The college catalog, dated March 1, 1919, outlines the system.

[7]The state's fifty-one colleges could prepare fewer than a thousand trained teachers each year. On the average, they taught fewer than three years each.

[8]In 1914 the federal Smith-Lever Act called for agricultural and home economics demonstration work in counties and communities across the nation. CIA sought authorization to supervise the home demonstration work. In keeping with the pattern established in other states, however, the Texas Legislature placed the supervision of both the agricultural and the home demonstration work under Texas A&M because it was a land-grant institution with a demonstration staff already established.

Many people objected to this arrangement because A&M admitted only male students and because they felt CIA best suited to work with women in their homes. A controversy developed, fanned by newspapers, college publications, and ex-students from both CIA and A&M. Bralley of CIA and Bizzell of A&M (and formerly of CIA) appeared before a special session of the Legislature to present their cases in what Ella Ernestine Lunday described as "an elaborate presentation with professional courtesy controlling the debators in as happy a way as was human." By a vote of sixteen to twelve, the Senate awarded the service to A&M; but the two Presidents continued their rather heated debate in educational journals in the fall of 1921.

[9]The revised course, issued February 1, 1918, reflected the impact of World War I with such topics as "The Patriotism of the Clean Platter," "Making the War Safe for Childhood," "Women Ambulance Drivers in France," "War, Women and American Clothes," and "What Are These War-Jobs for Women?" Whether related to the war or to other trials of the time, the bulletin also offered information about a "Sure Cure for Nerves."

[10]The undated bulletin, probably issued in 1918, admonished, "There is no more excuse for ugliness in dress than in manners, or morals, or anything else," and offered to provide both a lecturer and "dress exhibit as illustrated" to women's organizations or high school classes interested in "this much desired dress reform." Decrying the "paint, powder, beauty-spots, grotesque hair arrangements, cheap jewelry, transparent blouses, high heels, and extravagant use of silk hose as bears marked resemblance to a chorus rehearsal" which were widely in evidence in the average high school classroom, the bulletin illustrated a modest wardrobe which included a midnight blue or navy serge dress, a dark blue wool skirt and white blouse, a white cotton skirt and blouse, a gingham dress, a white cotton slip, a white petticoat and camisole, a dark underskirt, a combination suit (teddies), and knickers.

[11]The Regents' report to Governor James Ferguson (December 1, 1916) added that fewer than thirty-five per cent of the two million had even "a common grammar grade education."

[12]Among other recommendations was the information that "the amount of protein and fat present make cottonseed flour so very nutritious that it can be substituted for meat in the diet if not eaten too frequently." Research in the uses of cottonseed flour as a source of protein is still a major undertaking of the TWU Research Institute.

[13]"Program Material for Parent-Teacher Associations," issued December 1, 1921, addressed the problem; and the entire bulletin of August 1, 1922, "How May Texas Adequately Support Her Institutions of Higher Learning?" by C.D. Judd, Director of the Department of History and Social Science, discussed the problem at length, offering a number of alternative funding proposals along with research about the funding of higher education in other states and the effects of the advocated millage tax on the taxpayers of Texas. Bralley advocated a carefully deliberated permanent plan to safeguard "equality of educational opportunity, as well as economy and efficiency" with the admonition that Texas has thrown away several opportunities in recent years to provide permanently for a comprehensive and efficient system of public education." Judd warned that the institutions of higher learning must be placed out of the reach of "designing politicians and those whose faces are turned backward." Denouncing criticism of the gap between college teachers and public school teachers and between "college men and women and the humblest and most illiterate men and women" as "demagoguery, sheer nonsense," he advised, "It is time for us to shake off the parsimonious attitude we now assume, [and] look the question [of financing] squarely in the face."

[14]The addition of the new space, the installation of an elevator, and "the absolute fire-proofing of the entire structure" cost approximately $100,000.

[15]Nine teachers were instructing more than three hundred students in music under these conditions.

The greenhouse completed in 1918 is still in use today. The Rural Arts Building to its right has been demolished.

Mary Eleanor Brackenridge Hall (above) and Sallie B. Capps Hall were named for CIA Regents from San Antonio and Fort Worth, respectively.

[16]The college bulletin (October 1, 1923) described the pool as "a large tile-lined swimming pool filled with clear artesian water of even and suitable temperature. The water is kept clean and pure by frequent change and by use of a violet ray apparatus." Although the pool is no longer usable, the gymnasium building still receives some use as a training center for student athletes.

[17]When the Regents requested funds for the barn in 1916, they noted that the barn then in use had been erected soon after the College was established and "never was sanitary and adequate, and is now in a worn-out dilapidated condition." Besides, they reported, it was "located too close to the dormitories in which students reside." The college bulletin of March 15, 1918, which announced the completion of the greenhouse and dairy barn, described them as "the most modern and well-kept buildings of their kind in the country." The well-equipped barn could accommodate forty-four cows.

[18] See Chapter III, footnote 2. The demonstration cottages enabled students to assume the full responsibility for the management of a home. Living for short periods in groups of six seniors plus a faculty chaperone, each student in turn assumed full responsibility for buying groceries, preparing and serving meals, cleaning the house, and doing the laundering and other appropriate work. The college bulletin (September 1, 1917) noted, "Under no circumstances are the girls permitted to spend more than thirty cents a person per day, and the menus must represent that scientific combination of victuals known as the balanced ration for each particular group of girls." The girl responsible for the meals of the day rose at 5:30 to have breakfast ready by 6:30.

In addition to the day-to-day management of the house, each group entertained with two informal dinner parties and two informal afternoon teas to which they invited outside guests. Many students planned other picnics or outings for members of their groups.

The opening of the second demonstration cottage allowed juniors in foods and cookery to reside in the cottage for three weeks and seniors to return for a second three weeks for problems in administration and nutrition.

[19]Two senior students in the houseplanning section of the manual arts department designed the one-and-one-half-story frame cottage, and students of the fine and applied arts department planned the interior decorations.

[20]The dormitory was named for Mary Eleanor Brackenridge of San Antonio, who served from the time of her appointment to the first Board of Regents until 1924. A strong advocate of the advancement of women, she was president of the Texas Woman Suffrage Association, 1913-14. Built at a cost of some $126,000 plus $15,000 for equipment, the hall accommodated 147 students in its seventy-three rooms. A roofgarden with a covered stage and seating for more than 1400 people was a popular place for social gatherings and entertainment; and a large basement dining room served about 500 students—not only the residents of Brackenridge Hall but also the students in the Oakland Annex, Stoddard Hall, and nearby private rooming houses.

[21]They are the oldest dormitories remaining on the campus. The halls were named to honor members of the Board of Regents at the time of their completion—James H. Lowry, President; and Mrs. Sallie B. Capps, Secretary. The slightly larger Lowry Hall, which cost approximately $155,000 plus $30,000 for equipment, included 84 rooms to accommodate 180 students; and its basement dining hall served about 600 students—residents of Capps Hall and nearby private rooming houses as well as its own residents. Capps Hall cost about $100,000 plus $15,000 for equipment. It contained 72 rooms to house 159 students.

[22]See Chapter II.

[23]The *Daedalian Quarterly* was first published in January, 1915. It sold for fifteen cents. The *Lass-O* and the quarterly were published continuously from their first issue through the 1978-79 school year. In the 1979-80 school year, the *Daedalian Quarterly* merged with the yearbook (called *The Daedalian*) into an annual magazine called *Daedalian*. The *Lass-O* continues to be published four times a week. Following the establishment of the Journalism Department in 1925, that department assumed responsibility for the *Lass-O*. The college bulletin of March 1, 1925, reported that "practically all of the work on the *Lass-O*, including the composition, is done by students under the active supervision of faculty members, all of whom have had newspaper experience." Printing presses and four linotype machines were included in the journalism workshop.

[24]Since 1939, all undergraduate classes have prepared original stunts each spring in competition for a silver "stunt cup."

[25]Although many kinds of clubs were popular among the students, the Regents reported to Governor Hobby in 1919, "The authorities of the College have never permitted the organization of sororities among the students on the ground that such organizations usually characterize fashionable society schools for girls in which the democratic spirit finds small, if any, expression, and which tend to encourage social division and caste." Although the Regents noted that sororities at other colleges and universities had requested the organization

Life in a demonstration cottage was a formal part of a student's instruction.

James H. Lowry Hall was named for a CIA Regent from Honey Grove.

of sororities at CIA, they added, "It must be said in justice to the student body that they have never made a request to organize sororities."

The legislative committee which visited the campus and which the Regents quoted in their report also referred to the democratic spirit of education at the College: "The rich girl, who ought to know food values and whether her servants give her honest returns for her money and whether her garments are shoddy or genuine, studies these problems by the side of her less wealthy friend who will want to buy her own groceries and know what to buy, cook her own family's meals and know what to cook and how to cook it, and how to keep her own house and make her own home."

To foster a democratic spirit and to encourage economy, the College also required the students to wear uniforms, a practice planned before the College opened its doors and initiated in the second quarter of classes.

[26]See Chapter II for a discussion of the original Lyceum program. The College replaced the Lyceum with an Artists' Course in the fall of 1916.

[27]In 1916-17, the first year of the Artists' Course, the College brought Alfred Noyes, Giovanni Martinelli, soprano May Peterson, Oscar Seagle, Ethel Leginska, the Devereux Players, and the St. Louis Symphony Orchestra to the campus. Zimbalist, May Peterson, John Masefield, the Devereux Players, and art lecturer Frank Alvin Parsons appeared in 1917-18; and the bulletin of March 1, 1919, reported that the Flonzally String Quartette and the French Army Band had also appeared.

In 1920-21, contralto Merle Alcock, violinists Thelma Given and Eddy Brown, Count Ilya Tolstoi, composer and pianist Charles Wakefield Cadman, Indian contralto Tsiania, poet Rabindramath Tagore, pianist Ernest Hutcheson, lecturer Mrs. Forbes Robertson Hale, baritone Reinald Werrenrath, interpreters Mr. and Mrs. Charles Rann Kennedy, and Frank Alvah Parsons appeared at the College. The bulletin of March 1, 1922, reported that sopranos Helen Stanley and Frieda Hempel, violinist Albert Spalding, pianists Mischa Levitski and Wilhelm Bachaus, harpist Alberto Salvi, and the Sherniavsky Trio of Musicians had also appeared.

Artistic dancing was among the classes offered along with other "practical" and "literary" subjects.

[28]Never before suffering an illness of any consequence, Bralley became ill on August 7, 1924, apparently with a kind of influenza. Following several days of hoarseness and fever, he was taken to Baylor Hospital in Dallas. Reports of his improvement were issued; but his condition worsened, and he died at five o'clock on the morning of August 23 of myocarditis.

An estimated two thousand persons attended his funeral the following Sunday in the College Auditorium, which had been built during his administration. At the direction of his wife, who was herself confined to Baylor Hospital and unable to attend the funeral, Bralley's body was buried in the I.O.O.F. Cemetery in Denton rather than in the State Cemetery in Austin. His funeral cortege was reported to have been the longest ever seen in Denton.

This information comes from the biography prepared by Ella Lunday and from information supplied by Jewel Rattan-Bralley (see footnote 1, this chapter).

(Left to right) In 1915 Susan Cobb, Allie George, and Sallie Byrd completed the first four-year course of studies offered by CIA and received the first B. S. degrees awarded by the College.

A Period of Confusion   V

Following the death of Bralley, the Regents met August 25 to designate Dean Edmund Valentine White as acting President. Slightly more than a month later, on September 27, they unanimously elected Lindsey Blayney, Professor of German at Rice Institute, to begin service as President on January 1, 1925.[1] The choice was celebrated across the campus and throughout Texas.

In spite of Blayney's wide travels, his broad acquaintances, his distinguished academic credentials, and his dedication to the ideals which guided the College, however, Blayney quickly found himself embroiled in conflicts which he could not resolve. Governor Neff pledged his support, but Miriam A. Ferguson was elected Governor following a bitter campaign; and, according to E. V. White in his autobiography, *Lengthening Shadows,* local supporters of Governor Ferguson "sought to dabble in the affairs of the College and to place their henchmen in positions that they said should go to loyal Democrats only."[2] According to White, the supporters sought the discharge of faculty members who, they claimed, had bolted the Democratic ticket. In the meantime, White reports, Blayney attracted open opposition by discharging some faculty members and proposing to discharge others. In a long autobiographical letter to his sons (February 10, 1959), Blayney recalls the appointment of two Regents, characterized in the press as "incompetent henchmen" of James Ferguson, husband of the Governor and former Governor himself. By influencing a third Regent to vote with them, they could, Blayney says, tie the vote "at will, . . . rendering orderly transaction of most important business difficult or impossible."

White reports that faculty and students began to question Blayney's qualifications to remain as President; and he made countercharges of incompetency against the faculty who sought his removal, a "great majority" of the faculty according to White. The disruption had reached such a great state by the fall, 1925, that, according to White, the Regents decided in a heated meeting that Blayney was unsuited for the Presidency and voted to request his resignation to become effective June 1, 1926. In his letter to his sons, Blayney records his decision to resign after round-about suggestions that "the Governor would be glad to suggest replacements" for certain business officers of the College if Blayney would remove them; and he noted the continued support of many of the students who presented him a French clock inscribed, "In Affectionate Loyalty From YOUR Girls of TSCW." Newspapers throughout the state—from Van Alstyne, Sherman, and Quanah to Dallas, Houston, and San Antonio—lamented his departure.

Thousands of persons, including eminent citizens of Texas, gathered January 11, 1925, to participate in the installation of Lindsey Blayney as President of CIA and to hear him pledge "the best that is within me."

Virginia Carroll founded the YWCA movement at CIA.

The YWCA clubhouse named for her opened during the 1925-26 school year. An upstairs porch and room for rest, rooms for reading and writing, a kitchenette, a fireplace, and a large room for dancing made the house a social center.

In spite of his problems, Blayney was able during his short administration to accomplish substantial good. In fact, in his autobiography, *Recollections of a Texas Educator,* L. H. Hubbard, Blayney's successor, credits him with having basically sound ideas, which students probably favored. Hubbard suggests that Blayney's problems came because of his lack of tact and his attempts to move too quickly, but persons who knew Blayney later in his life praised his gentleness and generosity along with his high idealism.[3]

Since Blayney took office in a legislative year, he assumed responsibility for negotiating funds for the College. According to Blayney's report to the press, "We contended for, and received from the Legislature, the same maximum salaries as paid at the A&M College. Thoughtful critics credit us with having rendered thereby a signal service to the cause of education of women in the South."[4]

The Legislature approved a good appropriation bill, including funds for a library, but Governor Ferguson threatened to veto a number of items, which would be lost because the Legislature had adjourned. Through a personal conference with the Governor and her husband White and/or Blayney persuaded them to leave two threatened items in the budget—$150,000 for the library and $40,000 to pave Bell Avenue and to purchase land which would be used for athletic activities.

Another lasting contribution to the campus was Blayney's persuasion of the Board of Regents to employ Arthur A. Shurtleff, a noted Boston landscape architect who had designed the Wellesley College campus, to prepare a permanent plan for the CIA campus. Like the plan for Washington, D.C., the CIA plan was to guide the growth of the campus forever. The design called for three great courts—south, central, and north—surrounded by buildings and traversed by permanent cement walks and driveways.[5]

As in its early days, the College again came under attack from two groups of critics with almost opposite ideas. On the one hand, opponents

charged that the College was becoming a "Vassar," and on the other critics claimed it was "only an industrial school." To counter these criticisms and to provide effective administration, Blayney organized the College into five schools—Liberal Arts, Industrial Arts and Sciences, Home Economics, Fine Arts, and Education—and launched a major publicity campaign to win support for the College through a series of articles he circulated to newspapers all over the state.[6]

In his articles and in college bulletins, Blayney contended that the College offered the best of both practical and intellectual extremes without being extreme itself. He praised CIA for its originality, for its dedication to the ideals of the American home, and for its efforts to combine intellectual and cultural education with practical and vocational training.

Like his predecessors, Blayney was determined that the College would develop well-rounded students. As he reported to the press in the bulletin dedicated to them (June 1, 1925), "So long as the present administration is at the helm of this great Texas college the things pertaining to the head, hand, heart, and body will always be equally emphasized." Praising the democractic spirit of the College, he reported that "five of the last seven presidents of the Students' Association had earned a part of their college expenses by serving in the college dining rooms"; and he asserted that the fact that the College Students' Christian Association was the largest organization of its kind in the South or the Middle West was a direct refutation of the claim that state colleges were irreligious.

In spite of attacks on him, he even praised the "character, application, zeal, and devotion" of the students and acknowledged the faculty "who, with few exceptions, have shared the visions and the ideals to realization." He was also generous in his evaluation of the developers of the curriculum who, he said, "have not permitted themselves to be unduly influenced by tradition nor yet misled by unwise demands of the present, however insistent."

Although in his autobiography White describes Blayney's tenure as a "period of confusion" with "little time . . . given to curricular matters," there were areas of significant progress. Aroused by the controversy of Blayney's administration, the public demanded that holders of higher academic degrees be employed to upgrade the faculty. Preparatory students, whose numbers had declined throughout Bralley's administration, entered CIA for the last time in 1925-26; and in 1925 Blayney secured membership for the College in the American Association of University Women.

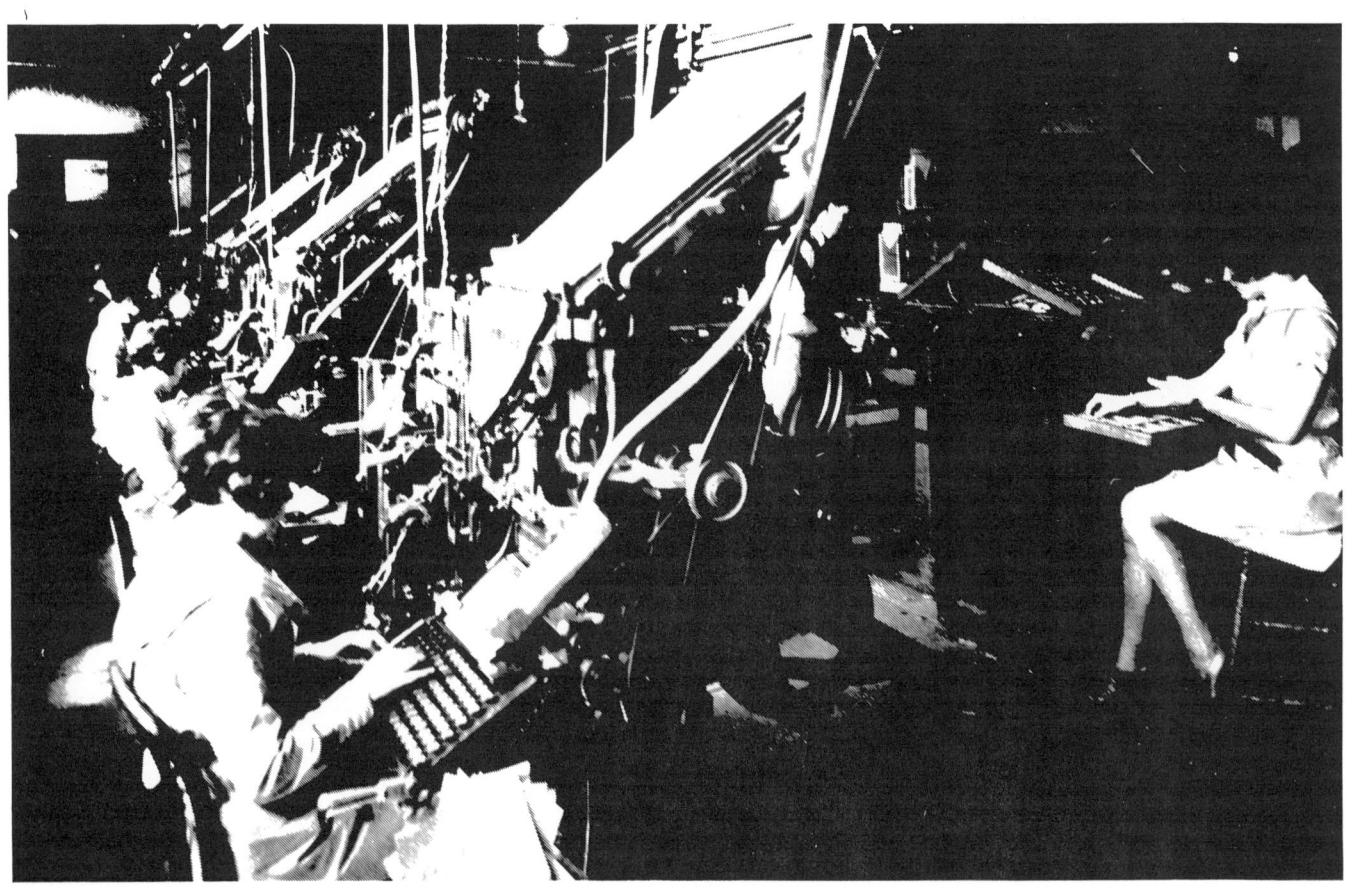

Students wrote, edited, typeset, and printed the Lass-O, *CIA's prize winning newspaper.*

In addition, with linotype training and the *Lass-O* firmly established, the College was ready in 1925 for the establishment of a Department of Journalism and a four-year program that led to a degree in journalism.[7] Working under the supervision of faculty members who had newspaper experience, students performed practically all of the work of the newspaper from reporting and editing to writing headlines and composing.

Among the events the students reported were a wealth of extracurricular activities. As Blayney reported to the press, twenty-two clubs were operating at the College, some limited in membership but most large enough to allow all students to belong to at least one. Blayney emphasized that there were "no secret societies or sororities at CIA." The clubs were designed to encourage friendship and to foster literary and artistic interests. Some groups engaged in philanthropic work as well: sending Christmas boxes to orphanages, establishing scholarships, and helping students who needed financial aid.

The James H. Lowry Club was affiliated with the League of Women Voters. The Department of Speech sponsored a Dramatic Club which performed plays, a Story Tellers' Club which offered recreational work such as twilight story hours and fireside groups, and a Debating Club through which students could compete intercollegiately. The Poets' Club published *The Blue Chambray Book of Verse,* a collection of poems by CIA students, in the spring of 1925; and the Round Table, composed of the presidents of all literary and special clubs, brought such poets as Cecil Roberts, Edgar Lee Masters, and Harriet Monroe to the campus.[8]

In spite of the opportunities available to students, however, the faculty, and even the people of the town, felt the effects of the Blayney controversy; and the next administration acquired the task of binding up the wounds from a bitter fight.[9]

[1]Thomas Lindsey Blayney was born December 3, 1874, in Lebanon, Kentucky. His father was pastor of the First Presbyterian Church in Albany, New York, at the time of Lindsey's birth; but Mrs. Blayney, an ardent Southerner, made the journey to visit her sister in Kentucky so that the child might be born there. From 1879 to 1881 when Mrs. Blayney died, the family lived in Europe where they had gone seeking medical help for her. Living on the French border with Italy, Lindsey learned French and Italian and, from his father, geography and other subjects. Seeking for the frail Lindsey a milder climate than that of New York where they returned after the death of Mrs. Blayney, the family moved to Frankfort, Kentucky, in 1884.

In 1894, Lindsey Blayney graduated from Centre College in Danville, Kentucky. (His father served as chairman of the board of trustees of the college for almost twenty-five years.) In the fall of 1895 Blayney began graduate studies in European universities, studying in France, Germany, Spain, and Italy. He married Gertrude South, member of a distinguished Southern family, in 1896. After enrolling at Heidelberg University in 1901, he graduated in 1904 with honors with M.A. and Ph.D. degrees in philology and comparative literature.

He was the second professor chosen when Rice Institute began classes in 1912, and he remained a member of the faculty of Rice until he accepted the Presidency of CIA. In 1914 the Albert Kahn Foundation chose him to be a traveling fellow in India, China, and Japan. During World War I, he volunteered for service, even though he was over draft age, and served with distinction from the English Channel to the Aegean Sea, attaining the rank of lieutenant-colonel. He was decorated by the governments of France, Serbia, Greece, Italy and, numerous times, by the government of the United States; and he continued his service in Europe, helping to establish peace after the war.

Upon his return to the United States, Blayney was widely respected as a soldier, an educator, a humanitarian, and a leader in the development of policies at both the local (Houston) and national levels. His strong and eloquent public stands against the Ku Klux Klan following the war won him admiration throughout Texas and the nation, resulting in his receiving the Doctor of Laws degree from the University of Notre Dame in Indiana, from Loyola University in New Orleans, from Southwestern University in Georgetown, Texas, and from Austin College in Sherman, Texas.

Biographical information comes from the *Lass-O* of October 4, 1924, and from typewritten materials provided to TWU President Mary Evelyn Blagg Huey. The typed materials include an autobiographical letter from Lindsey Blayney to his sons (February 10, 1959) and a biographical letter prepared by Ida Walz Blayney (December, 1972). Lindsey and Ida Walz Blayney were married March 24, 1948. Lindsey Blayney died March 13, 1971.

[2]Denton: E.V. White, n.d.

[3]Hubbard notes that Blayney had served with army intelligence during World War I, and he had developed a habit of making his pronouncements regarding improving standards at the College in the form of memoranda which resembled army orders. Combined with his statements of the need for a better faculty and his threatened reprisals against critics, Hubbard suggests, such "orders" may have fostered insecurity and lack of cooperation among the faculty. In his letter to his sons, Blayney quotes the Houston *Chronicle* (date not given) which said, "There were those connected with [the College] who resented his selection over themselves and the thwarting of their ambition for the position for which they were not fitted."

[4]Nevertheless, he noted, "It will be well that we Texans be reminded that the Legislature of the little state of Oklahoma, since 1915, has given to its State College for Women (only one-third as large as our College) one and a half times as much for buildings as Texas has given to its State College for Women"; and, he added, the total cost of CIA to Texans "since its establishment is less than five cents per capita per annum."

[5]The circular drive in front of the Administration Building (now called Old Main). Blayney had been chairman of Houston's first City Planning Commission.

[6]Although a dean was named for each school, the organization was short-lived. President Hubbard's administration quickly re-established departments as basic units of organization.

[7]The College had printing presses and four linotype machines which served as a laboratory for the department.

[8]Other artists of the first rank also continued to come to the campus. Among those reported in the college bulletin of March 1, 1925, were violinists Erma Rubenstein and Carl Flesch; sopranos Florence Macbeth and Rosa Ponselle; pianists Samaroff, Elly Ney, and Georgette LaMotte; baritone Oscar Seagle; the New York String Quartet; and Marion Rosenberg, Harriet Gilman, R.H. Griffith, William Allen White, and William Russell Clarke.

[9]From CIA, Blayney went to Carleton College in Northfield, Minnesota, where he was highly respected Dean of the College and Chairman of the Department of German until his retirement in 1946.

Turbulence characterized the brief tenure of President Lindsey Blayney.

An annual Valentine's Day dance allowed students to repeat the styles and dances of George and Martha Washington.

Order out of Chaos   VI

Even as early as the first spring of Blayney's administration, the fracas at CIA was of sufficient size and force to spread rumors to Austin where Louis Herman Hubbard was the Dean of Students at the University of Texas. Hubbard had long been interested in CIA, once applying unsuccessfully for a teaching position in the Department of English; but, according to his autobiography, *Recollections of a Texas Educator,* when word reached him that he might be considered as Blayney's successor, he was inclined to stay in the position he liked at Austin and stay out of the politics which would surround the selection of a new President.[1] Nevertheless, on the encouragement of Annie Webb Blanton and Mrs. Lee Joseph, Hubbard applied for the Presidency; and on his forty-fourth birthday (February 10, 1926) he returned to Austin from an overnight trip to Belton and found a student reading a special edition of *The Daily Texan* which proclaimed, "Dean Hubbard Elected President of CIA."

The task which faced him was no easy one. E. V. White records in his autobiography, *Lengthening Shadows,* that Hubbard had to try to bring "order out of chaos, to harmonize existing factions, and to bring respect again to the office of the President." In his autobiography, Hubbard notes that the problems were greater than he had realized; for not only were the faculty and students "at one another's throats, but also the entire citizenship of Denton had evidently gotten into the act under the leadership of a former local Regent and prominent attorney who had supported President Blayney."

Blayney made no offer of congratulation or help; but quickly contacting Hubbard, Dean White arranged to meet him in Waco. There the President-elect pledged to ignore past incidents, take no sides in the dispute, and judge people solely on their performance after his arrival on the campus on June 1. White returned to spread the news; and Hubbard was, according to White, "remarkably successful in healing old wounds in a short time. . . . Only a few months were required to give the campus its wonted appearance of cordial cooperation." A spirit of cordiality, hospitality, and geniality became the hallmark of Hubbard's administration.

No less determined than Blayney to upgrade the College, Hubbard succeeded where Blayney failed. One of the weaknesses of CIA was the small number of doctorates the faculty held and the large number of faculty members who held only baccalaureate degrees.[2] Hubbard adopted the master's degree as the minimum requirement for faculty membership and filled vacancies with persons who possessed doctorates whenever possible. He himself received the honorary Doctor of Laws degree from

"Uniforms" for students came to include many stylish variations.

L. H. Hubbard learned of his selection as President of CIA on his forty-fourth birthday.

Austin College in June, 1929, in recognition of his work as an educator and as President of CIA; and he earned the Doctor of Philosophy degree from the University of Texas the following year.

Although Hubbard acknowledged in his autobiography that "the academic mind cannot be stampeded; it must be led slowly," the early years of his administration brought rather quick changes to the College both academically and in the area of student life. Within a year of his arrival, the bulletin (April 1, 1927) reported the initiation of honors courses for "seniors who are capable of doing more independent work than is necessary to fulfill the requirements of their minor and major subjects"; and the College established a Committee on Students' Use of English, authorized to give oral and written tests when necessary to be sure that students who received the bachelor's degree could speak and write correct English.

Within another year the academic calendar had changed from a quarter system to a regular session of two eighteen-week semesters and a twelve-week summer session, and the following year the College initiated a nine-week and a three-week summer term. During the spring semester, 1929, the College established Honors Day for the public recognition of students receiving freshman and intermediate honors. The Honors Day included an address by a scholar of wide reputation. Seniors were recognized at graduation.

Again displaying its readiness to adapt to new needs, the College introduced a major in library science in 1929. The Southern Association of Secondary Schools and Colleges had announced that all accredited high schools in Texas would be required to add librarians to their faculties by 1930; and in response to the anticipated need for additional work for both public school and city and county librarians, CIA expanded its existing offerings in library science to a program which would lead to the Bachelor of Science degree.[3]

With the ending of preparatory classes in 1925-26, CIA established a demonstration school, which it maintained not as a "fitting school" or preparatory department of the College but as a laboratory for seniors who could teach, under supervision, physical education, public school music and art, expression, manual training, home economics for the grades and for high school, and other courses.

The capstone of the academic growth during Hubbard's early years in office was the addition of graduate studies. Blayney had been flatly opposed to graduate work at CIA. As he stated in the college bulletin of March 1, 1925, "The administration refuses to be tempted by the allurements and consequent dangers of graduate training and of highly specialized scholarship." But, in the spring, 1930, Hubbard announced, "There seems to the authorities of the College no reason why these requests from students who preferred not to do their graduate work in a co-educational institution should any longer be ignored." According to Hubbard, "Nearly every prominent woman's college in America offers graduate work." Following months of consideration, the Regents voted (March 22, 1930) to accept the recommendation of the faculty that CIA offer work leading to the Master of Arts degree; and the College inaugurated a graduate school at the beginning of the summer session, 1930.

At first the College added no new faculty and formed no separate organization for graduate studies. The President named a Committee on Graduate Study, appointed each year, to administer the work of the school, which originally offered majors in home economics, fine arts, English, American history, Spanish, and education and minors in each of these areas and in biology, business administration, chemistry, economics and government, mathematics, and physical and health education.[4] Within

home economics, students could elect majors in general home economics, foods and nutrition, or clothing and textiles.

Along with its academic growth, the College enjoyed modest growth in its physical facilities during the early years of Hubbard's tenure. Approved during the 1925 legislative session, the new library building was completed in February, 1927.[5] Its red brick construction and its colonial design were in marked contrast to the existing buildings of the campus, which were fairly uniform in style and color; but, as the bulletin of April 1, 1927, noted, "This contrast is that of dignity as it rightfully should be, considering the use made of the building, together with its dedication in memory of a beloved President of the College."[6]

Although neglected and underfinanced, the library had grown with the College. From 460 books housed in a single room on the second floor of the original college building, the library had expanded into a special section in the east wing of that building by 1916. As late as 1925, however, according to the remarks of ex-students in the college bulletin (December 1, 1929), "The books were few and the chances of getting one at the desired time were fewer." By the time the library building was completed, the library contained approximately 24,000 volumes; more than 7,000 classified pamphlets; subscriptions to more than 135 current periodicals plus government publications; the bulletins and pamphlets of many colleges, associations, and corporations; and leading newspapers.[7]

Designers of the library thought the capacity of the building for 75,000 books would make it adequate to serve the needs of the College for many years. By 1929, the library had been designated a depository for government documents; and by the time the College instituted graduate study in

The Bralley Memorial Library opened in 1927 with approximately 24,000 volumes plus pamphlets, periodicals, and government publications. The reading room and surrounding balcony accommodated three hundred students and housed the Round Table, where presidents of the literary and departmental clubs gathered. The table was made from the different woods of Texas.

71

Named for Governor Joseph D. Sayers, Sayers Hall opened in 1928 (Carruth Coll. photo).

1930, the library had increased its holdings to 40,000 volumes plus subscriptions to 225 periodicals. The bulletin of August 1, 1930, reported that the College spent $9,500 each year for books and magazines, "approximately five dollars per student."

Although student enrollment remained fairly stable during this time, the Fortieth Legislature approved $150,000 for another dormitory;[8] and the College continued to provide five Senior Houses through lease or purchase—the Neal House, Shadow Lawn, Los Alamos, Sin Cuidado, and Solana. By January 1, 1929, CIA had also acquired a residence near the campus which it equipped for the Nursery School. Auxiliary buildings added during 1929 included a one-story brick building, which the federal government leased as a sub-station post office, and an addition to the laundry, which almost doubled its capacity.

The new auditorium remained the social center of college life with "class plays, picture shows, and other forms of wholesome recreation and amusement." The Artists' Course continued to attract renowned artists. In addition to the Russian Symphonic Choir and the London String Quartet in 1926-27, the series included tenor Lambert Murphy, soprano Gianini, contralto Merle Alcock, violinist Raoul Vidas, pianist Levitzki, and lecturers Charles Brandon Booth and Ada Ward.[9] For informal social activities, the ex-students' number of the college bulletin (December 1, 1929) reported plans for picnic grounds at Lake Dallas on a twenty-acre lake front tract which the City of Dallas had granted to the College for use as a recreation ground.[10]

The College reflected its maturity in many ways by 1930. Its first students were now sending their daughters to CIA;[11] and whereas reports of the activities of early alumnae had reflected them first as homemakers and second as teachers, the ex-students number of the bulletin (December 1, 1929) reported recent graduates in varied professions. Journalists worked from El Paso to New York City. One alumna was "assistant director of a tile shop in New York City." Alumnae also included actresses. One played the roles of Juliet, Portia, and Ophelia with the Avon Players, a Shakespearean company which toured the southern states; and another had the leading role in a Broadway play. Other graduates included a member of the laboratory staff in a Dallas hospital, a graduate student in English at Columbia University, and a missionary to the criminal tribes in India.

Class days, like this one in 1928, included the senior promenade from the auditorium to Old Main with seniors bearing an oak chain as a symbol of their unity.

Accompanying curricular changes and expanding roles for women were major changes in fashions on the campus. Although students still wore uniforms, they had adjusted to changing times. The ex-students' bulletin reported, "Dame Fashion holds sway in the present day uniforms of CIA. . . . A description of the present uniform reads like the advertisement of an exclusive dress shop." Sport suits of blue silk canton, a three-piece outfit of white crepe for seniors, and a tailored blue serge replaced the sun bonnets, shirt waists, and floor-length gored skirts which flowed over the campus in 1903. And the modern gymnasium uniform substituted tailored knickers, a white shirt, and tennis shoes for the voluminous bloomers of 1910. The square tops (mortarboards), a part of the first uniforms, were gone; and hats were no longer required except for church services.

Along with the square top, the waist and skirt, and the ankle length chambray had gone the Sunday quiet hours; and with the new crepe and silk had come permission for students to have portable victrolas. In addition, the evening study hour was delayed from 7:25 to 7:40; and students were permitted to arrange their out-of-town visits through the dormitory offices without written permission from home.

When occasions required chaperones, seniors could chaperone younger students; and even younger students could go to town on Saturday and the first Monday without special permission. Underclass women could "go to the downtown picture show once a week at night" without special permission, and seniors could go on any evening "in groups of three or more without a chaperone." Seniors also had the special privilege of "riding with gentlemen callers on Sunday afternoon from 3:30 to 5:00, provided two couples go in a five passenger car, and have secured permission from the Dean of Women in advance."

The new social privileges reflected a maturity that the College was acquiring in many areas. Graduates in increasing numbers were seeking advanced degrees;[12] and CIA had instituted graduate courses to serve them. These graduate courses, the improvement of the library and the faculty, and the addition of new courses to prepare women for new careers carried the College into realms beyond those suggested by its name, College of Industrial Arts. Thus, as early as 1924 the Texas Survey Commission had recommended a name change; and Hubbard told the ex-students at their business meeting on June 1, 1929, that every visitor to the campus since the Commission had also recommended a change.

The proposed new name was the *Texas State College for Women,* a descriptive phrase used on publications of the College and in spoken references to it since early in its history. Noting that many other state colleges for women had already made the change, that the new name would help graduates who sought admission to graduate schools, that the change would not "invalidate in any way either diplomas or degrees that have already been conferred," and that CIA would be retained as a "pet" name, Hubbard secured unanimous approval of the change from the ex-students at the meeting. Support of the ex-students was a critical step; but official recognition of the new name would not come for five more years, years which saw a steady decline in enrollment.

[1]Hubbard described the selection process in his autobiography. Annie Webb Blanton, State Superintendent of Public Instruction from 1919 to 1923, told Hubbard that she had recommended him to a friend of hers, Mrs. Lee Joseph, a member of the CIA Board of Regents, if a woman were not to be considered for the position. If a woman would be considered, Blanton told Hubbard, she would apply herself.

At Blanton's urging, Hubbard contacted Mrs. Joseph, who promised her support if a woman would not be considered, if he would present a personal endorsement from the president of the University of Texas, and if he would call on the other Regents to indicate his interest and availability.

After visiting the other Regents, Hubbard again met Mrs. Joseph, who outlined a campaign strategy. She noted that the first vote of the Board would likely be indecisive. Because Board President Hugh Nugent Fitzgerald and Regent Mrs. E.P. Turner had maintained their support of Blayney, they would probably vote together on a candidate not backed by other Regents. J.W. Degan of Denton favored R.L. Marquis, President of North Texas State College; and C.U. Connellee, Vice President of the Board, would probably vote with him. Thus, Hubbard could only count on the votes of Mrs. Joseph and Mrs. William Capps, Secretary of the Board from Fort Worth.

Connellee had halfway promised, however, that he would support Mrs. Joseph's candidate on the second ballot; and he did so. Thus, when Connellee's vote gave Hubbard half the votes on the second ballot, Fitzgerald added his support to give the necessary majority; and Degan and Turner joined to make the vote unanimous.

[2]In his autobiography, White recalls Bralley's pride in announcing the employment of the first faculty member to hold a Ph.D. The pride was short-lived, however, when the announcement appeared in the college catalog and the institution which was supposed to have conferred the degree reported that it had not done so. Bralley called in the faculty member and summarily dismissed him.

[3]In 1938, the TWU School of Library Science became the first in the Southwest to be accredited by the American Library Association. It has remained continuously accredited since that time.

[4]The original committee consisted of W.H. Clark, head of chemistry; L.M. Ellison, director of English; Rebecca Switzer, head of foreign languages; and Margaret Gleason, director of home economics.

[5]See Chapter V.

[6]The Library was named to honor President F.M. Bralley, who died in office August 23, 1924. See Chapter IV.

[7]The Bralley Memorial Fund, plus appropriations and other funds, provided $40,000 for the purchase of books for the new library.

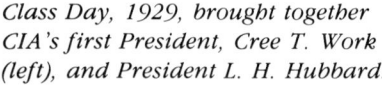

Class Day, 1929, brought together CIA's first President, Cree T. Work (left), and President L. H. Hubbard.

[8]The ninety-two room fireproof dormitory accommodated 202 students. First occupied in September, 1928, it was named Sayers Hall to honor Governor Joseph D. Sayers, who signed into law the legislation which created the College.

[9]The college bulletin of April 1, 1927, which listed these artists, also noted some of the other artists who had appeared in recent years: Schumann-Heink, Paul Whiteman's Orchestra, Tamaki Miuri in *Madame Butterfly*, E. Robert Schmitz, Olga Samaroff, Carl Sandburg, Vachel Lindsay, Edwin Markham, William Butler Yeats, John Gould Fletcher, Grace Noll Crowell, Karle Wilson Baker, Ada Salori in *Carmen*, Robert Frost, and Cyrena Van Gordon.

The college bulletin of March 1, 1930, reported appearances during the preceding year by Alfred Cortot, "renowned French pianist" who with Gounod was the only French musician to receive the Medal of the London Philharmonic Society; the fourteen-member Russian Cossack Chorus singing native songs and, at the end of the program, their interpretations of "several old Southern melodies"; soprano Mary McCormic, violinist Francis MacMillen, and the Pavley-Oukrainsky Ballet. In addition, the United States Marine Band had appeared; and Ruth St. Denis and Ted Shawn had danced in solo and duet performances.

[10]The plot, "situated on a cleared promontory above the lake," was about eight and a half miles from Denton on the Fishtrap Road.

[11]Estella G. Hefley, Dean of Women, began a list of daughters of former students. It numbered eighteen by December 1, 1929. They were invited to serve as hostesses at all ex-student meetings and entertainments on the campus. In 1928-29, Mary Margaret Fry, daughter of the first and only graduate of the Girls Industrial College, attended CIA.

[12]The college bulletin of October 1, 1929, reported the employment of Bertha Duncan, Ph.D., the University of Texas, in the Department of Philosophy and Education. She was the first CIA graduate to earn the Ph.D. degree.

A Spirit of Progress and of Pride

VII

"**U**ndaunted by the persistent cries of 'hard times,' the CIA miss buckles down to real work and continues her college education in spite of the economic condition," reported a college bulletin (October 1, 1930). Nevertheless, the College was not immune to the effects of the Depression which engulfed the country in the early thirties. The same bulletin noted that almost 800 girls had applied for 160 paid positions on campus. The average salary of sixteen dollars a month sometimes paid for a student's board and made the difference in whether or not she could attend school.

Many students who could not find work were unable to continue their studies, and enrollment dropped from a record high of 2,549 in 1929-30 to a sixteen-year low of 1,737 in 1932-33. To attract students and help them finance their studies, the College lowered costs and offered scholarships.[1] It liberalized admission requirements to bring them in line with changing requirements for high school graduation.[2] And it offered several loan funds. As always, college bulletins encouraged parents and students to be economical.

In 1932 the Board of Regents reduced the budget by $30,000 for the following year and passed the decrease along to students (reducing fixed charges from $361 a year to $321). A further decrease in charges for 1933-34 reduced the total expense for room and board, tuition, and optional fees to $289 even though the Legislature had raised tuition from $30 to $50 for nine months. Other miscellaneous expenses such as travel, uniforms, and laundry raised the total nine-month cost to between $350 and $500. Along with reduced charges, the College instituted a plan which allowed students to divide their payments into four installments each semester.

In an additional attempt to reduce expenses and encourage attendance, the College took over Smith-Carroll Hall in the summer of 1931 and converted it to a cooperative home.[3] The college bulletin of January 15, 1932, reported that fifty-seven students worked together in the dormitory, caring for rooms and halls and setting tables, serving, and washing dishes in the dining room. By working a maximum of one and a half hours a day, a student could reduce her expenses for nine months to $265, payable in installments.[4]

In the fall, a 4-H project introduced cooperative programs in houses near the campus where fifty girls lived in small groups with a hostess for each group. By the following spring, sixty-two girls (chosen from one

Students designed and created the lights, pews, windows, and other art works which adorn the Little Chapel-in-the-Woods (Carruth Coll. photo).

hundred applicants) were living in three homes—Wheeler, Shackleford, and Herbert Halls—sharing expenses and daily housework. Residents divided the price of rent and of food bought at cost from the college storeroom. Students who chose to bring food from home received market prices for the goods they brought.

Although maximum expenditures had been set at $15 per month, the college bulletin of March 1, 1935, reported that the largest monthly bill (all inclusive) had been $8.75. To correct any misconceptions about the nature of the system, the bulletin continued, "The cooperative home is no step-child. It is the apple of its college mother's eye and receives all the proud attention from the other halls that the youngest is wont to exact from older brothers and sisters."

Within a year 175 students were living in eight new twenty-room cooperative houses which had been built near Smith-Carroll, the central house for the units.[5] Hailed by a college bulletin of January 15, 1936, as "a history-making, forward step in the democratizing of higher education, by giving educational opportunity to many who could not attend college otherwise," the houses offered room and board—including light, heat, water, and laundering privileges—for $9 to $10 a month to approximately 275 students. Remaining a vital part of the residential system through the remainder of the decade, the cooperative homes increased to twelve in number by 1939.

As economic conditions improved somewhat and the College made its programs more easily accessible, enrollment rebounded dramatically. The summer enrollment of 918 in 1934 more than doubled the enrollment of the previous summer, and the jump of 650 (sixty percent) in the fall registration returned enrollment almost to its pre-Depression high in a rise that was to continue through the remainder of the decade.

If the Depression had brought problems to the campus, however, it had also produced programs which helped the College deal with some of the

The cooperative houses (in the center of the picture), clustered around the Methodist Dormitory, allowed students to attend the College for minimal costs. (Bell Avenue runs from south to north on the left side of the picture.)

shortages of facilities which had plagued it almost since its beginning. The total value of the buildings and properties of the College in 1933 was approximately $2.5 million, and the state had failed on several occasions to provide much-needed additions to the plant.[6]

Hubbard, however, was quick to realize the potential value to the College of the Public Works Administration (PWA) established in the summer of 1933. In his autobiography, *Recollections of a Texas Educator,* he records how he and the new business manager, Marvin Loveless, were waiting on the steps of the regional office in Fort Worth when it opened for its first day of business to present the needs of the College. By the fall of 1934, the College had secured grants of more than a half million dollars for the construction of four buildings—a dormitory, a hospital, and buildings for science and fine arts.[7]

The next January, following a three-week trip to Washington by Hubbard, Regents voted to accept additional PWA funds of $104,500 to be combined with the original amounts into one loan for the buildings. Within another year, the College secured another PWA loan and grant of $536,000 for the construction of the Music and Speech Building and of twin dormitories.[8] In all, PWA had made possible the addition of $1.25 million worth of buildings, a fifty percent increase in the total value of the campus.

The College began its biggest building program in 1935, a program that would effect a major change in its appearance and, as Hubbard predicted in the ex-students' newspaper of October 15, 1934, leave the College with "a physical plant in which we can take a real pride." The completion of the three new classroom and laboratory buildings doubled the instructional space of the College, and the new dormitories helped the College house all its students for the first time.

Although the earliest buildings on the campus were of a uniform color with the original building (Old Main), the library and Lowry and Capps Halls introduced red brick and a colonial style of architecture which was to characterize the new buildings as well. The first building to be completed, the infirmary—Hygeia Hall—was located in an oak grove north of the gymnasium and east of the new Fitzgerald Hall.[9] The infirmary had the appearance of a colonial residence rather than an institutional hospital. The $40,000 facility was put to use immediately upon its completion in early 1936, and the old Hygeia was converted to a rooming house.[10]

The dramatic increase in enrollment in 1934-35 and the anticipated continued increase for 1935-36 accented the need for additional residential space; and in the summer of 1935, the College spent some

PWA funds made possible the replacement of the original Stoddard Hall with a new dormintory, also named Stoddard Hall (foreground), and the addition of a fourth floor to Brackenridge Hall (background).

$60,000 of its PWA funds to eliminate the roof garden on Brackenridge Hall and add a fourth floor. The additional thirty-nine rooms accommodated some eighty-five girls to bring the total capacity of the hall to two hundred.

In spite of the great sentimental attachment to Stoddard Hall by students who had lived there or who had hoped to live there, this original state dormitory had long been proclaimed a fire-hazard; and the PWA grant made possible its replacement with a four-story Georgian structure. Razing the old hall began February 4, 1935; and by the following February senior students had moved into the new building on the old site even though the parlors were unfurnished and the dormitory itself was not completed.

After completion of the new Stoddard Hall, work began on the twin dormitories between Sayers' and Fitzgerald Halls which would complete dormitory row. Named Austin and Houston Halls to honor Texas heroes Stephen F. Austin and Sam Houston, the dormitories each cost approximately $175,000; and each accommodated approximately two hundred underclass students in one hundred rooms. The completion of these residential buildings enabled the College, even with its record enrollment, to house its entire student body on campus for the first time; and the College attained its long-cherished goal of being truly residential.

While residence halls and the hospital were being built to the north of the original College building, new buildings for science, fine arts, and music and speech were rising near the library on the south side of the campus. Each building was a three-story structure, built at a cost of approximately $175,000; each had a distinctive design in both appearance

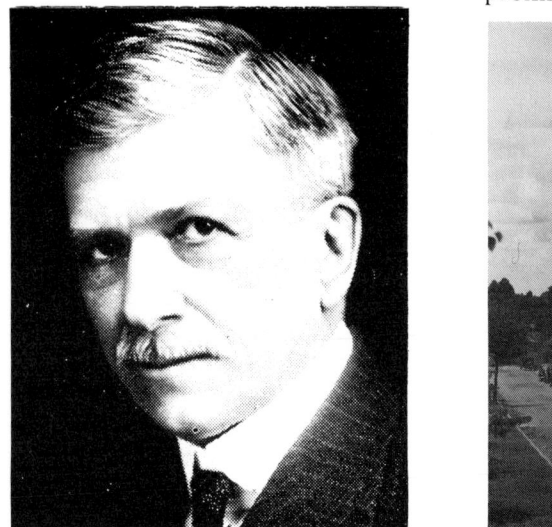

Fitzgerald Hall, named for Hugh Nugent Fitzgerald, former President of the CIA Board of Regents, completed "dormitory row."

and organization. The Science and Fine Arts Buildings were begun in 1935 and completed in the summer of 1936 prior to the construction of the Music and Speech Building.

The Fine Arts Building housed all courses in the fine arts—art appreciation, art in advertising, book-binding, costume designing, designing, drawing, history of art, house plans, interior decoration, mechanical drawing, metal work, modeling, painting, pottery, and woodworking. In addition it offered a locker room, a "lantern room," and twelve studios for classes. A wing on each end of the building provided museum and exhibit galleries.

The Science Building housed physics on the first floor, chemistry on the second, and biology on the third. In addition to its laboratories and classrooms, the building offered an attached auditorium to accommodate approximately five hundred people and a conservatory and animal room constructed in a tower above the third floor. A general museum, six photographic darkrooms, a culture room, and a cold room completed the facility.

Connected to the south end of the Main Auditorium, the Music and Speech Building formed an entrance to it and provided studios, classrooms, and a small auditorium for recitals.

(Top to bottom) While dormitories were being built north of Old Main, the Science Building, the Music and Speech Building, and the Fine Arts Building were completed to the south, giving the campus a distinctive red brick Georgian appearance.

The seven new buildings which the federal funds made possible were dedicated April 10, 1937. Although the College had adequate housing and instructional space for the first time, the facilities would not long contain the once-again growing student population. On November 1, 1938, the ex-students' newspaper reported that the Regents had voted to limit enrollment to 2,700 girls until the state could "provide additional dormitories and classroom facilities." In the same publication, Hubbard reported that the College had refused admission to at least two hundred girls in the fall "because of lack of accommodation."

The Regents petitioned the Legislature for new dormitories, a new home economics building, a dining and recreational hall, and an education building to replace the demonstration school.[11] But appropriations for the buildings were not forthcoming even though Hubbard reminded alumnae and Legislators that the College, unlike other state institutions, had not had a building funded by legislative appropriation since 1927.

Even without new buildings, however, the college bulletin of March 15, 1939, reported that the College was able to house all 2,850 students except those whose homes were in Denton in its fireproof dormitories and its cooperative houses. Housing was of great importance to the College, which relied on a complete residential system to promote social unity and loyalty.

The legislative session brought no relief, however; and *Lass-O* editor Isabel Warren commented in an editorial (September 22, 1939), "TSCW's crying need for greater housing and classroom space was voiced recently when the Board of Regents passed regulations, most of them effective in 1940, to discourage enrollment of out-of-state students." Warren also noted that some five hundred assurance fees had been turned down because of "the frugal budgeting that denies an institution the necessities of progress." In spite of protests, no new buildings would be forthcoming for the campus until the next decade.

The physical plant of the College had grown dramatically in the second half of the thirties, and course offerings at both the graduate and undergraduate levels had expanded as had the number of students who earned degrees after the early Depression years. The College awarded 274 bachelor's degrees in 1931, the year it granted its first thirteen M.A. degrees.[12] In 1940, 505 students received bachelor's degrees, and 44 received master's degrees.

Vocational home economics courses offered millinery more than thirty years after it made its appearance in the original curriculum.

An expanding and increasingly sophisticated curriculum led the College to seek a name change—from the College of Industrial Arts to the Texas State College for Women.

The thirties also brought major curriculum changes as the College made a concentrated effort to shift its emphasis from technical and vocational subjects to liberal arts areas. In 1934, on Hubbard's recommendation, the Board of Regents adopted a new name for the school: Texas State College for Women, a title used frequently in conversation and on college publications since 1906. Again, the College was criticized—this time for abandoning the principles on which it was founded—but Hubbard and other defenders championed the expanded and expanding role of the College which the new name proclaimed. Revisions in the curricula brought two major changes in degree requirements with the beginning of the 1934-35 academic year. First, overall degree programs achieved greater flexibility while the requirements in major and minor areas grew stronger. Second, by adding a minimum of liberal arts subjects, majors in technical arts subjects could earn the B.A. degree (or even the B.A. *and* B.S. degrees if they completed four and one-half years of study). In the spring of 1934, as the College worked out final details, E.V. White hinted to a group of alumnae in Fort Worth that the revisions would bring "changes greater than since 1916."[13]

Always ready to respond to public needs with innovative programs, the College began in the thirties to reap the rewards of some of its early experiments. It had been the first of the state colleges in Texas to develop degree programs in physical education, home demonstration and vocational home economics, speech, and library science. Innovation had also characterized the art and music programs of the College. And initiative in all these areas had placed graduates in positions of leadership throughout the state, particularly as the public schools looked for guidance in developing their own curricula in new areas.

White reported in his *Historical Sketch* (published as a college bulletin November 15, 1936) that graduates of the Department of Physical and Health Education "have had a potent influence in shaping the courses of physical education as they are now taught in the public schools of the State." Also in 1936 the State Department of Education designated TSCW as a center for special summer laboratory work in the development of curricula for art and music in the public schools of Texas.

The College had been one of only two state schools to offer vocational home economics the first year the federal government authorized the program; and the college bulletin of April 1, 1934, noted, "The demand

Initiated in 1932, radio broadcasts not only offered experience for students but also allowed the College to reach a new audience.

for vocational home economics teachers from the College has usually been much greater than the supply.'' Even during the Depression, the College was able to place all graduates of the course.

The bachelor's degree program in home demonstration, which was initiated in 1922, was still the only such program in the Southwest in 1934; and graduates of the program accounted for more than a third of the home demonstration personnel in Texas. Texas, in turn, employed ten percent of all home demonstration agents in the nation. The agents, who on the average reached some 2,200 persons, exerted major influence in the state.

Twenty years after the College offered its first two-semester-hour course in library methods in 1916-17, it remained the only state-supported college in Texas with degree programs approved by both the State Board of Education and the Library Committee of the Southern Association. In 1938, the program became the first in the Southwest to be accredited by the American Library Association.

The initiation of a four-year sequence leading to the Bachelor of Literary Interpretation degree in 1918 prepared the way for a strong Department of Speech by the thirties. The department's radio station WSAAN had listeners as far away as Australia, and on the campus the department sponsored little theater and children's theater productions and performances in an outdoor theater on a campus hillside.[14] The department attracted Interscholastic League and intercollegiate tournaments, debates, and recitals; served as host for college speech conferences; and encouraged intracampus competition by awarding a silver loving cup to the student who delivered the best original speech each year. A speech clinic provided treatment of speech disorders in children and adults.

Unique offerings in art led students and graduates to prominent positions as well. At a time when other colleges offered majors only in art education with art courses as service courses for home economics and architecture, CIA/TSCW was the only college to offer majors in costume design, interior decoration, art in advertising, ceramics, crafts, illustration, and painting. The claim of a college bulletin (March 15, 1937) that ''The Fine Arts Department offers work that is recognized to be equal to that offered by ranking institutions throughout the United States'' was supported by the accomplishments of students who captured top honors in national competitions. The crowning achievement of the art students of the period, the Little Chapel-in-the-Woods, still holds a place of honor on the modern campus.

In addition to the programs the College offered its regular students, it continued to reach people beyond the borders of the campus. Some programs offered college credit. Some offered only a chance to learn. Marking their twentieth year of uninterrupted programs in 1933, the extension services continued to offer bulletins, lectures, demonstrations, recitals, and contest judging for individuals and groups throughout Texas. The college bulletin of January 15, 1933, reported that the services had, during the past year, reached more than 54,000 people by faculty trips and released on request more than 12,000 bulletins on subjects ranging from art and international relations to home nursing and interior decoration. During the decade the number of topics for lectures grew as the number of bulletins declined, but bulletins proved the most economical method of disseminating information; and the college bulletin of May 1, 1940, reported that the College sponsored some 150 faculty trips each year for the extension service and distributed 127,000 pieces of literature. Designed primarily as a service for the women of Texas, the bulletins had widespread appeal. The bulletin of October 15, 1934, reported that the 113,964 publications distributed in 1933-34 had gone to forty-six different states and four foreign countries.

Although not incorporated as a part of extension services, the radio broadcasts initiated in 1932 provided a new way of reaching a new audience. Begun as a fourteen-minute weekly program over station WBAP in Fort Worth in early summer, the broadcasts each offered seven minutes of orchestra music and a seven-minute talk on topics which ranged from "Professions for the Trained College Woman" to "Christmas Carols" or "Chemistry in Every Day Life." In 1935 the programs moved to radio station WFAA in Dallas. The college bulletin of March 1, 1935, outlined a schedule of topics with a special emphasis on Texas for the remainder of the semester: Texas Historic Shrines, Texas Pioneer Women, Texas Composers, and similar subjects.

In 1936 the programs increased to thirty minutes—opening and closing with music under the direction of TSCW Professor William E. Jones with a ten-minute talk in the middle. The talks were grouped in series—one on Texas, one on parent education, one on social science. Through the rest of the decade the thirty-minute weekly programs on WFAA remained a standard feature of the fall and spring semesters, featuring students as well as faculty. Each February students and ex-students listened to the broadcasts which coincided with the annual commemoration of the founding of the College. The broadcast of 1939 included messages from two former presidents, Cree T. Work and William B. Bizzell, and from an original member of the Board of Regents, Helen M. Stoddard.

In 1937 TSCW initiated another program related to, but distinct from, the extension services. The college bulletin of February 1 announced the availability of correspondence courses in the departments of Bible, biology, business administration, economics and government, English, foreign languages, history, journalism, mathematics, philosophy and education, and physical education. The eleven departments offered 109 correspondence courses for persons who wished to earn college credits, who wanted to take business and vocational courses, or who wished to take non-credit work for information or for its cultural value.

As the extension services, radio broadcasts, and new correspondence program reached out, the College also drew people to the campus and expanded offerings through special institutes and workshops. In the summer of 1931, the College offered its first Summer Institute for Women. Announced in the alumnae newspaper of March 1, 1931, as "an adventure in adult education" with the "enthusiastic approval" of the Texas Federation of Women's Clubs, the PTA, Home Demonstration Workers, and other organizations, the course proved highly successful. For a minimal charge ($35.50 per three-week term, including room rent and meals in a dormitory) mature women could elect non-credit courses in practical homemaking or courses of cultural, social, or community value. The announcement for the second institute in 1932 issued a special invitation for daughters to accompany their mothers. By 1938 the institute had evolved into a ten-day Homemaker's Conference with full childcare facilities so that mothers could study and attend entertainment. Topics included clothing, food, expenditures, housing, pre-school and adolescent children, recreation, and the proper development of religious attitudes and practices in the home.

Beginning in 1932, the Department of Fine and Applied Arts offered a three-week summer school of painting (open to both men and women) at Taos, New Mexico, under the direction of Texas artist Alexander Hogue. Also in 1932, the Department of Home Economics inaugurated a two-month summer travel course in "Historic Costume and Textile Design." Students visited London, Bruges, Cologne, Venice, Rome, Florence, and Chartres to see lace factories, museums, blown glass factories, embroidery schools, weaving studios, and exhibits of tapestry, needlepoint, lace, and medieval costumes. The same year, the Department of Physical Education held its first camp to train counselors. In addition to nature study and campcraft, the camp featured sports—golf, archery, canoeing, swimming, horseback riding, and baseball—and dancing, including clogging and folk dancing. Two years later a "Councillor Leadership and Sports Camp" brought participants to live in the open in the campus woods.

In 1937 the Department of Speech began an Institute of Speech Activities which remained an annual event through the rest of the decade. Open to both men and women, the six-week summer program was designed to develop directors of speech activities for Interscholastic League competition. Participants polished skills from directing plays to coaching debate, broadcasting on the radio, preparing stage scenery and lighting, and coaching declamation and extemporaneous speaking. A unique feature of the institute was the involvement of high school students whom the institute participants could direct in the actual production of speech programs.

Responding to the changing needs of society with new educational programs, TSCW also found itself faced with the need to adjust to changing social values. The system of discipline which governed campus life had not kept pace with changing attitudes or even with the changing student body, which included students who were more mature than the young preparatory students who came when the College was new. In his autobiography, Hubbard frankly described the disciplinary system which was operating when he arrived as "antiquated"—and "certainly . . . out of place in a woman's college."

Working with the restive students to study the out-of-date system and to suggest changes, Hubbard fostered a gradual liberalization of the rules although the atmosphere that resulted was far from permissive. In 1931, following the wishes expressed by the popular vote of the students, the Board of Regents approved a new organizational plan which grouped junior and senior students together with the same privileges of dress and social life, privileges which went beyond those extended to underclasswomen. For example, underclass students could receive "gentlemen callers" on Saturday and Sunday nights only; juniors and seniors could receive callers on these nights and on Wednesday as well. Upperclass students also obtained the privilege of "riding alone with gentlemen in Denton on Saturday and Sunday afternoons until 5:30," according to the College bulletin of January 15, 1932, although parental permission was required for students to leave town or return in a private car with a gentleman. Weekend recreational opportunities were greatly expanded when the College made the golf course, tennis courts, swimming pool, and riding stable available for Sunday afternoon entertainment and opened the College cafeteria and tearoom on Sunday afternoon.

Relaxed rules opened the College tearoom to students on Sunday afternoons. Students operated the tearoom and a cafeteria.

By the 1933 commencement, the Regents had adopted significant changes, and Hubbard announced that the relaxed regulations would be implemented on an experimental basis with the College reserving the right to rescind the privileges with due notice. New freedoms included lengthened hours in which students could be away from campus, permission to be absent from dinner, and permission to go to doctors or dentists in town. Riding in cars continued, however, to be directed by careful restrictions. Night riding was to be confined within Denton city limits, and only upperclasswomen could ride in cars without special permission from home. Although the College did not forbid smoking, it discouraged it as a detriment to health, a fire hazard, and "a great drawback to those who seek positions, especially as teachers," the ex-students' newspaper of December 15, 1933, reported; and the College did not permit public smoking. The task of implementing a new system of discipline fell to a new Dean of Women, Mattie Lloyd Wooten.

One aspect of student life that had become increasingly vexing to some students was the wearing of uniforms. Inaugurated almost at the beginning of classes at the College, uniforms had begun partly as a means of economy and partly as a democratizing influence. To be worn from the time a student left home for Denton until she returned home, the uniforms had proved economical. However, several factors had contributed to dissatisfaction with the uniforms. Among objections were the rapid changes in styles, the difficulties of enforcing uniform regulations, and finally, the necessity for two wardrobes as the use of uniforms became increasingly restricted.

As students adopted a campus uniform and a civilian one, uniforms became an additional expense instead of a saving; and uniforms gradually ceased to be uniform in the sense that everyone dressed alike. Requirements came to call for an entire wardrobe of costumes for various occasions including recreation and sports; and, as the college bulletin of January 15, 1936, reported, there came to be "ample opportunity for every girl to express her own personality in her dress and yet conform with the uniform agreement."

Rigid regulations governing what students could and could not do in uniform often created hardships and ill feelings, and the fine points of uniform requirements contributed to unfortunate controversy and unnecessary confrontation. As Hubbard noted in his autobiography, a white fleck in a dark blue topcoat might disqualify it as uniform; and the number of permissible pleats in a costume led to great debates. The situation reached a climax when the editor of the *Lass-O* approached Hubbard to demonstrate that the "uniform" had well over a hundred uniform combinations provided for by the regulations.

Hubbard chaired a faculty-student committee to examine the problem; and it voted unanimously on January 26, 1938, for the abolition of the uniform. In a crowded auditorium the following day, after recalling the thirty-five-year history of the uniform, Hubbard discussed the reasons for the recommended change and then, amid cheers and tears, announced officially that the uniform would be abolished, effective immediately.

Sentiment was by no means entirely against the uniforms, however; and the president of the Student Government Association noted in a radio speech on February 15, 1938, that the uniform was "the oldest and most loved of all the College traditions" and that students had remained attached to the uniform in spite of its complex regulations and enforcement mechanisms. Nevertheless, she noted that students were willing to "sacrifice this personal sentiment for the sake of the College."

Although "uniforms" were abolished, the college catalog of March 1, 1938, advised students that one uniform dress would still be required, "a tailored white dress in any pattern or material to be worn on special

COLLEGE BULLETIN
of the Texas State College for Women, College of Industrial Arts, Denton, Texas

Uniform Information

Number 197   April 15, 1935
Issued semi-monthly by the College of Industrial Arts, Denton, Texas. Entered December 17, 1917, Denton, Texas, as second-class matter. Under Act of Congress, August 24, 1912.

By 1935 rules governing uniforms were so complex that the College issued a special bulletin to specify them.

occasions when the students are asked to assemble." The bulletin of January 15, 1938, advised that even though students were no longer required to wear the uniforms, they were "expected to maintain the College tradition of good taste, simplicity, and economy in dress"; and the bulletin of February 15, 1938, reported, "Although the uniform has been abolished, the College will encourage economy in dress as much as ever, and the spirit of democracy will call for simple tailored clothing for campus wear."

Restrictions in other areas also lessened. The bulletin of March 1, 1938, reported that students were allowed "for emergencies" a number of absences in a course per semester equal to the number of times the class met each week. This privilege was, however, short-lived. The college catalog dated March 1, 1940, reported, "The old system of allowing a specified number of absences in each class is abolished."

As students acquired confidence in their rights, they turned their energies to new projects. As the president of the Student Government Association noted in her Founders' Day speech in 1938 (February 15), "Activities of the students no longer are based upon a radical demand for students' rights. Instead, the Student Government Association is concentrating energy on using student privileges to contribute something valuable to higher education for women." The accomplishments of the students during this decade still bear witness to the success of their efforts on the campus.

In spite of the economic bleakness of the times, the love of beauty which President and Mrs. Hubbard brought to the campus combined with the initiative of faculty and students to produce amazing results. Even before the College was able to make a significant move toward obtaining basic necessities in housing and instructional facilities, students and faculty began physical improvements aimed at meeting the spiritual and social needs of students. By the end of the decade, botanical gardens and a chapel on the northern edge of the campus offered a retreat from studies and everyday pressures; an impressive statue and garden were installed in the circle surrounded by the library and the new Fine Arts and Music and Speech Buildings; major tree-planting projects added both shade and color to the campus; and students and alumnae were in the midst of raising funds to finance a Student Union Building.

Begun inauspiciously in 1930 by the Department of Biology under the direction of a committee consisting of Willie Birge, Fred Westcourt, and Mary Marshall, the gardens grew steadily in beauty and reputation. As a writer in the college bulletin of May 1, 1933, recalled, "In the dry March days of 1930 we planted our first seeds on the site of the old pig pens and peach orchard area." The location proved ideal. Although silk purses may not come from sows' ears, beautiful flowers did grow luxuriously in the old stock pens.

Located behind the new Fitzgerald dormitory and adjoining Lowry Woods (sometimes called "Hikers' Haven") on the north, the gardens offered both a formal and an informal area. The formal entrance to the gardens was marked by a rose-covered trellis, eight feet wide and nine feet high, completed shortly before January 15, 1932. The trellis ran the length of a fifty-six-foot flagstone path from the entrance to the interior of the formal garden with its hedged lawns.

Adjacent to the formal garden was a cultivated area with numerous wildflower sanctuaries. The investment in time and labor was sometimes greater than the financial cost of the plants, painstakingly collected from all over the state. By 1935 the seven-acre garden plot held more than three hundred native Texas flowers and shrubs, and annual plantings included hundreds of bulbs—gladioli, hyacinths, narcissi, and tulips.[15] The gardens served as a laboratory for biology students and as an instructional and recreational center for all garden lovers.

The abolition of uniforms in 1938 elicited joy and sadness from students and confronted them with decisions.

Willie Isabella Birge, Director of the Department of Biology, led the transformation of a weed patch into the Botanical Gardens of state-wide fame.

To the north of these gardens a sloping hillside became the site in 1932 of a rock garden with benches and terraces of native woodbine sandstone. The shaded rock garden with its strategically placed pools harbored shade and water-loving plants. High in the garden a spring pool with fern ledges fed a large garden pool and a lower lily pond, each of which was a garden in its own right.[16]

Campus beautification was a high priority for Hubbard, and he did not confine his efforts to the gardens. A select group of commemorative trees also contributed to the beauty of the campus as did major tree planting projects. On December 12, 1931, students gathered for the planting of an oak tree from Mount Vernon just south of the auditorium to the right of the circular drive; and the following February, the College inaugurated a ten-year plan to plant five hundred live oak trees—fifty each year—on campus.

On May 5, 1932, a second Washington memorial tree—a black walnut grown from a tree Washington had planted—was installed to the left of the circular drive. In October, 1934, the College planted a small pecan tree, grown from a tree Sam Houston planted at his home in Huntsville, in the circle; and before 1938 a fourth tree, grown from a pecan tree at the head of the grave of the late Governor James Stephen Hogg, was added to the area.[17] As the circle was prepared to receive the statue of the pioneer woman in 1938, three of the trees had to be transplanted. The black walnut was replanted southwest of the library, and the Houston and Hogg pecan trees were planted at the opposite ends of the Fine Arts Building.[18]

To the west of the Household Arts Building the pecan trees ceremoniously planted some fifteen years earlier contributed to the beauty of the campus; and, working with Fred Westcourt, Director of the Department of Rural Arts, Hubbard initiated a long-term plan to add hundreds of redbud trees to the campus landscape. Redbuds came to bank the margins of the campus woods and gardens and to line campus drives and walks. The College transplanted more than two thousand redbuds to the campus, and many citizens in town joined the campaign to make Denton a redbud city. As described in the the college bulletin of April 1, 1937, the campus delighted students and attracted thousands of visitors with its "driveways bordered with redbuds and scarlet poppies, its hillsides of bluebonnets, its tulip and cactus beds, its well-kept golf course; and the lake-part where students may camp or sail or row or swim and enjoy picnics or horseback rides along woodsy bridle paths."

To complement the natural and cultivated beauty of the campus, and to offer a retreat specifically dedicated to concerns of the spirit, students voted on November 4, 1937, for the construction of a small interdenominational chapel on the campus. Because the student loan fund contained $100,000 by this time,[19] an amount more than sufficient to meet the requests for student loans, money-raising projects which had previously contributed to the fund were designated for the chapel fund; and Hubbard announced at the following June commencement that Mr. and Mrs. W.R. Nicholson of Longview had contributed $15,000 toward the construction of the chapel.[20]

While students, alumnae, faculty, and others worked to secure the remainder of the funds needed to begin construction, preparations were underway in the circle bounded by the library and the new Fine Arts and Music and Speech Buildings for the receipt of a statue given to the campus to commemorate the centennial of Texas' declaration of independence.

On December 5, 1938, Mrs. John A. Hann, eighty-nine-year-old Denton County pioneer, unveiled the fifteen-foot tall statue, "The Pioneer Woman," by Leo Friedlander. Made of pure Georgia white marble, the statue was shaped in New York City in a three-year project that cost $25,000. Pat M. Neff, President of Baylor University and a former Governor of Texas, delivered a tribute to the spirit of the pioneer women of Texas; and Associate Dean Jessie H. Humphries read the inscription which she had written for the pedestal of the statue.[21]

The following January 1, the College broke ground for the chapel. Private contributions plus a grant from the National Youth Administration

The statue of the pioneer woman, unveiled in 1938, was a gift to TSCW to commemorate the centennial of Texas.

Dorothy LaSelle supervised more than three hundred students who created the art work for the Little Chapel-in-the-Woods.

Construction workers, paid by NYA grants, prepare the framework for the chapel, which was designed by O'Neil Ford.

(NYA) made possible the beginning of construction on January 23. The chapel was located on a wooded hilltop north and east of the wildflower garden.[22] Designed by Dallas architect O'Neil Ford, assisted by A. B. Swank of Dallas and Preston M. Geren of Fort Worth, the chapel was constructed of native gray fieldstone brought from Bridgeport. Dorothy La Selle, TSCW associate professor of art, was designated supervising director of the project. Master artisans supervised the work of some eighty Denton County boys in the stone, brick, and carpentry work; and Miss LaSelle supervised more than three hundred students in the design and execution of all of the art work in the chapel.

Ten stained glass windows, visible from the nave, depicted the theme, "Woman Ministering to Human Needs." Students began the windows

The rose window captured Texas' colors in an abstract design; and the motherhood window, the chapel's largest and most prominent, paid tribute to the ideal woman.

with sketches of living models and carried the work through the painting and firing of the glass.[23] The largest and most prominent window, the motherhood window in the chancel, is a triptych (10' x 15') dedicated to the ideal woman. Eight slender (2 1/2' x 17') windows—four on each side of the nave—are dedicated to women who distinguished themselves and benefited civilization through their professions—nursing, teaching, science, and social service on the left and speech, literature, dance, and music on the right. The tenth window, an abstract rose window above the entrance, signifies the renewal of faith through communion with nature.[24]

Rich in symbolism carefully explained in a published iconography, the windows feature both outstanding women in the professions and symbolic representatives of the professions along with appropriate quotations. Florence Nightingale, Helen Keller and her teacher Anne Sullivan, Isadora Duncan, Ruth St. Denis, Martha Graham, and Doris Humphrey are among the identifiable characters; and quotations come from Florence Nightingale, Mary Lyon (founder of Mt. Holyoke), Marie Curie, Jane Addams, George Eliot, and Psalm 149.

Although the windows are the most striking decoration of the chapel, students were no less careful in planning and executing the other features such as the saw-pierced and riveted brass lighting fixtures and woodwork executed in beech. Pews were made to accommodate approximately 150 people, and a small balcony seated about 25 people. Handmade rugs covered floors of rustic tile.[25]

Constructed more for private meditation and prayer than for formal services, the chapel has, nevertheless, become the setting for many student and alumnae weddings. The first marriage—that of alumna Esther Webb and John A. Houseman—took place on September 23, 1939, before an improvised altar in the unfinished chapel. The college bulletin of November 1 reported that the morning sun "streamed through spaces in the tough hewn stone walls onto the few witnesses who watched the ceremony," and President and Mrs. Hubbard entertained the wedding party with a breakfast in their home.

The chapel was still unfinished when Eleanor Roosevelt participated in the dedication ceremonies on November 1; but work had progressed far enough that the college bulletin of that date could report, "Critics pronounce this one of the nation's outstanding amateur art projects." Conceived as a work of art, the chapel also was planned to encourage students' spiritual development; and the heavy mahogany door was intended to be open at all times to all students.[26]

As the chapel neared its completion, Hubbard and the students and alumnae shifted their attention to securing a badly needed Student Union Building.[27] The college bulletin of March 1, 1935, had encouraged alumnae to determine ways they could help secure the building. Students were having to rent buildings in town for their social functions because Virginia Carroll Lodge, a small house which was the only facility on campus for such purposes, was far from adequate to accommodate the more than fifty organizations which offered social activities to some eighteen hundred students.[28]

By February 15, 1936, the Ex-Students Association had set a goal of raising $100,000 for a union building to house the Student Government Association, the Ex-Students Association, and student publications. In addition to a recreation center large enough to accommodate all the student body, the proposed building would offer reading rooms and club rooms, a cafeteria, and reception rooms for teas and reunions. In the meantime, makeshift projects provided a senior recreation room in Stoddard Hall, the addition of a larger kitchen to Virginia Carroll Lodge for use by clubs in 1938, and, by May, 1940, the transformation of Virginia Carroll Lodge into a central parlor for formal occasions.

Even without adequate social and recreational facilities, however, student activities flourished in the thirties. Old traditions received new vigor. Big sister-little sister adoptions and the lantern parade established ties between the new freshmen and their junior big sisters. Senior day activities included the oak-chain ceremony which bound seniors in friendship to their sophomore little sisters and provided seniors the chance to review their history and prophesy their future. The dining halls prepared special meals for holidays—Halloween, Thanksgiving, Christmas, Twelfth Night, and St. Agnes Eve. The Christmas dinner featured roast pigs, and St. Agnes Eve offered girls the opportunity to find out by divination who their husbands would be. Pancake Night in February also became a fixed part of the winter events.[29] Strong ties between TSCW girls and the boys of Texas A&M became even stronger; and in 1937, the TSCW Board of Regents made October 16, the date of the official corps trip of cadets to Fort Worth for the football game with TCU, an official TSCW holiday.

The decade was also rich in beginnings. President Hubbard instituted a formal convocation in early October each fall to open the school session. Students in their white dresses and faculty in full academic regalia gathered in the Main Auditorium for a processional, recessional, special musical numbers, and a speech by a prominent educator. Also on January 27, 1931, the College held its first mid-winter commencement, awarding seventeen diplomas. Twenty-six students had completed degree requirements in the fall; but nine chose to wait for their diplomas until spring commencement, which continued to be the time of alumnae homecoming with teas, luncheons, and entertainments. The 1931 spring

The Campus Serenaders, shown here in 1933, and the Modern Dance Group became popular entertainers.

commencement saw the presentation of the first Leman Award to a graduating student for artistic accomplishment.[30]

Students played a major role in college programs. Little Theatre presentations in one year ranged from a story of thirteenth-century Chinese intrigue to nineteenth-century English comedy. The college bulletin of December 15, 1933, announced the organization of an eleven-piece dance orchestra, "The Campus Serenaders," who, decked out in red and white striped blazers and white skirts, played for twice-a-week dances in the gym, for club programs and dances, for town activities, for stage shows at the Saturday night movies, and for ex-student engagements.[31] In 1937 the Modern Dance Group was organized as an extra-class club. Developing into the Dance Repertory Theatre, the group has performed to the acclaim of noted dance professionals throughout the eastern half of the nation and internationally. A forty-member choir and a fourteen-member stringed ensemble directed by William E. Jones, head of the Department of Music, made public appearances and performed in radio broadcasts from Dallas radio station WFAA. By 1939, the symphony orchestra had grown to eighty members, a full-complement of musicians.

Honorary and social clubs continued to increase in number. In 1931, eighteen members of the Mary Eleanor Brackenridge Club chartered a new literary-social club, the Aglaians, named for one of the three sister graces who in Greek mythology were the givers of charm and beauty. As the number of social, honorary, and other clubs increased, the College established a system of faculty sponsorship. The college bulletin of December 15, 1933, reported the first application of the faculty super-vision with the election of faculty sponsors for each of the four classes.

On April 18, 1936, the first chapter of National Collegiate Players ever installed in a woman's college was established on the campus. The college bulletin of April 1, 1937, reported some sixteen clubs which were affiliated with the Texas Federation of Women's Clubs.[33] The bulletin also recorded two additional honorary fraternities—Alpha Chi for upperclassmen and Alpha Kappa Delta for sociology majors; and the college bulletin of January 15, 1940, announced the organization of the Sarah Anderson Tuggle chapter of the Daughters of the American Revolution.[34]

To complement what students themselves could do, Hubbard ambitiously began to strengthen the cultural series which had been part of the College from its early days. Initiating a Concert and Drama Series which became the envy of other colleges and universities, TSCW became a true cultural center which served as host to myriad famous artists, poets, lecturers, musicians, dancers, actors, literary figures, dramatic companies, choruses, bands, and orchestras.

Beginning almost immediately following Hubbard's arrival on campus, the series moved slowly until 1930-31 when it reached full strength so that in the following twenty years it brought more than three hundred famous persons and groups to the campus. Poet Carl Sandburg and Russian pianist Vladimir Horowitz visited in 1933; and in 1934 Lily Pons, who was in her fourth season as leading coloratura soprano of the Metropolitan Opera Company, performed. American poet Edna St. Vincent Millay appeared in 1935 as did Judith Anderson, who performed on campus in the original New York production of the 1935 Pulitzer Prize winning play, *The Old Maid*. In the 1935-36 drama series Cornelia Otis Skinner appeared. For the 1939-40 season, Fritz Kreisler, Eleanor Roosevelt, the St. Louis Symphony, and William Rose Benet were among the thirty-two attractions scheduled. The series was not confined to the arts, however. Track's foremost miler, Glenn Cunningham, and the world's greatest archer, Russ Hoogerhyde, also appeared as did aviatrix Amelia Earhart and numerous other notable figures of the day.

As the series became firmly established, it lent itself to concentrated programs in certain areas; and in 1939 the Department of English organized a week-long Writer's Conference under the supervision of a committee chaired by Autrey Nell Wiley. In late February, British novelist Phyllis Bentley and six noted Texas authors including J. Frank Dobie and Walter Prescott Webb along with the poet-laureate of Texas, Grace Noll Crowell, came to the campus. Two hundred fifty selected students attended afternoon conferences and round-table meetings with the writers, and the entire student body was invited to evening lectures.[35]

Following the Writer's Conference in February, the College instituted another event which would become an annual highlight of the spring semester. In March, the week-long Redbud Festival complemented a Self-Development Week designed to improve students' poise and appearance. A nationally known specialist in fashion and grooming came to the campus to conduct open forums, and on Thursday a student-faculty committee chose a queen to be crowned the next day and honored by a ball given for her, her fifty-nine attendants, and their escorts.[36]

Cultural and social offerings flourished, and purely recreational opportunities kept pace. The college bulletin of October 1, 1930, reported the addition of horseback riding and miniature golf to the campus.[37] Physical education courses included horseback riding; and, the bulletin noted, "Any girl may secure horses for riding purposes." The old chicken barn was remodeled for an indoor riding circle, and bridle paths were laid out through the campus.

Ruth Vogel reigned as the first Queen of the Redbud Festival in 1939.

95

Lake Dallas provided boating opportunities and a cabin on a twenty-acre campsite for TSCW students. The lower photograph shows the installation of the cornerstone of the cabin.

The log cabins at the twenty-acre Lake Dallas campsite (only eight miles from the campus) were popular for swimming, rowing, and picnics. The college bulletin of December 1, 1932, reported that both faculty members and students planned weekend and evening cabin parties and fishing trips months in advance. Two camp houses were also built on the edge of the campus; and the college bulletin of January 15, 1933, reported seventeen clay-surfaced tennis courts and classes in golf.

The Women's Athletic Association organized outdoor recreation—seasonal intramural programs in volleyball, field hockey, soccer, basketball, baseball, swimming, dancing, hiking and outing, roller skating, ping pong, shuffle board, and ring tennis. Sailing, canoeing, and motor boating also became popular lake recreations.

The scope of the recreational, cultural, spiritual, and educational accomplishments of the College during the thirties was remarkable, particularly when viewed in the context of the shattering events which enclosed the decade like parentheses—the Depression which marred its beginning and the rumblings of war in Europe which became louder and more threatening as the decade neared its end.

Although war seemed a long way from Denton, faculty members, alumnae, and students experienced its threat. A foreign exchange student came to the College after she fled Spain where her father was a captive Loyalist. Faculty members who visited Europe in the summer of 1939 returned with exciting stories and a new appreciation for their country. In the college bulletin of November 1, 1939, Mary K. Sands, associate professor of speech, recorded her relief at seeing New York "after six days of zig-zagging and thinking every minute we would be torpedoed"; and Dorothy LaSelle noted, "I developed all kinds of sentiments about the Statue of Liberty and the New York skyline and America in general, although I am not a sentimental person." From alumna Aline Nicholson, who was teaching in India, came the report, recorded in the college bulletin of January 15, 1940, that "Prices are already beginning to soar in India. Patent medicines are now double in price and merchants are trying to take advantage of the war to put up prices on old stock. . . . Germans are being rounded up and put in concentration camps because they are Germans."

In America prices were rising because of the war, too; but Hubbard announced in October, 1939, that rising food costs would have little effect on the cost of living in the cooperative system which housed nearly twenty percent of the 2,700 students who were attending TSCW.

The decade which was nearing its end included numerous testimonies to the success of the College. The addition of graduate degree programs, the appointment of the first alumna to the Board of Regents,[38] and the changing of the name of the College reflected wide-spread recognition of and appreciation for the maturity of the institution. The decade which lay ahead would test that maturity.

[1]Designed to attract top students, the scholarships went to the highest ranking graduates of high schools and junior colleges; selected girl scouts and campfire girls; first, second, and third place winners in literary events in state Interscholastic League competition; and a girl from each district of the Texas Federation of Women's Clubs.

[2]Mathematics requirements were reduced from three to two units, and foreign language credit was made optional although students who entered without the credit had to take additional college-level courses.

[3]Operated by the Methodist Church, the dormitory was the oldest residence hall on the campus. See Chapter II.

[4]In February, 1934, the college bulletin announced that students who could not afford to pay room and board even in Smith-Carroll could make light housekeeping arrangements in town under the direction of the College. By May, 1936, however, these arrangements were discontinued after cooperative homes proved even more economical than light housekeeping.

[5]The College had purchased Smith-Carroll Hall and its surrounding acres in 1934. In early 1935-36 it built the cooperative halls on the Smith-Carroll property. The halls—named Austin, Bastrop, Crockett, Houston, Lamar, Milam, and Rusk for Texas heros—were two-story frame buildings constructed at a cost of some $6,000 each, not including equipment. With the construction of brick Austin and Houston Halls in 1936-37, the cooperative houses bearing these named were renamed for Bonham and Fannin. Another house, Bowie Hall, was a two-story frame building built about 1908 and purchased by the College for $2,250 in 1935.

[6]For example, Governors had four times vetoed legislative appropriations for an infirmary.

[7]About one-third of the grant ($130,000) was an outright gift. The remainder ($365,000) was a loan secured by a bond agreement with the federal government.

The College was able to secure an unexpectedly large loan (and a loan for non-revenue-producing buildings) because its system of dormitories was paid for and promised revenue to repay the loans. As the new buildings neared completion, an additional grant of $47,500 provided for furnishings.

[8]The $536,000 loan for the construction of the Music and Speech Building and of the two new dormitories included an outright gift of $241,360 with the remainder issued as a loan.

[9]Named to honor Regent Hugh Nugent Fitzgerald, the dormitory was built in 1931, financed under the new legislative authority for the College to issue bonds and pay for the building from local funds. The three-story brick building accommodated some 216 senior students in its 99 rooms. The $160,000 hall, located at the east end of a line running through Capps, Lowry, and Sayers Halls, was first occupied in September, 1931.

[10]The old two-story frame building, first occupied in 1908, was remodeled to accommodate about twenty-five students in September, 1935, and renamed Burnett Hall to honor one of Texas' heroes.

[11]The department had grown ten times as large as it was when the building was constructed in 1912. Dining facilities were serving more than twice as many as they were designed for; and the campus had no recreational facility large enough to accommodate even one class, much less the entire student body. Federal inspectors had condemned the demonstration school as a fire and health hazard.

[12]The College conferred its first six Master of Arts degrees in June, 1931—three in English, two in foods and nutrition, and one in fine and applied arts.

[13]Proving his remarks to be prophetic, the college bulletin of October 15, 1934, announced that the curricular changes effected in the last catalog had resulted in a 150 percent increase in the number of students obtaining the Bachelor of Arts degree (from 22 to 55) while the number of students obtaining the Bachelor of Science degree rose 6 percent.

[14]C.N. Adkisson, director of the Department of Physics, and one of a handful of original faculty members still on campus, supervised the building of the stage by college workmen during the summer session of 1931. Located west of the gymnasium, the open air theater included a lecture stage, "vita-phone," and moving picture equipment which featured short skits and newsreels in the summer as a supplement to, but not a replacement for, the Saturday night picture shows and other regular summer programs.

[15]Tulips from Holland were a regular addition to the campus. In 1938, a college bulletin (November 1) reported the arrival in early October of 11,500 tulips from Heemsted, Holland, to be planted in front of the gymnasium, east of the post office, in the president's garden, and in beds across from Sayers dormitory. The rock garden by the Little Chapel was the site of a wide variety of hardy bulbs and other plants.

[16]Among the plants listed in the college bulletin of May 1, 1933, are columbines, shooting stars, bleeding hearts, phlox, valley-lilies, botanical tulips, scilla, hyacinths, grape hyacinths, spiderworts, blood roots, trillium, ferns, snow drops, and Canterbury-bells. The banks of the stream which connected the pools were lined with young elder, birch, buckeye, yaupon holly, hibiscus, Japanese maiden hairs, and other shrubs and trees. Spider lilies, pitcher plants, switch cane, cardinal flowers, and wild water iris grew in the soft bog. Aquatics grew in the water gardens—water lilies (hard and tropical), water iris, cyprus, lotus, and caladium were massed; and Japanese iris were massed on the drip edges of the east bank.

The fifteen-foot statue of the pioneer woman has become the symbol of the spirit of GIC/CIA/TSCW/TWU.

First Lady Eleanor Roosevelt helped dedicate the Little Chapel-in-the-Woods.

Social activities ranged from informal hayrides to elegant dances where the uniformed escorts were members of the University of Oklahoma band on their way to the Texas-OU weekend in Dallas.

[17]Governor Hogg requested that a pecan tree be planted at the head of his grave and that the seeds of the tree be grown into nursery plants to be distributed to schools and colleges in Texas.

[18]The college bulletin of May 1, 1935, identified the tree at the northwest corner of the Library as one of the oldest on campus with a note that it had supposedly been the site of the hanging of a Negro during the Civil War—on the big limb that shades the sidewalk.

[19]A major boost to the loan fund came with the contribution of $50,000 stipulated in the will of Houston capitalist and philanthropist Will C. Hogg. His contribution of $1,000 had been the beginning of the Ex-Students' Loan Fund.

[20]The Nicholsons were parents of three daughters who attended TSCW.

[21]Following the retirement of H.G. Allen of the history faculty and C.N. Adkisson of the physics faculty in 1939, Miss Humphries remained as the last of the original members of the faculty.

[22]Ninety feet long by forty-two feet wide by thirty feet high, the chapel cost approximately $45,000—$15,000 contributed by Mr. and Mrs. Nicholson; $7,500, by students, alumnae, and others; and $22,500 representing the value of the work done by the NYA.

[23]A small signature window in the foyer graphically tells the story of the construction of the chapel. Beatrice Paschall initiated the stained glass window project in September, 1938. She established the glass workshop used through 1941, and she originated the visual and written iconographies for the *nurse* and *dance* windows which established the quality and style to be followed by subsequent glass crew designers. She received the M.A. degree in 1939. Marilyn Yates designed and executed the rose window.

[24]Miss LaSelle went to France in the summer of 1939 to study twelfth- and thirteenth-century stained glass cathedral windows.

[25]"Information, Please," a guide to the TSCW campus published by the College (n.d.), identifies faculty and student artists who worked on the Little Chapel. Members of the fine arts faculty include Dorothy LaSelle, supervising director; Mary Marshall, Mattie Lee Lacy, Elizabeth Mitchell, and Edith Brisac, mosaics; Thetis Lemmon and Dorothy LaSelle, brass work; Thetis Lemmon, front doors; Marjorie Baltzel, wood carving; Coreen Spellman, Lura Mae Burton Kendrick, and Marie Delleney, stencil painting; Edith Brisac, vestibule floor; Carlotta Corpron, photographic records; Dorothy LaSelle, supervisor, Coreen Spellman and Lura Mae Burton Kendrick, assistants, stained glass windows.

Student artists include Sammy Tate, Helen Solberg, and Margaret Green, lamps and altar pieces; Billie Marie Culwell, wood carving; Carmeta Drummond, front doors; Beatrice Paschall, Mary Ann Chadick, Ivy Mae Chollar, Mary Cook, Helen Crain, Eloise Carriker, Lucille Cudd, Elizabeth Miller, Nora Mae Pierce, Betty Winston, Marilyn Yates, and Billie Marie Culwell, stained glass windows; Mildred Bates, Edith Mae Rhodes, and Pauline Schoolroy, stencil painting; Nelda Bell, La Merle Quillian, and Marilyn Jones, mosaics; Helen Solberg, vestibule floor; Margaret Green and Patricia Fine, photographic records.

Lynn Ford, brother of architect O'Neil Ford, designed and made the furniture, railings, and pulpit.

[26]The chapel is believed to be the first in the nation to be built on a campus by a state college rather than by some outside religious organization.

[27]The College had moved toward providing a social center for faculty members by purchasing a Faculty Club House near the campus in September, 1933. The Faculty Club leased the house from the College.

[28]The story-and-a-half frame building had been purchased by the College several years earlier to serve as a student union under the direction of the YWCA; but it was totally inadequate for all-College socials and even class socials, forcing rental of the Woman's Club Building.

[29]Pancake Night was suggested by the medieval custom of wandering monks' returning to their monasteries one night each year to narrate tales of their travels. Their meals on these nights included a rare cake baked in a flat pan. In 1935 the observance was renamed Founders' Day at the request of alumnae who had for some ten years been celebrating the founding of the College during February.

[30]Brooks W. Leman of Chicago established the award in memory of his wife, the late Pauline Bishop Leman, a student at CIA in 1914. He presented the first awards at the 1931 commencement to Thetis Lemmon for her work as art editor of the *Daedalian* yearbook (1929); to Dorothy Milner, editor of the *Daedalian Quarterly,* for her poems and short stories (1930); and to Norma Hooper for a comparative study of two epic poems (1931).

[31]Margaret Hughston, senior public school music major from Dallas, organized the group.

[32]SMU, which was the other, conducted the initiation.

[33]After this date the literary-social clubs began to decline in number, and only two—Chaparrals and Aglaians—are still active on the campus. The Chaparral Club was formed in 1904.

[34]Named for one of Mrs. L.H. Hubbard's ancestors and organized in Mrs. Hubbard's home, the club limited its membership to TSCW students, alumnae, faculty members, and families.

[35]The conference proved highly successful and has been an annual event since 1939 although its format has changed from time to time.

[36]The Redbud Festival and Self-Development Week have, like the Writer's Conference, adapted to meet changing student interests while remaining an annual event.

[37]The miniature golf course was located behind Lowry Hall.

[38]Governor James V. Allred appointed Teresa Abney Charlton ('13) following petitions and a campaign by alumnae groups throughout Texas.

Students accepted the varied challenges of field hockey (above) and the demanding roles of Hedda Gabler, *which they presented in CIA's Little Theater.*

To Meet the
Exigencies of War   VIII

As the College approached its fifth decade, it experienced
both the joys and the pains of maturity. The college bulletin
of November 1, 1940, proclaimed, "Painted and pig-tailed
days are in the past of TSCW" as rushees presented a
"neat and dignified" appearance to conform to the Round Table decree
that informal club initiations should be conducted with "dignity and
discrimination."

No longer an awkward youngster, the maturing College could note with
pride the growing accomplishments of more than fifty thousand
daughters. In 1941 the College employed some eighty-five alumnae,[1] and
the Texas Legislature which convened in January, 1943, included its first
TSCW graduate. The Honorable Florence Fenley, Representative from the
Seventy-seventh District, was a 1917 graduate of the College, an
established author and lecturer.[2] The college bulletin of February 1, 1943,
reported that she expected to take a hand in "slashing through appropriations to cut down state expenditures—to help win this war."

Following World War II, graduates continued to advance in traditional
areas and entered the new fields which the war had opened to women. In
1946 TSCW graduates still comprised more than a third of the Home
Demonstration Agents in Texas, but they also ranged into many other
areas. After admitting its first pre-medical students in 1942, the College
reported five graduates enrolled in medical schools by 1946. In the same
year a Tessie modeled in a full-page advertisement in Holiday, and another
was a map artist for the National Georgraphic Society. While one graduate
danced in the Dallas Starlight operettas, another opened a school to teach
reading and speech to the deaf or hard-of-hearing. One practiced law in
Houston; another taught elementary school in Monterrey, Mexico; and
still another was Educational Director of the Dallas Museum of Fine Arts.

Perhaps the graduate who received the most acclaim during the period
was Margo Jones, who received the B.S. degree in 1931 and the M.A.
degree in 1933. Identified in 1939 by *Stage* magazine as one of ten outstanding young directors in the country (the only woman to be so
honored), Jones proved herself worthy of the honor in the following
years. After organizing and directing the Community Players of Houston,
she gained Broadway fame as director of *Joan of Lorraine,* the 1946 hit
starring Ingrid Bergman. In addition she co-directed Tennessee Williams'
The Glass Menagerie with Eddie Dowling; and then, supported by a grant
from the Rockefeller Foundation, she returned to Dallas to establish a civic

*Students developed a wide range of
new skills as both courses and informal programs prepared them to
contribute to winning World War II.*

101

repertory theater. Under her direction, the group opened in the Gulf Oil Theater on the State Fair Grounds for a ten-week dramatic season in June, 1947.

As graduates of the College entered a growing number of professions, members of the College family continued their advocacy of the rights of women. In September, 1944, the Texas House of Representatives served as the site of a Texas White House Conference presided over by District Judge Sarah T. Hughes. TSCW Dean of Women Mattie Lloyd Wooten opened the meeting on September 7 with a statement of the aim of the conference: "to give public expression to the desire of women to have a greater share in shaping the policies of Texas state government." It was the purpose of the meeting not merely to express this desire but also to take steps to increase the participation of qualified women in public affairs. The two hundred women who attended the meeting identified women qualified to serve on state boards and commissions and presented the information to Mrs. Wooten.

Continuing her crusade at the meeting of the Business and Professional Women in Colorado City a few months later, Dean Wooten, who was state president of the organization, encouraged the West Texas clubs to "decide what it is you want from your legislators, state and national, and then quit dawdling. Do something. . . . It is high time that this downright silly, childish discrimination against a woman's right to function as a person, regardless of sex or marital status, be removed."[3]

Within a few months, another proponent of the rights of women and of the good of the Texas State College for Women was dead. Jessie H. Humphries, the last original faculty member to retain a position with the College died at her home July 28, 1944. Characterized in the college bulletin of November 1, 1944, as a "champion of the cause of liberal arts and friend of students of TSCW for 41 years," the remarkable woman had left her imprint on the College and on hundreds of students. Author of the inscription at the base of the statue of the pioneer woman on campus, Dean Humphries was herself a pioneer in many respects. She had carried on many of the negotiations which resulted in the recognition of TSCW by various accrediting agencies and had promoted changing the name of the College of Industrial Arts to the Texas State College for Women. She had been one of the chief combatants for the abolition of uniforms and had worked to liberalize other regulations as well.[4]

Alumna Margo Jones (second from left) returned to the campus in 1946, fresh from her success as co-director of Tennessee Williams' The Glass Menagerie.

The passing of the old order was followed, however, by an event which re-emphasized the continuity of life at the College. In the fall of 1948, Janet Elizabeth Galt, freshman library science major from Oklahoma City, became the first third-generation student to enroll at the College. Her grandmother, Mrs. M.M. Mahaffey (Mattie Colley), had attended the College in its opening year; and her mother, Janet Elizabeth Mahaffey of the Class of 1930, was the first "daughter of an Ex" to attend. Approximately one hundred daughters of alumnae were enrolled in 1945.

The War

Like most Americans, TSCW faculty and students had been experiencing at least ripple effects of the war in Europe for some time before December 7, 1941. Alumnae throughout the world, traveling faculty members, and international students sent or brought news of the growing struggle as did daily radio reports like the one in early 1941 which announced that a German air raid had destroyed Allen and Unwin, Ltd., Publishing House in London and burned some 1.5 million books stored there. Among the books at the publisher's was TSCW English Professor Autrey Nell Wiley's recently completed book on rare prologues and epilogues to English dramas.

Her concern was great for, after giving one copy to the TSCW Library and another to the American Council of Learned Societies, she had only three copies of the book; and she had donated her royalties to the Lord Mayor's Fund for the Distressed of London. By May, however, her fears subsided as she began to receive reviews of the book from England, Scotland, and even Johannesburg, South Africa. The reviewers (some of whom mistook Miss Wiley for a man) were generous with their praise of the book, which was to become a standard reference in the field.

Within a few months, the attack on Pearl Harbor drew America directly into the war with an immediacy and horror that elicited support from every quarter. The College hastily concentrated its energies on war-related activities. A quickly-formed defense committee established in 1941 and renamed the War Council in the second year of the war was one of the most active campus groups during the period. Early activities ranged from the appointment of air raid wardens for dormitories and campus buildings to a scrap metal drive and contests for the best victory song, slogan, and cartoon. By early 1943 the emphasis shifted from *defense* to *victory* as reflected in various name changes. The "Defense Shelf" in the Library was renamed the "Victory Shelf," and the TSCW Defense Corps became the TSCW Victory Corps. At one point, in a move not readily assignable as an offensive or defensive effort, a project to fingerprint everyone on campus was launched. Whether the emphasis was on defense or victory, however, students, faculty, and townspeople rallied in support of American soldiers.

Some of the efforts, no doubt, provided a great deal of pleasure to participants. In late 1942, Universal Studios began production of *We've Never Been Licked*, a movie about A&M's contributions to the armed forces. Filmed largely on location on the A&M campus, the movie involved some two hundred Tessies who appeared as the Aggies' girlfriends.

Another popular activity was the county-wide rally held in the TSCW Main Auditorium. Admission to the pageant of patriotic songs, "Battle Songs of Freedom," required the purchase of war bonds and stamps; and the pageant and related sales collected about $2700 in November, 1942. The project was one of many through which the College contributed significant financial support to the war. The Student Finance Council sponsored the weekly sale of war stamps and bonds in dorms, a sale which col-

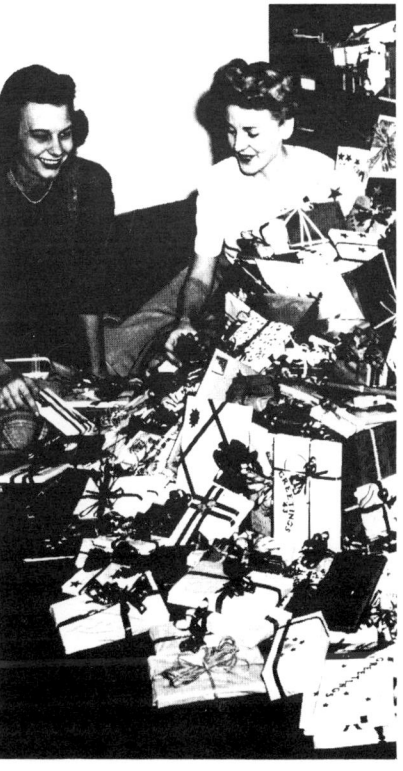

Tessies conducted a major drive to buy and wrap Christmas gifts for American servicemen.

Tessies bought this wedding dress, tiara, and veil, which they sent England where clothes rationing during the war made such gowns unattainable.

lected several thousand dollars during the course of the war. During February, 1944, ninety-seven percent of the students purchased at least one war stamp each week, winning the right to fly a Schools at War Flag in front of the Administration Building. The College was the first in Texas to receive such a flag, and it continued to fly as long as ninety percent of the students bought a ten-cent stamp or more each week. Brackenridge Hall alone contributed almost a thousand dollars during February, and a year later the College was still flying its flag without interruption. The student loan funds, which had attained a balance of more than $116,000 by May 15, 1944, invested $100,000 in War Savings Bonds; and the Student Finance Council appropriated several hundred dollars to a number of war relief funds, including the Red Cross. At the end of the war the Office of Peace Administration named TSCW the nation's model wartime educational institution.

In addition to making cash contributions, students, faculty, and townspeople also worked to provide other tangible support. More than a thousand girls enrolled in knitting classes or knitted in the Red Cross Knitting Room on campus, producing sweaters, kits, and other materials for the use of soldiers and the women of Britain. In the afternoons and evenings work in the Red Cross Surgical Dressing Room on campus produced bandages and surgical dressings.

In a rather radical departure from supplying bandages and sweaters, students in sixty-four campus organizations contributed money to purchase a bridal gown from Neiman-Marcus and, from A. Harris & Co., a seed pearl tiara which held a three-quarter-length veil. The students sent the gown to British girls in the armed forces who could not obtain formal wedding gowns because of clothes rationing. In another tribute to aesthetics in the midst of chaos, twelve art students and three professors contributed watercolor, oil, and photographic pictures to the American Red Cross to be used "for the duration" in service men's recreational buildings.

Other projects involved the conservation and recycling of resources. The dining halls instituted a "clean-plate policy" to conserve food. Dormitories adopted a rule which called for lights-out by 11:15 p.m. to save electricity and wear on the college power plant. And students mounted other drives to gather materials needed in the fighting. By March, 1942, the College had collected and baled two tons of paper. (The College purchased a baler the next January to deal with the waste paper which students salvaged.) In April, students launched a drive for old silk, nylon, and rayon hose to be used for powder bags for naval guns; and the following month College officials abolished the College tradition which had required wearing hose after six o'clock. To raise money to support beds in an English children's hospital, one campus organization collected cancelled stamps to be sold for dye. On May 8, 1942, like other Americans, students registered for sugar rations; and in October students signed up to ease the labor shortage by helping Denton County farmers pick their cotton.

Mary Jane Trail, President of the College Government Association, was clearly speaking for many when she wrote in the college bulletin of March 15, 1943, "With one accord we have pledged ourselves to win the war and to win the peace which is to follow." Along with their contributions of money and goods, many students determined to be completely prepared for whatever the war might demand of them. Thus, clean plates and early lights-out were designed to promote physical fitness as well as to save food and energy; and students sought new courses to prepare them for war emergencies. The college bulletin of October 1, 1942, reported, "War courses, defense and farm defense corps, and a date bureau led the list of aid-to-victory activities at TSCW this year." Not surprisingly, the date bureau, which arranged dates between soldiers and students, was popular. Some three hundred girls registered with the bureau while eighty registered to learn to operate farm machinery. Nevertheless, students were not by any means interested only in social opportunities. During January, 1943, 272 students joined the Women's Motor Corps;[5] and by mid-February, 456 girls were enrolled in various defense courses.

Courses included noncredit offerings in first aid, nutrition, home hygiene and nursing, motor mechanics, and canteen classes along with credit courses such as geography of the war, radio, group discussion and leadership, science, and other courses adapted to winning the war by raising morale and "training future civilian workers and leaders." As the war continued, the College added horsemanship, repair and conservation of household equipment, meteorology and navigation, bandage rolling, and other courses; and the government offered night driving, convoy driving, black-out driving, minor roadside repairs, map reading, and general courses. The Department of Health and Physical Education sponsored a Victory Corps and a program for physical fitness; and the Student Government Week focused on "Women in War Work."

The College also offered a number of student-faculty forums and featured speakers who could provide first-hand accounts of the war. In November, 1942, Lt. Lucy Wilson, one of ten nurses who escaped when Bataan fell, spoke on campus along with other WACs and WAVEs during War Week; and in the early spring of 1944 the Carnegie Endowment sponsored the Carnegie Professor Lectures at which thirty-seven-year-old Prince Hubertus zu Loewenstein discussed his speaking and writing campaign against the Nazis, which had forced him to flee Germany in 1933.

Not content to wait at home, numerous members of the College family joined newly established armed forces for women.[6] Betty Jane Sehmann of the Class of 1935 was the first Texas woman to qualify as an ensign in the WAVEs. Madeline Canova, assistant professor of library science, Mary Esther Wallace, long-time teacher and acting chairman of physics, and Mary Katherine Boone, instructor in physical education, were the first faculty members to join the nation's women's auxiliary service units.[7] Mary Paxton (class of 1943) became an honorary paratrooper when she designed the insignia for the 460th Parachute Field Artillery Battalion. By May 1, 1943, the College reported sixty-five ex-students in the armed services. The number grew to 158 by February 1, 1945. In recognition of its students' contributions, the College proudly displayed a service flag in the rotunda of the Administration Building.[8]

As the students ranged over the world, they reported their activities to their friends in Denton. The college bulletin of May 15, 1944, contained numerous accounts—accounts which did little more than hint at some of the frustrating experiences that accompanied the women's attempts to gain acceptance in what had been completely a man's world. Thelma I. Mehart, a class of 1931 foods major, wrote that she had been placed in charge of Ship's Service Stores in the Fort Security Command because of her experience in quantity food purchasing and because of the scorn of the "Old Salts" who didn't want women "getting fancy" with their cooking. She added, perhaps a little triumphantly, that as more SPARs entered the field, dietitians had been placed in charge of the commissaries.

Some of the complaints were little different from those voiced by some men in the same situations. Hazel L. Watts wrote, " 'Join the Navy and see the world' is, of course, pure propaganda. For I ended up in Oklahoma." Nevertheless, she was fulfilling the main role intended for the women in the services by freeing a man to go from Oklahoma to a battle front.

Other young women wrote of breaking new ground with surprising success. Janet Sanders, a costume design major of the class of 1937,

Contributions to the war effort were not always sublime. Here students in Brackenride Dining Hall are "rooting for rutabaga" as a part of their food conservation drive.

Journalism student Dorothy Gould works with Henry Blagg to prepare the Lass-O *for the college presses.*

reported, "Our group of WAVE mechs (grease monkeys) were the first in the instrument shop. I overhaul the directional gyroscope and it still surprises me when I finish and it works." Pfc. Josephine J. Rice, class of 1943, asked about the white redbud trees by the little chapel before reporting, "I suppose it is rather a far cry from teaching music, but I teach machine guns. . . . I was the first girl to do this work here at Cherry Point." Others served as teachers (one taught in the Army physical therapy school), dietitians, and storekeepers throughout the country.

As the end of the war approached, a report came of the release of Elizabeth Oxford Plowman (honors graduate in art in 1933) and her small daughter from Los Banos, a Japanese prison camp in the Philippines; and following the end of the war, Lt. Beth Andrews reported her wartime services as a dietitian, a job which had taken her from Casablanca where she saw Humphrey Bogart open Rick's Cafe to an audience with the Pope and to service in a hospital in Bologna on both VE and VJ Days.

The war had brought hardships and tragedies to the campus, but it had also brought unexpected growth to the College. As American men went to the war by the hundreds of thousands and women by the tens of thousands, enrollments in men's and coeducational colleges dropped rapidly. By the end of the fall semester, 1942, three-fourths of the Yale undergraduates had enlisted; and the class of 1943 had been graduated early to allow college-deferred students to go to war. The TSCW bulletin of February 1, 1944, reported that TSCW was the only state college in Texas to have an increase in enrollment (almost ten percent) while other colleges declined by thirty to fifty percent.

With a minimal number of men available to perform their customary work, women surprised themselves and others with their ability to fill vacancies in all kinds of new jobs. Norman Rockwell created the gently satirical Rosie the Riveter to portray the 3.5 million women who joined men on armament assembly lines, turning out cargo ships and bombers at almost unbelievable rates. In Texas, Tessies found new fields opening that offered not just war-time employment but long-range professional careers.

Before the invasion of Pearl Harbor, a puzzled writer reported in the college bulletin of February 1, 1941, that more than half the TSCW graduates were settling down within two years of graduation to "lead lives of pure domesticity with occasional dabbles in club work. Men are not the only people who cannot understand women." Exactly two years later, however, the bulletin noted that even though the number of girls who married during the year had doubled since 1941, the TSCW Placement Bureau had placed eighty-five percent of its 972 registrants. Slightly more than two-thirds of the applicants had taken jobs in some teaching field, but 31.5 percent (principally majors in home economics and business) had taken commercial positions.[9] The bulletin also reported a marked movement of art majors into drafting work in both governmental and commercial organizations.[10] Spanish majors were becoming translators and censors for the government. Science majors were entering commercial fields instead of teaching, and both government service and business were requiring increasing numbers of women.

A year later a college bulletin reported that the Placement Bureau had received twelve requests for health and physical education majors to coach football during the past year; and the state, which only a few years before had experienced a surplus of teachers, faced a teacher shortage. Many of the women who entered the job market during the war continued to work at its conclusion. The college bulletin, *Vocational Opportunities for Women,* published December 1, 1949, reported that the number of women in responsible positions almost doubled during and after the war, and the Bureau of Labor Statistics estimated that eighteen million women, one-third of the women in America, held jobs.

106

Seasons and fashions change, but the pioneering spirit of the first students and faculty members endures.

Lantern parades at home
and concerts halfway
around the world make
strangers into friends.

Students, alumnae, faculty members, and buildings stand as tall symbols of the traditions and accomplishments of TWU

Centers in Dallas and Houston and the main campus in Denton . . .

. . . are rich in academic and social life.

TWU and its students . . .

—teaching, learning, building, and growing together—are fulfilling the founders' dreams.

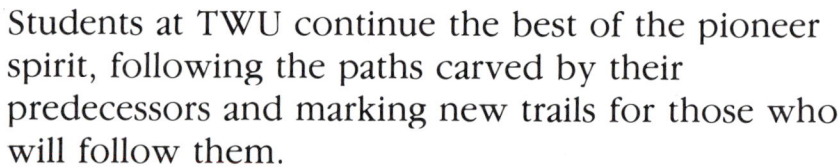

Students at TWU continue the best of the pioneer spirit, following the paths carved by their predecessors and marking new trails for those who will follow them.

The Curriculum

The College felt the impact of the war in every area of its operation, including the curriculum; but a traditional emphasis on timely and practical instruction minimized the need for major wartime changes. Characteristic of the efforts of the College to stay abreast of current needs and interests was the Regents' approval in 1940 of a new plan through which students could earn the Bachelor of Science degree in nursing[11] and the addition of aeronautics to the college schedule. The 142 students who quickly applied to take flying lessons at the Denton Municipal Airport testified to their faith in the claim in the college bulletin of November 1, 1940, "The sky is no longer the limit for opportunities offered at TSCW." The nursing program attracted significantly fewer students (only twenty-seven) in its first year, and the decline to twenty nursing majors by 1945 gave no indication of the future importance the program would attain. It was, in fact, overshadowed by the Music Department, which was observing its silver anniversary in the winter of 1940.[12]

Enrollment figures from 1940 to 1945 reflected distinct changes in the interests of TSCW students. Several areas traditionally associated with women declined sharply in the number of majors they attracted. Library science majors declined by three-fourths (from 139 to 32). Education, philosophy, and psychology majors fell by half (from 205 to 103). And home economics majors dropped approximately thirty percent (from 569 to 403). The number of English majors declined from 97 to 61, and history majors decreased from 24 to 15.

On the other hand, a number of areas which men had traditionally dominated showed increased enrollments although their enrollments still lagged behind those of more traditional fields. Mathematics and the sciences experienced significant growth. Biology grew from 75 to 86 majors, chemistry from 31 to 79 majors, physics from 0 to 2 majors, and mathematics from 23 to 38 majors. Economics and business outdistanced home economics to become the largest department of the College (growing from 330 in 1940 to 427 in 1945 with a high of 501 in 1944). Journalism grew dramatically from 78 to 127 majors, and pre-medicine majors (recorded for the first time in 1942) grew from 20 to 33. The Department of Sociology almost doubled its enrollment (from 65 to 126).[13]

These changes would require post-war adjustments, but during the war TSCW concentrated on the courses in which traditional emphases proved most timely. The production and conservation of foods; food substitutes; nutrition; budget making; the economics of consumption; and the selection, care, renovation, and repair of clothing were subjects of courses and of college bulletins such as "Hints on How to Live in a War Economy," prepared by members of the TSCW War Council and issued by the College April 15, 1943. Physical fitness programs continued to offer instruction in personal hygiene, first aid, home nursing, and the safeguarding of health by preventive measures. Even courses in the fundamental arts and sciences had regularly encouraged application to home uses and to industrial activities so that they were well-suited to the current needs. Thus, the College avoided panic and, according to the college bulletin of March 15, 1943, was "in the midst of all the adjustments attendant upon full participation in the War Effort, . . . calmly proceeding, with all the wisdom it has or can summon, upon its fundamental and permanent function, that is to give the young women of Texas an educational program that will result in developing purposeful, dynamic citizens, worthy and typical of the civilization we are striving to perpetuate."

In many ways, the College found itself in perhaps the most enviable situation of its existence. Technical education, which had been greeted

Frances McDowell Wagner pursued a degree in nursing and learned to fly while her husband flew supplies overseas.

107

with scorn in many circles when the College accepted its assignment at the beginning of the century, was now hailed as essential to the waging of a successful all-out war. Similarly, a liberal education, which the College had secured for its students in spite of strong opposition in its formative years, was regarded as essential to the development of leaders both for the war and for the post-war period.

Thus, Hubbard must have taken special pleasure in his message in the college bulletin of March 15, 1943: "It is gratifying to realize that the Texas State College for Women, from the day it opened its doors forty years ago, has been a leader in both of these important phases of higher education [technical and liberal]. . . . So much is this true that the College has found it necessary to make only minor changes in its curriculum to meet the exigencies of the war. It has, indeed, been a pioneer in the field of higher education for women. . . . The Texas State College for Women is keeping, I believe, abreast of the times, and is offering a curriculum to its students that will furnish them with such a fund of useful knowledge and of democratic ideals that they will be equipped to make a real contribution toward the winning of the war and the establishment of an enduring peace."

Courses as diverse as nursery education and music would make their contributions to the war efforts. Summer sessions especially attempted to help women prepare for the new roles in which they found themselves. The 1943 summer session emphasized instrumental training for public school teachers who had majored in music education only to find themselves placed in charge of bands and orchestras when men conductors went to the war. That summer also offered special courses to help home economics teachers establish high school Victory Corps groups, and the Department of Health and Physical Education offered a Victory Corps Institute to help in the physical fitness phase of Corps work.

Although nursery education may, at first glance, seem remote from military victory, it proved to be an important consideration during the war. As women worked outside their homes for the first time in large numbers, the need for trained nursery school supervisors to oversee children grew dramatically. By 1944, TSCW, which had offered its first child development course some ten years earlier, was offering a twelve-course major in child development and nursery education, the first such major in Texas. A new nursery school provided a laboratory where students could gain experience with two nursery school groups and

With the war over, students could redirect their energies to creating equipment which would be more useful for teaching young children than for fighting enemies.

108

simple model equipment which they could easily copy for use in other nursery schools.

As the war progressed, needs for special wartime and post-war services became clear, and TSCW led the way in adapting existing courses and developing a limited number of new programs to train students to meet some of these needs.

Among the fields which opened in new directions during the war was foods and nutrition. Demands for dietitians for the armed forces added to the regular needs of school lunchrooms, college dining halls, and commercial eating places; and TSCW offered a pre-training program for foods and nutrition majors who wished to become army dietitians. In 1943, following a required year of probation, the College received approval from the American Dietetics Association (ADA) for a fifth-year training program for dietitians studying institution management. Only five other colleges in the nation had the program at the time—the University of Texas, Oklahoma A&M , the University of Washington, and sister schools Boston Women's Educational and Vocational Center, and Mills College in California. ADA approval of the program meant that graduates were eligible for membership in the ADA and qualified for positions under Civil Service specifications for staff dietitians. Within five years, TSCW home economics graduates who wished to obtain hospital dietetics training were receiving appointments for fifth-year administrative training courses in hospitals and universities all over the country.

Men and women returning from service in the armed forces were also demonstrating needs for new therapies—recreational, physical, and occupational. In response to those needs the TSCW Department of Art initiated an occupational therapy major in the fall of 1943. Under the direction of Mary Marshall, head of the department, the program required the completion of the usual liberal arts work on campus. A great deal of the training occurred in the Art Department with additional work in psychology and biology and in health, physical education, and recreation. Courses led to the Bachelor of Science degree. The American Medical Association (AMA) required an additional year's clinical work in hospitals before registration with the Occupational Therapy Association (OTA).

The introduction of the new course was a major step for TSCW. No other college in the Southwest offered such a program. The nearest occupational therapy course was at the University of Kansas, and the only other in the South was at William and Mary. By May, 1945, the appointment of eleven Dallas physicans, all medical teachers at the Southwestern Medical Foundation, as special lecturers broadened the students' training. Campus buses transported students to the medical classes offered in Dallas at the Southwest Medical College of the the University of Texas.

By November, TSCW had concluded tentative arrangements with two large hospitals in Dallas to serve as interning centers for graduates, but students continued their clinical experience at hospitals throughout the United States as well. By 1947, the program had won accreditation from the AMA Council on Medical Education and Hospitals and from the American OTA, accreditation which it has maintained continuously to the present.

The Department of Health and Physical Education also met an obvious need during the war years with its instruction for personal fitness, and it took its place as a national leader in the preparation for post-war adjustments. Wartime living pointed up the need for improved fitness among both soldiers and civilians in a time of limited equipment and teachers, and TSCW responded to the cry which was sounding for effective health and physical education programs in the schools.[14]

The department also contributed to the development of the occupational therapy major in the Department of Art and offered baccalaureate studies in physiotherapy; but it adopted recreation as its own special contribution, adding the term to the name of the department and abbreviating the name to HPER. College bulletins noted that a bachelor's degree in HPER met the prerequisites for advanced study and licensure in physical therapy and for training in recreation therapy.

On December 7, 1945, the Curriculum Committee of the College approved new majors in both recreation and recreation administration in anticipation of a nationwide expansion of postwar recreation programs in hospitals, community centers, churches, schools, industry, communities, and states. Specialists also expected a rapid growth in camping and outing interests as civilians found increased time for leisure and relaxation. Again TSCW was in the forefront of a movement. Only three other colleges in the country, all in California, offered recreation programs at the time—the University of California, the University of Southern California, and Mills College. Nine new courses in recreation added twenty-four semester hours to HPER offerings.

Not all studies during the first half of the decade were war-related, however. In the summer of 1941, TSCW instituted a four-week summer school in Saltillo, Mexico, just west of Monterrey. Students resided in a large private home and ate at the Hotel Casa Colonial during their stay. The program offered not only liberal exposure to the language and culture of

Students' experiences in TSCW's summer program in Saltillo, Mexico, ranged from the serenity of Casa Villareal to the ruggedness of picturesque mountains.

Business students mastered the latest machines.

Saltillo but also optional trips to Monterrey and Mexico City. The basic cost of the four-week program—including two nights' lodging in a hotel room in Laredo, bridge toll, first class bus fare to and from Saltillo, rooms and meals in Saltillo, tuition, tutors, eight picture shows, and tips—was $95 in 1941.

The course proved extremely popular. Not only did it continue uninterrupted each summer throughout the war, but it grew significantly in size. Enrollment increased from sixty-one students in the first session to approximately 155 in 1945, a figure which had to be established as a maximum limit.

In addition to the last Saltillo school in 1948, the College offered a Spanish audio-visual workshop in Denton. By 1950 the summer program offered several hours of daily Spanish conversation in a language laboratory, a "theoretical but practical" study of phonetics, advanced grammar and composition, lectures on contemporary Spain, and Hispanic folksongs along with instruction in audio-visual aids and laboratory techniques. The nearest remnant of Saltillo was *Casa Espanola,* a small campus dormitory with a Spanish-speaking hostess. The mature students who resided there spoke only Spanish during their stay.[15]

Another popular extension program, the Summer School of Painting at Taos, New Mexico, did not survive the war. The college bulletin of

November 1, 1943, reported that the school would be suspended during the war; and the bulletin of March 1, 1946, announced that the school would be re-established "when conditions permit"; but the school never reopened. The closing did not, however, reflect a declining interest in art at TSCW. During the period from 1940 to 1945, the number of art majors increased by more than fifty percent (from 245 to 374).

In the fall of 1945, interests of the War Council quickly gave way to those of the Curriculum Committee, which scrutinized course offerings in a series of meetings ending December 7, 1945. Out of the meetings came not only the new majors in recreation and recreation administration already mentioned, but also new majors in psychology and social work, a new degree (the Master of Education), new courses in most departments for 1946-47, and the strengthening of liberal arts requirements for a number of majors already in the catalog. The committee established additional economics, history, sociology, natural science, mathematics, philosophy, or fine arts requirements for many majors for the B.A. degree. The College added news editorial and advertising majors in the Journalism Department by the following fall; and in the fall of 1948, it offered a new radio-journalism program which blended journalism, radio, and speech courses. Even before the new program was formalized, however, students had been gaining firsthand experience in programming, performing, and managing the TSCW radio station, WCST.[16]

Additional graduate degrees and majors reflected a growing emphasis on graduate studies. Beginning with the 1949 fall semester, the Department of Library Science offered a program leading to the Master of Library Science degree, and the Graduate Council approved a major in school social work for the Master of Arts degree. Offered for the first time in the 1950 summer session, the program was designed primarily for teachers who worked as visiting teachers and school social workers. In 1950 the Department of Economics and Business also offered courses leading to the new Master of Business Education degree for the first time.

The Campus

In spite of the major expansion of campus facilities during the thirties, the College continued to need more space. As the thirties drew to an end, TSCW officials broke ground (December 18, 1939) for a new one-story education building to be completed in approximately a year on the southeast corner of the campus. Contributions from WPA would support another significant addition to the physical plant. Consisting of six classrooms, an auditorium (which could be converted into two classrooms), a library, a kindergarten room, and a manual arts room, the building housed a demonstration school for student teaching.

Less than a month later (January 10, 1940) construction began on two other buildings on the opposite end of the campus. The new $44,000 storeroom-bakery-butchershop building on Hennen Drive on the north side of the campus increased storage capabilities by seventy percent and doubled the capacity of the campus bakery. Adjacent to the storeroom, a $25,000 building housed carpentry, painting, electrical, and plumbing shops. The fireproof buildings were constructed of reinforced concrete floors, walls, and roof slabs, and all-steel window frames.

By August 20, the buildings were completed and ready for use. As they had earlier worked on the Little Chapel, NYA boys worked on the construction of the new storeroom and workshop, on a gardener's cottage behind the chapel, and on two cooperative dormitories. The gray sandstone which was used in all buildings was quarried at Bridgeport to match the nearby Little Chapel. The boys, who began as unskilled laborers, did

Alumnae contributions and a grant from the WPA helped finance a new Student Union Building. The first dance in the SUB Ballroom was the Redbud Formal in 1942.

East of the new SUB a swimming pool, complete with a beach and umbrellas, was popular with students following its opening in the summer of 1942.

electrical work, plastering, finishing, and rock masonry and also made cabinets and furniture for the buildings.

WPA additions to the campus continued in 1941. During the first week of February, officials broke sod for a Gymnasium Annex north of the cooperative dormitories. Built on Bell Avenue, across from the gymnasium, the $150,000 recreation building was used as a Student Union Building for a number of years. WPA contributed about $43,000 to the project.[17] The building, which measured 150 by 82 feet (outside dimensions), offered club and activity space on the first floor with instructional space for the physical education department on part of the first and all of the second floor, which also contained two large dance studios. The third floor contained a spacious foyer and an 8500-square-foot ballroom which, with its capacity to accommodate a thousand couples, became the center of campus social life. The college bulletin of March 15, 1943, boasted that the building offered "all the indoor recreation facilities you have dreamed of—even a beautiful soda fountain." A tunnel under Bell Avenue connected the annex directly with the gymnasium building.

By May of the same year, WPA had poured the walls of a 50 by 150-foot swimming pool to the east of the Annex. Scheduled for completion by September, the $50,000 pool, which ranged from four to fourteen feet deep, offered special underwater windows for making pictures, underwater lights and floodlights for night swimming, a high-diving tower, a sandy beach (complete with umbrellas) on the south side, and a tile walk around its circumference.[18] Students could dress in the gymnasium and go to the pool through the Bell Avenue tunnel. Men dressed in an outdoor bathhouse.

Preston M. Geren of Fort Worth was the architect for the Gymnasium Annex and for the new $50,000 Journalism Building begun February 17. NYA again provided labor for the two-story tile building on Bell Avenue, just north of the original college building. The building housed the journalism, extension, and publicity departments of the College, the college print shop, two regular classrooms, an advertising laboratory, an

On Saturday nights, students could dance at the College Club and enjoy its snack bar until midnight.

editorial room, a general reading room, a photography laboratory with four air-conditioned dark rooms, a reporting laboratory, a journalism office, a publicity office, a general publicity workroom, and special offices for student publications. Copy traveled through a chute from the copy and editing rooms to the print shop. The one-story print shop (40'x70') on the west side of the first floor had sky-lighting and ceiling ventilation plus a storage room. The College hailed the shop as one of the most modern in North Texas.

Early in 1941 NYA boys also constructed a home management house at the corner of Hennen and Bell Avenues. Built of the gray sandstone which matched the Little Chapel, the home was named for Margaret Gleason, director of the Department of Home Economics from 1919 to 1935. The home housed eight senior home management students and one advisor.

Amid these additions, TSCW initiated still more requests for building funds. During the 1941 legislative session, the College asked Legislators for $300,000 to construct a new Home Economics Building. At the time of the request some seven hundred students were majoring in home economics, and all students were encouraged to take basic homemaking courses. The department, which had a faculty of twenty-four and which had awarded one hundred master's degrees by this time, was the largest in the state; and it had trained more than one-fifth of the home economists in Texas even though some eighteen colleges offered home economics courses. Although the 1913 Household Arts Building was woefully inadequate, it was not until the end of World War II—in fact, almost the end of the decade—that plans could be completed and funds obtained so that Regents could let the contract for the new building.[19]

Plans for other new buildings continued (Hubbard appointed a building committee approved by the Regents to plan additional dormitory and dining facilities), but new construction slowed during the war.[20] Nevertheless, the students who entered TSCW in the fall of 1940 saw significant changes in the campus before their graduation. An audit on September 1, 1943, established the value of all property belonging to the College at $4,700,764.66—$335,207.01 for lands and campus, $3,498,878.18 for buildings, and $866,679.47 for equipment.

On December 8, 1944, College officials and the Board of Regents outlined a proposed post-war building expansion program for legislative consideration the following February. The $2 million plan included a request for appropriations of $950,000—$450,000 for a new Home Economics Building and equipment, $350,000 for an Economics and Business Classroom Building and equipment,[21] and $150,000 for library

The new Journalism Building housed the journalism, extension, and publicity departments of TSCW and a modern print shop.

114

expansion. The second part of the plan called for the issuance of revenue bonds in the amount of $1.25 million to finance the construction of three $250,000 dormitories to house two hundred students each and a $500,000 centrally-located dining unit to accommodate 2,500 persons. In supporting the plan, Hubbard noted, "The College has reached its capacity enrollment and only through an additional building program can we hope to take care of the increasing number of students who wish to attend. . . . It was necessary this year to turn down many applications for entrance and from present prospects this condition will prevail next year."

Once again the College looked to federal financing, and in 1945 the Federal Works Administration announced an advance of $37,500 to finance the preparation of plans and specifications for three new dormitories and a new dining hall to be built at an estimated cost of $1.35 million. The college bulletin of February 1, 1946, included a drawing of the new dining hall along with a report that Regents had postponed final action on the $2 million plan. Of primary concern was the ability to secure needed materials; and, as Hubbard noted, the situation was also complicated "by the present cost of construction. . . . Many colleges are hesitating to enter into a program of construction at this time because of the conditions."

By late April, Regents had approved a $4.23 million improvement and construction program. The expected cost of the Home Economics Building and equipment had risen to $600,000. The estimated cost of the dining room and equipment had risen to $950,000. Anticipated costs for the new dormitories had dropped to $659,000; but the plan called for an additional $250,000 for the reconstruction of the Administration Building, $120,000 for power plant replacements, $50,000 for remodeling classrooms, and $10,000 for permanent improvements and repairs. By late fall the Civilian Production Administration had authorized the building of

Completed early in the decade (see p. 112), the Education/Demonstration School Building marked the southeast corner of the campus. The Home Economics Building, north of the Demonstration School, was called for as early as 1944 but was not completed until the early fifties.

the central dining unit and a three-story addition to Capps Hall to house two hundred freshman students. The College had also acquired three new frame dormitories—Anson Jones and Burleson Halls on Austin Avenue and Cynthia Parker Hall on Oakland Avenue across from the Music Building—and thirty acres east of the campus for future recreational use.

While plans for these changes continued, work was well underway on other major projects. By late 1945 the heating system in the Art Building was being rearranged in anticipation of the addition of darkrooms and conference rooms in the basement. A year later the basement of the Music-Speech Building was being finished for practice rooms and a speech room.

In early 1946, Hubbard Lake between the Library and the Demonstration School was filled in to make a smooth slope (it had been drained the previous spring); and on November 1, 1946, the college bulletin reported the completion of the outside walls of an addition that would increase the capacity of the Library from 75,000 to 200,000 volumes. The college bulletin of January 1, 1948, reported that the recent enlargement had doubled stack space and that the library holdings included a collection of 100,000 volumes exclusive of approximately 60,000 government publications.[22] The bulletin also pictured the proposed Economics and Business Building, a building that was never built.

Exactly a year later, the college bulletin reported progress on "A $3,000,000 Building Program." The College had completed construction of a new power plant. Officials expected completion of the addition to Capps Hall by fall. South of Dormitory Row, construction was well under way on the giant air-conditioned dining unit, which the bulletin described as "unsurpassed in the nation." The building's four distinctly decorated dining halls could each accommodate four hundred fifty people at one time. In addition, the building contained tea rooms, parlors, food and meat storage rooms, a bakery, a machine shop, and a refrigerated garbage room.

Hubbard Lake had to be filled to allow the eastward expansion of the Library toward the Demonstration School.

116

President Hubbard laid the cornerstone for the dining hall, the last of the buildings to be completed during his administration and the one to bear his name.

The north end of the ground floor was set aside for a new laundry (the old one would be torn down); and the third floor was planned to include a small banquet room and space for the relocation of the home economics cafeteria from the Household Arts Building. In February, 1949, Hubbard predicted, ''The new dining room will revolutionize the life on the campus and will enable us to greatly improve our meal service. For the first time we will have kitchen and dining room equipment that will be strictly modern.''

In the spring of 1950, students helped carry chairs from the old to the new dining hall, and on May 12, Governor Allan Shivers delivered the main address to dedicate the new $1.75 million facility, which easily covered a city block. Named Hubbard Hall, the building provided a kind of climactic capstone to Hubbard's tenure at TSCW. Like the other buildings constructed during his presidency, but larger than any of them, Hubbard Hall contributed both in appearance and in use to the air of gracious sophistication and culture which Hubbard had cherished and nurtured for the Texas State College for Women.

As completion of the dining hall approached, Regents let contracts for two new buildings—the long-needed Home Economics Building and a new dormitory. By November, 1949, work had begun on both buildings— the Home Economics Building to the south of the original college building and directly east of the Science Building and the new dormitory directly across Bell Avenue from Stoddard Hall on the site of the former Smith-Carroll Hall.[23] Completion would come under Hubbard's successor.

The Students

During the forties, social life on the campus centered on the "literary clubs," which were essentially social. The college bulletin of May 1, 1948, reported, "There are no national social sororities on the campus, thus reducing closed organizations to a minimum, yet in the various teas, receptions and dances the girls exercise the social graces so valuable in later life." The Round Table, a federation composed of the presidents of all campus clubs and organizations and sponsored by a faculty committee and the dean of women, organized social activities on the campus. Reflecting some of the maturity that one might expect at a thirty-seven-year-old institution, the Round Table decreed in 1940 that informal club initiations should be conducted with "dignity and discrimination so that [they do] not intrude into classrooms, dormitories, dining rooms, and auditorium."

Activities of the literary clubs on campus included both traditional initiation pranks and formal teas.

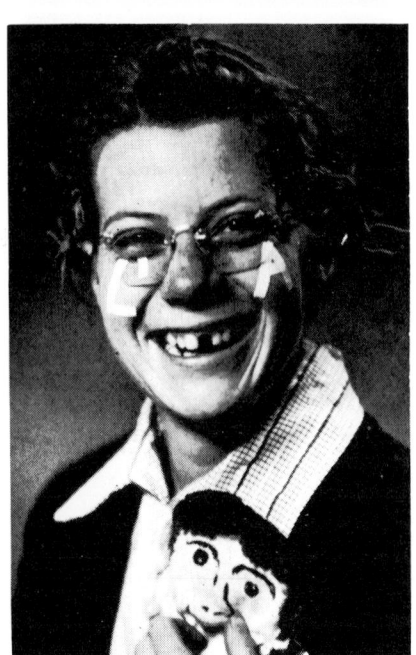

Along with the literary clubs, the Women's Recreation Association (WRA) also played a major role in campus social life. In the spring of 1941 students voted to add a fifteen-cent fee each semester that would make every student a member of WRA .[24] The organization helped start each academic year in grand style with a full range of activities during the first week of school. Among the festivities were New-Comers' Night, an all-college dance, the Villagers' Club program, the WRA Carnival, a faculty concert, and the traditional lantern parade.

Throughout the year TSCW offered additional picnics and all-college dances, and each class sponsored its own special event—the Freshman Frolic, Sophomore Harvest Moon, Junior Hay Ride, and Senior Breakfast. Stunt Night provided inter-class competition; and the Redbud Festival, concluding with a Coronation Ball, continued to be a social highlight.

At one time or another during the decade, individual leisure activities available on campus included archery, dancing—ballroom, folk, and modern—tennis, volleyball, basketball, badminton, softball, soccer, fencing, tumbling, and indoor and outdoor swimming. In addition to hard and clay tennis courts, the College also maintained a riding stable and academy,[25] a hockey field, and regulation-sized rifle ranges on campus. Just east of the campus the College golf course varied from nine to eighteen to twelve holes. The college bulletin of January 1, 1949, claimed the twelve-hole course was "the best course for women in the country."

Some of the activities were of more than casual interest to the students involved. The college bulletin of May 1, 1941, reported that the TSCW Rifle Team had defeated the Aggies' club for the second time in two years. In a "shoulder-to-shoulder shooting match" on the rifle range under Houston Hall, the Tessies secured a two-point victory. By May, 1943, news of the team's prowess had spread throughout the world with pictures of the shooters appearing in newspapers from Iceland to India's *Sunday Statesman*. The College even received a letter from a young woman in Russia who had seen pictures of the marksmanship class.

A furnished camp cabin continued to be an inviting rustic gathering place, and Virginia-Carroll Lodge offered a beautifully furnished living room and adjacent kitchen where students could arrange private social affairs without charge. The new Student Union Building[26] included rooms that were set aside on Wednesday and Saturday nights for games and dancing with dates, and it frequently entertained two to three hundred couples. Service men received special social considerations during the war through a date bureau which arranged dates on Saturday afternoons. With parental approval students could voluntarily participate in the bureau or attend dances at nearby army camps, which sent buses chaperoned by professors and their spouses to collect the girls.

The war, which necessitated some travel restrictions, imposed certain constraints on social activities. In compliance with requests from the Office of Defense Transportation ex-students cancelled their annual homecomings; and the student body voted to omit spring vacation in 1945 to help relieve overcrowded conditions on trains and buses. Even canoeing, sailing, and picnicking at the Lake Dallas camp only five miles from the campus were suspended for the duration of the war.[27]

By February 1, 1946, however, President Hubbard and Charlotte Cornell, President of the Ex-Students Association, could report to alumnae, "The College is rapidly returning to its normal activities after the storms of war have finally been quieted."[28] To support its activities TSCW added a forty-five-passenger and two forty-passenger army surplus buses to its exising fleet of two twenty-three-passenger buses and took to the road. By the fall of 1946, girls in hats, gloves, and high-heeled shoes were boarding the buses for regular trips to the Dallas Symphony and theater, to the Metropolitan Opera in Dallas in the spring, and to the State Fair and

Southwest Conference football in the fall. In addition, the buses provided transportation for field trips and carried TSCW ensembles such as the Caperettes, Vocalaires, Serenaders, Orchestra, Modern Choir, and modern dance troupe throughout the state to perform. Fort Worth and Texas A&M were also popular destinations; and the buses made even longer trips to help girls reach their homes during the Thanksgiving, Christmas, and Easter holidays.

Early in its history, TSCW had developed a close relationship with Texas A&M. Maintaining their distinct instructional undertakings—the one designed to serve the needs of the young women of the state and the other, the young men—the colleges had long looked to each other to provide social contacts for their students. Nevertheless, faced with a declining enrollment as both returning GIs and young women flocked to coeducational institutions, TSCW, which had always emphasized the educational benefits of a woman's college, found it necessary to address the social implications of a campus without men.

The college bulletin of March 1, 1948, devoted an entire section to the problem. The section—"What! No Men?"—boasted, "The College provides the ideal arrangement of freedom from masculine diversion during class time and adequate social life when desired." The College reiterated its claim in its bulletin of December 1, 1949: "TSCW is a woman's world as far as its classroom work goes, but there is no shortage of college men on the campus when social hours roll around." To back up its claims, the 1948 bulletin noted that three thousand men (two-thirds of them veterans) attended North Texas State College, just two miles west of TSCW in Denton—"on the same city bus line, too." In addition, the bulletin pointed to the seven thousand Aggies "who visit TSCW so often."

"Rare is the student who does not know several of these boys," continued the bulletin, whether meeting them on the TSCW campus or in her hometown. To demonstrate the closeness between the brother-sister schools, the bulletin described the annual TSCW Corps Trip to Fort Worth or Dallas to see A&M compete against Texas Christian University or Southern Methodist University in football. School closed one day each fall to allow the Tessies to root for their brothers in these games, and the Aggies selected a Tessie as football sweetheart to be presented between the halves of the game. The bulletin attempted to describe "this indefinable something that puts a lump in the throats of Tessies when the Aggies sing 'We are the Aggies'. . . or the 'Aggie War Hymn.' " In spite of these and many other promotional campaigns, however, TSCW which had boomed during the war years, found itself in serious trouble by the end of the decade.

Like the University of Texas and Texas A&M, TSCW had been designed to serve students throughout the state, and in 1943 the State Board of Education identified the three schools as the most nearly "State" institutions because they drew students from all over the state. In addition, students came to TSCW that year from thirty other states and three foreign countries. The typical student of the period was in many ways similar to the very early CIA students. According to a statistical analysis of the TSCW freshmen conducted by sociology instructor Catherine Bentinck in September, 1943, and reported in the college bulletin of May 15, 1944, "Frances Freshman" was a Texas girl graduated from a high school in a hometown of fewer than 2500 inhabitants. The federal census classification would, thus, have identified her as a "country gal." On the first day of registration, "Frances" was seventeen. Her father, who had been to college, and her mother, who had been only to high school, were both church members (probably Methodists); and they were both living and living together. "Frances" had 1.7 brothers and sisters.

A&M students annually chose a Tessie as football sweetheart and presented her at the Corps Trip to Fort Worth or Dallas.

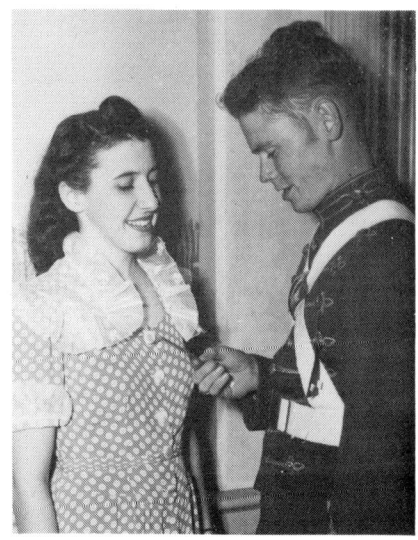

Although Miss Bentinck's analysis did not include data related to family income, students she surveyed seemed to be more prosperous than were the students at the beginning of the decade. The college bulletin of February 1, 1941, reported that more than one thousand students (almost forty percent of the total enrollment) earned a part of their expenses at jobs which ranged from washing test tubes for the NYA to "slinging hash" in the college dining halls. In addition five hundred girls shared rooms and duties in the cooperative homes designed to provide economical housing on campus. At the time of the 1943 survey, however, eighty percent of the freshmen stated no need to borrow money or to work in order to attend college, and only 12.3 percent became a part of the cooperative housing system.[29] Enrollment for the 1944-45 school year reached 2760, a number which made TSCW the largest residential college for women in the United States and the second largest college in Texas.[30] Summer students increased the total to 4027, the largest enrollment during Hubbard's administration.[31]

Although TSCW continued to draw from a large geographic area after the war (the college bulletin of January 1, 1948, reported students from 223 counties in Texas; and the bulletin of November 1, 1948, reported students from seven foreign countries and twenty-nine states besides Texas), enrollment began a precipitous decline. Hubbard reported an almost-twelve-percent decline in enrollment in the bulletin of November 1, 1947, and encouraged alumnae to direct promising girls to TSCW. Putting a good face on the situation, the college bulletin of January 1, 1948, boasted that being a woman's college had enabled TSCW to avoid "the serious post-war crowded conditions characteristic of most other institutions due to large veteran enrollments"; but College officials were deeply concerned.

Hubbard candidly reported to the alumnae again in the college bulletin of May 1, 1948, "Many of you will no doubt be surprised to learn that your Alma Mater which was filled above capacity during the war, is now facing a serious shortage of students." A number of factors contributed to the decline. Hubbard suggested that some students might have been discouraged by reports that TSCW was overflowing with students and applicants and could not accommodate any more—reports that may have continued after the war-time surfeit was over. Probably more important considerations, however, were the rapidly growing public junior colleges[32] and the fact that all senior coeducational colleges in the state now provided dormitories for women whereas at one time only TSCW and the University of Texas had offered such accommodations. Hubbard suggested that wartime enrollments at TSCW might have been somewhat inflated by students and parents who considered the campus a sheltered refuge from the war conditions, but as the GI Bill attracted large numbers of returning soldiers to coeducational institutions, these institutions, in turn, attracted large numbers of women students. Identifying some of the causes of the problem and soliciting the help of alumnae in dealing with it, Hubbard concluded his message, "I am sincere when I tell you that in my judgment the situation is critical." The bulletin included a list of accomplishments, distinguishing features, and attractions that the College offered with the admonition to alumnae to "Boost Your College." Hubbard reported the decline from 2779 students in the 1946-47 long session to 2414 in 1947-48 and gloomily projected an enrollment of below 2000 for the next session.

Major recruitment efforts had some success, however; and in the fall, Hubbard thanked the alumnae for helping to minimize the loss of enrollment which was down only 195 students from the previous fall. Nevertheless, enrollment problems remained a primary concern. During the 1950 Easter holidays more than seven hundred students were excused from classes a day early to participate in a booster program. Armed with special kits of bulletins, pamphlets, and programs assembled by the staff of the Extension Department, the students returned to 267 high schools in eleven states to talk to girls about attending TSCW.

Other recruitment efforts included an extensive program of workshops in the summer of 1950. The Department of Business and Economics co-sponsored a third annual business education conference with North Texas State College. The Department of Education offered workshops in counseling and guidance, adolescent growth and development, and special education. The Department of English offered a workshop on current trends in English. A sports clinic for high school and college coaches of girls intramural and interscholastic teams offered instruction in basketball, softball, volleyball, and tennis; and instruction in officiating led to National Officials' Ratings. The American Red Cross directed a national aquatic school in senior life saving and boating, advanced swimming, first aid, accident prevention, and leadership training. And the Department of Home Economics offered workshops related to school lunch problems, problems and practices of the Future Homemakers Organization, and teaching family relations in high school.

The 1948 Daedalian *celebrated new relaxed rules.*

No lights off!—12:15 privileges on Saturday night!—Secret ballot voting!—"Coke" machines in the dormitories! —— President Hubbard's "Grievance" Sheets—½ day earlier on holidays! Smoking rules changed!

Perhaps partly in response to the declining enrollment and certainly in response to a changing society, TSCW again decreased its restrictions on student behavior. On February 26, 1947, the recommendation of a faculty-student conference that juniors and seniors be allowed dates any night from 5:30 to 11:00 p.m. without special permission was approved and implemented on an experimental basis; and the following spring proposed revisions for the handbook which regulated student life on campus were approved. The reduction in regulations was designed to give freedom to students without the College's relinquishing "necessary" controls. Hubbard stated his philosophy in the college bulletin of May 1, 1948: "I believe that they are an improvement on the present regulations, and that the students will prove worthy of the increased trust placed in them. If, however, the plan does not work, it can be changed."[33]

The statement was typical of Hubbard's attitudes about every aspect of college operations during his tenure. Believing always in the possibility for improvement, he expanded the physical plant beyond all expectations, attracted exceptional faculty and students, and enriched their stay with a wealth of cultural and intellectual offerings unmatched before or after his tenure. Also believing that a plan that did not work could be changed or that an adverse situation could yield some benefit, he was admirably suited to lead the College through the difficult years of the Depression and World War II.

Like his predecessors, he seemed exceptionally talented at finding some bounty even in the lean years and at balancing the two-fold responsibility of the College to educate its students both liberally and practically. The facilities constructed during his administration offer concrete evidence of his ability to blend the practical with the aesthetic. They range from the essential maintenance and storage buildings to the spiritually satisfying Little Chapel and Botanical Gardens. In between, a host of instructional, residential, and other buildings combined utility and graceful charm. Less concrete, but no less real, is the lasting impact which the combination made on the students of the era.

When Hubbard announced his retirement in the spring of 1950, he had served as President of the College for longer than all of his predecessors combined, more than half the life of the College. Like them he had accepted the uniqueness of the institution, marshaled its resources to greatest advantage, and capitalized on its strengths. After a rather rugged youth, the College had in Hubbard a man who could smooth away many rough edges to produce a polished surface. It would be the job of his successor to bring new strength and vitality to the delicate and fragile institution he was leaving.

CHAPTER VIII—NOTES

[1]The forty-five alumnae on the faculty comprised forty-eight percent of the total female TSCW faculty, and women comprised approximately half of the total faculty. In addition, twenty-one secretaries, five librarians, four dorm hostesses, four dietitians, two hospital workers, two employees in the journalism department, one pianist, and the director of extension were alumnae.

[2]Specializing in the Texas pioneer, she attempted to perpetuate the language and character of the old cowboy. J. Frank Dobie, who reviewed her book *Oldtimers* in the Dallas *News* called it "the most faithful report I have ever read." Her election to the Legislature came exactly twenty years after Edith Eunice Therrel Wilmans of Dallas was the first woman elected to the Texas House of Representatives.

[3]Among the situations that disturbed Dean Wooten was Governor Coke Stevenson's contention that women should not serve on juries because courthouses were not equipped to care for women overnight.

[4]In 1896, she had become the first woman graduate of Howard Payne College, which conferred the honorary Doctor of Literature degree on her in 1941. Teaching in Dallas, she had read in the newspaper of the founding of the Girls Industrial College, but she did not apply for a job until President Work visited her class searching for a history teacher. Arriving for the first class at the College, she remained active on the campus (except for two years on

leaves-of-absence) until her death. She served as head of a department in the social sciences from the time of her initial appointment. She had retired as Director of the Department of Sociology and Associate Dean of the College (the Regents named her Associate Dean emerita), but she continued her appointment as professor of sociology to the time of her death.

[5]The feminine contingent of the Texas Defense Guard was later renamed the TSCW Defense Corps and then the TSCW Victory Corps.

[6]Secretary of War Stimson authorized Oveta Culp Hobby to organize the Women's Army Auxiliary Corps (WAC) in May, 1942. On March 5, 1943, the first WACs to come to the TSCW campus for training arrived. Housed in Capps and Lowry Halls, the women attended classes in rooms not being used by the College. Other military services also established feminine branches—the Women Marines, the naval WAVEs, and the Coast Guard SPARs.

[7]F. L. McDonald, Director of the Department of Journalism, enlisted very early in the war. He returned to Denton in the spring of 1944 as a lieutenant colonel on leave with a Purple Heart for wounds received aboard an army transport which was strafed by low-flying Japanese planes in New Guinea. Ms. Boone, who graduated from TSCW in 1931 and received her M.A. degree from TSCW in 1937, was the only woman in the United States at the time who held a permanent certificate as an instructor in rifle shooting from the National Rifle Association.

[8]Carlotta Corpron, assistant professor of art, designed the flag, which was constructed by C. E. Burke in the drapery department of H. M. Russell and Sons Co. of Denton. The flag (54" x 95") consisted of a red border and a white background with a large blue star within which snap-on numerals represented the latest number of students and ex-students enlisted. The numbers represented enlistments in the WACs, WAVEs, SPARs, Marines, and members of the Nurse and Dietetics Corps.

After the war, on November 11, 1947, Oveta Culp Hobby dedicated a permanent bronze memorial tablet to the students at an assembly of the entire student body in the Main Auditorium. Measuring 36 by 54 inches with raised figures of the American Eagle on crossed branches and the official U.S. shield enclosed in the dates 1941-1945, the tablet bore the inscription, "Dedicated to the graduates and former students who as members of the armed forces and in other services contributed to our victory in World War II by their grateful Alma Mater the Texas State College for Women." The tablet has been installed on the west wall of the entry to the Old Main Building.

[9]Home economics majors formed the greatest number of teachers followed, in order, by education, library science, English, music, fine arts, physical education, speech, business administration, foreign languages, history, mathematics, science, journalism, sociology, and government.

[10]Catherine Cloud Edwards (class of 1932) joined Humble Oil Company in October, 1942, as the first woman draftsman in the company's civil engineering department, contributing to the production of gasoline for the war and paving the way for a number of alumnae to join the firm.

The Daedalian *of 1943 captured the sense of readiness that permeated the campus.*

WACs disembarked early in the day at the Denton Depot to prepare for their parade through Denton to TSCW.

[11]The Regents established the nursing program in response to requests for additional academic training for nurses. The five-year program called for a year of prescribed courses on campus, three years of training in a recognized nursing school (after which the student could qualify as a Registered Nurse), and a final year at TSCW for prescribed courses which emphasized sociology, science, or a combination of the two.

[12]The Music Department experienced a golden age during the forties. The college bulletin of February 1, 1945, reported that students and faculty musicians were performing an average of five shows a week during the previous semester. Performances ranged from camp and hospital shows to a performance in the Dallas Museum of Fine Arts. Performers varied from soloists to small ensembles to a one-hundred-member choral club, a select choir of thirty-six voices, an eighty-piece band, and an eighty-piece orchestra with full symphonic instrumentation. The orchestra was the official orchestra of the Texas Federation of Women's Clubs. Musicians and musical groups responded to requests to perform in concert throughout the state; and some, particularly the orchestra, broadcast regularly over the radio. In 1943 a highlight of the annual Music Festival on campus was the presentation of the College Symphony Orchestra in the first public performance of Carl Wiesemann's "Panoramic Rhapsody for Piano and Orchestra," which was dedicated to Hubbard and the TSCW faculty and student body.

[13]Enrollment figures come from a report in the College Bulletin of November 1, 1945.

[14]Enrollment in the department had declined about ten percent in each of the first two years of the war, but by 1945 the enrollment of 115 was slightly higher than the 109 majors of the department in 1940.

[15]Among other accomplishments of the department during the war was the establishment of the "Realia Room," a museum-library, in 1943; and the college bulletin of May 1, 1943, reported Spanish shorthand as the newest subject taught at TSCW.

[16]A radio broadcasting studio had been constructed in the northeast corner of the Main Auditorium in 1935. Beginning in November, the station broadcast a thirty-minute program on the Texas Centennial each week for twenty-six weeks through a wire extension hookup with radio station WFAA in Dallas. Direct broadcasts from the stage of the auditorium were possible. By 1949 the college bulletin of December 1 could boast, "From the four studios of the campus radio station it is possible to channel programs to WCST, the campus station, to KDNT, the local AM-FM station, or by wire to any of the commercial stations in Dallas or Fort Worth."

[17]Upon completion of the Little Chapel, alumnae had turned their attention to raising funds for a Student Union Building (see Chapter VII). The Ex-Students Association (at the suggestion of Marion Rowland Roberts, union building fund chairman) adopted a theme of "Buy a Brick for the Union Building" and received contributions toward the construction of the facility. The association also accepted donations for the purchase of furniture to be used in the new building and then transferred to the SUB when it was completed.

[18]The College had first requested $25,000 for the building of the pool in 1935. The pool is still in use.

[19]The college bulletin of May 1, 1942, reported that Hubbard had been notified by Senators Tom Connally and W. Lee O'Daniel that $99,743 had been approved for WPA Project No. 15217, a new Home Economics Building. Beginning of work was dependent on the approval of the state WPA director and the availability of materials.

[20]One small but significant addition to the campus was a small (20' x 30') photography studio, under construction by early 1942. Built with materials salvaged from the old studio and speech shack, the new studio offered four dark rooms, a print finishing room, a projection room, and a storage room. Mary Esther Wallace, instructor in physics, noted that the building made it possible for TSCW to offer photographic training at a time when there was no photography school in the South.

[21]The Economics and Business Department had grown to the largest in the College by this time.

[22]Special holdings included approximately two thousand volumes in the Woman's Collection, which was begun in 1930, and a thousand books plus a number of valuable out-of-print books not kept on open shelves which comprised the Texas Collection begun in 1928. In addition, membership in the North Texas Regional Libraries, organized April 16, 1943, and comprised of TSCW, NTSTC, SMU, TCU, Southwestern Baptist Theological Seminary, and the public libraries of Dallas and Fort Worth, made approximately 810,000 volumes, including 79,000 bound government documents, available to students. A cooperative plan with NTSTC approximately doubled the number of books available to students of each college in Denton alone, and the two libraries offered a combined periodical list of almost 1400 publications.

[23]Smith-Carroll, the first dormitory for the College, had become the center of the co-operative housing system (see Chapters II and VII).

[24]Some six hundred students belonged to WRA at the time of the action.

[25]Students who successfully completed Branche Williams' stringent course of formal riding instruction in the TSCW riding stable and passed a thorough examination received their choice of a pair of spurs from Miss Williams.

[26]The Gymnasium Annex served this function until the completion of a new Student Center in 1969.

[27]In the spring before Pearl Harbor, the College had four canoes, and the Denton Sailing Club provided five snipe class boats and one sea gull type boat for students to use at the lake. By January, 1949, the College was again able to tout the joys of steaks, boat rides, sailing, and singing around a campfire for girls who spent the weekend at one of the three rustic cabins on the twenty-acre campsite on the east shore of Lake Dallas.

[28]At its 1946 homecoming, the first in four years, the Ex-Students Association elected Vada Frances Hale president. For the next four years, her energetic leadership provided the impetus for significant growth. The executive board employed a part-time secretary for the association on February 1, 1947; and two years later, Mrs. Hale reported that the expansion program of the association had resulted in sufficient growth to enable the organization to employ a full-time secretary. Gwen Beene was the part-time secretary. Zou Aikin was the first executive secretary.

The association instituted a "class agent" plan to gather news of former students and bring them closer together with the November 1, 1947, issue of the college bulletin. By the following spring, Regents had approved a request that Bowie Hall on the corner of Bell

Vada Frances Hale (right) presides at a meeting of the Board of the Ex-Students Association in 1947.

Avenue and College Street be designated as headquarters for the association. Shaded by oak trees, the two-story white colonial building had been purchased by the College in 1935 to house students in the cooperative system. The college bulletin of May 1, 1948, proudly announced, "For the first time in their history, TSCW Ex-Students will have their own center at the College."

All of these changes pointed to the developing sense of unity, loyalty, and true organization among the alumnae of the College that was evident as the TSCW prepared to celebrate its fiftieth anniversary. At the 1949 homecoming business meeting, Mrs. Hale announced the appointment of Lura Mae Burton Kendrick as chairman of the Fiftieth Anniversary Committee.

[29]The system, initiated for economy during the Depression, continued to offer a decreasing number of students substantial savings on room and board into the 1950s.

[30]Completing the list of the top ten women's colleges were Florida State College for Women (2194), Woman's College of North Carolina (2117), Smith (2081), Wellesley (1606), Vassar (1481), Winthrop (1399), Mary Washington (1365), Simmons (1283), and Mount Holyoke (1113). The University of Texas had 6432 students; and, with many of its students away in the war, Texas A&M had fallen to third place in the state with 2152 students.

[31]The enrollment of 2847 in 1938-39 and 2855 in 1939-40 surpassed the 1944-45 long-session enrollment, but smaller summer registrations pushed the yearly totals to only 3950 and 3990, respectively.

[32]The state's 31 junior colleges had a total enrollment of 30,860 at this time.

[33]Typical of the kinds of changes were the revisions regarding smoking which were reported in the college bulletin of May 1, 1948: "Students may smoke on the campus in dormitory bedrooms, Recreation Room of the Union Building, Little Cabin-in-the-Woods, Golf Club House after class hours, and drama rehearsals at night. On College-sponsored trips, smoking off the campus will be left to the discretion of the sponsor. Otherwise smoking off the campus will be left to the discretion of the student." A poll conducted at the time showed almost three-fourths of the students in favor of changes in the policies related to smoking.

Students performed roles as varied as Sir Toby Belch in Shakespeare's Twelfth Night *and the Madonna in the campus nativity play.*

Operating Confidently IX
and Aggressively

To follow the man who had served as President of the College longer than all his predecessors combined, the Board of Regents selected forty-four-year-old John A. Guinn, the first President to be younger than the College. Guinn would, in his turn, serve even longer than had Hubbard.[1]

The new President's career had been full of challenges, and his latest position would be no different. The declining enrollment during the last years of Hubbard's administration made the College vulnerable to attack, and Guinn immediately directed his attention and energy to attracting students. Adopting strategies very much like those of President Work, who had had the responsibility for making the public aware of a brand new College and its purpose and for bringing the first students to the College, Guinn embarked on a vigorous personal speaking campaign. Unlike Work, Guinn could also enlist the aid of students, faculty, and alumnae to help spread the word about what TSCW had to offer.

Even before he officially began his duties, the new President had put people to work in Denton. Catherine Cloud Edwards, President of the Ex-Students Association, reported in the college bulletin of August 15, 1950, "In cooperation with Dr. John Guinn, we wrote and sent to our entire mailing list a promotional letter for the College. This 'Talk TSCW' letter has received a great deal of favorable comment, and to date the registrar's office has filled 246 requests for information on the College as a direct result of the letter." By the following spring TSCW had instituted a year-round booster program, sponsored by the Student Council, through which students would work with alumnae in their hometowns to spread the word about TSCW to high school girls.

The College also expanded its long-standing program of publications which described career opportunities for women and explained how TSCW could help young women prepare for these careers. Frank C. Rigler of the Department of Journalism prepared a colorful bulletin which described in words and pictures the social, recreational, and intellectual advantages of TSCW. It was ready for distribution September 1, 1950. Although the College had used similar brochures before, the publications had never matched the current offerings in number or variety.

Guinn's early days in office took him across the state to speak at all kinds of gatherings, from ex-students' meetings to groups of teachers, business men and women, and students—some thirty speeches during the 1950-51 academic year alone. Wherever he spoke, his message revealed his

New President John A. Guinn (left) visits with his predecessor, L.H. Hubbard. Like Hubbard, Guinn became President when he was forty-four and served a quarter of a century.

A full-page illustration from the 1934 Daedalian *demonstrates students' responses to an earlier attempt to change the College.*

unqualified belief in the future success of TSCW. Among his often-repeated remarks was the statement which he shared with the ex-students in the college bulletin of November 15, 1950: "The College will operate confidently and aggressively in the knowledge that [the] harmonious duality of its total mission in higher education, the unique character of its historical objectives, and the unequalled overall effectiveness of its methods and organization are more than ever indispensable to the higher educational health of Texas."

In spite of his confident statements, however, and in spite of the "air of newness and expectancy" which Alumnae President Edwards described in the college bulletin of November 15, 1950, TSCW would face many serious difficulties in the next few years. The first threat surfaced quickly when the Legislature convened in January, 1951. Based on enrollment losses and predictions of continued declines, the Legislature prepared to reduce the TSCW budget by $1 million during the next biennium.[2]

To combat the threat, Guinn enlisted the aid of alumnae. Charting the enrollment of the College since its founding, he identified an overall upward trend with occasional declines which are invariably followed by larger enrollment gains than those experienced before the losses. Showing no surprise or alarm at the current decline, Guinn confidently predicted that the trend would turn upward in the fall and show a steady increase during the next few years. His predictions proved accurate; and he proudly announced enrollment increases each year during the rest of his administration even at times when state and national enrollment trends were downward.

On February 10, 1951, the Board of Directors of the Ex-Students Association pledged full support of the college administration and agreed to oppose strongly any cut in appropriations for the College. In the college bulletin of March 1, 1951, ex-students were urged to "Raise your voices for TSCW," in a story headlined, "All Exes Called to Aid of College in Crisis." In the story, Mrs. Edwards explained the problem: "It seems that some state officials and members of the Legislature do not realize the importance of TSCW to the women of Texas and would, in their efforts to economize, approve an unreasonable cut of more than a million dollars in the college appropriations for the next biennium." She called on all ex-students to "let them know that there is a definite place in Texas for a woman's college" and to let them know that it deserved funds to assure "that the purpose for which it was established will be held inviolate." By February 27, Representative Henry Rampy, Chairman of the House Appropriations Committee, reported, "I have had any number of letters from people saying they understood the Legislature was out to ruin Texas State College for Women."

State Representative Doug Crouch of Denton came to the support of both TSCW and NTSC on March 18, labelling the appropriations cuts "false economy" which would result in the loss of one-half the faculty at TSCW and one-third of the faculty at NTSC; and an editorial in the Denton *Record-Chronicle* of the same date attacked the "short-sighted and false economy ax wielding" that, it warned, could set Texas education back ten years.

On March 23, the *Record-Chronicle* warned again that federal bureaucrats would "do the job" if Texas Legislators failed to provide adequate support for higher education. The final appropriation established by the House-Senate Conference Committee totaled $1,302,450 for TSCW, a drastic reduction from appropriations for the previous biennium even though it was a significant increase over original proposals.[3]

Although Crouch labeled the appropriation insufficient, Mrs. Edwards reported in the college bulletin of August 1, 1951, that "an adequate appropriation has been made, and the College will continue to offer all courses now in the catalogue without any lowering of standards or advantages.''

In spite of financial difficulties, Guinn announced in the college bulletin of October 15, 1951, ''The opening of the 49th annual session at Texas State College for Women has been characterized by manifestations of very strong institutional morale.'' Enrollment was up; and the President reported, ''TSCW has recently crossed the threshold of an era of significant new developments that will maintain the College in its traditional role as an educational pioneer.'' Among the developments he identified were the large conventions which would be coming to the campus during the year,[4] the dedication of the new College of Household Arts and Sciences, and the establishment of the TSCW Foundation, which would provide a coordinated program to secure scholarships, gifts, grants, and other benefits for the College.

Conditions were improving when the College began its Golden Anniversary celebration in the fall of 1952. As the college bulletin of March 15, 1953, observed, the College now combined ''the wisdom of maturity with the vigor of youth.'' For its fifty years of existence it could claim fifty thousand ex-students of ''unswerving loyalty'' and more than fifty ''firsts'' in its role as a pioneer in higher education in Texas.

January, 1953, brought a new legislative session; and Guinn appeared before the House and Senate subcommittees on higher education on February 10 and 11 to testify with regard to TSCW's budgetary needs for the 1954-55 biennium. According to the college bulletin of May 1, 1953, both committees congratulated the President and the College on its recent progress; and Guinn reported an increase in TSCW enrollment at a time when many other schools were losing students. ''The fact is,'' Guinn announced to the TSCW Ex-Students Board of Directors on March 7 in Denton, ''that TSCW is the only institution in the state of Texas, public or

Beulah Kincaid Fry, first graduate and first President of the Ex-Students Association, visited the campus from her nearby home to participate in Golden Anniversary activities.

private, which has had a substantial increase in enrollment of girl students the last two years."

Nevertheless, a bill introduced January 24 by State Representative Bert Hall of Rio Vista threatened the very existence of the College. Hall apparently hoped that the institution created by the combination of North Texas State College and the Texas State College for Women and named North Texas University could become the Texas state university which would share the permanent fund with the University of Texas and Texas A&M. Protests began to flow to the offices of the TSCW Ex-Students Association and the TSCW President; and the college bulletin of March 1, 1953, condemned the bill and urged alumnae once more to rally in support of their alma mater.

In a widely-circulated statement, Guinn declared that Hall's proposal reflected "an utter lack of understanding of the program, character, atmosphere, objectives, services, and achievements of the Texas State College for Women" and predicted that "the good judgment of the other members of the Legislature will prevail to the end that the proposal will be unceremoniously buried."

Hall had apparently taken his inspiration for the bill from Governor Allan Shivers' call for the coordination of higher education in the state.[5] Although Guinn repeatedly emphasized the "enthusiastic willingness" of TSCW to work with the Governor and other leaders in cooperative efforts, he charged Hall with distorting the Governor's intent and misleading the people about what his bill would do.

Guinn contended that the Governor's message did not suggest mergers, "especially a merger that would destroy the only woman's college that serves a state of 8,000,000 people." According to Guinn, Shivers "had in mind the elimination of competition and duplication of facilities at colleges racing to grow larger and larger, each at the expense of others"; and Guinn claimed, "Representative Hall's thoughtless and spontaneous action, in fact, probably has been embarrassing to the Governor," before reaffirming TSCW's energetic support of the Governor's program.

Marshaling all the arguments in favor of TSCW, Guinn pointed to its high academic standards and reputation, its length of service, and most importantly its uniqueness: "The Texas State College for Women is unlike any other college in the state. Our institution, which is this year celebrating its golden anniversary, has a unique mission and a unique program. The quality of its work is unexcelled, many of its curricular offerings are exclusive, and its pattern of organization defies duplication. By the very nature of things TSCW simply cannot merge with any other institution."

Noting that expectations of increased efficiency or economy through mergers were ill-founded, Guinn pointed out that the official audit figures for 1951-52 showed that the overall per capita cost for full-time student equivalents at TSCW was below the same costs at the state's three largest educational institutions and at a number of others as well. Attacking the bill as "a shocking example of immature thinking and irresponsible action," Guinn continued, "Fortunately, the majority of our state legislators are more farsighted and better informed on the broad aspects of economy and the necessity of building, not tearing down, the state's higher educational system."

Then, Guinn turned his attention to the author of the bill: "Occasionally, an individual like this young man goes off on a tangent because of an emotional lack of understanding of the mission of women's colleges. He did not consult members of the staff of TSCW or anyone else who might enlighten him on some of the aspects of educational standards and the need for a woman's college in Texas. As an uninformed student still in school, his immature thinking is understandable."[6]

Accusing Representative Hall of allowing his "selfish interests" to "blind him to the purpose of a woman's college," Guinn insisted that "the girls who come to TSCW do so because they WANT to attend a woman's college. If not, they could and would enroll at coeducational institutions near their homes throughout the Southwest"; and he predicted that if TSCW were to be eliminated, the girls would be "driven" to other states that had women's colleges.[7]

Another argument against the merger was Guinn's reply to the reasoning that two colleges in one town might operate as one: "[Hall] fails to point out that the two campuses are two miles apart—at the opposite edges of the City of Denton." Ironically, TSCW had frequently capitalized on the idea that the proximity of the other college offered easy access to added library resources and social opportunities. Guinn's conclusion to his argument, however, that the two institutions were "completely unlike in nature and purpose" was telling.

Condemning Hall's bill as an "ill-conceived and ill-considered measure" of the kind typical of people who "have no respect for tradition and success" and who "distort information to achieve selfish ends," Guinn predicted that the only effect of Hall's bill if it should pass would be to "abolish TSCW and obliterate all the important and necessary services TSCW has rendered and is continuing to render to the State of Texas."

But, he promised the students, alumnae, and friends of TSCW, "The Texas State College for Women does not expect to yield its identity as a woman's college, second to none in the nation"; and he urged them to "heed the call when it comes to let the Legislature know how they feel about the need for a woman's college in Texas."

In an editorial of January 27, 1953, the Denton *Record-Chronicle* endorsed the need for a separate women's college: "We think the measure [merger] would serve no good purpose, and hope that the Legislature refuses to pass it, as it has refused to pass similar bills in the past." To support its position, the paper noted, "In the East, where educational standards are higher, as a rule, than in the Southwest, the values of women's colleges are never disputed."[8]

A newspaper poll of TSCW and NTSC students, reported in the *Record-Chronicle* of February 5, showed eighty-three percent of them opposed to the merger; and the paper of February 20 reported that even though state auditors would come to Denton to survey the facilities of the two colleges, Legislators seemed "cool" to the merger.

The merger proposal, called by Guinn "Mr. Hall's 1953 version of an old story," failed as had previous proposals; but the issue did not die. Merger rumors resurfaced in the spring of 1954. In response to reports in several state newspapers late in May, Governor Shivers released to the press an open letter to President Guinn with copies to the TSCW Regents. Emphasizing his unqualified support of a strong and independent TSCW, the Governor praised "the glorious history and record of achievement of the College" and recognized the "key position in the State's higher education system" which TSCW occupied and the "distinctive and useful service to the State" which the College rendered. The letter concluded unequivocally, "I have never favored the merging or closing of TSCW— and it is not my intention to do so now, nor in the future. To the contrary, I stand ready to help build a bigger and better TSCW."

In spite of the rumors and threats, which one would expect to drain some of the institution's vitality, TSCW developed new vigor in the first years of the fifties. To aid in the development of the College, Guinn held as one of his highest goals the establishment of a foundation which would insure funds for college enrichment.

As Mrs. Code E. Edwards reported in the college bulletin of March 1, 1952, "Just when TSCW needs more support than ever, world conditions

Members of the TSCW Foundation first met May 13, 1952: (back row) Harold Volk, Francis W. Emerson; (center) Grover C. Bullington, John A. Guinn, Nelda C. Stark; (front) Catherine Cloud Edwards, Mary Beard.

and public sentiment are adverse to using public funds for anything more than basic education. . . .Thus a new concept of responsibility for the continuation of the things that make TSCW great is developing. Individuals and groups, recognizing the urgent need of the type of education offered young women at TSCW, are realizing that they have a responsibility in enabling TSCW to grow. . . .''

To provide a means through which individuals and groups could contribute to the College, Guinn announced in the same bulletin that work was near completion on the organization of the TSCW Foundation, "an incorporated body which will promote the development of TSCW by providing a financial method of educational expansion of the College." At the meeting of the Executive Board of the Ex-Students Association on March 29, Guinn announced that Texas Secretary of State John Ben Shepperd had approved the charter for the foundation.

Among the goals of the foundation reported in the college bulletin of May 1, 1952, were "the establishment of scholarships and fellowships, funds for research, projects, endowments for chairs and lectureships, additions such as rare book collections in the library, and funds for publicity, public relations and promotional activities." Membership of the Foundation Board would consist of the Presidents of TSCW, the TSCW Board of Regents, the TSCW Ex-Students Association, and the TSCW College Government Association (CGA). In addition, the board would include a faculty representative and four lay members, two of whom would be alumnae.[9]

President Guinn called the organizational meeting for the foundation in early May to adopt policies, select objectives, and initiate programs of immediate action. In his letter to the ex-students in the May 1, 1952, college bulletin, he reported the principal purpose of the foundation, recorded in its charter: "to encourage a program of benefactions to the Texas State College for Women, and to provide an agency authorized to receive and administer donations of money or other gifts designed to increase the renown, extend the services, improve the facilities, or promote in any way the welfare of the Texas State College for Women."

In May, the foundation received its initial contribution, $2,500 from the Ex-Students Association, an amount that was matched by Mr. and Mrs. H. Lutcher Stark of Orange. Following the first Gold Rush Carnival in November, 1952, the CGA added $2,500; but other contributions were slow to arrive.[10]

Regular support for the foundation from the annual CGA-sponsored Gold Rush[11] and from alumnae continued through the spring of 1956 when the foundation began a $250,000 five-year fund drive. The drive focused on six major goals: funding of additional scholarships and graduate fellowships;[12] augmentation of religious life through special lectureships, forums, publications, and other activities; construction of a Margo Jones Dramatic Arts Building;[13] purchase of out-of-print books and periodicals for the Library; funding for basic research; and support for promotional activities directed primarily toward recruiting students. By May 1, faculty pledges totaled $17,231; and by July 1 students had pledged or contributed $3,645.

In addition to attempting to build enrollment and strengthen the financial position of the College, faculty and administrators also focused their attention on the curriculum. Hubbard had developed a strong faculty including almost fifty members who held doctorates; and the curriculum during his administration had grown to encompass a solid program of graduate studies at the master's level. In the fall of 1950, TSCW offered sixty-three different groups of courses which led to the B.A. and B.S. degrees and thirteen majors which led to master's degrees.

With its fiftieth anniversary just in sight, many of the fifty "firsts" which the College boasted were in its curriculum. As the college bulletin of September 1, 1950, reminded readers, the College was the first in Texas to offer college credits and degrees in advertising, art education, commercial courses, costume designing, designing, drawing, health and physical education, interior decorating, kindergarten-primary education, occupational therapy, painting, and public school music. It was also the first to give degrees in library science, music and applied music, nursery education, and speech.

Unique in the Southwest, the occupational therapy program provided students experience with patients in Dallas medical centers like Parkland Memorial Hospital.

Of immediate importance to the future growth of the College was its ability to build on two very important "firsts." TSCW was the first college in the state to give degrees in home economics (including such degree programs as home demonstration for county agents, institutional management, and dietetics); and it was the first woman's college in the nation to offer graduate work leading to master's degrees.

As a leader and innovator in the study and teaching of home economics since its earliest days and as a mature institution with a solid program of graduate studies, TSCW was ready to take another major step; and the new President was ready to lead it toward national prominence as a center for home economics research. TSCW had taken some tentative steps in this direction following legislative approval of the Moffett Bill which created the Texas Cotton Research Committee in June, 1941;[14] but it was not until some eight years later (January 1, 1949) that a college bulletin announced the addition of new equipment in the Department of Home Economics for research in textiles, foods, and nutrition; and it was not until 1951 that the College brought together the people, incentives, and support to establish a large scale research program.

When the Department of Home Economics moved from its old building to a new four-story building on Bell Avenue in 1951, it assumed new leadership, a new name, new responsibilities, and new stature. The department became the College of Household Arts and Sciences (CHAS) with Pauline Berry Mack as its dean and director of research.[15] Guinn's announcement of the new college-within-a-college reminded readers of the college bulletin of October 15, 1951, that "TSCW has been a leader in the teaching of household arts since the beginning."

Among the work of the new college were research projects in nutrition, textiles, and household science conducted by a staff of trained research engineers. Dr. Mack supervised the work; and graduate and undergraduate students assisted in the projects, supported by grants from commercial and industrial organizations. As director of several research projects. Dr. Mack brought with her to TSCW several assistants from Pennsylvania State College and thousands of dollars in grants.[16]

At the formal inauguration of the College of Household Arts and Sciences on March 27, 1952, Guinn spoke of the "splendid beginning" which had been made on "possibly the most dramatic of our recent pioneering ventures . . . namely the first major program of research to be undertaken by a woman's college." Already, he reported, "an advance guard of seven full-time research scientists is . . . at work. In coming months the number of such workers will double, then double again."[17]

Household Arts and Sciences Dean Pauline Beery Mack and President Guinn examine the results of a three-year exhaustive study of nutrition among teenagers.

A student participant in nutrition research undergoes a basal metabolism test.

Both the new building and the old Home Economics Building provided extensive space for the scientists. The ground floor of the new HAS Building provided laboratory space and equipment to test household equipment. The second floor included facilities for testing foods. And the third floor housed textiles research space. The top floor also contained an animal laboratory.

The college bulletin of August 1, 1952, described the conversion of the old Home Economics Building into facilities for the TSCW Research Center which included "laboratories for human nutrition studies and for nutrition studies using experimental animals; modern laboratories for experimental cookery and food analyses; textile and clothing laboratories for advanced study, including a modern constant temperature and constant humidity research laboratory; laboratories for study of household materials and equipment; a nursery school; and facilities for measuring the effectiveness of teaching techniques and procedures."

The building also included an air-conditioned reading room for graduate students, and it became the home of the Nelda Childers Stark Laboratory for Human Nutrition Research. Beginning in 1953, TSCW alumna Nelda Childers Stark and her husband, H. Lutcher Stark, contributed generously to make the laboratory not only the sole research center of its kind in the Southwest but also one of the best equipped centers in the nation.[18]

With new facilities, new faculty, and new programs of research, the new college-within-a-college was prepared to expand its curriculum; and it became the first component of TSCW to offer doctoral degrees. To accommodate the expanded scope of graduate studies, the Graduate Division, which had supervised graduate work, became the Graduate School in 1952 with its own Graduate Council and dean to set and administer policies related to graduate study.

The college bulletin of August 1, 1952, announced the first TSCW majors to lead to doctoral degrees. Students could study foods and nutrition, textiles and clothing, clothing and costume design, and home economics education to earn the Ph.D. degree; or they might earn the Ed.D. degree with a major in home economics education or the Master of Home Economics Education degree.

In June, 1953, the year of the Golden Anniversary, the College of Household Arts and Sciences and the Texas State College for Women came of age with the awarding of the first Ph.D. degrees. Alice Knapper Milsom, who majored in dietetics and nutrition, and Mae Yoder Moore, who majored in textile technology, were not only the first women to earn the Ph.D. degree at TSCW but also the first women to receive the degree in household arts and sciences from a Southern college.[19]

The College of Household Arts and Sciences paved the way for other colleges-within-the-college, and the TSCW bulletin of June 15, 1954, announced a new academic organization which included six colleges: Arts and Sciences; Education; Fine Arts; Health, Physical Education, and Recreation (HPER); Household Arts and Sciences (HAS); and Nursing. The Graduate School would administer the graduate sequences in each college.[20]

Each of the colleges except the College of Nursing represented programs of study which had been major parts of the curriculum for many years. The College of Nursing, however, was a new venture which represented the determination of the new President and the life-long commitment of TSCW to prepare students to meet current needs.

In April, 1952, Guinn had announced a $60,000 grant from the Samuel H. Kress Foundation to establish a practical nursing program to be in operation by the fall. The pilot program, one of only five in the nation, was designed to help alleviate a growing shortage of registered nurses by training practical nurses. The Foundation provided $10,000 for the initial equipment and the installation of a nursing practice lab, nursing demonstration and lecture room, offices for a director and instructors, and reference material. The grant provided an additional $10,000 each year for five years to cover instructors' salaries and a recruitment program.

The college bulletin of November 1, 1953, reported students from seventeen to fifty years of age enrolled in the one-year course. Participants studied child care, personal and community health, nursing care, and personal and vocational rehabilitation for seventeen weeks on campus and then practiced for thirty-two weeks in hospitals under the guidance of registered nurses.

Mae Yoder Moore (left) and Alice Knapper Milsom (right) received the first doctoral degrees awarded by TSCW.

The practical nursing program complemented the five-year degree program in nursing instituted at TSCW in 1940,[21] but a newer and better alternative to both programs was to develop soon. The college bulletin of December 1, 1953, announced a TSCW School of Nursing "pointed toward the development of a superior professional nurse." In keeping with the dual purpose of TSCW from its beginning, the nursing school was designed to offer students both the best of a liberal arts education and the best of practical professional training. By the time it admitted its first students in the fall of 1954, the *school* had been elevated to the rank of a *college,* one of the six colleges which represented a new and more complex academic organization for TSCW.

Approved by the TSCW Board of Regents, the Board of Managers of Parkland Hospital, the State Board of Nurse Examiners, and the Dallas

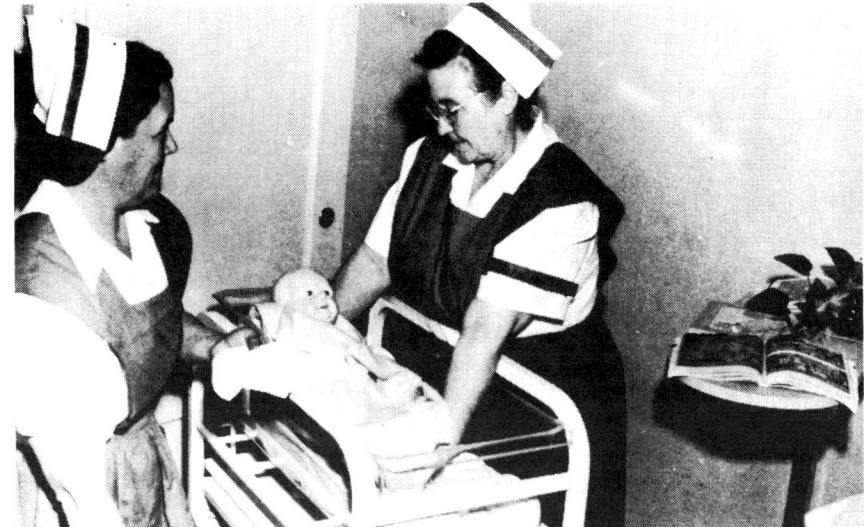

The Kress Foundation provided hospital units as laboratories for practical nursing students. Students pursuing degrees and licensure as registered nurses received clinical training at Parkland Hospital in Dallas.

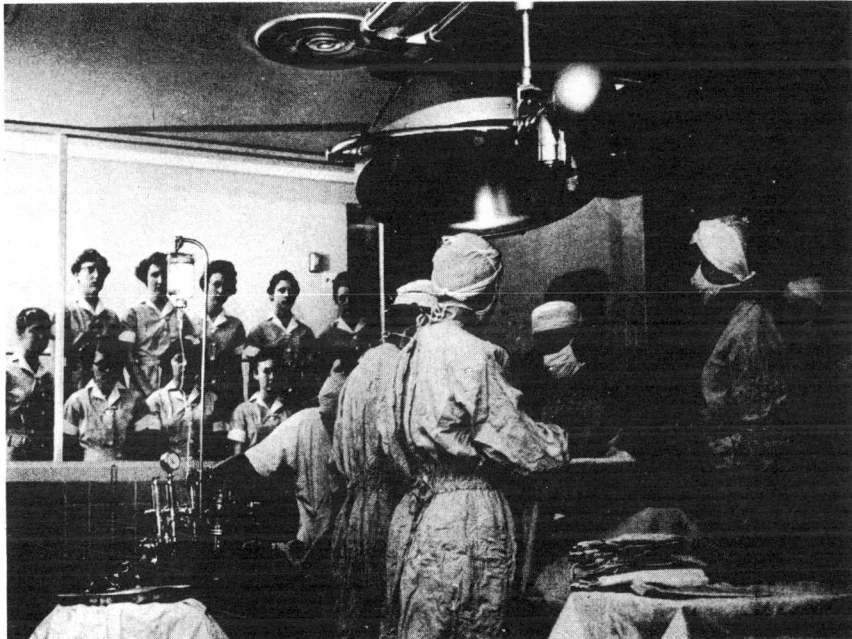

County Medical Society, the new program combined the facilities of TSCW in Denton with those of the new $11 million, 663-bed Parkland Memorial Hospital in Dallas beginning in September, 1954.

Freshman students lived in the TSCW dormitory system and attended classes in Denton during a full academic year and summer session before moving to Dallas for approximately two and one-half years of professional study. In Dallas, students lived in the new million-dollar staff residence immediately adjacent to the hospital, but they were encouraged to return to Denton, only thirty-five miles away, to participate in campus activities. The college bulletin of December 15, 1953, which promoted the new program, emphasized, "Students have no more than a 44-hour week— including classes and clinical practice."

Students returned to the campus in Denton for the final semester during their senior year and received the B.S. degree with their class at the regular June commencement. Thus, by enrolling each summer, students could meet all requirements for a degree in less than four calendar years and be prepared to take the State Board examination for licensure as a registered nurse. In addition to compressing the studies into four years, the new program insured the availability of adequate hospital facilities for training and offered economic advantages since the Parkland Hospital paid for room, meals, uniforms, and laundry during the two and one-half years of professional study, leaving the student to pay only college tuition and fees and then regular expenses during her time in Denton.

The merger of the two existing nursing programs to form a TSCW College of Nursing proved to be of great benefit to both institutions. Faye Pannell, director of the Parkland school, brought her expertise to the directorship of the TSCW college; and the Parkland school brought with it a record of continuous operation as a three-year diploma program since 1917, continuous accreditation by the State Board of Nurse Examiners, and accreditation by the National League for Nursing since 1950 when it became the first nationally accredited school in Texas.

On the other hand, TSCW, which had been charged in the founding legislation with providing nursing training, could complement the existing Parkland program by offering academic instruction which would lead to regular academic degrees and, eventually, to graduate degrees.[22] Thus, graduates would be prepared to assume positions of greater authority and responsibility in their profession than would nurses who held only a nursing diploma.

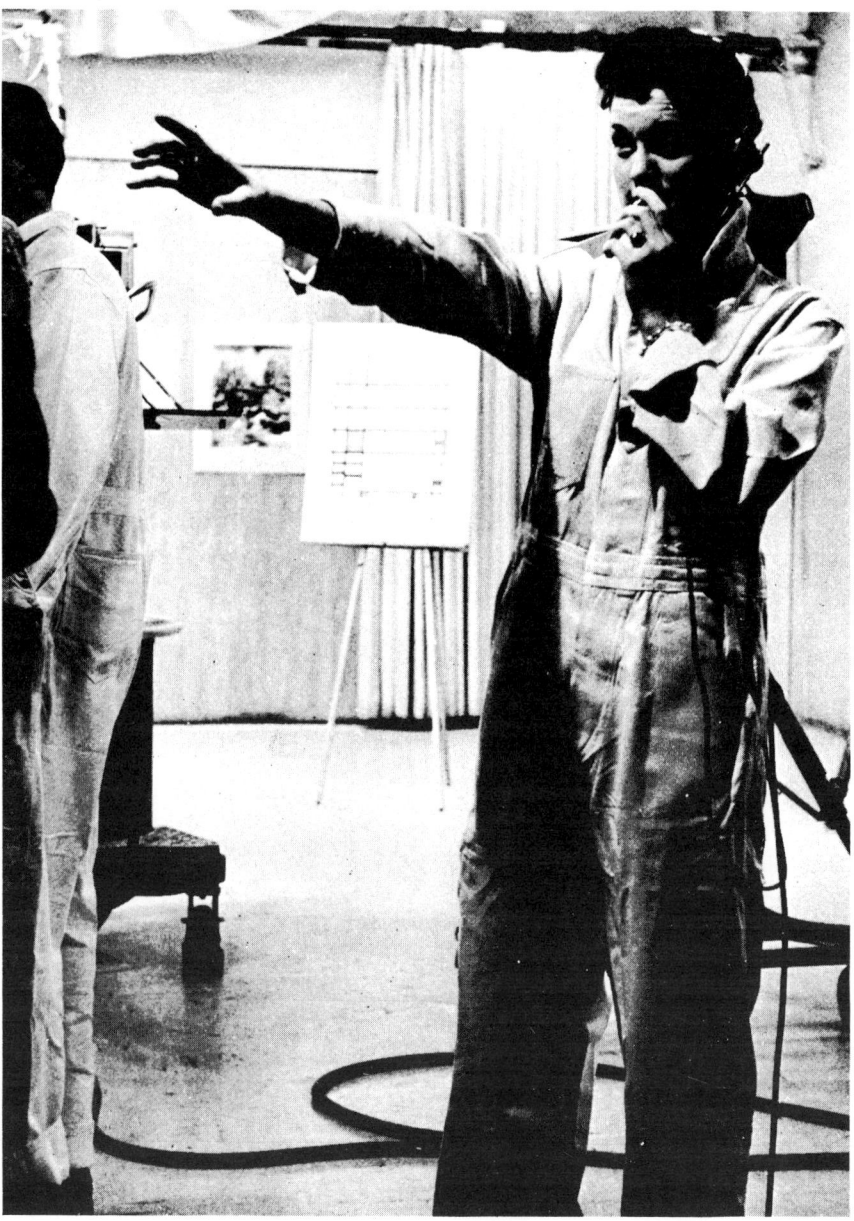

Students wrote, cast, directed, and produced weekly radio and television shows which were broadcast on KRLD in Dallas.

The original faculty for the new program consisted of thirteen members (only one fewer than the original faculty of the entire Girls Industrial College),[23] and registration for the first class was limited to eighty-five students (approximately half of the original enrollment of GIC). The success of the new nursing college was phenomenal. Enrollment climbed to 140 in the fall of 1955, in spite of an announced limit of 100, and reached 428 by the end of the decade when the college added a second clinical training center at the Texas Medical Center in Houston. The number of nursing majors to receive degrees grew from one in 1950 and eight in 1952 to sixty-five in 1960.

Although major triumphs such as the new College of Nursing and new doctoral studies and research programs received the greatest attention, TSCW was not without growth in other areas as well. Guinn headed a faculty committee which liberalized curricular requirements beginning in the fall, 1951. The revisions eliminated some required courses and provided greater freedom in choosing electives. The changes were designed to be especially helpful to junior college transfers who were more likely to be able to complete their studies in two additional years than they had been under the old curriculum.

Other curricular changes involved modernization at the departmental level. The college bulletin of October 1, 1951, announced, "TSCW now joins the progressive colleges entering the field of recreational music." Students in the program worked under medical direction with music therapists to plan and direct both recreational and rehabilitational musical work in a variety of settings. Building a program entirely around existing courses in the Department of Music, J. Wilgus Eberly, director of the department, was able to announce in the fall, 1953, the addition of a music therapy major.

Other therapies also were playing an important part in the training of TSCW students. In addition to working closely with handicapped children's centers in Fort Worth and Dallas, TSCW had maintained since 1948 its own Speech and Hearing Clinic to provide laboratory experience for students and both individual and group therapy to children and adults who needed remedial help. The clinic operated in Shadow Lawn (formerly a small dormitory).

Although the College would not have its own School of Physical Therapy until the middle of the next decade, graduates of TSCW's College of HPER were eligible to enter one-year training courses at accredited schools of physical therapy; and many TSCW graduates took their places in hospitals, clinics, camps for the handicapped, and military operations around the world.

In other areas, TSCW was advancing toward new horizons also. Beginning in the fall of 1953, students in the Department of Speech participated for the first time in television programs. Through arrangements with KRLD-TV and KRLD AM and FM radio of Dallas, students, under the direction of speech faculty member Josh P. Roach, wrote, produced, and participated in "Seminar," a series of fifteen-minute weekly television shows and thirty-minute radio shows about college life.

Another first of the period was a traveling literary workshop offered by the Department of English from 1955 to 1962. Under the direction of Eleanor James, the course was designed to increase students' appreciation of American literature by taking them to places which have figured prominently in American fiction and poetry. Described in the college bulletin of March 1, 1955, as "an extended field trip or laboratory course, combined with a week's residential work," the first month-long workshop traveled almost five thousand miles across the Old South and the Eastern United States. The cost of all required expenses, including tuition but excepting food, was $284.

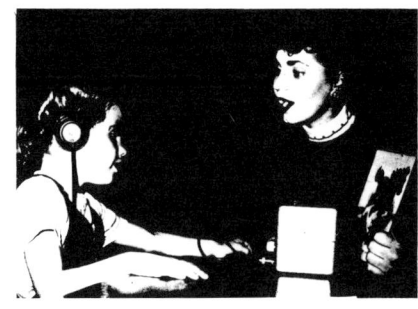

TSCW Speech Clinic therapists helped children correct hearing losses.

141

Recognition of the quality of educational programs at TSCW came in various ways. Seventeen-year-old Madelon Pulver came to TSCW from Saratoga Springs, New York, according to the college bulletin of November 1, 1952, because she read about TSCW in an article about golf and then discovered the College's high scholastic standing. Word had made its way to the west coast as well to attract Maryann Stephens, who traveled in a trailer for three days to reach Denton and lived in the trailer to work on her Master of Library Science degree.

In addition to these kinds of personal recognition, various components and programs were winning official recognition as well. In 1952 the Department of Speech was granted affiliation with the American Speech and Hearing Association, and in 1954 the degree program in social work received approval of and affiliation with the Council on Social Work Education. The American Chemical Society approved the TSCW chemistry program in the fall of 1955, and in the same year the College of Education became a member of the American Association of Colleges of Teacher Education.

Also in 1955 the new College of Nursing became an "agency member" of the Department of Baccalaureate and Higher Degree Programs of the National League for Nursing (NLN). The TSCW college attained full accreditation from the NLN Collegiate Board of Review in 1958 and initial accreditation in public health nursing in the fall, 1959. The School of Library Science, which had been continuously accredited by the American Library Association since 1938, was re-accredited, under the revised 1951 national standards, as a graduate school of library science in 1957.

Increasing national recognition of both academic and research programs, the maturing of important graduate sequences leading to master's and doctor's degrees, and the organization of TSCW into component colleges and schools made the *college* a *university* in fact even before Governor Price Daniel signed the bill on May 21, 1957, to change the name of the Texas State College for Women to the Texas Woman's University (TWU) on August 19.

Explaining that "the provisions of the law creating TSCW laid the foundations for its character as a multipurpose institution exclusively for women," Guinn affirmed in the college bulletin of August 1, 1957, that this "distinguished American university" would continue to train "homemakers and top women careerists" "in unique ways and in a unique setting."

During this time students were involved in what were probably the most demanding studies the institution had ever offered; for TSCW, like virtually all Americans of the period, was keenly aware of the scientific progress of Russia. At mid-winter commencement in January, 1956, Guinn reminded the graduates, "Scarcely a day passes without a publicized speech in which some prominent American points apprehensively at the strides Russia is making in university training for top-flight scientific personnel." But, he said, TSCW was ready to meet the challenge and was, in fact, "unexcelled anywhere" in preparing women "for all the greater responsibilities indicated for them in the future." It was the following November that Russian leader Nikita Khrushchev promised the American people, "We will bury you."

Threats such as Khrushchev's combined with memories of the destructive power of the atomic bomb to create an atmosphere of anxiety, a decade in which many people considered the construction of a backyard bomb shelter merely sensible homemaking. However, the decade which brought the Korean War, Joseph McCarthy's House Un-American Activities Committee, and Estes Kefauver's televised congressional investigations of organized crime also brought hula hoops, 3-D movies, crinoline petticoats, and ducktail and poodle-cut hairdos; and TSCW

students played as hard as they studied.

At the 1954 commencement exercises on May 31, President Guinn described life at TSCW as "a marvelously rich experience." The first class to enter and graduate during his administration had, he noted, had the opportunity to participate in some 164 events. Commenting on the long-standing rejection of Greek-letter social sororities on campus, he explained, "Enrollment at TSCW entitles a student to become a full-fledged member of an outstanding sisterhood of superior university women living in an honestly democractic atmosphere."

In that atmosphere, the College felt, young women could develop their self-reliance, a quality of great value in the business world and in family and community life. The college bulletin of October 1, 1951, noted, "Although girls still are leaving football to the boys, they are attempting a greater share of many other campus activities. This is particularly true at TSCW where girls hold all the offices usually occupied by men."

The independence of TSCW students was not meant to suggest, however, that there was no place for men in their lives. College bulletins of the early fifties demonstrated through both words and pictures the many social opportunities available to students. The bulletin of February 15, 1953, emphasized that a TSCW student "will have her share of dating." In fact, the bulletin reported, "The TSCW initials sometimes are said to mean 'Texas' Sweetest Collection of Women' "; and other bulletins of the period reported the recognition of numerous students for their beauty and talent in national as well as local pageants. An unidentified survey reported in the college bulletin of March 15, 1956, that "TSCW graduates marry earlier and with greater permanence than do women graduates of coed institutions."

Life at TSCW, however, was not designed to prepare students just for marriage or just for careers, nor did it attempt to provide a magic formula for success in either arena. As Guinn told the 177 graduates at the 1955 spring commencement, "In the great epics which form part of our cultural heritage the heroes and heroines often possess magic weapons. The Texas State College for Women does not try to furnish its students with magic swords or cloaks of invisibility to assist them in the trials of life or career." On the other hand, the College did not leave its graduates defenseless either. Students would acquire, Guinn said, the weapons of "knowledge, competence, leadership ability, and understanding. In place of a cloak of invisibility," he continued, "the College seeks to enrich their store of fortitude, perseverance, high purpose, intellectual and spiritual resources." In place of "dragon's blood to toughen the skin," the College offered, he said, "the lasting protection of poise, of good grooming, good manners, and good taste."

Some of these qualities were developed in the one-hour course entitled "Personality," which was required of all freshmen for the first time in the

Possum hunts promoted competition and cooperation among students for more than a decade.

Dean Francis W. Emerson traditionally presented the silver "Stunt Cup" to the winners of the competition among classes in Stunts.

fall, 1953. Others were developed through the students' opportunities not only to participate but also to take the lead in myriad campus activities.

All students became members of the Campus Government Association and the Women's Recreation Association (WRA) upon enrollment; and elected representatives served on the Student Council, the Student Council of Religious Activities, the Student Finance Council, and the Student Council of Social Activities. In addition, some one hundred departmental clubs, honorary scholarship organizations, literary-social clubs, religious organizations, regional clubs, and special-interest organizations were represented by their presidents on the Round Table, a group designed to assist in scheduling club activities so that each student could participate in several organizations.

For the most part, social activities in the early fifties were a continuation of long-established traditions which have, in many instances, maintained their popularity to the present. Class activities included the sophomore "harvest moon," the junior hayride, and the senior breakfast. Stunts, which had long been a part of campus life, had been a formal competition between classes since 1938, giving every student a chance to work on a twenty-minute script, design and make costumes and scenery, and even perform on stage as the classes attempted to win the silver loving cup which went to the best original skit.

All-campus activities included all-college night, the lantern parade to welcome new students, the WRA Carnival, the Corps trip to Dallas or Fort Worth each year to the Aggie football game where a Tessie would be crowned Aggie Sweetheart, the Howdy Dinner, picnics, Religious Emphasis Week, caroling during Christmas week, dormitory open houses, self-development week, the Redbud Festival, and the Corn Huskin' Bee with activities from folk dancing to husband calling and hog calling.

To provide a feeling of unity for the College, the Student Council and the Daily *Lass-O* began a search for a proper TSCW mascot. Five finalists—

144

a swan, a peacock, a calf, a canary, and a lamb—were selected from
hundreds of suggestions ranging from horses and tigers to turtles and
birds; and a little white lamb to be called "Tessandra" was chosen as the
winner.[24] Mr. and Mrs. Herman Trietsch of Denton presented a live six-
week-old two-foot-tall lamb to the College, and it made its initial appearance at Stunts in late February, 1951. Tessandra resided in the converted cook's dressing room behind Brackenridge Hall.

Special celebrations brought thousands of visitors to the campus during
the early fifties. Among the early festivities was the celebration of Guinn's
inauguration on April 27, 1951. The College issued more than 2,500 invitations; and hundreds of guests, including representatives from some
150 colleges and universities and civic leaders from throughout the state,
attended the inauguration.

College departments held all-day open houses; and Mrs. Carney B.
Fletcher, member and secretary of the Board of Regents, presided at the
luncheon at which Emily Taft Douglas, former Congresswoman and wife
of the incumbent Senator from Illinois, Paul Howard Douglas, was the
principal speaker.

Following the luncheon, members of the senior class hooded Guinn in
Stoddard Hall, and then the academic procession made its way down
Redbud Lane to the Main Auditorium, accompanied by the College Band
seated under a canopy west of the Science Building. Dean W. H. Clark
presided at the inauguration. D. S. Campbell, President of the Florida State
University delivered the principal address, "The Measure of a Man";[25] and
Carl Runge, Chairman of the TSCW Board of Regents, installed the sixth
president. After the inauguration, President and Mrs. Guinn greeted guests
at an informal reception in the SUB Ballroom,[26] and the Modern Dance
Group presented an original recital in the evening.

A second inauguration came the following spring, the inauguration of a
new college and program of research. The dedication of the new Smith-

145

A new Smith-Carroll Dormitory was built on the site of the original Methodist Dormitory.

Carroll dormitory and of the New Household Arts and Sciences Building and the inauguration of the new academic and research programs were scheduled to coincide with Redbud activities, the week of March 27. The ceremonies brought hundreds of visitors, including some sixty experts in fields related to chemical and home economics research to conduct symposia and career conferences.

The principal speaker in the Main Auditorium was Francis M. Law, Chairman of the Board of the First National Bank of Houston, who described women as "the cornerstone of society, a cornerstone which TSCW is helping build stronger," and predicted that the "great industries of the Southwest will benefit materially from the findings of your outstanding new research program."

Chairman of the TSCW Board of Regents, Carl Runge, dedicated the new buildings and presented them to the College, reminding the audience that in spite of decreased legislative support based on predictions that enrollment would decrease, "TSCW, unlike most other Texas colleges, suffered no loss in enrollment, thus establishing the faith of Texas in this institution and the need and desire for a state college exclusively for women." The audience burst into applause when he predicted, "I think that we may rightfully expect more support from the Legislature in the future."[27]

In accepting the buildings, Guinn reaffirmed the important role of TSCW in pioneering new programs such as that of the new College of Household Arts and Sciences. "TSCW views its future with confidence," he asserted. "Its mission as a woman's college is more important than ever in the life of Texas . . . It is the nation's foremost woman's college, the only one with a top-level university program. . . . In its record for producing women, TSCW takes off its hat to no one."[28]

Perhaps the most festive of all the ceremonies was the celebration of the fiftieth anniversary of TSCW. The College proclaimed the 1952-53 school year its Golden Anniversary Year, a year filled with special commemorative projects. Beginning October 1, 1952, and continuing through the anniversary year, the local post office used a cancellation which read "50th Anniversary, Texas State College for Women" on all mail which left the city. The special cancellation brought requests from stamp collectors in thirty-six states and Canada.

The Botanical Gardens and flower beds throughout the campus bloomed with gold and yellow blossoms—tulips, daffodils, narcissi, Dutch irises, and crocuses—to celebrate the anniversary; and various departments sponsored special activities. The Music Department presented seven Golden Anniversary Recitals during the year. The TSCW Art Galleries exhibited a month-long display of art by ex-students.

Alumnae sponsored the creation and sale of aniversary plates designed by alumna Marie Delleney of the TSCW art faculty. The plates, in an edition of one thousand, depicted the Administration Building (the original College building), the Student Union Building, the Library, Hubbard Hall, and the Little Chapel-in-the-Woods with the Hubbard Memorial Chapel Garden arranged in a composite "campus scene."[29] Vernon Kilns of Los Angeles made the plates, which sold for three dollars.

A faculty committee, headed by alumna Mamie Walker of the Department of English, prepared a Golden Anniversary Almanac. Students in Eleanor James's English class (including Gretna Cobbs Davis, a memer of the graduating class of 1905) gathered historical data and college songs and yells as a part of their studies in informative writing and methods of research. And forty former students had poems, short stories, essays, and narratives published in the 50th Anniversary issue of the *Daedalian Quarterly.*[30]

146

Ceremonies to launch the Golden Anniversary celebration officially began on November 6, 1952, with a TSCW Band Concert at 9:15 in the morning. At 10:00, an academic procession opened the convocation, which featured five speakers who reviewed the history of the College and examined its present role: Mrs. Van Hook Stubbs, President of the Texas Federation of Women's Clubs; Carl Runge, President of the TSCW Board of Regents; Congressman Ed Gossett, husband of a TSCW alumna, Mary H. Moseley; and M. T. Harrington, President of Texas A&M. TSCW President Guinn provided a look at the future of the College.

Following the convocation, Mrs. Edgar Deen, TSCW Regent and well-known Fort Worth newspaperwoman, served as mistress of ceremonies at a luncheon which featured novelist and lecturer Nora Waln. College departments offered demonstrations, exhibits, and guided tours of classroom work in the afternoon; and the evening offered open houses in the dormitories and offices.

Festivities continued on November 12 when the College sponsored its first all-day Gold Rush Carnival, designed to raise funds for the TSCW Foundation.[31] Supported by Denton businessmen, the carnival began with a morning parade through the Denton business district. Reminiscent of the gold rush days of the Old West, the event included booths, side-shows, rides, food stands, square dancing, a program by TSCW Demonstration School students, and a six-hour variety show by TSCW faculty and students on the south side of the campus. Children throughout the county received free tickets; and hundreds of children and parents attended the event, which raised $2,500 for the foundation.

The Ex-Students Association joined fully in the Golden Anniversary celebration. In the college bulletin of May 1, 1953, Ex-Students President Mae Wadley Boyd reported "fifty thousand Tessies in fifty Golden Years" and challenged every alumna to magnify her influence by uniting and "Talking Turkey for Tessie." Looking at the anniversary as a challenge, the association set its goals for the year: to increase (almost double) the number of chapters to fifty, to change the name from *ex-students* to *alumnae,* to coordinate and integrate the foundation and the association, and to employ an executive secretary.

By homecoming, the association had its fifty chapters. At homecoming it adopted the new name, *Alumnae Association* and voted to eliminate general association dues and encourage annual donations to the foundation with the understanding that the first dollar of each contribution would go to the association for its work.[32]

Officers of the Alumnae Association conducted business in the Alumnae Center, which served as a rooming house as well as headquarters for the Association.

147

The Golden Anniversary Homecoming brought hundreds of alumnae and families (from every class except 1910 and 1911) back to the campus. Among the visitors was Beulah Kincaid Fry, the first graduate of the College and the founder of the Alumnae Association, and one of the few surviving members of the original college faculty, C. N. Adkisson.

While the inauguration of a new president and a new research program, the dedication of new buildings, the celebration of the fiftieth anniversary of the College, and the continuing Concert and Drama Series brought outstanding people from many fields and thousands of visitors to the campus, the College was sending its outstanding faculty and students throughout the nation as well.

The Chapel Choir, organized in the fall, 1950, presented free music services to Texas churches of any denomination. The Modern Choir performed throughout the state and was invited to perform with the Liverpool Philharmonic in the fall of 1956. The Modern Dance Group, organized by Anne Schley Duggan as an extra-class club, had become a regular performing group which appeared at numerous national conventions and on regularly scheduled concert programs of colleges and universities in the South. The group developed and performed original dance compositions under the supervision of Dr. Duggan and her assistants. Notable critics compared the dancers favorably with professionals both in performance skills and in the maturity of their choreography.[33]

The Modern Dance Group earned national recognition.

Among the triumphs of the group was its appearance as the only non-professional performers at the ten-week Jacob's Pillow Dance Festival at Lee, Massachusetts, in 1956. Near that time the group also opened the International Convention of Physical Therapists and appeared on a coast-to-coast television broadcast on NBC's *Home* show.

The TSCW Symphony Orchestra, which had boasted eighty members and full orchestration in the mid-forties, had declined to twenty-one members by the fall, 1953; but it had "big ambitions" according to the college bulletin of November 1; and it set a membership goal of one hundred. The limited size of the group necessitated a change from its performance of symphonies and overtures to smaller classical and simi-classical pieces.

In other areas students were proving their individual talents and the value of their studies in ways that were practical as well as aesthetically pleasing. In the fall, 1954, Cone Mills began a search for new designs that

would make denim a highly fashionable fabric. Furnished material, TSCW flat pattern and draping classes, under the supervision of Bethel Caster (a recent graduate of TSCW's new doctoral program) created all kinds of clothes from evening dress to a man's lounging robe—all from denim. In competition which included a number of colleges, TSCW students took the top three prizes for the best designs. The garments received widespread television and newspaper publicity; and twelve TSCW students were invited to model their self-designed, self-made denim garments during the Texas State Fair.

For purely recreational activities, students gathered in 1950 at the soda fountain on the first floor of the Student Union Building to enjoy pool, ping-pong, or other table games or to dance to the music of the juke box. By 1953 television and an automatic record player had been added to the recreation room, and "The Pub" had been installed between the post office and the book room on the ground floor of Brackenridge Hall. The Pub included a CGA-operated snack bar which served coffee, cokes, sandwiches, and other refreshments. An outdoor theater provided motion picture entertainment on summer evenings.

Outdoor recreation facilities which also accommodated instructional uses on campus continued to include tennis courts and various other athletic fields, the olympic-sized outdoor pool, and the eighteen-hole golf course. The College also continued to maintain its three cabins on the twenty-acre campsite on the north end of Lake Dallas; and when that became unusuable in 1953 because of a drought, the College leased a 118-acre tract on Lake Texoma, north of Whitesboro, from the Army Corps of Engineers for $1 per year. The college bulletin of March 1, 1953, described the tract on the west shore of the Big Mineral Arm of the lake as a "perfect camp ground, well-covered with trees and with deep inlets for boats and a continuous sand beach."

The background for the curricular and extracurricular activities of the time was an extensive physical plant, much of which had been built, expanded, or begun during Hubbard's administration. Some sixty

The new Household Arts and Sciences Building included display space for gowns of Texas' first ladies.

buildings with a book value of approximately $10 million and a replacement value of approximately $20 million belonged to the College when Guinn began his tenure.[34]

Remodeling of Capps and Lowry Halls was completed just before the 1950 fall semester, and a $700,000 addition to Capps Hall increased its capacity to almost four hundred freshmen. Among the attractions of the new wing of the dormitory, according to the college bulletin of September 1, 1950, were "built-in-drawers, cabinets, and mirrors [to] give additional floor space." Innerspring mattresses, foam rubber chairs, and telephones for intra-hall communication were in each room along with double desks built in the College workshop and equipped with fluorescent lights. The second, third, and fourth floors of the building included student lounges and adjoining kitchenettes; and each floor had phones for outside calls. The service elevator in the dorm was changed to a self-service elevator.

Smith-Carroll Hall, which was begun in 1949 and built at a cost of approximately $595,000 was located on the site of the old dormintory of the same name on Bell Avenue. Opened in the fall, 1951, the red-brick Georgian dormitory contained 134 rooms to accommodate 268 junior students. Like the addition to Capps, the new dormitory boasted built-in chests-of-drawers, wardrobes, and dressers. The lounge on the main floor included a spacious living room with three adjoining date parlors, student kitchens, a lobby, office, conference room, and elevator. Each floor contained an air-conditioned student lounge, and each room had a phone for intra-hall communication.[35]

Also ready for occupation in the fall semester of 1951 was the new Household Arts and Sciences (HAS) Building. In addition to extensive space and equipment for research described earlier in this chapter, the new building contained an air-conditioned auditorium to seat two hundred people, a student lounge, a dining room, a weaving laboratory with looms, three fitting rooms for clothing classes, two outdoor terraces, in keeping with Texans' love of out-door living, and "ample" lecture classroom space. The building housed eleven complete kitchen units, four of which were all-electric.

Special features of the building included shallow glass cases in the halls, which were used to display the large china and crystal collections of the new College of Household Arts and Sciences,[36] and a museum to house the inaugural gowns of the wives of Texas Presidents and Governors which the Texas Daughters of the American Revolution had presented to TSCW. Students and faculty worked together to select classroom furniture which would emphasize comfort.

Completion of the new building made space available in the old Home Economics Building for the TSCW Research Center and for the Department of Occupational Therapy, which occupied most of the main floor. One room of the old building was set aside for individual studio space for the Art Department, and a third floor office was designated to house the state files of the American Association of University Women.

The new HAS Building was to be the last on the campus until the future of the College could be insured against the loss of students and against merger with another college. In 1954, however, following official word that constitutional tax funds would be available to each state-supported college for construction projects, a faculty committee began plans that would make the best use of the new funds. Regents gave preliminary approval on March 27 to a proposed $1 million building plan which included three instructional buildings, an administrative building, and a new home for the presidents.

Page, Southerland, Page Architects of Austin designed an administration building, a general classroom unit, and new buildings for the College of HPER and the Library School. Arch Swank designed the president's home

and supervised its construction.[37]

Begun in the summer of 1954, the president's home was completed by the fall. East of Bell Avenue, near Highway 380, the home sat in a grove of twenty-five post oak trees on top of a hill overlooking the college golf course. The location offered natural privacy and beauty, and Fred W. Westcourt of the College of Household Arts and Sciences capitalized on the setting with his use of native plans in the landscape design.[38]

Contracts for the other four buildings were announced in the spring of 1955, and by August the new steel frameworks marked a noticeable change in the style of the campus. Of red brick, which blended in color with the predominant architecture of the campus, the new buildings displayed an austere contemporary style that would characterize new construction through the remainder of Guinn's tenure. The modern architecture symbolized the College's determined look to the future.

Each building was air-conditioned, and each revealed the influence of faculty members who worked with architects to employ art works and other furnishings created by TSCW students, faculty, and staff. Marie Delleney and Coreen Spellman of the art faculty joined with other faculty members and administrators to plan and coordinate the colors, interiors, and furnishings for the new buildings. The two women chose the colors for exterior and interior surfaces, wood finishes, floor tiles, decorative accessories, leathers, rugs, and furnishings for the administrative and classroom units and designed many of them; and the woodworking, metal-working, and painting shops at TSCW executed many of the original furniture, metal trim, and woodwork designs.

The largest of the new buildings was that designed to accommodate the College of Health, Physical Education, and Recreation. Burnett Hall

Architects' designs for the new Administration Building (above) and the new HPER complex (left) foreshadowed a marked change in the appearance of the campus.

151

between the original gymnasium and Hygeia was torn down to make way for the three-level building which faced Bell Avenue. Overall dimensions for the complex, which formed a quadrangle around an open courtyard, were 185 by 255 feet.

Along Bell Avenue, the first level of the east wing of the building housed faculty and administrative offices and a faculty lounge and dressing room. To the north of this wing, toward Hygeia, a second level included three soundproof classrooms (two seated fifty students, and the third accommodated twenty students). Behind this wing to the west, a new gymnasium formed the northwest corner of the quadrangle. The gymnasium floor (108' by 88') offered twice the floor space of the old gymnasium and seating space for up to five hundred people on light-colored wooden bleachers which could be pushed flat against the south wall and locked. With the bleachers pushed back, the gymnasium floor was marked with two basketball courts, three volleyball courts, six badminton courts, and an exhibition tennis court. An unbroken wall on one end provided space for skills tests and for other testing and research.

The gymnasium was designed to be a sports center for general students, for majors in HPER, and for visitors. According to the caption which accompanied the architect's drawing of the new building in the college bulletin of March 1, 1955, "Even the ancient Greeks would admire the large modern gymnasium to be built on the TSCW campus."

Along the west side of the quadrangle ran two curtained dance studios which measured 63 by 32 feet. Each studio contained a mirrored wall, a practice bar, and a hinged bench of light wood along one wall; and each opened onto the patio. Space between the studios provided storage for music, instruments, and costumes. One studio was set aside for folk, tap, and ballroom dancing; the other, for modern dance.

Beneath the studios was a marble and tile shower and locker room with rows of individual showers, makeup tables, hair driers, dressing areas, and lockers. Storage space for sports equipment was adjacent. The locker area connected by tunnel with the old gymnasium, which still housed an indoor pool, a library, staff and club offices, and a gymnasium floor with

Ruth St. Denis was one of numerous internationally famous dancers who have appeared in concert on the campus and conducted master classes. She is pictured here in the fall of 1956.

152

basketball, volleyball, and badminton courts, and fencing strips. Covered walkways ran around the inside perimeter of the courtyard, and the south wall of the quadrangle was left open for the future addition of a modern indoor swimming pool.

Throughout the building, ramps facilitated movement between levels; and built-in shelves, work counters, show cases, and bulletin boards added to the convenience of faculty and students. The complex was designed to accommodate needs which ranged from simple practice space for general students to space for competitive tournaments and to research facilties for graduate students engaged in the study of dance, sports, motor abilities and skills, physical fitness, and health education.

Across the campus to the south, the smallest of the new buildings, that for the School of Library Science, would become the nation's first separate building for library science instruction.[39] It, too, was built around a courtyard; and it connected with the Bralley Memorial Library to the north by a forty-foot latticed breezeway. On the north side a library-study (60' x 40') and a lounge (18' x 36') overlooked the courtyard through ceiling-to-floor glass with sliding panels. The library had its own microcard and microfilm machines, professional holdings of more than 6,000 books and extensive pamphlets, and regular receipt of 142 professional periodicals. The lounge area included a stove, sink, and refrigerator along with its regular furniture. The south side of the building included two multipurpose seminar-laboratory-conference rooms, complete with audio-visual equipment; and offices, file rooms, and a student typing room constituted the east side. Unused space was set aside for additional classrooms.

A striking feature of the new facility was the brick mural which formed a structural part of its exterior west wall. At the request of the architects, various members of the art faculty submitted ideas for a mural. Kenneth B. Loomis, director of the department, created the design which was chosen.[40] Intended to serve as a transition between the contemporary Library Science Building and the nearby traditional Art Building, the mural (12' x 23') incorporated twelve colors and a variety of abstract shapes united by a theme of Southwestern colors and forms of nature.

The remaining two new buildings, the new classroom unit and the administration building, were located on the west edge of the campus near its center, just north of the Little Theater and south of Hubbard Hall, between Oakland Avenue and Redbud Lane.

The two-story classroom unit was built around a semi-open courtyard which contained a pond and white concrete benches on pebbled cement squares. Covered walkways circled the inner passageways on both floors, and a checkerboard roof of colored plastic panels partially shaded the courtyard. On the north and south sides of the courtyard, three classrooms on each floor (a total of twelve rooms) opened onto the inner passageways as did seven offices. The east end of the building was completely open with iron grillwork and a gate to the courtyard on the first floor and a railed walk on the second. Entrances at the north and south corners of the west wall also provided access to the courtyard.

The new classroom building came to be known as the Patio Building because of its partially covered courtyard. Coreen Spellman designed the brick mural on the west wall of the building.

154

Faculty members of the art department designed decorative tiles of fired clay, pewter, and metal to fit into the wrought iron framework in the building,[41] which also included on its west wall a "Star Motif" mural designed by Coreen Spellman of the art faculty. Like the mural on the Library Science Building, the star mural was a part of the wall it decorated. Against a background of multi-colored brick, the mural was created mostly of yellow sand-colored brick with other bricks in complementary tones, all laid in straight courses.

Immediately north of the classroom unit was the new administration building, designed to give a "modern front" to the campus.[42] Of all the new buildings, it reflected most extensively the work of faculty and students. Metal figures, water colors, collages, and other student art work decorated the staff and administrative offices; and faculty members created all kinds of works from ceramic ashtrays with TSCW monograms to planter boxes for the president's office, the regents' room, and other areas of the building.[43] The president's office was furnished in walnut, and the new regents' room was decorated in a contemporary Chinese motif, which included walnut furnishings with ebony and brass trim and persimmon-colored leather chairs. Two panels (15" x 48") of ceramic pieces, brass, metal, and wood made by Marie Delleney and Coreen Spellman completed the decoration of the room.[44]

Dedication ceremonies for the four new buildings on May 9, 1956, included a library science symposium, "What's Ahead in Librarianship,"[45] and special exhibits—the history of TSCW library science, original lithographs and manuscripts of "Cotton Farm Boy" and "Texas Ranch Boy" by Merritt Mauzey, five hundred fifty of the year's new junior books presented by twenty-six publishers, and more than fifty story book characters in costume.[46] Open house in the new HPER Building included exhibits, films, and demonstrations of badminton, volleyball, basketball, tap dance, folk dance, and modern dance.

The new buildings plus the CHAS Building made available air-conditioned classrooms to accommodate all summer classes, and by the summer of 1957 Smith-Carroll Hall had been air-conditioned throughout its bedrooms and lounges to accommodate students of all classfications; Houston Hall offered some air-conditioned rooms for graduate and mature students; and Stoddard Hall offered some for undergraduates. Air-conditioning was also added to the reserve reading room of the Library by this time so that students could attend summer classes in comfort.

New buildings, new programs, and new plans characterized the institution which assumed its new name, the Texas Woman's University, in 1957. In achieving its new mature identity, the institution had lived through trying times. Fortunately, it had had the leadership of presidents and the support of faculty, alumnae, and friends who believed wholeheartedly in the worthiness of its mission, the education of women to their fullest potential.

And it had in its latest president, John A. Guinn, a man single-mindedly dedicated to developing the institution itself to its greatest potential. Thus, under his confident and aggressive guidance, an institution threatened with obscurity and even annihilation reached heights of achievement that earned it a rightful place as one of the first institutions of higher education in the state and the first woman's college in the nation to achieve university status. The years of challenge and growth were, however, far from over.

President and Mrs. Guinn posed with their children at the new President's Home.

New President Guinn meets Carl Runge, Chairman of the Board of Regents.

CHAPTER IX—NOTES

[1] A native Texan, born in New Braunfels and descended from pioneer Texas families, Guinn received the bachelor's and master's degrees from the University of Texas at Austin. Following graduate work at Heidelberg, Germany, in 1931 and at the University of Chicago in 1936, he returned to the University of Texas to complete work for the Ph.D. degree in 1939. His major and minor areas of study were English, education, and history.

Serving as an instructor in the Advanced Naval Intelligence School and in combat intelligence in the United States Navy from 1942 to 1945, he earned the rank of lieutenant commander and won five battle stars and two citations for combat activities in the Pacific. Upon his return to Texas following World War II, he accepted the superintendency of the Alice public schools, which had suffered badly from the war and from a rapidly growing population. During the three years he was in Alice, Guinn transformed the system into one of the best in Texas, attracting visitors from throughout the nation to see the improvements which he had brought about in the school's plant, its efficiency, its financial and community support, its curriculum, and its morale. Frank Lloyd, president of the Board of Trustees for the Alice schools described Guinn for the Denton *Record-Chronicle* of April 26, 1951: "Dr. Guinn is honest in his thinking, in his dealings with his faculty, and the community admired him for his straight-forward methods."

From Alice, Dr. Guinn went to San Angelo College as its president. During the single year he was there (1949-50) he built community and regional support for and interest in the college so that enrollment increased and a successful bond issue led to the construction of three new buildings. When the San Angelo trustees learned of Guinn's selection to head TSCW, they told the Denton *Record-Chronicle,* "We knew we couldn't hold a man like that for very long."

Coming to TSCW September 1, 1950, Dr. Guinn brought with him his wife, the former Bessie Alice Mitchell from Bay St. Louis, Mississippi, and three children—a six-year-old son, John, Jr., and four-year-old twin daughters, Denise and Diana. The entire family quickly became involved in campus life. Mrs. Guinn became a photography student; John, Jr., a student at the TSCW Demonstration School; and Denise and Diana, students in the college nursery school.

[2] Amid threats of war in Korea and extreme inflation at home, the Legislature which convened in January, 1951, was dedicated to economy. Newly-elected Governor Allan Shivers even cancelled the traditional inaugural parades, balls, and receptions to set a "strictly-business" tone for the session. The Legislators proved somewhat hostile to colleges in general because of supposed extravagance at some colleges and because of sharply declining enrollments. World War II veterans, who had crowded the colleges, were completing their studies; and with the prospect of a new war many students were enlisting in the armed services. A New York *Times* survey of one-hundred colleges showed anticipated declines of twenty-five to fifty percent in the spring and summer of 1951; and the Denton *Record-Chronicle* of February 18 hinted relief that NTSC had declined "only" 885 students, from 4999 to 4114, for the spring. Colleges and universities had requested $96.5 million for the next biennium, $34 million more than the last appropriation.

The Legislative Budget Board recommended a reduction in total college appropriations of more than $6,788,000 dollars from the last biennium. The appropriation for TSCW during the last biennium was $2,512,286. The Legislative Budget Board recommended $1,394,750 for the next biennium. The Senate Finance Committee recommended $1,597,026 in a bill that called for the reduction of the salary for college presidents and deans and increased pay for faculty members.

[3] On March 22, pointing out that the TSCW faculty was the lowest paid in the state, Representative Crouch missed by only two votes (56 to 54) securing an additional $598,450 in the House for teaching salaries for TSCW. Critics responded that TSCW, which had experienced an enrollment decline of forty-one percent during the past five years, had only a twelve to one student-faculty ratio whereas the average for the state was nineteen to one.

[4] The college bulletin of May 1, 1952, reported more than four thousand participants in conferences and conventions on campus during March and April alone, exclusive of participants in Redbud and in the ceremonies for the dedication of new buildings and the inauguration of the new college. Typical events ranged from Future Homemakers conventions to organ and landscaping workshops.

[5] The call for coordination did not, however, originate with Shivers. In the face of what it viewed as wasteful spending by the colleges, the 1951 legislative session sought tighter control of locally collected funds such as tuition and other fees; and a House proposal called for the denial of any new courses or degrees not offered before October 15, 1950. Callan Graham of Junction had also introduced a bill that would establish a single board to coordinate the activities of higher education.

On January 27, 1953, Governor Shivers called together representatives of all seventeen colleges in Texas to emphasize the need for them to coordinate their activities voluntarily before the Legislature mandated coordination and warned that the Commissioner of Education would expand his role from public school to higher education as he was empowered to do if the Legislature did not remove his power during the current session.

[6]Guinn was quick to question both the motives and the judgment of Hall, a recent student of North Texas State College who had enrolled only the previous fall in the law school of the University of Texas. NTSC President J. C. Matthews told the Denton *Record-Chronicle* the day following the introduction of the bill that the college had not sponsored the bill but would be happy to comply with the decision of the Legislature and the Governor.

[7]Paradoxically, another of his major arguments for the College was that it offered many courses and programs that were not available at any other single-sex or coeducational institution in the state or even in the Southwest.

[8]The value of all-male education at Texas A&M was coming under question, however. On March 3 the House of Representatives approved the admission of women students to A&M, but the Senate rejected the proposal on March 5.

[9]Members of the first Board were Guinn, Carl Runge of the Board of Regents, Mrs. Code E. Edwards of the Ex-Students Association, Mary Beard of the CGA; Francis W. Emerson, registrar, for the faculty; Mrs. H. Lutcher Stark (Nelda Childers, '30) of Orange, Mrs. J. W. Walker (Lucile Hill, '21) of Planview, Harold Volk (husband of Dorothy Lucille Hill, '46) of Dallas, and Grover C. Bullington (former Regent and father of two ex-students) of Wichita Falls.

[10]On February 1 the College began its annual Founders' Day Fund Drive; but of the more than ten thousand ex-students contacted fewer than four hundred had sent contributions by April 1, and the contributions totaled only $1283.

[11]The 1955 Gold Rush, the most successful to that date, realized a gross profit of $3,957.99, according to the college bulletin of November 15, 1955.

[12]The college bulletin of November 15, 1955, recognized Annie Hughey of Denton as the first person to establish a permanent scholarship through the TSCW Foundation. Interest on her $3,500 contribution would provide an annual scholarship for a TSCW student.

[13]Alumna Margo Jones' death from uremic poisioning on July 24, 1955, cut short her distinguished theatrical career. She founded and served as producer and director of Dallas Theater which helped boost William Inge and Tennessee Williams to Broadway fame; and her direction of Broadway plays led *Theater Arts* magazine to identify her as one of the four leading directors in the U.S. (see Chapter VIII).

[14]The bill provided for the University of Texas to conduct pure research, for Texas A&M College to conduct agricultural research, and for Texas Technological College to conduct textile research. The purpose of the program was to improve cotton and increase its desirability as a fabric of high quality. The role of TSCW was to popularize cotton, not as a substitute, or second-best, fabric but as a material that was suitable for all uses.

To this end, TSCW graduate student Lucille Finley of Amarillo, directed by Gladys McGill, TSCW home economics professor, designed two complete cotton wardrobes to meet all campus requirements for an entire school year—classroom, dormitory, and social—and a freshman and senior student were selected to wear the clothes. To publicize the desirability of cotton, the College distributed news stories about the wardrobes to four thousand daily and weekly newspapers and sent radio scripts to 250 stations. The College, in this instance, served to translate the findings of the other institutions for popular dissemination rather than to conduct research itself.

[15]Before coming to TSCW, Dr. Mack was director of the Ellen H. Richards Institute of the Pennsylvania State College, and she had for the past fifteen years been director of the Pennsylvania Mass Studies in Human Nutrition. Her research, principally in nutrition, had brought her international recognition; and in 1940 she was elected the first Marie Curie Lecturer.

[16]By the fall of 1953, the college was involved in detergency research; in the improvement of hand irons; in studies in child development, family living, and family housing; and in skeletal studies. The Industrial Textile Mill of Kaufman, a manufacturer and nationwide distributor of industrial toweling, sponsored a project for the development of a fabric for cotton towels which would have improved strength, abrasion resistance, and absorbency.

Another project of much larger scope was a ten-year study of teenage nutrition, supported by a grant-in-aid from the Good Luck Margarine Division of Lever Brothers Company. In the spring of 1953, Dr. Mack completed the work she had begun in Pennsylvania and reported her findings in New York.

[17]Among the researchers who accompanied Dr. Mack to TSCW were George Sims Wham to direct textiles research (conducting tests for color fastness, dyes, and style combined with durability), John A. Balong to conduct detergency (cleansing) studies, and George P. Vose to conduct bone density research. In February, 1952, Joseph Sherrill came to TSCW to direct detergency research, including projects on power laundering and household washing. Among the equipment he tested was a sonic washing machine, which used sound waves instead of agitation to force dirt out of clothes. The following September researchers Enid Bever, Leland Baughman, Helen Campbell, and May Yoder Moore and statistician Murray L. Richards joined the research staff of the college.

[18]Mrs. Stark had earned the B.S. degree in bacteriology and medical technology in 1930. Governor Allan Shivers appointed her to the TSCW Board of Regents in 1955.

The Starks' first contribution of $25,000 established the laboratory and purchased miscellaneous items for clinical examination rooms, additional x-ray equipment and supplies

Pauline Beery Mack gathered a team of scientists who established a major program of research in varied areas of nutrition and textiles, securing national attention and paving the way for research in additional fields.

157

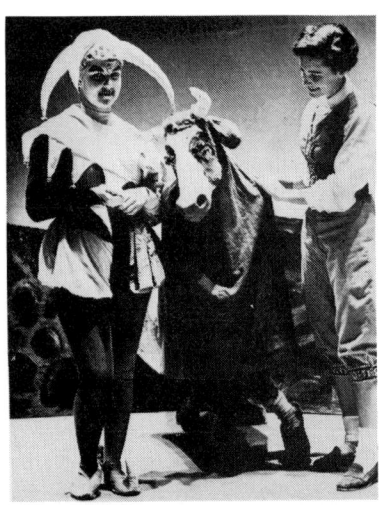

Drama students' roles ranged through Jack and the Beanstalk *for children to Lillian Hellman's* Little Foxes. *Students staged the plays from lighting and scenery to makeup and performed all roles, including those of male characters. (Right) Students designed and sewed fashionable clothes.*

and other major items such as a Beckman quartz spectrophotometer, a highly sensitive gramatic balance, a biomicroscope, and various centrifuges. In 1954 the Starks gave $2500 to purchase a refrigerated tank unit and accessories for the x-ray darkroom so that nutrition studies could be conducted under favorable conditions year-round.

In 1956, a second contribution of $25,000 supported the development and construction of improved equipment to be used in bone density research. Pauline Berry Mack had developed the x-ray technique and equipment for early detection of bone changes in children and adults. The Stark grant made possible the incorporation of the most recent electronic advances into the bone density measuring equipment currently in use. Dr. Mack and Professor George Vose designed and built what would be the fifth model in a series of such machines. Physicists on the staff of Leeds & Northrup in Philadelphia cooperated in the construction of the machine, which made possible the most sophisticated research to that date in the building and maintenance of the human skeleton.

[19]Including TSCW, only four institutions in the nation were qualified to offer doctoral degrees in the field at this time.

[20]Fourteen departments comprised the College of Arts and Sciences: Bible and Religion which offered no major, Biology, Business and Economics, Chemistry, English, Foreign Languages, History and Government, Journalism, Library Science, Mathematics, Occupational Therapy, Physics, Sociology, and Speech. The Departments of Art and Music comprised the College of Fine Arts. The remaining colleges were not departmentalized. Later in 1954, the Department of Library Science became the professional School of Library Science; and in 1956 the Department of Occupational Therapy became the professional School of Occupational Therapy.

For the fall of 1954, all regular departments of TSCW offered the Master of Arts degree, and certain departments offered the Master of Education; the Department of Business and Economics offered the Master of Business Education; and the Departmrnt of Library Science offered the Master of Library Science. The Colleges of Education, HPER, and HAS offered advanced (six-year) certificates as did the Departments of Business and Economics, English, Music, and Speech. Both the Colleges of HPER and HAS offered Ph.D. and Ed.D. degrees.

[21]See Chapter VIII.

[22]Beginning with the 1954-55 session, the diploma course at Parkland School was phased out over a three-year period; but all students who had completed diploma studies at Parkland were eligible to earn a TSCW degree by completing required supplementary work by 1960.

[23]The original nursing faculty included three members with master's degrees—Dean

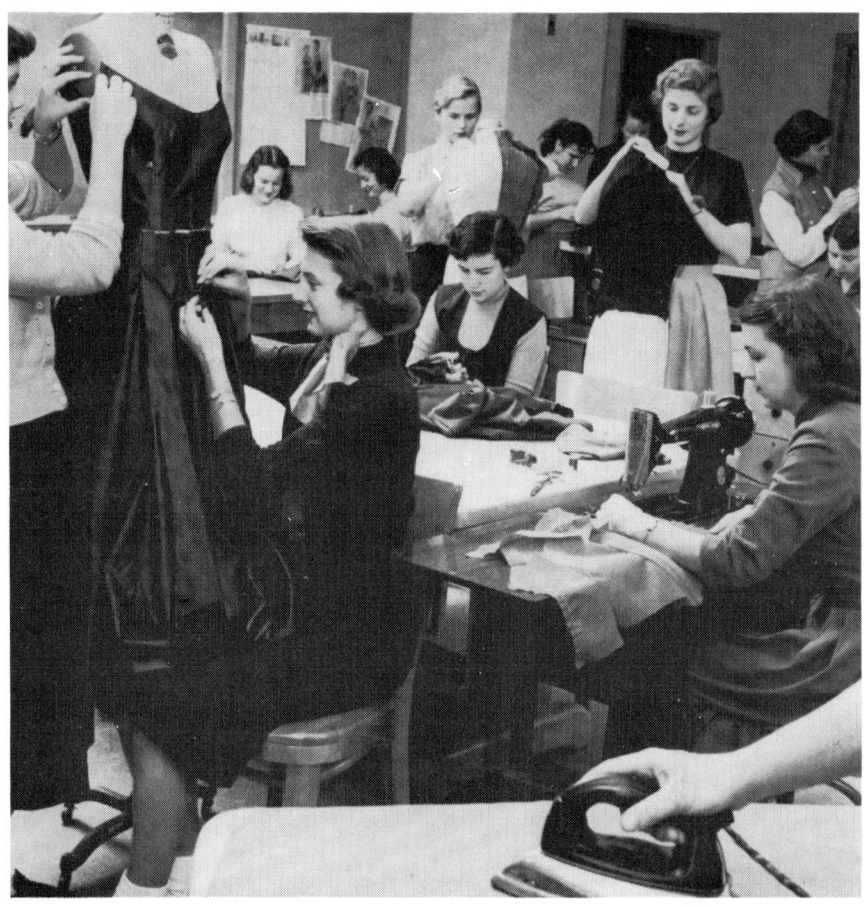

Pannell, her assistant Gesine Franke, and Grace Theresa Gould. Six faculty members had bachelor's degrees; one had an associate degree; and three had diplomas.

[24]Senior home economics major Mary Lamb suggested the mascot because she felt it had femininity suitable for a girls' college and because she thought souvenir stuffed lambs could easily be manufactured.

[25]Campbell, in his tenth year as President, had led the institution, formerly the Florida State College for Women with an enrollment of 1800, to become a coeducational university with about 6500 students.

[26]Dean Clark chaired the general committee on arrangements for the inauguration. Faculty members were Anne Schley Duggan and Josh Roach; and Mrs. Fletcher, Reagan Houston, III, and Mrs. Edgar Deen comprised the committee membership from the Board of Regents.

[27]The 1953 Legislature appropriated $1,735,840 for the College, more than $400,000 more than the 1951 appropriation but some $500,000 less than the College requested.

[28]Other speakers on the program included TSCW Dean Willis H. Clark and Ruth O'Brien, Assistant Director of the Bureau of Human Nutrition and Home Economics, U.S. Department of Agriculture. Gladys A. Emerson of the Merck Institute for Scientific Research represented research scientists. W. T. White, Superintendent of the Dallas Independent School District, represented the public schools of Texas. Mayor Mark Hannah brought congratulations from the City of Denton. Dixie Young, Director of the Department of Biology, represented the TSCW faculty with brief remarks; and Mary Beard, President of CGA, represented the student body. Mrs. Code E. Edwards, President of the ex-students, spoke on their behalf.

[29]The Executive Board of the Ex-Students Association approved plans for a garden near the Little Chapel-in-the-Woods to honor former President Hubbard and the late Mrs. Hubbard in June, 1951. Lura Mae Burton Kendrick of the class of 1931 was named chairman of the Hubbard Memorial Committee. With the theme, "Dollars to honor a scholar," alumnae raised the money for the construction of a flagstone terrace with appropriate evergreen shrubs and other plants and with a thirty-two-inch limestone statue of St. Francis and the Birds created by Jo Roper in the spring, 1952. With President Hubbard in attendance, the garden was dedicated at homecoming, June 1, 1952.

[30]More than 160 alumnae responded to requests for contributions to the *Quarterly*. Among the works selected were poems by Mrs. Henry Blagg of Denton and her daughter Mary Evelyn Blagg of the class of 1942, who was studying toward the Ph.D. degree at Duke University. (Mary Evelyn Blagg Huey became the seventh President of the University in 1976.) The work of future distinguished alumna Laura Lane of the class of 1933 was also included.

[31]The carnival has, with some modifications, continued to be an annual fall event.

[32]As a first step toward coordination, the association and foundation had employed a joint secretary, Vivian Wallace McCracken of the class of 1920, who assumed her duties March 9, 1953. The action of the alumnae at the homecoming business meeting made all former students members of the association with no dues except those required by individual chapters. A five-dollar donation to the foundation made the giver a voting member for the rest of the foundation's fiscal year, and a one-hundred-dollar gift brought life membership.

[33]Members of the group through the years have taken places on television and Broadway, in professional concert dance groups, and in high school, college, and university teaching and administrative positions.

[34]Instructional buildings included Burnett Hall, Bralley Memorial Library, and the Administration Building (the original college building), which housed the offices of the president, dean, dean of women, and registrar and classrooms for sociology, education, economics and business, foreign languages, English, history and government, and mathematics; the Demonstration School, Nursery School, Gymnasium, and Rural Arts Center; and the Fine Arts, Home Economics, Journalism, Music-Speech, Science, and Union Buildings.

Service buildings included the auditorium, college hospital (Hygeia), Hubbard Hall, the Little Chapel-in-the-Woods, the Little Theatre, and the Ellen H. Richards, Margaret Gleason, and Mary M. Bralley Cottages.

Dormitories provided space for some 2550 students. The main housing units were three-story fireproof brick units: Austin, Brackenridge, Capps, Fitzgerald, Houston, Lowry, Sayers, Smith-Carroll, and Stoddard Halls. Smaller units provided supplementary housing for overflow and for mature and graduate students: Anson Jones, Burleson, Los Alamos, Oakland, Shadow Lawn, Sin Cuidado, Travis, Turrentine, and Zavalla halls. And the cooperative system, which provided especially economical housing for students who wished to do their own cooking and household work, included Bastrop, Bonham, Crockett, Ellis, Fannin, Lamar, Milam, Reagan, and Rusk Halls.

Among the miscellaneous holdings of the college were cabins in the woods and at Lake Dallas, the Ex-Student Center, a golf clubhouse, greenhouses, a model cottage, a photography studio, a post office, a power plant, workshops, Virginia Carroll Lodge, and the president's residence.

[35]In the midst of this construction, the old power plant behind Hubbard Hall was leveled and the ground cleared for parking. The new dining hall also made possible the elimination of individual dining rooms and kitchens in each dormitory; and at the beginning of the spring

Dramas were presented in the Little Theatre.

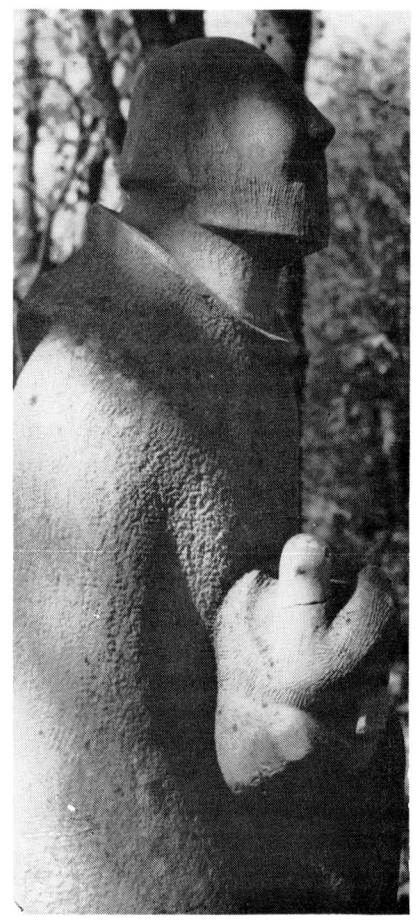

Alumnae financed a statue of St. Francis in the Botanical Gardens to honor former President and Mrs. Hubbard.

159

Regents moved from their early quarters (above right) to modern space in the new Administration Building (below right).

During nine-week shifts, students in Gleason Cottage, named for Margaret Gleason (below), applied budgeting, buying, cooking serving, and other homemaking skills learned in their home economics classes.

semester, 1952, the post office and bookroom were moved from the Administration Building (the original college building) to the basement of Brackenridge dormitory in the space formerly used by the dining room and kitchen. In 1956 a new modern front was added to the post office.

[36]Margaret Gleason, former director of the Department of Home Economics, had brought most of the collection while on summer tours.

[37]With O'Neil Ford, Swank had designed the Little Chapel-in-the-Woods. Projected costs were $375,000 for the HPER Building, $350,000 for the classroom unit, $175,000 for the administration building, and $70,000 for the Library Science Building.

[38]Foundation planting included varieties designed to provide changing features with the changing seasons. Yaupon holly from East Texas bore berries during the winter, and ceniza (ashplant) bore little miniature orchids during the summer. Other foundation plants included mountain laurel, agarita (chaparral berry), and yucca. Gardenias were planted along the redwood fence which enclosed one side of the patio, and waxleaf ligustrum formed a hedge that would grow to shield the outdoor living area from the street and still permit breezes to pass.

To the east, a large livingroom picture window looked over a low bed of turf lilies, across a valley planted in Texas bluebonnets to the TSCW golf course. From the living room one could also view the individual groups of redbud and crabapple trees planted on the terrace slope.

[39]Organized as the Department of Library Science in September, 1928, the TSCW School of Library Science was the first in the Southwest to receive accreditation by the American Library Association. Beginning with a 31-hour major to be taken in the senior year, the department added a fifth-year B.S. in L.S. in the 1938-39 academic year and then inaugurated a master's degree program in 1941. It remained the only department in Texas to offer an advanced library science degree for many years.

[40]Loomis had designed murals for the Chicago World's Fair in the early 1930s and the New York fair in the late 1930s, but the TSCW mural was his first in brick.

[41]Edith Brisac, Carlotta Corpron, Toni LaSelle, Mabel Maxcy and Kenneth Loomis designed

more than forty brick-colored terra cotta tiles to be set in the decorative framework of the courtyard. Designs included abstract and geometrical shapes, campus scenes, and, in Miss LaSelle's tiles, "Great Moments in the History of Civilization" ranging from the invention of the wheel to the design of airflow aircraft. Thetis Lemmon designed and made abstract openwork pewter squares to be fitted into the eastern gateway of the courtyard.

[42]The new concentration of buildings near the center of the campus, along with the increasing number of cars, called for new parking and roads; and the college bulletin of March 1, 1955, reported the widening of Redbud Lane and Oakland Avenue for parking. The bulletin of August 1, 1955, reported the addition of parking on Bell Avenue, the addition of paving and curbing to two parking areas immediately west of the old gym, and the opening of a road from Bell Avenue to Hubbard Hall. All parking was head-in.

[43]Students created many decorative pieces. Linda Crawford and Jo Ann Spann created bright abstract watercolors for the office of the dean of admissions. Ann Gillespie designed an abstract fish of gold metal for the wall of the comptroller's office. Joyce Britton, Natalena Shelton, and Maria Paez created collages which picked up the color schemes in the office of the dean of women. Collette Colbert made a collage for the reception room. In an oil-on-masonite panel, Roberta Heffner enlarged a detail of the drapery pattern on the east wall of the president's office to decorate that room.

Faculty contributions to the building were sometimes utilitarian as well as aesthetic. Faculty members designed book end tables and conference tables, one of which was a modified rectangle, larger at one end than the other to enable the person seated at the head to see all other persons seated around the table.

[44]After administrative offices were moved to the new building, the old administration building (the original college building) was remodeled to accommodate the College of Education.

[45]Speakers included Janice Kee, executive secretary of the public libraries division of the American Library Association; Robert Trent, president of the Texas Library Association; Luella Higley, chairman of the schools section of the Texas Library Association; and Dr. Gould Clark, president of the Texas Chapter of the Special Libraries Association.

[46]Prior to the dedication, library science students and ex-students presented the school a six-piece silver coffee service to be used in the new lounge.

Students in Gleason Cottage (above) gathered to meet class requirements while dormitory residents (below) met to play or study.

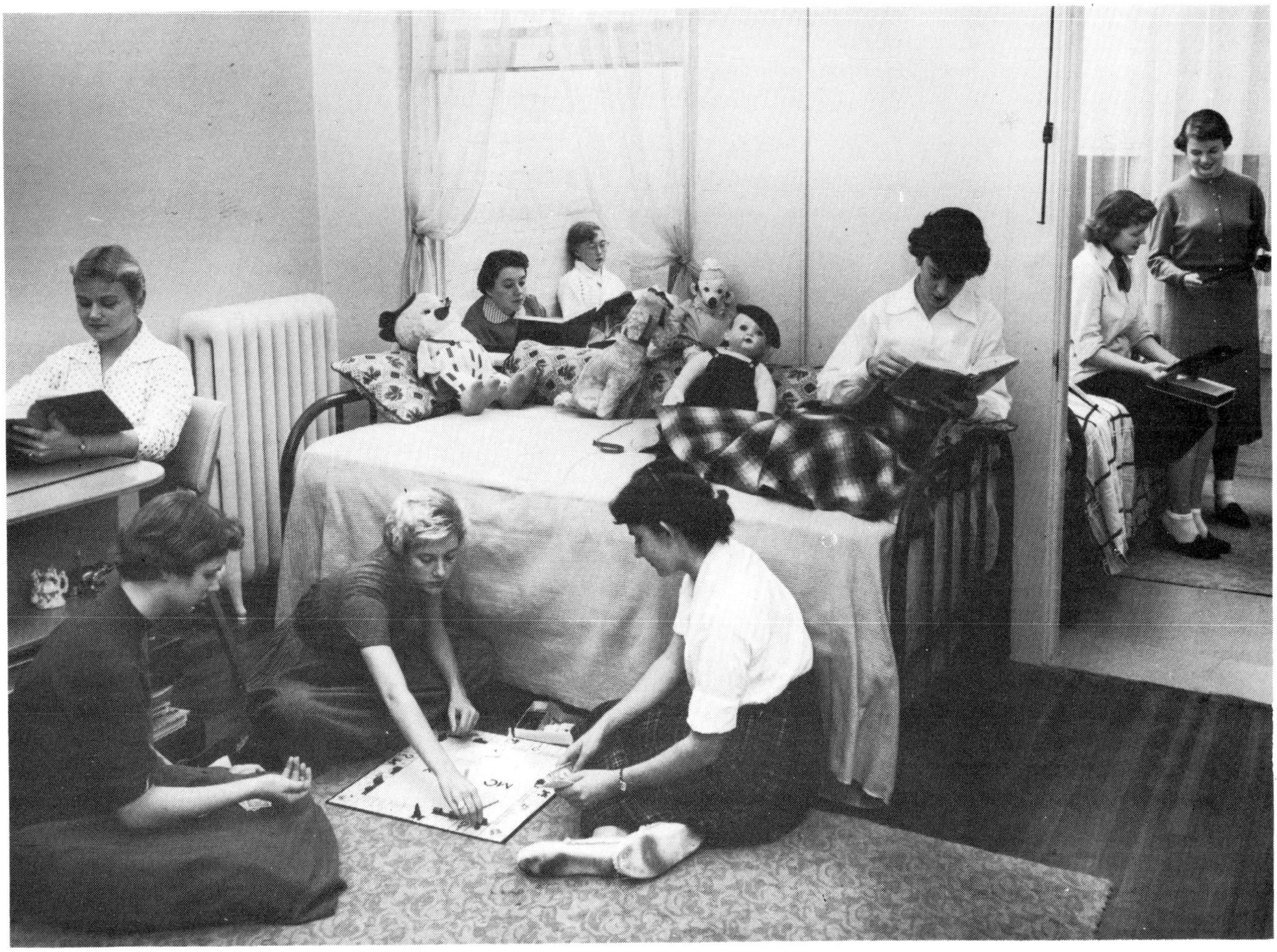

A Citadel of Culture and a Fortress of Learning

X

Following official legislative recognition of its status as a University in 1957, TWU entered a decade of major growth. Curriculum and research activities expanded to meet new needs as the world entered the space age and the age of unprecedented attention to the health and welfare of its inhabitants. Growing curricula attracted students who, in turn, required additional classroom, laboratory, and research facilities and additional residential space.

Overseeing and directing the growth in every direction was a man of vision and determination, a man characterized by Judge Robert A. Hall, Chairman of the TWU Board of Regents, as "the Upgrader." In remarks on November 10, 1966, Hall described President John A. Guinn as a man who charted a course around any obstacles which threatened to bar his way. The growth of TWU during Guinn's middle years of service bears witness to the effectiveness of his methods.

Guinn was conscious of the past. He told graduates at commencement on June 5, 1960, "You are inheritors of a proud tradition." But his mind was on the future; and before his audience could become too reflective, he directed their thoughts there: "We shall not tire in our efforts nor weaken in our determination to push the developmental activities in which we are continuing to make excellent progress."

Speaking at each commencement, he used his platform to reaffirm his belief in the value of TWU and its distinctive work and to urge always an intense drive toward growth and excellence. His description of TWU at commencement on May 28, 1961, as "a citadel of culture and a fortress of learning" reflects the tone of the period in which the nation found itself, at least figuratively, besieged and anticipates the late sixties and the seventies when many colleges and universities would be beleaguered by physical and philosophical attacks from within and without.

Obstacles and difficulties would never change Guinn's opinion about TWU, however. The university bulletin of December 15, 1965, quoted him: "After fifteen years as president of TWU, I am able to affirm with greater pride and confidence than ever my belief in the distinctive values of our university exclusively for women."

First Lady Lady Bird Johnson toured the campus when she received her honorary doctorate from TWU in 1964.

By the time he made this statement, he could look around him at spectacular growth in enrollment, in research, and in facilities on the TWU campus in Denton and to extensions of that campus through clinical centers in Dallas and Houston. As he had remarked in 1958, "Building is a symbol of progress"; and evaluated on that criterion alone, the decade from 1957 to 1967 would be a progressive success. However, the President understood that a University is more than bricks and mortar; and he noted, "We must not only construct new buildings, but we must build our curriculm and interpret our institution to the public." In these areas, less readily measured than buildings, the University proved itself as well.

In 1957, at his seventh spring commencement as President of TWU, Guinn conferred 245 degrees and reported, "The future is rosy with promise." By 1957-58 the number of students had risen from a sixteen-year low of fewer than two thousand during Guinn's first year as President to 2493.

The university bulletin of August 1, 1960, reported a 7.57 percent enrollment gain during the past year, an increase that was topped by only two other state institutions. On November 15, 1963, the university bulletin announced a record fall enrollment of 3,196 which made the "dorms bulge." Francis W. Emerson, Dean of Admissions, reported one of the biggest freshmen classes ever—1133, almost twice as many as the next largest class, the 631 sophomores.

When the fall enrollment of 3380 set a new record in 1964, Guinn admitted in the university bulletin of November 15, "We anticipated an increase, but the number was a little more than we were prepared for"; and TWU had to arrange temporary housing for some forty students.

According to the university bulletin of July 15, 1966, the Coordinating Board, Texas College and University System, projected an enrollment of 3789 students at TWU in 1966 and 7,797 in 1978.[1] Both estimates proved to be conservative. The 1966 fall enrollment was 4408; and the spring enrollment for 1978 was 8339.

Rising enrollments required campus expansion and made possible other improvements as well. Faculty salaries, which had plummeted with the enrollment, rebounded with the enrollment. *The T-A-C-T Bulletin* published by the Texas Association of College Teachers in November, 1959, carried the announcement by the Texas Commissioner of Higher Education that teachers' salaries at TWU had increased 41.7 percent during the last five years. Increases and projected increases in enrollment would enable TWU to obtain a fair share of the anticipated $200 million to be distributed among the state-supported schools for construction.[2]

A number of factors contributed to TWU's growth and influenced its direction during the decade. Among the earliest were two events in late 1957 which startled the world and gave a new direction to American education. Russia first announced the creation of an intercontinental missile for the rapid delivery of nuclear bombs and then, five weeks later, revealed the successful launching of *Sputnik,* the first man-made satellite to circle the earth.

Only a few months after Guinn had looked into the "rosy future" of TWU, he addressed a university assembly on December 12, reflecting the sense of anxiety that characterized the period: "We must come to grips with the critical realities that face our nation in this time of perils and pressures which may be expected to continue for years to come."

Although he sensed the anxieties of the age, however, he viewed them as a rousing challenge, not an apocalyptic menace. As always, he looked for the proper role for TWU and predicted, "I say, as I have often done in the past, that womanpower can be the answer to certain publicized shortages of manpower." Recent graduates were working in that direction already. Members of the class of 1957 were, according the university bulletin of August 15, employed from San Angelo to Washington in jobs that ranged "from computing to probating."

Predicting a "vigorous new era of development," Guinn announced that TWU was ready to expand its curriculum laterally and vertically, not by duplicating programs of other institutions but by filling unmet needs. TWU's new emphasis on science and on diverse areas of health care served as a catalyst to the University's development.

In the first summer (1958) after *Sputnik*, TWU joined educational institutions at all levels in attempting to meet the demand for better science instruction. Although it offered nineteen workshops on topics as diverse as current trends in English and piano methods, perhaps one of the most significant workshops was that for women science teachers. Not only could they receive refresher work in fundamental scientific principals, but they could also enjoy a special emphasis on such developments as atomic power, rocketry, space medicine, and radiation effects. Special speakers and guest scientists from government and industry stressed the potential for women in science and engineering.

By the following summer, the National Science Foundation (NSF) was involved in a major federal program which would pour millions of dollars into attempts to improve the teaching of science throughout the nation. That year TWU, with NSF, sponsored a special summer science training program for high school girls and an experimental summer program of institutes for science and mathematics teachers and supervisors in elementary schools. The program for high school students continued through a number of summers; but in the summer of 1960 TWU, with NSF, replaced the institute for elementary teachers with the first of a series of summer institutes in science and mathematics for junior high and high school teachers.[3]

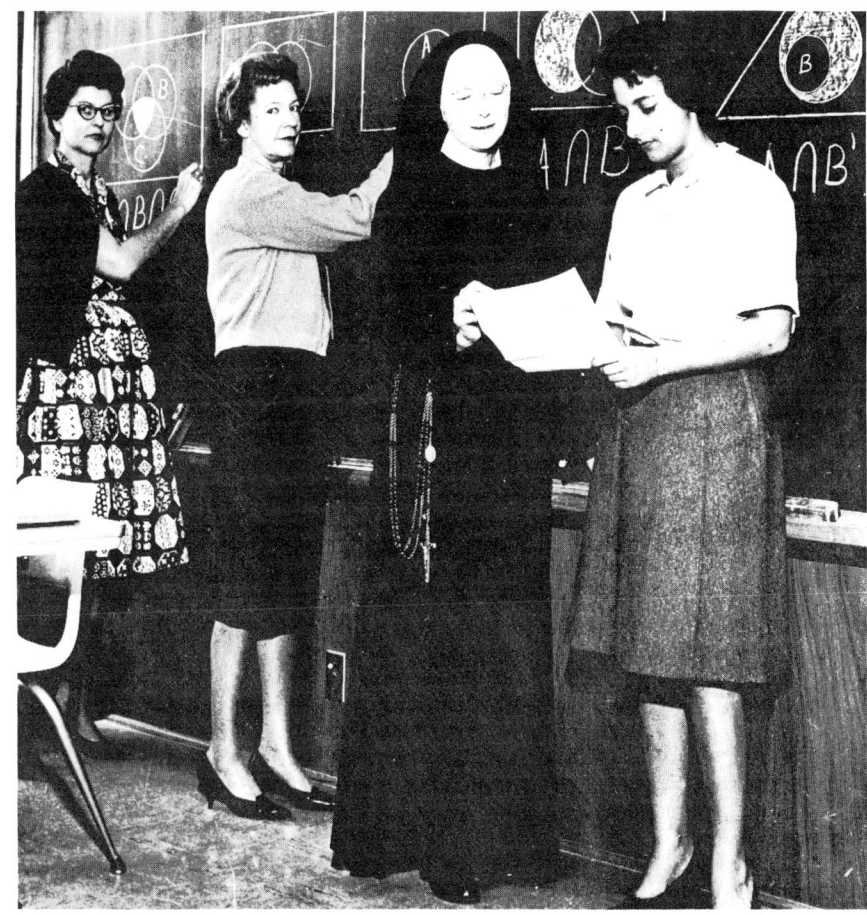

Saturday seminars offered teachers a way to stay abreast of trends in mathematics.

Bone density studies involved X-raying the foot and other parts of the body.

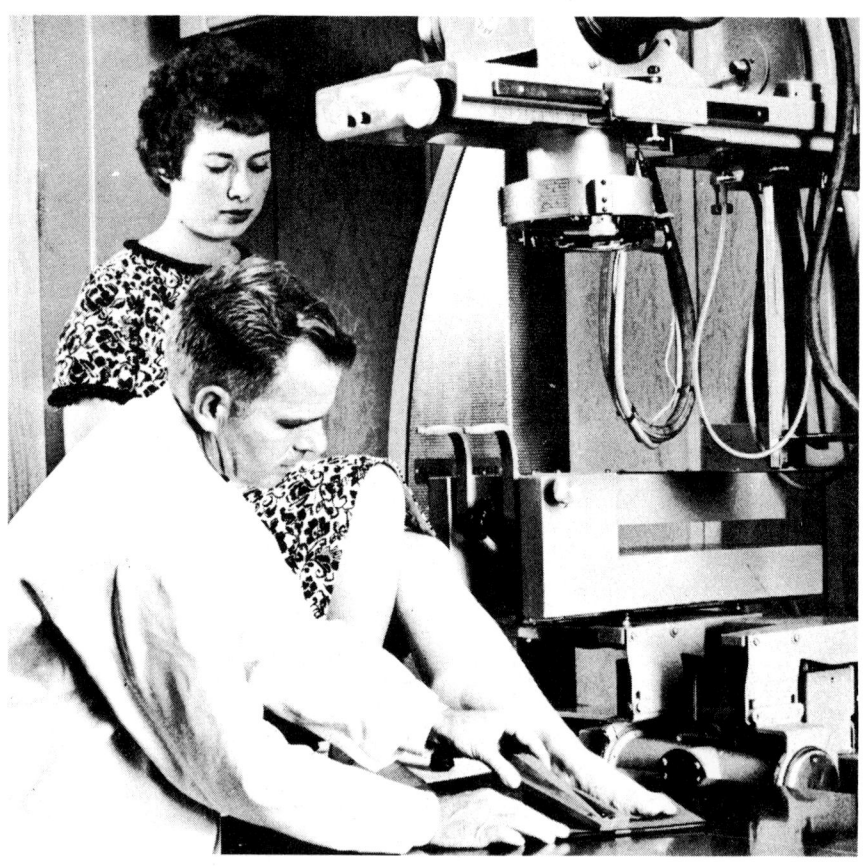

While TWU reached out to help the women who were preparing future scientists, its current students and faculty were involved in timely scientific research. The University, which ten years earlier had had virtually no research program, had by the fall of 1960 a fully-equipped radiation laboratory and strong research and teaching programs in both radiation biology and radiation chemistry.[4]

Among the research projects was an extensive study of bone changes in animals that were subjected to low potency gamma radiation, which the university bulletin of August 15, 1958, described as "representative of the type of radiation characteristic of atomic fall-out." Grants from the Surgeon General's Office and the National Institutes of Health (NIH) sponsored the research in this area.

TWU also cooperated with the Oak Ridge Institute of Nuclear Studies, and several members of the TWU faculty and staff had performed research at Oak Ridge in the summers before TWU formally applied for membership in the Institute in the summer of 1959. On October 18, 1960, Guinn telegraphed the *Lass-O* from Oak Ridge, Tennessee, that TWU had become the thirty-ninth member of the Institute.[5] The university bulletin of November 15, 1960, reported twenty-two members of the TWU faculty and staff engaged in studies which involved the use of radiation in chemistry, physics, biology, nutrition, textiles, and textile technology.

On July 13, 1964, the Texas Commission on Higher Education authorized TWU to grant Ph.D. degrees in radiation biology and radiation chemistry. In reporting the approval in the university bulletin of July 15, 1964, Guinn noted, "We've been getting ready for five years, so we're ready to get started with the programs this fall." The first students completed the new sequences in 1968.

As TWU directed major efforts toward nuclear studies and research, it also focused attention on a project that would help the United States in its race to the moon. The university bulletin of March 1, 1964, described

TWU research for the National Aeronautics and Space Administration (NASA) into the causes of the loss of calcium in the human skeleton during long space flights or other long periods of immobility.[6] Studies had been underway on the campus for almost six months, using four young men selected on the basis of extensive medical and psychological tests.[7] Three classrooms in the Education and Research Building (Old Main) were converted into living quarters and a laboratory for the study, which included controlled diets and two-week bed rest periods, comparable to the length of the projected Gemini space flights.[8] Studies continued during the next several years, using primates as subjects; and TWU was issued a research contract in 1967 to determine the effect of weightlessness and cockpit confinement on bone demineralization during the Apollo flight.[9]

These research projects and projects for state hospitals and other institutions and in fields such as biology and radiation biology, chemistry and radiation chemistry, dietetics, human nutrition, child growth and development, textiles, and detergency brought hundreds of thousands of dollars of support to TWU during the period. As the university bulletin of August 1, 1960, noted, TWU's research was "very large in proportion to the size of the institution." (Enrollment for the 1961-62 school year was 2,785). The university bulletin of July 15, 1962, noted that industrial, governmental, and private grants in these areas had totaled $1,131,750 during the past five years, that the budget for research and related programs in the fiscal year drawing to a close was $368,500, and that some sixty thousand feet of floor space was in use for research.

Although nuclear threats, satellites, and space travel provided the most dramatic potential crises throughout the world, a critical shortage of qualified nurses produced real and immediate problems at home. By the

The "tilt" table test, applied here to a bed rest subject after thirty days of total rest, was also given to astronauts immediately before and after their orbital flights.

167

fall of 1958, enrollment at TWU's Dallas Center had reached capacity, and TWU Regents accepted an invitation to provide training for nurses at the Texas Medical Center in Houston, where the shortage of nurses was especially acute. According to the Houston *Chronicle* of October 10, 1958, Texas (with 108 registered nurses per 100,000 persons) ranked thirty-ninth among all the states in the nation. The paper estimated that Texas had only sixty percent of the registered nurses it needed, and Houston had only fifty percent.

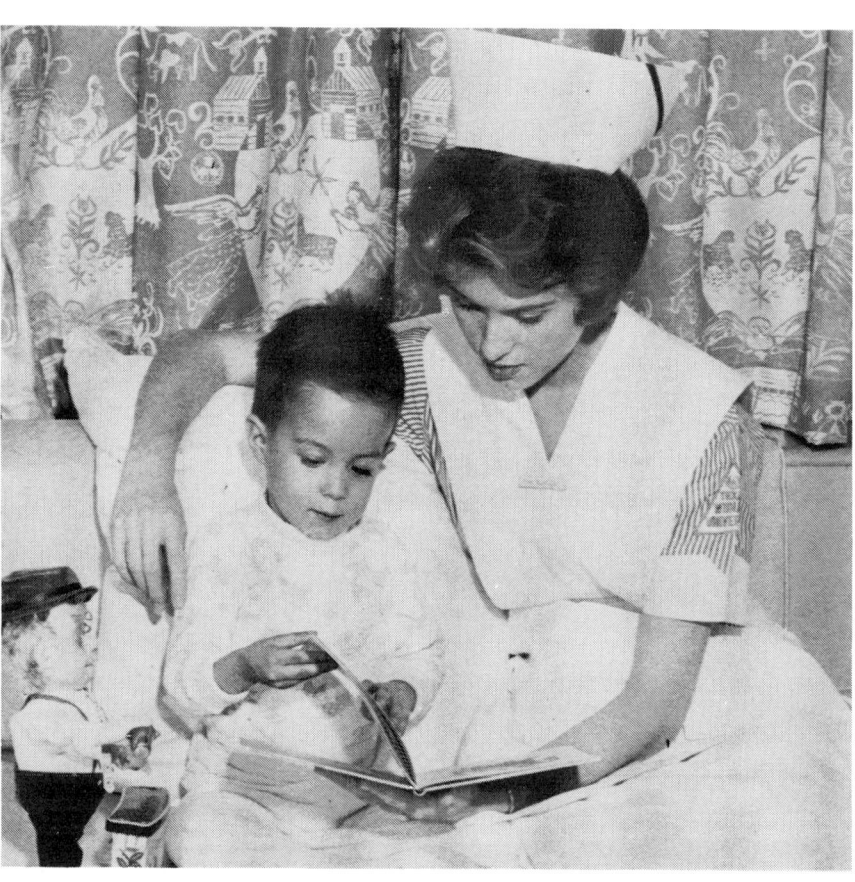

The development of a TWU Houston Center allowed nursing students to work with patients in the Texas Medical Center.

Nursing students of the class of 1963 were the first to receive clinical training at the Houston Center. The building on the left contained classrooms, laboratories, and offices. Recreational and residential facilities occupied the six-story structure on the right.

Although the Medical Center had extensive research, educational, and treatment facilities, it had no program for training nurses. Thus, it offered to build a $1.5 million classroom building; and the Good Samaritan Club of Houston promised to build multimillion-dollar housing for nursing students and Medical Center nurses. In turn, TWU would cover instructional and administrative costs and provide up to three hundred young women who wished to obtain a college degree in nursing.

The Houston *Chronicle* of October 10, 1958, praised the project as "one of the finest examples of co-operation toward a desired goal that has been undertaken here for some time." Nevertheless, the project had encountered difficulties; and progress stopped until Attorney General Will Wilson ruled that state law did not require that the Texas Commission on Higher Education approve the nursing program in Houston.[10]

With the legal obstacles removed, TWU moved ahead; and by mid-November, 1958, architects were designing a residential and instructional building for student nurses at the Texas Medical Center. On July 1, 1959, fewer than fourteen months after Medical Center representatives first approached TWU officials, Guinn turned the first spade of dirt for the new $1.75 million building, which would enable the University to double the number of nurses it could train. Financed by grants from the M.D. Anderson Foundation and Houston Endowment, Inc., the facilities for the program cost the state nothing.

Nursing students who enrolled at TWU in the fall of 1959 completed their first year of studies on the Denton Campus. At the first summer term, 1960, however, they were assigned to the Dallas Center or to the Houston Center when it opened in September, 1960." With the expansion made possible by the new facilities, the TWU College of Nursing became the largest in the state.[12]

In 1963 TWU received authorization to offer the Master of Science degree in nursing. Like the undergraduate program, graduate studies in nursing grew rapidly. The University awarded the first four graduate degrees in nursing in 1968. The following year it awarded seventeen degrees, and in 1970 it awarded twenty-four. The National League for Nursing accredited the program in January, 1969.

The nursing program proved to be effective not only in attracting students but also in contributing to the growth of the nursing profession as well; and, as its founders had hoped, the nursing program in Houston produced nurses who chose to stay in the area.[13] Nevertheless, the shortage of nurses in the state continued to be a serious problem, a problem that was, in fact, worsening.

On November 10, 1966, Governor John Connally spoke at the dedication of a new seven-story residence hall at the TWU Dallas Center. He praised the TWU College of Nursing not only as the largest such college in the Southwest (it had grown from 68 students in 1954 to 1,070 in 1966)[14] but also as one of the finest in the United States.

"Let me remind you, however," he said, "that we've only begun. In spite of the progress being made, Texas ranks 46th among the 50 states in

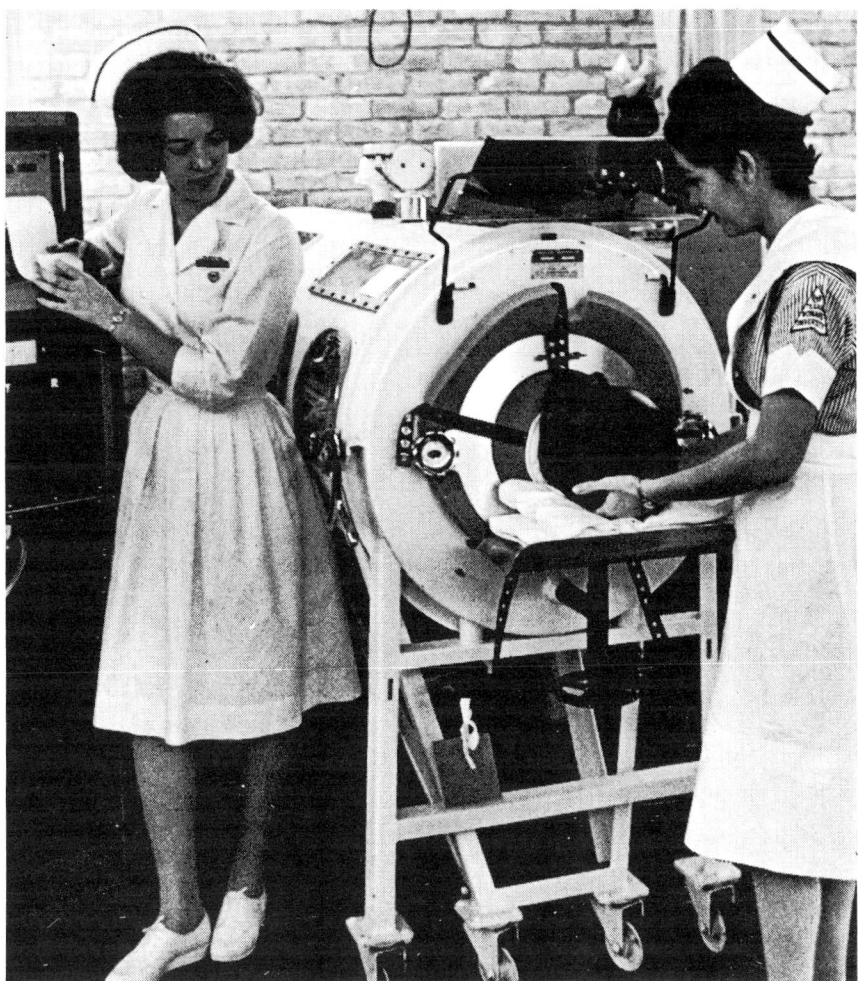

Nursing students at the Houston Center developed skills for handling diverse situations, including (here) a patient in an iron lung.

the number of nurses in relation to the population." Pointing out that Texas was short by 10,500 nurses in the current year, Connally predicted that the state would need fifty thousand nurses (three times as many as it currently had) by 1980.

By 1967, the Houston Center had reached its capacity, and Regents authorized planning for a second dormitory and instructional building. TWU officials were also involved in negotiations for a new nursing center in the Amarillo Medical Center to be ready for students by the fall of 1969. Plans, which never bore fruit, called for the construction of residential and instructional buildings like those at the other clinical centers.

Although plans for a center in Amarillo never became more than plans, the existing clinical centers enriched areas of the curriculum in addition to nursing. TWU affiliations with Parkland Hospital enabled students in food and nutrition, dietetics, and institution administration to gain experience in such fields as quantity cooking and diet therapy. The Department of Biology also developed a combined major in medical technology whereby students completed University and departmental requirements plus twelve consecutive months of clinical training at Parkland. The department also announced in the university bulletin of July 15, 1960, a program of preliminary training in which a student could earn a baccalaureate degree that would prepare her to pursue the Master of Medical Art degree at a medical school.[15]

For many years TWU's College of Health, Physical Education, and Recreation (HPER) had offered pre-professional training for students who wished to attend a school of physical therapy following receipt of a baccalaureate degree. In 1965, however, in response to pressing needs, the Coordinating Board authorized TWU to establish its own School of Physical Therapy. Here, professional course work was introduced during the student's first year and continued throughout her studies instead of being concentrated at the end of baccalaureate study. Seven students enrolled in the program in 1965, and by 1971 enrollment in the program had grown to more than one hundred. Students in the program received a part of their clinical instruction at the Houston Center and then spent the

Students at the Dallas Center could board a TWU bus outside their residence hall to travel to nearby Parkland Memorial Hospital for clinical experience.

final semester of their senior year in clinical affiliations at physical therapy departments in Texas. Students in the School of Occupational Therapy also spent the fall semester of their senior year at the Houston Center, and in the spring of 1967 the school added the spring semester of the junior year to the studies to be completed at Houston.

TWU also received support for the expansion of another innovative therapy program on the Denton Campus. The university bulletin of January 1, 1959, reported the establishment of a Music Therapy Training Center under the joint sponsorship of the Hogg Foundation and TWU. TWU had worked for many years in music therapy activities and had initiated a music therapy major in the fall of 1953. The new center would provide, according to the bulletin, "an eminently qualified teacher, supervisor of clinical training, and coordinator of research."

Students involved in clinical training and in scientific research were extending the University motto, "We learn to do by doing," into ever new fields; but the purpose of the Texas Woman's University could still be expressed as it had been in the founding legislation which charged the Girls Industrial College with teaching "such . . . practical industries as from time to time may be suggested by experience"; and the University had not forgotten that the first charge of the legislation was to provide "a literary education."

Guinn reiterated the dedication of the University to its dual mission in his commencement address on May 28, 1961: "As surely as we shall continue to be champions of liberal or general education . . . we shall also continue to develop further our traditional emphasis on education for unusual competence in occupations and professions, particularly those which are heavily dependent upon, or predominantly staffed by, university-trained women."

As the new age demanded steadily increasing emphasis on technical occupations and professions, however, many people felt that technical programs were being offered at the expense of conventional liberal arts studies. To enrich offerings in traditional subjects TWU joined a growing number of institutions which offered especially challenging studies through an honors program. Following lengthy discussion by the faculty, students, and administrators, seven programs in the College of Arts and Sciences—biology, chemistry, economics, English, French, history, and mathematics—instituted honors courses in the fall of 1965 for freshman students.[16] The university bulletin of March 15, 1966, described the program: "Honors courses will begin, as a general rule, with enriched programs in the basic courses and will become progressively more specialized, particularly in the junior and senior years." A student who enrolled in honors courses early in her studies would be able to complete enough honors courses to receive her degree as an honors graduate.

New programs, new emphases, even new campuses demonstrated the new freedoms for women and the new possibilities for humanity which characterized the age, an age which looked more to the future than to the past. Nevertheless, TWU students of the age were an inextricable part of what one alumna described in the university bulletin of July 15, 1962, as the "long chambray line."

The students of the late fifties and early sixties were both like and unlike their predecessors. Kitty Newton wrote the alumnae class agents in the university bulletin of April 1, 1961, "At first humorous, then sad, are remarks like 'Oh, it's not like the good old days' when a smartly dressed figure alights from a shining sleek automobile, lovely head cocked to one side. 'Thank goodness' should be the next thought. The University is doing a brilliant job of combining our heritage and tradition with her progress."

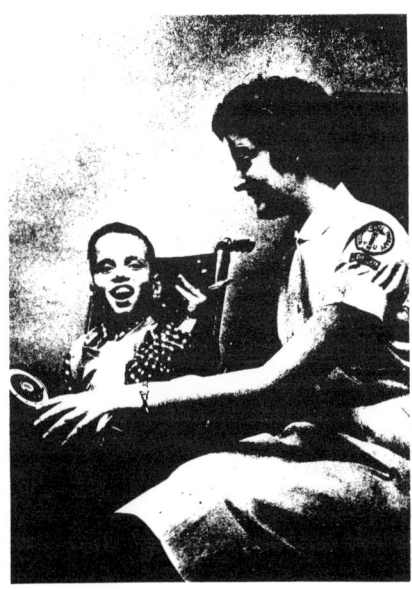

Programs at the Dallas and Houston Centers came to include occupational therapy and other programs in the health sciences.

Alumna Nelda C. Stark received the first honorary doctorate for TWU.

Mary Gibbs Jones received the second LL.D. degree awarded by TWU.

The alumna who wrote in the 1962 bulletin had no difficulty in identifying with the younger Tessies. "The models are newer and prettier—but they are still the same basic girl," she wrote. "Those of us who are part of the 'long chambray line' are glad to discover, as we see the University graduates, that the hallmark is still stamped on the girls."

In 1962, alumnae and students still had the original member of the long chambray line to measure themselves against. Beulah Kincaid Fry, the first graduate of GIC, lived in Denton, older than the Texas Woman's University but as modern as the age in which she lived. In the university bulletin of April 1, 1961, she reported her first jet plane flight to visit her children at Christmas. In 1964, she was honored at homecoming when the University for the first time recognized a sixtieth anniversary class. She was its only member.[17] Faculty members also had a link with the past through Lucy E. Fay, the only surviving member of the original faculty following the death of Charles Noble Adkisson on March 14, 1959.[18]

TWU graduates of the recent and distant past were not just alive, however; they were assuming and continuing their places in important careers throughout the country.[19] Kate Adele Hill, Chairman of the Past Presidents' Council of the Alumnae Association in 1961, compiled a report on the number of TWU alumnae identified as distinguished American women in the first edition of *Who's Who Among American Women* prepared by Marquis Who's Who, Inc. According to the report, printed in the university bulletin of November 15, 1961, Marquis listed 314 women from Texas. With sixty-eight alumnae listed, TWU had a higher percentage of its graduates included than any other college or university in the state.[20]

The second edition listed sixty-seven TWU alumnae, thirty-nine of whom were second-time entrants. Again Dr. Hill compiled information about the distinguished women and reported it in the university bulletin of July 15, 1962. The TWU women were scattered from California to Connecticut and from Arkansas and Florida to New York and Washington, D.C. Most of the women graduated in the twenties and thirties, but the list included women who graduated as early as 1911 and as late as 1954 as well as several women who received master's or doctor's degrees from TWU in 1959. The class with the greatest number of entries (five) was 1929.

Proud of its distinguished alumnae and of other outstanding women, TWU awarded four honorary doctorates to women between 1957 and 1964. The University conferred its first honorary Doctor of Laws degree on June 3, 1957, on alumna Nelda Childers Stark for "singularly and exceptionally high civic and humanitarian achievements." With her husband, H. Lutcher Stark, who was in the audience to see her receive the degree, Mrs. Stark had been successful in extensive business enterprises; and the two had shared their success generously. Their philanthropy ranged from small gifts for individuals to major contributions to institutions such as TWU.

The following year, the University gave its second LL.D. degree to Mary Gibbs Jones on June 1 for "singularly and exceptionally high personal, civic, humanitarian, and philanthropic achievements." Mrs. Jones, widow of Houston businessman Jesse H. Jones, had for some years been a special patron of women in education. Some thirty colleges and universities in Texas offered Mary Gibbs Jones Scholarships for women in nursing, home economics, liberal arts and sciences, American history, pediatrics, occupational therapy, physical therapy, business, and teacher training. She also financed scholarships and fellowships for research in geriatric nutrition, and she had recently given Rice Institute a handsome building for women students, The Mary Gibbs Jones College.

The first two honorary degrees were awarded at regular commencement exercises; but the third, the Doctor of Letters, was awarded Edith Alderman Deen in a special convocation November 4, 1959. Like Mrs.

Stark a TWU alumna and member of the TWU Board of Regents, Mrs. Deen was a pioneer journalist and a highly successful writer of inspirational books. The convocation coincided with the publication of her second book, *Great Women of the Christian Faith.* Her first book, *All of the Women of the Bible,* published in 1955, was in its fourteenth printing, soon to reach a circulation of 200,000 copies. Mrs. Deen pioneered the woman's page of the Fort Worth *Press,* writing the lead column from 1924 until her resignation in 1954. She received the B.A. degree from TWU in 1953 with an English-journalism major, and she was enrolled in master's studies when she received the honorary doctorate.

The fourth and final honorary degree to be awarded for a dozen years was conferred upon the first lady of the United States, Lady Bird Johnson. She received the LL.D. degree from TWU on March 31, 1964, for "magnificent achievements symbolic of the lofty goals for which the University strives in its educational programs for women leaders of the future." A special academic procession and convocation highlighted her five-hour visit to the campus; and she wrote to President Guinn upon her return to Washington, "I know of no honor that has ever come to me that has pleased me more."

As the long chambray line reached out to include a first lady of the United States, campus activities continued to reflect the long and strong ties which bound the TWU students of different generations together and began to demonstrate some of the differences which separated the contemporary students from their predecessors. Extracurricular events continued to center on old traditions, but many failed to elicit the widespread support and enthusiastic participation they had enjoyed in the past. Nevertheless, abundant activities continued for students who wished to take part.

The mid-September opening week of school described in the university bulletin of August 15, 1958, was typically busy. Monday's orientation for new students preceded a campus sing and free movie in the evening. Tuesday included registration and a musical concert by the faculty. The President held a reception for new students and other newcomers on Wednesday; and classes began on Thursday, which also included an afternoon assembly. The Women's Recreation Association sponsored Fun Night on Thursday, and on Friday students participated in the Lantern Parade and University Review.

Jo Greshman, President of the Student Council of Social Activities, described University Review in the university bulletin of April 15, 1967: "This brief skit will give you a small glimpse of what is in store for the coming year. At the close of the skit the SCSA President will introduce to you the head yell leader from Texas A&M, Student Body President, the Memorial Student Center President and the Commanding Officer of the Corps. These Aggies will give you a few tips about what can be expected at Aggie football games and will teach you a few Aggie yells." The annual Corps trip to Dallas or Fort Worth continued, and Aggies continued to select a "Tessie" sweetheart.

The rest of the fall semester remained almost as busy as the first week with the Student Finance Council sponsoring a rummage sale and a Howdy Dinner in September. Local churches sponsored parties; seniors were honored with a breakfast in late September; and myriad students worked on the Gold Rush Carnival in October.[21]

In early October, new students became a real part of the campus when they were allowed to remove their beanies at the Freshman Frolic; and literary-social clubs held a Pre-Rush Open House for interested students. Rush parties were scheduled about a month later. The number of literary-social clubs had dwindled to eight by the end of 1957, but all eight continued their affiliations with the Texas Federation of Women's Clubs.

Alumna and pioneer journalist Edith Alderman Deen received the University's third honorary doctorate.

First Lady Lady Bird Johnson visited the campus to receive the LL.D. degree in 1964.

A representative of the Texas A&M Corps "pins" the TWU student selected 1964 Aggie Sweetheart.

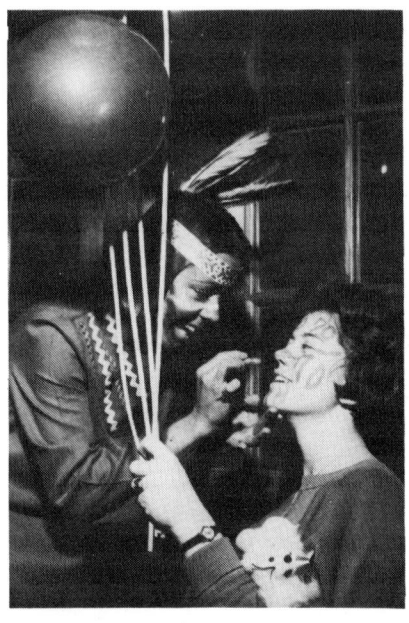

Stunts (above) and the Redbud Pageant (right) proceeded through their second decade.

Springtime traditions continued to center around Stunts and Redbud. The university bulletin of December 1, 1957, reported Stunts as a kind of second homecoming for alumnae. In 1960, the class of '60 became the first class to win the Stunts competition three times in a row and retire the silver loving cup. The class, which won with a blackface production of "Mighty Fine," was the first senior class to win since 1948.

Stunts hit a slump, however; and the university bulletin of March 15, 1966, included a letter from Kay Williams Goodman, writing under the pseudonym Agatha Exe, that reports had come that "death was hovering . . . over an old and dear friend of mine [Stunts]." Mrs. Exe explained the problem: "A stroke of apathy-plexy had greatly weakened her and the writer warned, she might not last the year." Making a desperate trip to Denton, however, Mrs. Exe found Stunts "in high good spirits. . . . She was bright and gay and clever. . . . Her death, if ever it is to come, seemed far away." Again that year, a class ('67) won Stunts for the third consecutive time; but when it attempted to accomplish a four-year sweep the following year, it lost to the sophomore class production of "Chalice in Blunderland."

More than twenty-five years old, Redbud, like Stunts, suffered from apathy; and the university bulletin of March 15, 1966, reported, "Following a study of the decreasing interest in TWU's annual Redbud Festival, an entirely new pageant has been chosen to replace it." The new pageant, to be known as Merienda, was held in place of Redbud in the spring of 1966 with a theme of "Carnival in Rio." It was proposed that the pageant be moved to the fall with a new theme each year, but Redbud returned the following spring. Most of the changes called for in Merienda were abandoned, but the number of princesses was reduced to thirty-six upperclass students and six freshman ladies-in-waiting, a reduction of approximately half.

The general lack of enthusiasm for extracurricular activities was reflected in other ways as well. Although college bulletins boasted a rich array of entertainment and cultural activities for summer school students, for example, a senior student who had attended summer school for two summers reported in the bulletin of May 1, 1959, "As a rule, sunbathing, reading 'that book you never got around to', and sleeping are the most preferred pastimes."

In the fall of 1963, to encourage attendance at the Concert and Drama Series, the University established the Earl C. Bryan Fine Arts Award through which the dorm with the highest percentage of its residents in

attendance each year would receive a plaque.[22] Homecoming activities were rescheduled in 1963 from their traditional commencement date to late April so that students might participate.[23]

Although some activities lagged, however, some traditions remained popular and strong. The university bulletin of August 1, 1957, reported, "More than a thousand weddings, varying from the most formal to the simplest day time ceremony with the bride in a traveling costume, have been held since the Chapel was built in 1939." Each wedding was carefully recorded in the chapel bride's book with its heavy copper cover inset with turquoise stones.

Traditional activities were designed to encourage widespread participation on campus, and selective performing groups gave talented young women opportunities to travel throughout the world. In 1962, fourteen Choraliers attended the second summer session to prepare for a four-week fall tour of U.S. military bases in the Caribbean.[24] Their tour included Guantanamo Naval Base in Cuba, where tensions were building toward an American-Russian showdown.

Folk tunes, western songs, and popular numbers from Broadway musicals comprised the group's repertoire; and the Choraliers proved so popular that they were among the first groups to be invited for a second tour. In September, 1964, fifteen girls—more than half of whom had participated in the Caribbean tour—left for a five-week tour of the Northeast Command—Newfoundland, Labrador, Greenland, and Iceland.

In mid-November of the following year, the TWU Serenaders, the University's fourteen-member stage band, began a seven-week tour of U.S. military installations in Germany, France, and Italy; and in the summer of 1966 the Lass-O Choraliers made their third tour, a two-month visit to military bases in France, Germany, and Italy.[25]

Although the Lass-O Band was too large for the USO tours, it was becoming an outstanding performing group. After only three years in existence, the band was almost as large as the TSCW Symphony had been in its heyday; and the university bulletin of September 15, 1959, reported, "It is being compared to the best bands in the country."[26]

The TWU Band reached a peak in size and reputation.

175

Bermuda shorts were an innovation in campus dress, worn only in limited situations.

The construction of the Arts and Sciences Building south of the Patio Building completed another courtyard on the campus.

Although uniform dress had been abolished more than twenty years earlier for TSCW students, students of the late fifties and early sixties were still expected to conform to dress codes, which were relaxed on only special occasions. The university bulletin of December 15, 1959, described Bermuda Night. On Tuesday nights, the SUB Rec Room, which was normally open to TWU students and their dates, was restricted to TWU students, who were permitted to wear sports clothes. In the university bulletin of April 15, 1961, Student Finance Council President Lou Ann Sebesta advised prospective students, "If you are a lover of casual attire, Bermuda Day will be a must for you. Wear bermudas plus an SFC tag and enjoy a cool, comfortable day in May."[27]

Like other colleges and universities of the period, TWU also enforced a strict residence requirement. The University mandated that all undergraduate students under twenty-three years of age live in its residential system unless married or actually living with parents or a court-appointed legal guardian. Strict enforcement of the rule necessitated extensive additions to the University's housing accommodations at the same time that the growing enrollment required new instructional and research space.

As the 1955-56 building program approached completion, TWU officials were planning to accommodate new needs. Following a year and a half of study, Guinn announced in the university bulletin of August 1, 1957, that Regents had approved a two-year $2.5 million expansion program for the University.[28] By December he could announce a loan of an additional $450,000 from the federal Community Facilities Administration to build a dormitory to house students in the cooperative system.

First priority in the six-building project, which began in 1958, was a new three-story unit of some 52,000 square feet of classrooms and offices.[29] An addition to the east side of the Bralley Memorial Library would double its capacity and virtually turn it around by changing its entrance from the west side, which faced the Pioneer Woman Statue, to the modern east side, which faced the Household Arts and Sciences Building.

A new dramatic arts facility just north of the University Hospital on Bell Avenue would provide a much-needed small auditorium and laboratory facilities for speech, drama, and radio majors. The addition of an aquatics unit with an indoor swimming pool would complete the three-sided HPER complex. And to the north of the golf course, away from the main campus, a new Demonstration School would provide facilities to train teachers of kindergarten through the sixth grade and of special education.[30] A new dormitory, located to the north-east of the tennis courts north of the Student Union Building, would accommodate 240 girls.

The university bulletin of August 15, 1958, reported work progressing rapidly on all six new buildings; and the bulletin of the following November 15 described the "mounds of mud, masses of steel framework, detailed blueprints, complicated machinery and busy construction crew" which characterized the site of work on the new classroom unit. The university bulletin of August 1, 1959, announced the completion of the Demonstration School and predicted that most of the new space would be ready for the opening of the fall session in mid-September. On April 1, 1960, the University dedicated the six new buildings and the Therapies Building, which was the old Demonstration School remodeled. The dedication marked the completion of a second major building program in three years.[31]

The new classroom unit, called the Arts and Sciences Building, was located to the south of the Classroom Unit constructed in 1956 and connected to it by covered walkways along the east and west sides of a courtyard. The new unit consisted of a three-story wing of classrooms and laboratories along the south side of the courtyard and a two-story wing of offices along the east side. The 1956 Classroom Unit bordered the courtyard on the north, and a long colonnade, parallel to Oakland Avenue on the west side, connected the two buildings.

Although the new unit was designed to be flexible enough to accommodate any component of the University, the original use of the building assigned the first floor to the English Department, the second floor to the Department of Business and Economics, and the third floor to the Department of Foreign Languages with classrooms and offices available on each floor for other departments such as sociology, history and government, and mathematics. The rapidly growing College of Nursing would soon offer its Denton courses in the unit formed by the Arts and Sciences Building and the 1956 Classroom Unit.

The building included a small automatic elevator for use by persons who because of physical disability could not use the stairways, and each floor was designed with central corridors and a lounge for women faculty members. All classrooms were given either north or south windows to make use of the most desirable natural light. Only offices had east or west windows, and roof overhangs protected west windows from the hot afternoon sun. Like all the instructional buildings still to be built, the Arts and Sciences Building was completely air conditioned.[32]

The building blended in color, design, and material with its neighboring Classroom Unit, and architects once again called on art faculty members concerning certain "embellishments." Herbert H. Tyrnauer of the Art Department selected the color schemes for the new building, and other selected members of the art faculty chose furnishings and general finishing of the interior.

Faculty members had their office equipment and other belongings moved to the new offices during the Christmas holiday of 1959; and before students in English, business, economics, and foreign languages left for the vacation, they were instructed to report to classes in the new building upon their return.

The university bulletin of March 15, 1960, attributed the need for the new Arts and Sciences Building to "the pressures of the growing enrollment of the University." Accompanying the growth of the student body and the growth of research activities and graduate studies was the growth of library holdings; and the university bulletin of August 1, 1959, carried Guinn's report that "The present library is full, with no more room for the very many books acquired each year."[33]

A $500,000 project added a new wing to the east of the existing library, more than doubling its capacity; remodeled, modernized, and redecorated all the old library except for a small part of the basement; and air conditioned both the old and new wings of the building. The result was a unified structure which attempted to blend the contemporary style of the new wing with the traditional style of the existing library.

In addition to doubling the library's storage capacity for books and periodicals, the new wing provided extra carrels and other spaces for advanced students, a work center for library services, and a large high-ceilinged reading room with tall windows. Exterior louvers controlled the sunlight, eliminating the need for interior shades. The new wing also joined with the old to form an interior reading patio.

Whereas college bulletins before the addition had reported some fourteen thousand books on open shelves, the university bulletin of December 15, 1959, advised that nearly all books, including books for reserve readings, and almost all current and bound magazines were readily available to students in open stacks or on open shelves in the reading rooms. The bulletin promised, "Only rare books and books whose use is limited to the building are in closed racks."[34]

Growth had demanded an expanded library; but even though the University's main auditorium had for many years been filled to capacity on

Again overcrowded, the Library received a major addition and a new face on its east side.

numerous occasions, TWU now needed not a larger auditorium but a smaller one for lectures, recitals, opera workshops, group meetings, and theatrical productions which lent themselves to an intimate setting. Thus, the University built the Redbud Auditorium Building, named for TWU's spring festival and contemporary in every way.

Behind the stage were the spaces that made the building functional for instruction. Radio and television studios featured special acoustical treatment, including double walls and ceilings and isolated foundations for soundproofing. Adjacent to the studios were equipment control rooms, observation rooms, and class areas. By the fall of 1960, Mr. and Mrs. H. Lutcher Stark had contributed closed-circuit television equipment for the use of students in the Speech Department and for experimental use as an instructional resource in other areas.[35]

Costume storage space and dressing areas connected with the stage by an enclosed passage; and a laboratory stage shop for building and painting sets adjoined the stage, which was described in the university bulletin of August 1, 1959, as one of the most modern in the South.[36] Elaborate controls regulated both stage and audience lighting, and removable traps in the stage floor opened into a full trap basement for use in the productions and for the storage of equipment. Seating consisted of 332 comfortable auditorium seats, padded, covered in a soft blue cloth, and arranged in tiers. The foyer of the auditorium looked toward the east through large glass windows and glass doors into a small courtyard, shielded from Bell Avenue by a serpentine wall.

The construction of the Aquatics Center formed the southern boundary of a much larger courtyard that was already bordered on three sides by the existing HPER complex. The major part of the center was the sound-proof pool room from which one could look through a full glass wall into a landscaped courtyard to the north. The south wall of the room was occupied by a gallery with a seating capacity for some five hundred spectators. Under the raised bleacher seating were classrooms, offices, and equipment storage.

The completely-tiled pool was the standard AAU size (42' x 75') with two one-meter diving boards and a three-meter diving board. Radiant heating insured that swimmers would be uniformly comfortable in the pool and on the surrounding deck. A control room for a sound system and for underwater and overhead general lighting overlooked the pool, and an underwater observation window allowed controlled viewing of swimmers and provided for underwater photography. An enclosed passageway connected the dressing room for the pool with the original Gymnasium Building.[37]

The new Demonstration School featured a number of special safety features such as a one-story design that eliminated the use of stairs by small children, off-street drives and parking, and a fenced playground. It also included four classrooms especially for mentally retarded and orthopedically handicapped children, and certain areas of the building included handrails for the handicapped.[38] The large classrooms were well lighted both naturally and artificially; and each room had not only built-in work cabinets, storage work counters, and clothes cupboards, but also a sink and drinking fountain. The building included a library; and Hubbard Hall served food in the cafeteria area, which could be converted to use as a group meeting room with the addition of a portable stage.

The Demonstration School was the first of the new buildings to be completed; and as soon as the old Demonstration School at the corner of Bell and Texas Streets was vacated, remodeling began to make it suitable for occupancy by the Nursery School, the School of Occupational Therapy, and the speech therapy division of the Department of Speech. Among the new features of the building were clinical areas equipped with

(Top to bottom) Redbud Auditorium provided new dramatic arts facilities. An indoor pool completed the HPER complex. A new demonstration school displaced two of the holes of the golf course north of University Drive (U.S. 380) to provide instruction for students in kindergarten through the first grade and for special education.

one-way glass panels for viewing from elevated observation galleries and a large shop laboratory for occupational therapy students. The building was renamed the Therapies Building following its remodeling.

In the midst of the construction that was making marked changes in the Denton Campus, the University was also building instructional facilities almost three hundred miles away in Houston. Financed by contributions from the M. D. Anderson Foundation and from Houston Endowment, Inc., construction of a multistory instructional and residential building in the heart of the Texas Medical Center in 1960 approximately doubled clinical training facilities for TWU nursing students. Constructed mainly of brick with exterior decorative solar tile, a two-story instructional wing sat atop a garage for faculty cars and adjoined a seven-story student residential wing.

Five years later, late in the summer of 1965, TWU, which had been conducting its Dallas nursing instruction in Parkland Hospital facilities, began construction of a one-story instructional building, adjoined by a seven-story residence hall. Located in the Parkland/Southwestern Medical Center complex near the intersection of Inwood Road and Stemmons Expressway, the $2.5 million project was dedicated on November 10, 1966, with Governor John Connally as the principal speaker.

Although construction, except for residence halls, virtually ceased on the Denton Campus in the few years after 1960, planning did not stop. The razing of the old Home Economics Building (the second oldest building on campus) in 1960 made space for a proposed modern biology building.[39] By March 15, 1965, plans for an $800,000 building to be used for graduate research had been formed, and the University had received a grant of $130,625 from the National Science Foundation to be matched from funds already on hand and from moneys expected in the near future. The grant stipulated that the building be used for no less than five years for graduate research in biology and chemistry.

By the following spring the University had received a second grant, $134,654 from the U.S. Office of Education, to apply toward the building, where a basement and ground floor would provide more than 23,000 feet of floor space. The plan subsequently included a third floor, which increased the cost of the building to more than $1 million. Construction began in the winter of 1966, and the new Graduate Science Research Building opened in the fall of 1967.

In addition to providing instructional and research facilities for its students, the University continued to build dormitories; for it had since its earliest days prided itself on being a residential campus where young women could learn in their homes as well as in their classrooms and laboratories. Since 1934, the University had provided special economical housing in a cooperative system of small frame buildings where girls did their own cooking and cleaning.

In 1957 the University received a federal loan to construct a two-story brick dormitory, Mary Hufford Hall, to house 240 girls and replace the eight frame buildings which comprised the cooperative system at the time.[40] Different in design from the existing dormitories, the building— designed by Page, Southerland, Page, Architects—offered a preview of features that would become almost standard in the remaining dormitories to be built on the Denton Campus.[41]

In place of the long corridors characteristic of the existing dormitories, the new hall was arranged in fifteen clusters of four rooms. Each cluster had its own outside entrance. Each room accommodated four girls. And all rooms had either a north or south exposure for ventilation and lighting. Each room had its own bath, separate built-in dressers, desks, bookshelves, and clothes hanging spaces. Curtain dividers separated study areas from sleeping areas in the room.

Mary Hufford Hall, named for a TWU faculty member and Dean of Women, provided a residence for students formerly housed in the nine-building cooperative system.

A new senior dormitory (above) was named for Mary Gibbs Jones. Her portrait in oil was presented at the dedication of the hall (below).

Because girls in Hufford Hall would continue to prepare and serve their own meals under professional supervision, the dormitory had its own kitchen and dining hall where meals were served cafeteria-style. According to the university bulletin of September 15, 1959, girls spent about an hour a day "planning menus for the week, making the living room shine, and stirring up cookies for supper." Between meals the dining hall could serve as a study room.

With new cooperative housing completed in 1959, Guinn announced in the university bulletin of November 15, 1960, plans for a $1.1 million dormitory to be located between, but to the east of, Smith-Carroll Hall and the Student Union Building. It would stand on the site of the old frame buildings of the Rusk Cooperative System.

Rising enrollment had filled all the University's dormitories when Guinn made the announcement; and senior students, for whom the dormitory was planned, voted to live in temporary housing on campus during its construction. Work progressed rapidly from groundbreaking on February 22, 1961, to completion in November, 1961, and dedication on December 11.[42]

Named Mary Gibbs Jones Hall, the new 2 1/2-story structure was designed to accommodate 332 students in double rooms. Among special features of the building were "ample parking" and a patio. Like all the residential and instructional buildings which would be built during the rest of Guinn's tenure, the dormitory was centrally air conditioned and heated. Upon completion of Jones Hall, Stoddard Hall was converted to the use of sophomores.

At about this time the newly widened and paved Bell Avenue increased traffic through the campus, creating hazards for the growing number of students who lived to the east of the busy street. Thus, in late 1961, the University approved the general design by Page, Southerland, Page of an overhead pedestrian bridge. Financed by the federal Housing and Home Finance Agency, construction on the bridge across Bell Avenue just south of the old gymnasium and the SUB began in the spring of 1962.

Even with the new residence halls, dormitory space was barely keeping pace with the needs of the growing enrollment. The university bulletin of November 15, 1963, reported "bulging" dormitories; and Housing Coordinator Herb Gibson said, "All of the dormitories are comfortably filled." According to Gibson, Smith-Carroll Hall was filled to capacity; Mary Hufford was overflowing into Reagan Houston Hall; and "Mary Gibbs Jones has fewer vacancies than ever. . . . There are only a few vacancies in the entire housing system."

The university bulletin of March 15, 1964, reported that TWU Regents had authorized construction of another "ultra-modern million-dollar-plus dormitory for 300 undergraduate students" to be located adjacent to and east of Mary Gibbs Jones Hall. By mid-summer, construction was underway; and students first occupied the dormitory, John A. Guinn Hall, in September, 1965.[43] Seventy-five suites of two double rooms accommodated three hundred students in considerable privacy. Each suite included a private bath, and each room had a jack to allow the installation of private telephones.

Visitors to the new dorm were generous with their praise. The college bulletin of February 15, 1965, recorded the comments of English faculty member Gladys Maddocks at the time of the dedication on October 5, 1964: "For once I'm speechless. . . . At last they've solved the problem of noise in the halls. I love the view from the balconies and the green grass everywhere you look. It wasn't like that in my days. I lived in Capps."

Less than a year after the third new dormitory, Guinn announced at spring commencement, 1965, the most ambitious project to date on the campus—another dormitory. The proposed 21-story tower would change not only the skyline of the campus but that of Denton as well, for it would be the first skyscraper in the city.[44]

The $3.2 million project, financed by revenue bonds issued by the University, was named to honor alumna Nelda C. Stark. The building, which would rise near the intersection of Bell Avenue and University Drive, would be, according to Guinn, "symbolic of TWU's pioneering spirit as it looks forward zestfully to new and wider horizons of service."

Groundbreaking ceremonies on December 27 were a time of self-congratulation for members of the TWU family. The university bulletin of March 15, 1966, captured the feeling of many in the remarks of Harriett Cobb, President of the Young Democrats: "Congratulations to us all. We're on our way UP."

The ground floor of the new building included office space and a large reception area, and two mezzanine apartments housed the directors of the hall. Each of the remaining stories provided sixteen double rooms for student residence; and floors were arranged in pairs to create the effect of living in a two-story dwelling. Even-numbered floors included a living room area with a small kitchenette. Residents of the odd-numbered floors could look over an inside balcony to the living room area below. They also had access to outside balconies; and odd-numbered floors had space for typing, storage, and other uses. Each room had a private bath and jacks for the installation of private phones.

With each pair of floors creating a comfortable unit for sixty-four young women, the building could accommodate 640 undergraduate students—almost twice as many as the next largest dormitory. Because the building was remote from the central dining unit, a one-story dining room joined the tower on the west. All noisy equipment used in food preparation and dishwashing was isolated in a basement under the dining room.

In addition to the more or less regular features such as a coin-operated laundry, storage rooms, and an intercom system, the hall had four high-speed elevators and, atop the building, a sun deck. It also provided special security advantages and a spectacular view of Denton and its surroundings.

Ramona Stark participated in the groundbreaking ceremonies for the twenty-one-story residence hall which would bear the name of Nelda C. Stark.

Rayzor Hall, just south of the Denton square, provided housing and meals for graduate students.

When students moved into the new tower in the fall of 1967, the charges for room and board reflected the luxury of the new hall. Costs ranged from $380 to $435 per semester, according to the TWU housing bulletin of August 15, 1967. The least expensive accommodations at the time were in Mary Hufford Hall, the cooperative dormitory, where costs ranged from $230 to $250 per semester. On dormitory row freshmen could live in Sayers Hall for $270 to $310 per semester; and upperclassmen could live in Fitzgerald Hall for $280 to $310 per semester. Accommodations in Guinn Hall were nearest in price to those in Stark, ranging from $370 to $390 per semester.[45]

Although Stark Hall was the tallest building on the campus, even the tallest residence hall in the nation, it was not the University's first venture into high-rise construction. A seven-story dormitory in the heart of the Texas Medical Center in Houston had housed TWU nursing students there since its completion in 1960. The ground floor of the building featured a large reception-recreation area, guest rooms, and offices. The building included 118 double rooms and four rooms which would each accommodate three girls.

Also in 1960 the University acquired a five-story air conditioned building located less than a mile from the campus near downtown Denton to serve as one of the first residence halls for graduate students in the South. The sixty-room Southern Hotel was closed for business on February 24, 1960. Effective March 1, the owners of the hotel, Mr. and Mrs. J. Newton Rayzor of Houston, leased the building to the TWU Foundation, through an arrangement which provided for the eventual transfer of title to the Foundation.

Because of difficulties in securing adequate parking for student residents, the Rayzors contributed $20,000 to the Foundation so that it could purchase a parking lot across Locust Street from the property. By summer, the University had the Graduate Student Center in operation with rooms available for summer students and, in time, for other mature students and some women faculty members.

Named Rayzor Hall to honor the University's benefactors, the building offered economical housing in forty-one single rooms and six double rooms. Prices for single rooms quoted in the university bulletin of August 15, 1967, ranged from $168 to $195 per semester plus meals, which were served a la carte in the hall's coffee shop/dining room every day except Sunday. Parking was provided at no cost, and students who shared one of the double rooms could stay for $136 to $175 per semester plus meals.

Only months before the beginning of construction on Stark Hall, the University also began a seven-story dormitory for nursing students in Dallas. Its 160 double rooms contained private baths, jacks for private telephones, and outside balconies. As the fall semester, 1967, began, TWU housed most of its undergraduate students and a few graduate students in more than a dozen large dormitories.[46]

While new buildings made marked changes in the appearance of the campus, other changes were occurring inside some of the buildings. On June 1, 1958, Guinn announced to the sweltering commencement crowd in the Main Auditorium that Nelda Childers Stark, who was present with her husband, had given funds to air condition the building. Work began almost immediately on the project so that it could be completed in time for the orientation of new students in the fall.

In the SUB, a new student lounge, described in the university bulletin of December 15, 1959, as "semi-modern" opened from 8:00 to 5:00 each day for students, clubs, and organizations to gather; and the bulletin of March 15, 1962, reported that a new kitchen in the SUB with stove, refrigerator, silverware, dishes, and even a kitchen sink had made a long-standing dream of CGA officers come true.[49]

In the fall of 1965, remodeling of the basement of Hubbard Hall converted the Little Theater area into a new dining hall with an atmosphere completely different from that of the other dining rooms in the building. The hall featured new lighting and a color scheme of white, blue and gray with accents of red, yellow, and blue. Double lines speeded up service.

Even the University's oldest building bore evidence of progress as the university bulletin of November 15, 1966, reported that the fifty-year-old manually operated elevator in the Education Building (Old Main) "has carried its last passengers." Carl Hill, who had served both as the elevator operator and as a kind of informal information center for the past thirty years, took another assignment on the campus; and one of the first elevators in Denton retired to make way for an automatic, push-button model.

Changes in other areas reflected that TWU was continuing to fulfill its original legislative obligation of preparing its students "for the practical industries of the age." Whereas original college equipment had included churns, ironing boards, and cream testers, the atomic age required scientific equipment such as that described for the Department of Chemistry in the university bulletin of January 1, 1964: "such items as a neutron source, a 1500 curie cobalt-60 gamma irradiator, infra-red spectrophotometer, Cary spectrophotometer, hydrogenation equipment, gas chromatograph, aerograph autoprep, automatic titrimeter, scintillation spectrophotometer, other types of counting equipment, and automatic fractionation equipment."

Whereas the original curriculum had included theoretical work in laundering and dairying, the university bulletin of November 15, 1960, described facilities for "teaching the principles of neutron detection, neutron reactions, and chemical analysis by neutron activation." In spite of the many and dramatic changes which had occurred, however, TWU still taught many of the subjects that it had always taught although they had come to have modern applications that were undreamed of when GIC began classes. Long-established subjects such as woodworking, mechanical drawing, pottery, clay modeling, and china painting were still offered in the occupational therapy laboratories; and the early "theoretical work in laundering" had developed into sophisticated research in various phases of textile chemistry and detergency.

Nonscientific areas were keeping pace as well. Along with the highly technical equipment added for scientific research was a seventy-seven-rank Sipe-Yarbrough pipe organ, announced in the university bulletin of September 15, 1967, as an addition to the Main Auditorium for the use of students and faculty.

The needs of TWU were becoming increasingly complex and expensive. Guinn told the alumnae at their homecoming luncheon in 1962, "For a country school, I think that we are doing pretty well"; but, he hastened to add, "We are not interested in size but in quality. . . . This is not a time when we can afford the luxury of being idle or taking things for granted." Neither Guinn nor the University under his leadership was likely to make such a mistake.

As TWU reached the end of its first decade as a University, it was still looking toward the future with plans for its first high-rise instructional building, a fourteen-story tower of classrooms and offices, and for other additions to meet projected expansion. Early in the spring semester of 1967 Guinn announced plans for the general-purpose classroom and office tower, for a second tower dormitory, and for a student center and mall.

In addition, plans called for the finishing of the library basement, which had been constructed at the beginning of the decade and left unfinished until it was needed. It would accommodate some sixty thousand volumes, making increased space for reading, storage, and library staff work available on the ground floor.

By mid-summer, excavation for the tower office and classroom building had begun; the post office and University Book Store had been moved from Brackenridge Hall so that it could be demolished to make way for the new Student Center; and the University had received a grant of almost $54,000 for an addition to the Library Science Building because the library science program, especially at the graduate level, had outgrown the building constructed for it only eleven years earlier. The future of TWU continued to look ''rosy with promise,'' but it would not be without its shadows.

On June 4, 1967, TWU conferred 469 degrees at its spring commencement, almost twice as many as it had awarded ten years before. The Main Auditorium was jammed. The occasion was joyful. But the tone of the President's remarks was somber: ''It is my deep concern and earnest prayer that all those many forces, internal and external, which are working overtime to undermine our national strength and national resolve will never prevail.''

CHAPTER X—NOTES

[1]Assistant Commissioner of Higher Education David Hunt predicted a total enrollment of 147,050 students at state-supported institutions in 1966 and projected an enrollment of 368,000 students in 1978.

[2]A constitutional amendment election in the fall of 1965 had secured approval of an increased allocation from ad valorum taxes for college construction. These funds were expected to provide approximately seventy-five percent of the $200 million, with the remainder coming from federal funds. Eighty-five percent of the funds would be distributed June 1, 1966, with the remainder allocated in 1972.

[3]Although science received the most publicity, other areas remained strong. High school girls could participate in the all-girl band and choral school in the summers. By 1965 the federal government had broadened the scope of its interest, and TWU received grants of more than $72,000 from the United States Office of Education to add summer institutes for secondary English teachers and for elementary and secondary school librarians.

[4]Grants from the Atomic Energy Commission and from Mr. and Mrs. H. Lutcher Stark enabled the University to equip the laboratory, which included a sub-critical neutron source. Guinn estimated the value of equipment at $550,000 in the university bulletin of July 15, 1964.

[5]TWU is the only woman's institution to be accepted for membership in the Institute, a combination of selected universities and the U.S. Atomic Energy Commission to work toward peaceful uses of atomic energy. The organization is now known as the Oak Ridge Associated Universities.

[6]See Chapter IX for the background of TWU in bone density studies.

[7]Bill Odom from Denton had completed two years of study in pharmacy at the University of Texas. Rondle Littlejohn from St. Louis, Missouri, was just beginning studies in business administration. Bryce Kraft from Lewisville, Nebraska, had taught elementary school near Sitka, Alaska, and planned to enter the Peace Corps. John Odom was from Sanger, Texas. Each young man received financial aid toward his college studies as a result of his participation in the research.

[8]During the rest periods all activity ceased. The subjects had no visitors and engaged in no activities. Although special glasses enabled them to read or watch television while lying flat on their backs, orderlies had to change the television channels and turn the pages of the books. They also spoon-fed the subjects, bathed them, and even brushed their teeth. Between the bed rest periods, subjects did some work in the research labs. Frequent x-rays compared bone density values while the men were engaged in normal activities with values during periods of inactivity.

[9]Pauline Beery Mack and her assistants made periodic x-rays of the astronauts' feet and hands during a ten-day pre-flight period up to 220 minutes before launch at the Kennedy Space Center and at scheduled post-flight intervals at the manned Spacecraft Center until the bone density values returned to preflight levels. George Vose assisted by taking x-rays on the primary ship immediately after the recovery of the astronauts and on the recovery ship from forty-eight to seventy-two hours postflight.

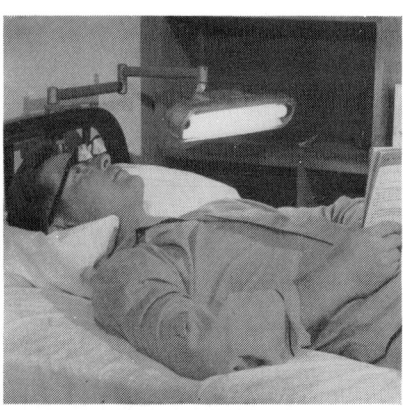

Prismatic glasses allowed participants in research projects which demanded complete bedrest to read, but someone else had to turn the pages.

Grady Dozier and B. J. Stover assisted Dr. Mack. Others who assisted in the project where Ralph E. Pike, Elsa Dozier, and Walter Gilchrist, who conducted metabolic analyses during the bed rest studies; Betty Alford, who served as chief nutritionist; and Jessie Ashby and Reba Fry, who conducted the statistical analysis of data.

[10]The Commission was the forerunner of the Coordinating Board, Texas College and University System.

[11]Texas students who lived in Jeff Davis, Pecos, Crockett, Schleicher, Menard, Mason, Llano, Burnet, Williamson, Milam, Robertson, Madison, Walker, San Jacinto, Polk, Tyler, Jasper, or Newton County or counties to the south of these in Texas and students who lived in Louisiana were assigned to the Houston Center. Students who lived to the north of these counties in Texas or in New Mexico, Oklahoma, or Arkansas were assigned to the Dallas Center. Students from other states were assigned to whichever center their parents chose.

[12]In addition the University continued to offer the Kress Foundation Practical Nursing Program. The university bulletin of August 1, 1960, reported that the program had received full accreditation by the National Association for Practical Nurse Education and Service, Inc., following a survey visit; and the university bulletin of June 15, 1962, reported accreditation by the Texas State Board of Vocational Nurse Examiners.

[13]The University bulletin of July 15, 1965, reported the results of a follow-up study of the graduates of the College of Nursing. The program had graduated four hundred students since 1958, and seventy-eight percent of the graduates responded to a questionnaire. Of the respondents, 71.89% (243) were employed, and 73.25% of those (178) were employed in Texas. Seventy-six percent of the students who studied in Dallas were still in that area, and seventy-five percent of the students educated in Houston remained in Harris County. The greatest number (59.26%) were employed in civilian hospitals with nine percent in federal hospitals, eight percent in public health nursing, eight percent in doctors' offices, seven percent in schools of nursing, five percent in school health, and four percent in other jobs.

[14]Robert A. Hall, Chairman of the TWU Board of Regents, reported the figures in his dedicatory remarks on that date and cited TWU as the largest nationally accredited college of nursing in the entire South.

[15]The program has been transferred to the Department of Art.

[16]Courses would be offered for freshmen and sophomores by the fall of 1966; for freshmen, sophomores, and juniors by the fall of 1967; and for all classes by the fall of 1968.

[17]Guinn read to the assembled alumnae a telegram to the class and the University from the four children of first CIA President and Mrs. Cree T. Work: "Our parents were proud and fond of their G.I.C.-C.I.A. girls. We follow the success and achievements of your great university with warm interest always. All good wishes to the first graduating class of Texas Woman's University and to those who followed." The telegram was signed by Florence Work Gillis, Telford Work, Isabel Work Huycks, and Arch Work.

[18]Adkisson had retired in 1939; but he lived in Denton and continued his close ties with TWU. Lucy Fay lived in Chapel Hill, N.C. In the university bulletin of April 1, 1961, she reported that she nurtured her interest in politics by listening to the radio and reading the newspaper with a magnifying glass. The University received word of Miss Fay's death in January, 1968.

[19]Perhaps the most widely-publicized alumna of the period was Janie Foster Fletcher of the class of 1919. Many papers throughout the nation carried the front page story in early 1962 of her response to President Kennedy's invitation to the American people to serve their country and the world. After serving as a home demonstration agent in the State Extension Service for twenty-three years, Mrs. Fletcher had retired only to return to home demonstration work in Brazil where she would work for the National 4-H Foundation under contract to the Peace Corps to teach farm wives and prospective housewives to use their resources and to maintain good health. Mrs. Fletcher had received bachelor's and master's degrees from TWU. She was a former member and secretary of the TWU Board of Regents and past president of the TWU Alumnae Association. She was included in the first and second editions of *Who's Who of American Women*.

[20]With ninety-four graduates listed, the University of Texas was the only school in the state with a greater number of former students included. Its larger enrollment, however, gave it a smaller percentage than TWU.

[21]The carnival attracted large crowds to the campus and continued to add significant contributions to the TWU Foundation treasury. The university bulletin of November 15, 1958, reported, "Despite a rainy opening, the University's annual Gold Rush Carnival drew a crowd of approximately 6,000 persons"; and the downtown parade contained fifty-one entries including dormitory floats decorated with fantasyland themes. The following fall seven thousand persons attended in spite of rain which delayed the carnival two days, and individual dormitory displays replaced the downtown parade.

[22]After thirty-three years of service to the University, Earl C. Bryan had retired as Director of the Department of Speech the previous year.

[23]One area of renewed interest during the period was the Daughters of Alumnae Club. Organized in 1946 with more than fifty members, it had remained active through 1956. The club was reactivated November 6, 1961, with the election of Judy Connor as temporary chairman. She was not only the daughter of an alumna, but the niece of four alumnae (her

This float won Capps Hall freshmen second place in the 1957 Gold Rush Carnival Parade.

185

Windows and lighting made underwater photography possible in the indoor pool.

The addition to the Library included a major reading/reference area.

mother's sisters), one of whom, Florence Langford, was and still is a member of the faculty of the College of Nutrition, Textiles, and Human Development.

[24]According to the university bulletin of July 15, 1964, the first group to tour during the first year of the project, sponsored by the National Music Council and the USO, was the Choraliers.

[25]On their way to Europe, the group serenaded Senator Ralph Yarborough, Congressmen J.J. Pickle, George Bush, Jim Wright, and Abraham Kazan, and staff members of other members of the Texas delegation with a concert in the rotunda of the Senate Office Building in Washington, D.C.

[26]Along with contributions for research and campus improvements, Mr. and Mrs. H. Lutcher Stark also contributed funds to equip the Lass-O Band.

[27]Although uniforms were no longer required for general wear, there was a rapidly growing number of students (nursing, occupational therapy, and other majors) who were required to have uniforms. The university bulletin of January 15, 1964, advised, "The [nursing] students will be required to purchase one uniform, including shoes and hose, at the beginning of the spring semester of the freshman year." At the beginning of the fall semester of the sophomore year, students needed, in addition, five uniforms, five University decals, eight aprons, eight fichus, and four caps. Total uniform costs were approximately $75.00; and students also had to purchase "a watch with a sweep-second hand, a Taber's Medical Dictionary, [and] a tailored navy blue or black coat."

[28]Expansion would be financed from the constitutional tax amendment fund shared by all state colleges.

[29]Page, Southerland, Page, Architects designed the buildings and supervised their construction.

[30]The school would occupy the space which formerly accommodated two holes of the University golf course. The two holes were moved across to the south side of the highway.

[31]A dedication convocation preceded open houses and programs at the various new facilities. The Demonstration School displayed student works; and Frank L. Williams, assistant superintendent for instruction for the Dallas Independent School District, delivered the dedicatory address in the evening. The Aquatics Center offered a demonstration of water sports, competitive swimming, life saving, diving, and swimming instruction. Redbud activities included the presentation of the freshman theater class in *King Woodenhead's Crown,* an original children's play by faculty member Josh P. Roach, tours of the building, and an evening concert by Dr. and Mrs. Wilgus Eberly.

[32]The first floor included ten classrooms, two seminar rooms, and an English study hall plus seven single offices. Seven classrooms on the second floor housed modern typing and business equipment; and the floor included fourteen single offices, eight double offices, and a quadruple office. The top floor included faculty offices plus eight classrooms and laboratories equipped with the latest electronic machinery for language study. In addition, to meet a growing need for larger classes, the floor included a lecture room with 194 seats arranged in a tiered semi-circle.

[33]Among the additions to the library holdings were two special collections. The university bulletin of March 15, 1960, reported the gift of rare cookbooks and additional miscellaneous items by Mrs. P.R. Gilmer of Shreveport, Louisiana. The collection consisted of three main sections—cookbooks dating back to the 1850s; loose-leaf binders of recipes and clippings for kinds of food and reports of food served on special excursions; and hundreds of menu cards from hotels, restaurants, and clubs and from rail, air, and steamship lines.

The second collection was established in 1965 by the TWU Alumnae Association. As the first step toward establishing TWU Archives, the alumnae initiated a collection of all books written by graduates of CIA, TSCW, or TWU. Edith Deen was the first to contribute, giving the three books she had written. By the fall of 1966 the collection included more than forty books, which were shelved in a specially built mahogany book case near the front door of the main reading room in the Bralley Memorial Library. The collection continues to grow steadily.

[34]By August, 1966, regular library holdings had grown to 288,160 volumes and 1350 periodical subscriptions; and the American Library Association rated the library "141 Per Cent Adequate," according to a report in the university bulletin of March 15, 1967. Of Texas' twenty-two tax-supported institutions, only the University of Texas (150%) and Sul Ross State (101.8%) besides TWU were judged one hundred percent adequate.

Library facilities at the clinical centers were provided through the staff library and unit library in each clinical area at Parkland Memorial Hospital and through the Texas Medical Center Library located in the Jesse H. Jones Building, which opened in the summer of 1954.

[35]The University bulletin of November 15, 1960, reported the installation of three television cameras, two monitors, audio and switching units, cable and all accessories needed to make the equipment operational. Students immediately put the equipment to use.

The College of Nursing also used the facilities when it established its new nursing laboratory in the basement of Lowry Hall. The university bulletin of March 15, 1965, reported that the use of closed circuit television enabled all students in the lab to have an equally clear view as they watched their instructors and other students employ nursing skills with "patients" in the lab.

[36]The storage and dressing space was built in 1917 as a dairy barn. Eventually known as Willard Hall, it was converted from a dairy barn to a storeroom for canned goods used in the Lowry and Brackenridge dining halls. Then it was remodeled and used for a time as an isolation ward for hygeia before it was completely redone for the nursery school.

[37]By 1964 gymnastic equipment such as a trampoline, balance beams, a vaulting box and vaulting horse, uneven parallel bars, tumbling mats, stall bars, and other equipment had been added to the facilities in the old gymnasium.

[38]Shadow Lawn, which had served as TWU's school for handicapped children, was destroyed by the first fire on campus for many years during Easter vacation, 1958.

[39]The wrecking company cleaned and sold the bricks and lumber from the building, but TWU stored its towering columns for later use.

[40]The dormitory was named to honor the TWU Dean of Women who died in a Houston hospital April 23, 1959, during heart surgery. Daughter of a distinguished Texas educator, C.H. Hufford, Dean Hufford had earned the B.A., M.A., and Ph.D. degrees from the University of Texas at Austin. A member of the faculty of the TWU English Department from 1929 to 1949, Dr. Hufford served as Dean of Women from 1949 until her death.

Requests continued to exceed the 240-girl limit so that students had to be carefully screened for evidence of need and, if approved, housed temporarily in a frame building while they waited for space in Hufford Hall.

[41]Page, Southerland, Page served as architects for all dormitories subsequently built on the Denton campus and for the dormitory at the Dallas Center.

[42]Funds for the dormitory came through a federal housing loan program of the Housing and Home Finance Agency, which enabled colleges and universities to obtain long-term loans and low interest rates for housing.

[43]At the 1964 homecoming, alumnae greeted Kate Adele Hill's suggestion of naming the dorm for the TWU President with a standing ovation and unanimously approved the idea at their annual business meeting. The Board of Regents adopted the name at a subsequent meeting.

For Guinn's fifteenth anniversary as President of TWU, Regents commissioned Dallas artist Victor Lallier to paint a portrait, which was hung in Guinn Hall on November 10, 1966. At the unveiling ceremonies, Judge Robert A. Hall, Chairman of the TWU Board of Regents, described Guinn as a man "who knows where he is going and how to get there." According to the university bulletin of November 15, 1966, Guinn received the praise and the portrait rather modestly, apologizing to the residents of the dormitory, "I am only sorry that here in Guinn Hall you could not have had something like George Hamilton or Gregory Peck."

[44]The placement of elevator housing and other equipment on top of the building gave it the height of a twenty-second story.

[45]As it had from its earliest days, TWU attempted to minimize students' costs. Characterizing charges as "very moderate," the university bulletin of September 1, 1957, estimated total costs for nine months at $648. The cost covered a room in a regular dormitory, meals, tuition, textbooks (which the University provided at no cost), medical and linen fees (the University provided bed linens and laundered them for students in the regular dormitories), and activity fees which included a season ticket to all Concert and Drama Series programs.

Ten years later, students could still attend nine months for as little as $721 in the regular system or $641 in the cooperative system, an increase of approximately twelve percent. According to the university bulletin of February 1, 1967, TWU had added a $10 charge for the rental of textbooks; and student services fees had risen from $40 to $52; but tuition remained fixed at $50 per semester, and students could still receive room and board for as little as $520 per year plus a sales tax of $7. Costs for room and board at both clinical centers ranged from $340 to $370 per semester according to the university bulletin of August 15, 1967.

[46]Students over twenty-three years of age were not permitted in the undergraduate dormitories, but they could live in Rayzor Hall or in one of the University-owned apartments which TWU maintained for graduate students with families.

[47]Mary Ann Odom, an interior design graduate of the class of 1959, planned the lounge. She had also designed a popular TWU emblem to be worn on blazers.

For his fifteenth anniversary as President of TWU, Regents presented the University a portrait of President Guinn to hang in the dormitory named for him.

Seniors lead classmates in a traditional yell.

Bright with Promise and Exhilarating with Challenge

XI

When *Lass-O* editor Sharla Marks asked President Guinn in the fall of 1967 what his biggest problem was, he responded, "At the moment the rate of growth and development and diversification with the University is so great we don't quite keep up with it in terms of staff. Growth is our biggest problem." Projections estimated an increase in enrollment of more than one hundred per cent at TWU and across Texas during the next dozen years on top of the increase at TWU during the seventeen years of Guinn's administration. The growth demanded increased facilities, staff, and course offerings; and the changing nature of the student body called for adjustments in both the University's academic and nonacademic services. As Guinn approached the end of his twentieth year as President of TWU in the spring of 1970, he wrote for the Denton *Record-Chronicle* of February 10, "The prospects for the '70's are bright with promise and exhilarating with challenge." The promises and challenges would be virtually inextricable, and they would affect every aspect of campus life.

Although TWU students and alumnae for many years had sung in their "Alma Mater" about the buildings, "crowned with majesty" which rose on "broad and rolling plains,/'Neath Texas skies," none of the buildings had risen more than four stories on the Denton campus and seven at the Dallas and Houston centers until Stark Hall opened with its twenty-one stories in the fall of 1967. In the next ten years, buildings of ten, thirteen, and twenty-four stories would rise on the Denton campus; and the facilities at the Houston Center would rise to twelve stories. Construction would also begin on a seventeen-story tower on the Denton campus. The towers stood as visible symbols of the growth and changes that the University was experiencing. Somewhat less obvious, however, were the changes going on inside these buildings and in their shadows.

By the mid-sixties, many American colleges and universities were experiencing student dissatisfaction. Rice University Chancellor Carey Croneis was quoted in a Dallas *Morning News* editorial on November 3, 1966, to the effect that "bad morals, bad manners, and belligerent, if not sadistic, behavior patterns" on too many campuses were serious threats to higher education.

President Guinn reviews the drawings of the first of several high-rise buildings constructed on the campus during his tenure.

189

Like students at other colleges and universities, TWU students demanded new rights.

Traditional student-administrator squabbles about social restrictions on dormitory hours, tobacco, cars, alcohol, and dress were entering new areas. Students questioned curricula, grading, finances, admission, and even faculty composition; and college campuses became political battlegrounds where students demonstrated and fought for and against the war in Vietnam and for and against civil rights.

The *Congressional Record* of June 24, 1969, reprinted a congressional report to President Richard Nixon which addressed this "major national problem," classifying campuses across the nation into categories which ranged from "tranquil" with "no history of, and little likelihood of, disruption" to "paralyzed" with "civil war and open military siege."

TWU fell between these two extremes—primarily uneasy with some discontent and even, from time to time, troubled with relatively mild incidents of "group civil disobedience." The 1969 spring semester ended with tensions between black and white dormitory residents threatening possible violence in the fall. Campus Government Association (CGA) President Kathy Dunn answered alumnae questions in the TWU bulletin of July 15, "TWU is not without student unrest. Fortunately, however, we have been able to meet our problems in an orderly and constructive manner."

CGA conducted a series of open hearings and forums at which students made suggestions which were, in turn, considered by the committee of students, faculty, and administrators charged with revising the student handbook which outlined expected student behavior. By the time students registered for the 1969-70 school year, the handbook, the *University Woman,* had incorporated significant changes. Dress rules, which previously had largely forbidden the wearing of slacks and bermuda shorts, were relaxed and allowed casual dress in all but five areas— classrooms, dining rooms, dormitory living rooms, the Administration Building, and businesses not located on Oakland Avenue. The handbook also lifted restrictions on traveling in a car at night, being absent from the campus overnight, traveling by airplane, horseback riding, spending the day or night in adjacent communities, and going home. In addition, the TWU bulletin of November 15, 1969, also reported, "The white cards containing the eight-line honor code that students were required to sign at registration last year were not in evidence. There is no copy of the code in the *University Woman."* The bulletin was quick to note, however, "There is . . . still an honor code in effect at this university."[1]

When the Alumnae Association Board met in the fall, Dean of Women Lurline Lee advised them,

> We have quit complaining about the apathy of students, for today they are demanding many changes. . . .
>
> Students recently drew up a list of most desired privileges, which included no nightly room check for seniors, the right to regulate their own hours, the right to visit in friends' apartments or residences, the right to attend unregistered and unchaperoned parties and the abandonment of sign-out requirements in dormitories.
>
> Today, the University no longer acts as a parent, but nevertheless, the University must accept a degree of responsibility for its students.

The following year brought additional changes, some of which CGA President Annella Wright discussed in the alumnae bulletin for the fall, 1970. The *University Woman* had been renamed the *Student Handbook* for 1970-71, she explained, because "the book is not supposed to be a 'bible.'" Aspects of student life as diverse as clothes and honor would cease to be governed by arbitrary written "codes." For dress, she said, "We want to create a realistic and workable standard . . . based on reason and good judgment." The elimination of the dress code did not eliminate expectations among faculty, administrators, alumnae, and even older students about what was appropriate attire. Mandates became suggestions, though, and by October 27, 1971, *Lass-O* staff writer Lillian Gonnell rejoiced, "Students no longer need someone to tell them what is proper, both to wear and to think."

Looking back to a time more than sixty years earlier when uniform dress served as a symbol of membership in a group, Gonnell viewed the present styles of dress as symbols of individuality. Contrasting past and present, Gonnell recalled that the seniors, "ladies," of 1912 wore white shoes to symbolize their title whereas the ladies of 1972 might wear no shoes at all. "The Ladies of 1912 would indeed be shocked by our blue jeaned, barefooted, bra-less companions," she remarked. "Even the Ladies of 1969 would take a double look." Those ladies had had to wear dresses to class and hose and heels to concert and drama presentations and to Sunday dinners. Instead of the de facto uniforms of shirts, sweaters, hose, and heels which had followed the mandated uniforms, students of 1971 modeled, according to Gonnell, "long flowing skirts, short blowing skirts, pants suits from Neiman's, and cutoffs from too many summers ago. Barefeet and adorned feet, crepe blouses and army fatigues."

TWU students were concerned about social and personal changes, but they were also, like students throughout the country, interested in large political and moral issues. The official position of TWU concerning the national Moratorium Day on October 15, 1969, to protest the war in Vietnam, was "business as usual." The University emphasized that no departures from normal activities had been authorized and that standard policies and regulations would prevail on October 15 "as on every other day of the academic year." In mid-November, however (when a quarter of a million protesters demonstrated in Washington, D.C.), fliers announced a gathering of TWU students and faculty "to express concern for the world situation" through fifteen minutes of silence in front of Hubbard Hall.

Near the end of the fall semester, 1970, mounting tensions led to a clash between students and police. Some twenty women and two men were arrested at Guinn Hall for disorderly conduct when they refused a police order to disperse. By the following morning they had been released on small bonds; and the Denton *Record-Chronicle* of December 18, 1970, reported that "Texas Woman's University was like most any other college campus Friday morning. . . . Students were hurrying to classes, taking end-of-the-semester exams and getting ready for the Christmas holidays." Attributed variously to end of the semester tensions and to festering racial problems, the incident received extensive publicity in the press of Denton, Dallas, and Fort Worth.

Other incidents expressed a growing discontent on the campus through the last years of the sixties in spite of attempts to accommodate students' new needs and wants. The *Lass-O* of September 2, 1971, reported that campus leaders had established the theme of "The Liberated Woman" for the year's activities, and editorial writer Jackie Grey set the tone for the year: "Although TWU may find itself filed under 'conservative' in comparison to other colleges and universities, the significant fact is that definite strides have been made toward liberation—liberation in the sense of providing a more relaxed atmosphere for learning and growing with the times."

If the atmosphere was relaxed for learning and growing, however, the times were not; and on September 21, Grey wrote, "Our educational preparation is pretty scary. . . . For us the future becomes a long list of

Demands for greater freedoms led to the elimination of dress codes in the early seventies.

191

question marks." The immediate past offered few answers, for recent history was punctuated with the exclamation points and question marks of disorder at Watts, Kent State, and Attica.

It is not surprising that the bleak view of past and future bred frustration and dissatisfaction with the present. On September 24, a *Lass-O* editorial complained, "The students at Texas Woman's University have no power," before citing a list of irritations. Accusing TWU of clinging to "ancient restrictions," the editor criticized choices for the Concert and Drama Series, lamented restrictions on religious activities on campus, and rejected "an administrator's" labeling of "songs having to do with sex, beer, grass, woman's lib and others" in the University Review as "unnecessary." Specifically attacking a recent committee decision to change the student-selected Gold Rush theme from "The Changing Woman" to "America the Beautiful," the editor charged, "They're 10 years behind time. With public opinion being so against the war and so dissatisfied with the American government, how can anyone honestly want to display the old red, white and blue without getting smirks from outsiders."

Although the writer's attitude was not unique, it was not universal either. Letterwriter Jan Pair represented the opposing point-of-view when she defended patriotism in the *Lass-O* of September 28 with a reminder that "Liberated (or Changing) Woman' wouldn't be free from smirks from outsiders either."[2]

Through the fall, the *Lass-O* urged student activism. Parking and bookstore prices came under attack, and frequent drives urged students to register to vote. The Student Council voted not to elect class beauties. In spite of complaints, however, students were experiencing increased freedom from University-imposed restrictions. Complaints about meal service had led to the establishment of a system which enabled students to purchase either a fifteen-or twenty-meals-per-week plan so that students who regularly went home for the weekends would not be charge for meals while they were away from the campus. Students were permitted for the first time to vote for campus movies.

The new student handbook listed new hours for students. Curfew for freshmen was extended to 11:30 p.m. on weekdays and 1:00 a.m. on weekends. Sophomores and juniors with parents' permission had open hours, and all seniors had open hours. An early curfew of 9:00 p.m., however, was imposed on freshmen who received two or more failing slips.

Although students expected and demanded new freedoms, alumnae on the opposite side of the "generation gap" did not always understand their young sisters' concerns. Agatha Exe wrote in the TWU bulletin of November 15, 1969, "The only marching I ever did on campus was the year I got to be a soldier in the Nativity Pageant and the day I graduated." Fourteen years after her graduation, Agatha met an old friend on the TWU campus in October, 1971, and reported in the alumnae bulletin of that fall, "We visited the campus government offices where the big words were 'relevancy' and 'meaning' and we found that we appeared lacking in both." Comparing her past with the present, Agatha recalled, "Freshmen in my day were concerned with things immediate. We thought the 'establishment' was the drug store across the street from the dorm."

Under the twin watchwords of relevancy and meaning, however, students continued to press for changes. Across the nation students rejected dormitory living in their quest for greater freedom. Highly prized housing units built for growing enrollments only a few years back became albatrosses to the institutions as students refused their accommodations. Vacancy rates of twenty-five percent were common.

When students petitioned Guinn for relaxed housing requirements, he attempted to explain the economic considerations that determined

Students' protests ranged from housing regulations to social injustices.

housing policies. Having assumed large debts to build the dormitories, the University had to insure that they be occupied so that the debts could be paid. Nevertheless, chafing under the restrictions, students finally challenged them in a law suit. The court ruled in favor of the University, which continued to require all undergraduate students under twenty-three years old to live on campus unless married or living in the home of parents or guardians. As increasing numbers of students qualified for the exemption and chose to live off-campus, Transportation Enterprises, Inc., initiated student commuter bus service between Denton and Dallas and Fort Worth in the spring of 1971.

Students expressed their anger and dissatisfaction with University policies in a number of ways that ranged during the fall of 1971 from other law suits to a bomb threat in Guinn Hall and small fires in Stark Hall. Following the troubled fall, a writer in the *Lass-O* of February 1, 1972, described the "watchful stance" of the pioneer woman statue as "a symbol of endurance for the University." The spring would continue to test that endurance.

On March 9 about a hundred students, mostly black, gathered on the lawn of the president's home to present a list of a dozen grievances after Guinn failed to respond to an ultimatum to meet with them in his office. The students began to disperse after about an hour; but *Lass-O* staff writer Rhonda Fullbright reported in the paper of March 14, "What began as an NAACP demonstration against disciplinary actions taken by the University has now become the Students' Human Rights Movement." Other student leaders, including CGA President Cherri Lott, joined members of the NAACP in a rally on March 14, which attracted some five hundred students to the lawn in front of Hubbard Hall.

Unaware of the tensions on campus, U.S. District Court Judge Sarah T. Hughes delivered the Woman's Day Colloquium keynote address that evening to an audience which overflowed Redbud Auditorium. Some students watched on closed circuit television as Judge Hughes spoke of "Women as a Political Force." "I am pleased at signs of rebellion. It's up to you to decide whether or not the rebellion will be successful," she told the responsive audience. On feminists, Hughes, stated, "I glory in what they have done, because they realize the great waste of women power in this country"; and she challenged her listeners at the end of her address, "Get up! Get up! It's later than it's ever been."

Following close behind Judge Hughes, Frances "Sissy" Farenthold, Democratic gubernatorial candidate, spoke to an overflowing crowd in the Student Center Lounge on March 21. After encouraging women to get involved in local and state politics, Farenthold received a copy of the grievances of the Student Human Rights Movement and promised to review them with TWU Regent, Mrs. William Bowers.

Two days later feminists Gloria Steinem, Margaret Sloan, and Joanne Edgars visited the campus. On February 2, Steinem had spoken at East Texas State University. TWU student Odilia Mendez reported in the *Lass-O* the following day that in response to her question about the place of a woman's university in the women's liberation movement, Steinem had said, "It can serve as one big radicalizing place where women learn about their history and where they can develop the self confidence they might otherwise lose." Apparently interested in helping make TWU such a "radicalizing place," the three women spent March 23 from noon to midnight on the Denton campus, visiting with students, and, in the evening, delivering their message of sisterhood, liberally punctuated with obscenities.

At commencement exercises on May 18, Guinn publicly responded to the charges and pressures which had built through the previous year. Acknowledging the necessity for modern universities to respond to

(Top to bottom) Outstanding women such as Judge Sarah T. Hughes, gubernatorial candidate Frances Farenthold, and activist Gloria Steinem encouraged students to become involved in their world.

changing times and demands, Guinn, nevertheless, warned against overreacting to "loud-mouthed agitators." "We do not intend," he said, "to waste an undue amount of time in analyzing or evaluating all of the discordant shrieking, or caterwauling, of faddists who seem more concerned with what is wrong rather than what is overwhelmingly right in well established American colleges and universities."

By the fall TWU and campuses across the nation had left behind most of the violence and stridence that characterized the unrest at its peak. *Lass-O* managing editor Jackie Grey wrote in her editorial of September 15, 1972,

> The stormy period of the youth revolution has passed. No longer do we hear of mass marches and protests . . . and confrontations between this group and that.
>
> With the exception of the political arena, few murmurings are being heard from the 18-25 age bracket.

In the midst of turmoil, traditions like the lantern parade (top) continued; and new activities like the Miss TWU competition (bottom) were begun.

Claiming victory, Grey said, "Things have changed." Prominent among the changes she identified were those in dress: "Five years ago, wearing jeans to class at TWU was a fantasy. Today, it's a habit." Pierced ears and bicycles were also popular on campus, and students who no longer participated in marches and vigils wore POW/MIA (Prison of War/Missing in Action) bracelets to demonstrate their continued interest in the American soldiers who were not accounted for following the war in Vietnam.

New concerns claimed the students' interests also. Students who had only recently won the right to smoke in public now faced objections not from administrators but from other students. A *Lass-O* headline of December 5, 1972, proclaimed, "Non-smokers want clean air."

Students still continued to press for changes in University policies. Gloria Barboza reported in the *Lass-O* of May 1, 1973, that the CGA was displaying in its office a list of 161 goals which ranged from the ability to live off campus at age twenty-one or upon the completion of sixty hours to open visitation in the dormitories, a refrigerator program, and a centrex phone system. By the time of the story, Guinn and the individual dormitories had agreed to a visitation policy which allowed males to visit students in their dormitory rooms by signing in and out during pre-arranged visiting hours; and an unsuccessful bill to lower the mandatory age for dormitory residence had been introduced in the Texas Legislature.

Both the goals and the methods for attempting to fulfill them reflected a new maturity on the part of TWU students. Preparing for her first visit to the TWU campus since her graduation in 1956, alumna Shirley Abbott Tomkievicz studied a number of issues of the *Lass-O*. In an interview with Gloria Barboza, published in the *Lass-O* of May 1, 1973, Tomkievicz said, "I found stories that made me think you (the student body) had changed a great deal. The sweet and girlish tone that characterized student pronouncements in my day is gone. I frequently heard the voices of young women, not little girls; of adults, not children." Surprised that students complained in editorials and articulated problems in by-line stories, Tomkievicz noted that a number of the pieces she had read could not have been printed in the early 1950s when she was a student; "But in any event, none of us could have written them," she added. Tomkievicz regarded the change as "one of the heartening developments in education in the past few years" and praised the new attitude that "college students are now expected to be adults, fully in control of their own morality and their own style of life."

Changes did not, however, mean the complete rejection of everything from the past. As Guinn reminded the audience at the spring commencement of 1973, TWU was engaged in "a conscious striving to prevent the erosion or elimination of enduring values." The TWU bulletin of the following July 15 stated the University's expectations for its students: "To obey the law, to show respect for properly constituted authority, to perform contractual obligations, to maintain absolute integrity and a high standard of individual honor in scholastic work, and to observe conduct appropriate for a community of scholars."

With students concentrating on bringing about institutional and societal changes traditional student activities diminished in popularity, but they did not cease. Tracing its origins back at least to 1911 when the CIA "Middlers" presented a circus in which members of the student body performed as clowns, rope walkers, wild animals, jugglers, and trained horses, "Stunts" continued to attract participants.[3]

In the mid-sixties the Lantern Parade in which upper classmen shared the "light of friendship" with entering freshmen entered its fifth decade as an official University activity; and the Corn Huskin' Bee began its fourth decade of contests in corn husking, singing, dancing, log sawing, nail driving, and peanut shelling. Like the other traditions, the Redbud Festival had undergone changes in its more than thirty-year history, and the change in the 1970 pageant reflected the growing individuality of students. The University bulletin of March 15, 1970, reported that princesses would choose individual gowns instead of "dressing alike according to classes as they did in the past." Styles in general had changed, too, as the bouffant hoop skirts and layers of net, tulle, and lace gave way to slim A-line and empire gowns. A soft, natural look, replaced darkly painted makeup; and hair styles changed from waves to curls to straight to the "do your own thing" look of the period.

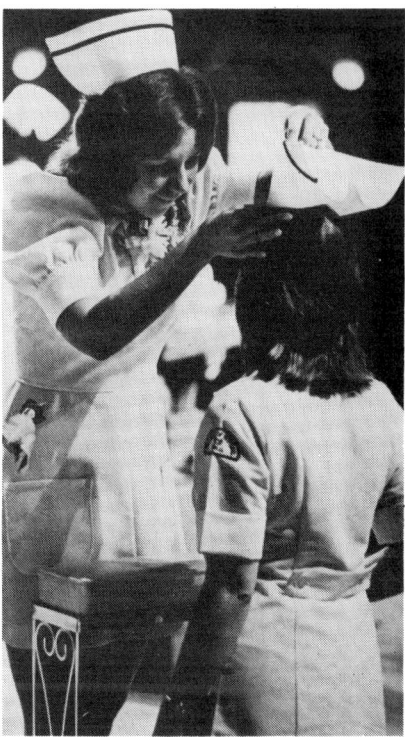

(Above) the capping ceremony signified a major step for nursing students.

(Left) Ties with Texas A&M remained strong when TWU student Kathy Heldman reigned as the Cotton Bowl Queen in 1968.

Literary-social clubs continued to play a part in campus life, and the merger of L'Allegro and the Mary Eleanor Brackenridge clubs in 1966 resulted in the formation of the newest, Alpha Omega, with its phoenix mascot and its motto of "Looking to New Horizons."

New horizons brought new activities and services and the beginning of new traditions. The Woman's Day Colloquium was instituted in the spring of 1968. In conjunction with homecoming in 1970, the College of Nursing initiated a convocation in Denton to recognize all TWU nursing students. Commencement audiences outgrew the newly air-conditioned Main Auditorium so that by the spring of 1970 commencement had to be moved outside to the lawn of Hubbard Hall, which would seat four thousand people. By the spring of 1974, the commencement audience had grown to 6,500. The alumnae bulletin of the summer of 1971 reported the creation of a new Counseling and Testing Center. Joggers formed a club in the fall

Part of the eight-week tour which carried the Lass-O Choraliers throughout the Orient, was a performance aboard the USS Yorktown.

of 1971. And the *Lass-O* of September 24, 1971, reported that the delivery of the *Daedalian* yearbook had been changed from spring to summer so that it could reflect the activities of the whole school year.

Musical groups continued their international tours. The *Lass-O* of February 3, 1970, reported that the Serenaders had just completed their third big tour, performing some seventy times for fifteen thousand servicemen in Japan, Korea, Okinawa, and the Philippines; and in the fall of the same year the Choraliers completed an almost-two-month tour of Europe, their fourth major concert tour. In mid-November, 1974, nine Choraliers began another extended trip, this time singing throughout the Mediterranean area.

Athletic competition achieved a new scope and intensity at the end of the sixties. In the spring of 1969 the TWU track team captured the first National Intercollegiate Track and Field Championship for Women by defeating second-place Texas Tech and Indiana University. Although the TWU athletes failed to place first in any single event, the team accumulated seventy-eight points in fourteen events to surpass the second place teams, which each earned sixty-one points. By the following spring, construction of a new outdoor track and field area had begun; and by the summer of 1975, the track team had captured two more national titles (in 1972 and 1974), two second place finishes, and one third place in the national competition. To support and guide the emerging athletic program, the Board of Regents approved the establishment of an athletic department and the appointment of an athletic council in May, 1974.

As Guinn began his third decade in office, student unrest made the headlines; and student accomplishments, though impressive, received measured attention. The heart of the University, its academic program, was far from the thoughts of most Texans; but it was changing, and in one case attempting unsuccessfully to change, in dramatic ways.

The lateral and vertical curricular expansion that had intensified early in Guinn's administration continued through the last years of his tenure. New faculty, new courses, new degree programs, new departments, and a new academic structure reflected TWU's efforts to meet new challenges.

New courses reflected new student concerns. *Contemporary Problems,* an advanced history course introduced in the fall of 1967, probed such topics as "Vietnam—how did we get there?, the pill and politics, the alienation of the intellectual from the church, urbanization, and other topics," according to the TWU bulletin of November 15, 1967. The

196

University catalog for 1974-75 listed the first women's studies course at TWU, *Women in American and World Society,* a sociology course designed, according to the catalog description, to explore "woman's role" with emphases on "socialization and sex roles, world cultural variability, biological and psychological differences, occupational structure, and law."

By 1970, curricular growth had extended beyond the bounds of the existing system for numbering courses. As the TWU bulletin of March 15, 1970, noted, some sequences had no numbers left for new courses; and current numbers were inadequate to describe some new levels of courses. Therefore, the University instituted its present numbering system at the beginning of the 1970-71 academic year.

Along with a wide array of individual new courses, TWU also initiated a number of new degree programs both at the baccalaureate and graduate levels. The TWU bulletin of July 15, 1968, reported a new master's degree program in occupational therapy, a new six-year program in library science, and doctoral programs in special education. Students could earn either the Ph.D. or the Ed.D. in special education with concentrations in mental retardation, speech pathology, learning and language disorders, and the mentally disturbed.

Degree offerings were burgeoning on college and university campuses throughout the state, and the Legislature had created the new Coordinating Board, Texas College and University System, to coordinate the growth of the state's institutions of higher education. In late 1968, the Board proposed the creation of what was variously described as an urban university system, a "super" urban university, a multi-university, and a megaversity in the Dallas-Fort Worth area. An Associated Press report from Austin, November 12, 1968, described a tentative proposal to put the Texas Woman's University, North Texas State University, the University of Texas at Arlington, and the proposed branch of the University of Texas in Dallas under a single board of regents. Each institution would issue baccalaureate degrees in its own name, but all graduate degrees would be awarded in the name of the system.

The story reported opposition from each of the universities involved, from East Texas State University, and from the Chambers of Commerce in Dallas, Fort Worth, and Arlington. The Houston *Chronicle* of the same date reported the unanimous opposition of the Dallas County legislative delegation and the opposition of Fort Worth Representative W.C. Sherman and the regents of the University of Texas.

In response to the proposal, TWU, ETSU, and NTSU developed a counter proposal which TWU President Guinn presented to the Coordinating Board at its November 11 meeting. At a special called meeting in Austin, December 3, the Coordinating Board adopted the counterproposal, which called for the formation of the Federation of North Texas Area Universities, an organization in which each member institution maintained its own governing board and conferred its own degrees in its own name. Cooperative efforts would focus on graduate programs. On January 13, federation representatives from the three universities met in Dallas with Bevington Reed, commissioner for higher education, and elected Guinn chairman.[4]

In the TWU bulletin of March 15, 1969, Guinn expressed this satisfaction with the arrangement: "We are very happy with the decision because we not only get to keep and develop all existing programs," he said, "but we also have an open door for new programs here and in cooperation with other universities." Although the Coordinating Board or the Federation did not assign restrictive or exclusive areas of concentration to any of the participating universities, the agreement called for future expansion of graduate programs to be recommended through the

In 1969, 1972, and 1974, TWU athletes won the National Intercollegiate Track and Field Championship for Women.

197

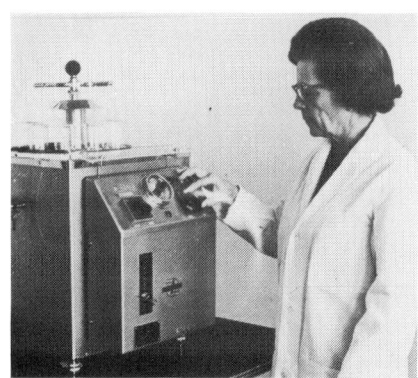

Textile research continued to be of major significance.

Students learned video-taping skills.

Federation to the Coordinating Board.

A part of the adoption of the plan was a definition by the Coordinating Board of the special roles of each of the member institutions. As reported in the TWU bulletin of March 15, 1969,

> TWU was authorized to continue its present master's level and doctoral programs and was assigned areas of primary responsibility in home economics, women's physcial education, radiation biology and radiation chemistry.
>
> The board decision also gave TWU and NTSU joint responsibility for graduate work in library science and special education.

By the fall of 1969, TWU and NTSU had joined in a cooperative program to offer the only Ph.D. in library science in the Southwest and one of the few in the country.

As external cooperative arrangements developed, TWU also developed internal cooperative efforts through multidisciplinary programs. The TWU bulletin of February 15, 1968, described the new TWU Institute for Mental and Physical Development, which provided diagnosis, treatment, training, and education for children and some adults with physical or mental handicaps. The Institute served a two-fold purpose—to train TWU students majoring in health-related disciplines and to serve patients. The Institute regularly offered service in pediatrics, psychology, special education, speech pathology, occupational therapy, biochemistry, nutrition, physical therapy, music therapy, therapeutic recreation, adapted physical education, home economics, sociology, social work, genetics, cytology, nursing, counseling, and audiology; and other disciplines provided consultation upon need for patients who applied or were referred to the Institute.

For more specialized problems, the Center for the Study of Learning opened in June, 1969, under the direction of Aileen Griffin. A practicum facility for the College of Education, the center had a two-fold purpose— to provide firsthand experience for students studying learning problems and to help TWU students and young people in the community improve their reading and communication skills. Through the center, education students could study children's learning problems by observation, micro-teaching, and laboratory or clinical work with an individual child. These experiences helped students learn to diagnose, teach, and evaluate children's progress in reading and related language arts studies.

Located on the first floor of the new CFO Tower, the center included a curriculum library which provided textbooks, children's books, programmed materials, and an abundance of audio-visual materials for use in reading and language arts studies and teaching. The library could accommodate about thirty students, and twelve small study rooms were available for elementary education majors who sought to learn how children learn. Students could also practice their teaching before classes of youngsters and a video-tape machine which enabled them to evaluate their performance afterward.

Other disciplines were developing new programs as well. At its meeting on January 20, 1969, the Coordinating Board gave preliminary approval for the B.A. and B.S. degrees in social work.[5] *A Summary History of Texas Woman's University: 1901-1971* reported 197 social work majors by 1971.

The TWU bulletin of July 15, 1969, described developmental activities on a new bilingual education program offered in cooperation with the Fort Worth Independent School District. The Bilingual Education Centro de Accion (BECA) had twenty-four students by the fall. Divided into two groups, the junior students attended classes at TWU and worked as teachers' aides in Fort Worth public schools on alternate weeks to acquire skills in both Spanish and education as they prepared to teach in elementary schools. Proud to be "pioneering" a new program, the students compared themselves to the TWU pioneer woman in an interview published in the TWU bulletin of November 15, 1969.

Also introduced in the fall of 1969 was a new degree program in a old subject. The State Board of Examiners made economics, which had been combined with business or social studies as a teaching field for teacher certification, a separate teaching field in 1967. The TWU bulletin of November 15, 1969, reported, "Students wishing to obtain a B.S. or B.A. degree in economics and perhaps go on to get a master's degree in the field may do so for the first time this year at TWU," following approval of both provisional and professional programs by the State Board of Education on October 4.

In the summer of 1970, the College of Nursing introduced a new approach to an established subject. Thirteen students enrolled in a pilot program which would enable them to earn a master's degree in psychiatric and mental health nursing by attending four sequential summer sessions. The winter alumnae bulletin of 1971 described the program as the "first of its kind in Texas."

In 1971, following five years of study, TWU applied for and received Coordinating Board approval to institute the first full four-year B.S. degree program in dental hygiene to be offered by a state university. The program received full accreditation from the American Dental Association in 1972. Also introduced in 1971 was the new B.S. degree in Medical Record Administration. Sixteen students enrolled under the program's director, Mildred Ford. Following three years of study on the Denton campus, students in medical records proceeded to the Dallas Center and to affiliations with Dallas hospitals.

Along with expansion at the undergraduate level, TWU was introducing new graduate programs, particularly at the doctoral level. The TWU bulletin of May 15, 1970, listed new Ph.D. degrees in molecular biology, rhetoric (a field of concentration in English), sociology, and early childhood education. Both Ph.D.s and Ed.D.s were available in five major areas of concentration in the College of Health, Physical Education, and Recreation (HPER): dance and related arts, health education, physical education, recreation administration, and therapeutic recreation.[6]

In October, 1970, the Coordinating Board approved the Ph.D. degree in nursing at TWU; and the Board approved a doctoral program in psychology in the fall of 1971. The TWU bulletin of April 1, 1972, listed specific areas of concentration for doctoral studies in the College of Household Arts and Sciences. Students could earn either Ed.D. or Ph.D. degrees with concentrations in child development, clothing and related arts, home demonstration, or home and family life. In addition they could earn the Ed.D. degree in home economics education or the Ph.D. degree in food and nutrition, institution administration, nutrition, textile technology, or textiles.[7]

At the undergraduate level, home management houses had given way to newer buildings; but students still obtained practical experience. The *Lass-O* of September 23, 1972, reported that students in the home management course required of all home economics education majors would learn "what it takes to feed a family at the lowest possible cost." Students in the course lived on the third floor of Guinn Hall for seven weeks not only to practice budgeting and the use of equipment but also to learn the management of food, time, and energy. Students who were married practiced their skills in their homes.

(Top to bottom) Academic programs ranged from bilingual education, to dental hygiene, to scuba diving.

Accompanying changes in the curriculum were changes in the academic organization of TWU. In the fall of 1969, the Coordinating Board approved a reorganization of the TWU College of Education which called for the combination of the psychology and philosophy departments and the creation of four new departments—Educational Foundations, Curriculum and Instruction, Counselor Education and Personnel Services, and Special Education. Departmentalization of two other colleges was effected by the fall of 1974. The College of HPER included the Departments of Dance, Health Education, Physical Education, and Recreation; and four departments comprised the College of Nutrition, Textiles, and Human Development (formerly the College of Household Arts and Sciences)— Child Development and Family Living, Home Economics Education and Consumer Sciences, Nutrition and Food Sciences, and Textile Science and Clothing.

Although these changes were significant, they did not have the impact on the University that the establishment of the new Institute of Health Sciences in 1972 had. The TWU bulletin of July 1 announced the Coordinating Board's approval of the Institute as a major academic component of TWU. The institute consisted of the College of Nursing, the Schools of Occupational Therapy and Physical Therapy, and the new School of Health Care Services.[8] The Institute was distinct from other components of the University in its admission policies. The bulletin which announced the Institute also announced a change in TWU policy: "There will be no discrimination on the basis of sex in the admission of qualified individuals to any of the programs offered by the Institute of Health Sciences."[9]

The following fall, the first male students (nine) in the history of TWU enrolled. As *Lass-O* editor Patricia Couch noted on September 29, 1972, "It is not quite as exciting as being the first man on the moon . . . , but having male students on the . . . campus is definitely a notable occurrence."[10] At spring commencement, 1975, for the first time, TWU awarded degrees to males (ten) who had completed their studies in the Institute.

Title IX of the Higher Education Act Amendments of 1972 required a second modification of University admission policies; and the TWU bulletin of June 15, 1973, reported that beginning with the second 1975 summer term, "There will be no discrimination on the basis of sex in the admission of qualified individuals to any of the programs offered in the Graduate School."[11] Thus, by the fall of 1973, men were eligible to enroll in two of the University's three major components. The third, the University General Divisions, was allowed by federal statute to limit its enrollment to women since it had historically and traditionally been so limited.[12]

The phenomenal success of the health sciences programs initiated at TWU during the more than twenty years of Guinn's tenure and the national shortage of doctors led the University to plan and propose the establishment of a TWU Medical School.[13] The proposal, which was submitted to the Coordinating Board, Texas College and University System, in late January, 1973, proposed the establishment of a TWU medical school in the Dallas-Fort Worth area. The focus of the school would be on the health problems of women, health problems of the disadvantaged—the elderly, minority groups, and the physically and mentally handicapped—and environmental health—health concerns related to pollution and over-population.

As it had done consistently throughout its history, TWU sought to solve an important problem of the state through an innovative educational program. Whereas existing medical schools focused on highly specialized training with a heavy emphasis on research, the proposed TWU school would attempt to prepare family practitioners for direct and immediate

service to persons in need of health care.

At its meeting on February 17, the Coordinating Board's Advisory Committee on Medical Education reported no need for a "new free-standing medical school at this time"; and when the Coordinating Board met in March, it tabled the TWU proposal. The Board also heard at its March meeting, however, a suggestion from the advisory committee that a new medical school linked with an existing Veterans Administration hospital "may be of benefit to the state, should the program be funded."

The federal government was, at the time, seeking eight locations across the nation for the establishment of state-supported medical schools in connection with Veterans Administration hospitals. Passed the previous October, Public Law 92-541, the Veterans Administration Medical School Assistance and Health Manpower Training Act, appropriated $25 million for the establishment of the schools; and the Texas Legislature had in May, 1971, given the Coordinating Board the power to negotiate and contract with federal agencies for the establishment, operation, and maintenance of such a school.

At its meeting of April 13, the Coordinating Board advised any schools who wished to apply for federal funds to present affirmations of their intentions from their governing boards. On April 24, TWU Regents adopted a resolution which called for the completion of all necessary steps to insure the timely submission of a formal proposal to the Coordinating Board: "Knowing that it [the medical school] has the enthusiastic backing of administrative staffs and faculties of the university, [the Board] pledges full support in material resources and in cooperative endeavor to the plan for a new medical school to be operated in conjunction with Veterans Administration medical facilities."[15]

In late May, TWU and Texas A&M, which had also submitted a proposal, each presented three hours of testimony before the Coordinating Board's Program Development Committee, which unanimously approved Texas A&M's proposal to establish the medical school in Temple.

An Associated Press report on May 24 noted that "committee members wondered how attractive the female emphasis on the university's name would prove to male students"; and Dallas *Times Herald* staff writer Tracey Smith reported on the same date that TWU "was turned down because committee members felt the school's name would not prove attractive to male students." When bluntly asked whether he would be prepared to change the name of the University, Guinn had responded, "No"; and the vice president of TWU's Institute of Health Sciences, Margaret Harty, pointed out that law required the admission of male students on the same basis as female students.

Looking back on the decision a year later, education writer Joyce Hopkins analyzed the choice in the Denton *Record-Chronicle* of June 20, 1974:

> When the Texas Legislature chose A&M as the designated state school for a proposed VA-financed program last year, it made the sort of decision families used to make when they had a son and a daughter and the money for only one to go to school.
>
> Just as the brother got the nod and the sister made do, legislators gave the spot to A&M instead of its sister school.

Nevertheless, in spite of a second setback in a matter of weeks, TWU continued to work toward approval for a medical school, even in the face of mounting opposition. Dallas *Times Herald* medical writer Joe Taylor reported on November 11, 1973, "A source close to the Coordinating Board . . . said some state medical school leaders have expressed doubts about the need for another medical school in Texas"; and the article quoted unidentified "leaders" who expressed their reservations, citing both an influx of foreign doctors and the increased production of doctors at existing medical schools as ways of meeting the need for more doctors.

But support for the school grew apace with opposition; and on June 19, 1974, Fort Worth Mayor R.M. Stovall and Fort Worth Chamber of Commerce President J.C. Pace announced the dedication of a sixty-acre tract of land valued at more than $1 million as a location for the new medical school.[16] Optimism mounted as many people thought that this contribution plus pledges of additional support might tip the scales in TWU's favor when it again sought action on the proposal which had been pending for some eighteen months.

But Carl Freund predicted in the Dallas *Morning News* of June 21 that TWU's proposal for a medical school on the new site would "accelerate a fight for state funds for training doctors," a fight which would, he said, "reach a climax during the 1975 legislative session." Freund quoted a regent of the University of Texas system: "The pie simply isn't big enough for everybody to get the portion he wants. That means the Legislature must decide who gets the biggest slices."

The receipt of the land and other support marked the beginning of a major public campaign to win approval for the school which, supporters emphasized at every turn, would concentrate on the delivery of health care rather than isolated research or highly specialized treatment. By the fall, TWU had the support of Governor Dolph Briscoe who was quoted in the Fort Worth *Press* of September 22 as saying that he "heartily approve[d]" of the TWU plan to build a medical school in Fort Worth and that he "look[ed] askance" at reports that the state had enough medical schools. Reporter Pat Patrick quoted the Governor, "When you have a harder time finding a doctor in Austin than we used to in Uvalde, it's hard to believe there are enough doctors in Texas."

Armed with new information and new financial and political support, TWU presented its case again to the Coordinating Board. On October 17, the Program Development Committee recommended approval of the TWU proposal by a vote of 4-3; but on October 18, following a 7-7 vote of the entire Board, Board Chairman Harry Provence voted in favor of the staff recommendation to deny the TWU request.

Obtaining permission to address the Board following the defeat, Guinn said, "We have talked things out; we have provided information; and there has never yet in these 24-plus years [of my presidency] been a dissenting vote on our board. I think there won't be a dissenting vote on the board of the Texas Woman's University this time either on the subject of our determination—and I'm not saying this antagonistically, sir. I'm simply saying that we are going to pursue in a proper and a legal and a dignified way our dream of achieving the medical school which was not approved this morning by the Coordinating Board."

Returning to the campus, Guinn concentrated not on the defeat but on the fact that the tie vote reflected a great deal of interest and support among Coordinating Board members. When the TWU Regents met November 19, Beeman Fisher of Fort Worth met with them to pledge the continued support of the leadership of Fort Worth businessmen; and, according to the *Lass-O* of November 20, "indicated they were 100 per cent behind the goal of Dr. Guinn and his colleagues and agreed that the approval of support be recorded." On December 7 the Board of Directors of the TWU Alumnae Association formally championed the cause by adopting a resolution "That the Alumnae Association go on record with their support and approval of the quest for a medical school for Texas Woman's University."

When the Texas Legislature convened the following January, Fort Worth Representative Doyle Willis submitted House Bill 254 and Senator Bill Meier introduced Senate Bill 234, both of which called for the establishment of a TWU Medical School in Fort Worth. Alumnae, faculty, staff, students, and other supporters of the proposal engaged in an all-out campaign; but Governor Briscoe's earlier pledge of support crumbled. In an Austin press conference on January 30, the Governor said he "strongly favor[ed]" more medical education for the state and was kindly disposed toward TWU's proposal. However, he also supported increased authority for the Coordinating Board; and he stated, "Until the Coordinating Board approves, I'm not in a position to approve [the school]."

Accusing the Governor of "copping out," a Fort Worth *Star-Telegram* editorial of February 1, questioned the wisdom of increasing the power of the Coordinating Board and asked, "Governor, if the medical school proposal was a good idea last year, why isn't it a good idea now?" Reminding Briscoe of his earlier remarks—"Good idea, said the governor last year. Heartily approve, said the governor last year. I'll back the proposal whenever possible, said the governor last year"—the editorial concluded, "Governor, the medicine you've dispensed is hard to swallow."

The Dallas *Morning News* described the Governor on February 9 as being "caught in a political crack" and reported that he was trying to persuade the Coordinating Board to reconsider its decision: "And he admits there is a 'possibility' that if the legislature created the TWU school, he would let it become law without his signature."

By mid-March, the Legislature found itself facing four medical school proposals—one for the TWU school in Fort Worth, two (one in Corpus Christi and another in the Rio Grande Valley) which had never been presented for Coordinating Board action, and one which would merge the Texas College of Osteopathic Medicine (TCOM) in Fort Worth with North Texas State University and then expand TCOM.

Opponents of the new schools predicted a surplus of doctors (twice as many as needed) by 1980. Proponents of the bills noted that almost two-thirds of the doctors licensed in Texas between 1968 and 1973 came from states other than from Texas or from foreign schools and that the number of doctors who entered Texas to practice was almost exactly the same as the number of doctors who were trained in Texas but chose to practice elsewhere.[17]

Proponents of the TWU school noted the availability of the land, the existence of support systems—both facilities and programs—and the promise of other support; but skeptics remained unconvinced. Fort Worth Senator Betty Andujar, wife of a doctor, opposed the TWU school on economic grounds. She did not, according to Robert Heard in an Associated Press story of March 13, believe that there would be a doctor surplus; but she did not believe TWU could support the medical school either: "Saying you've got the land is like saying you can buy a car because you can afford the tires," she said. Andujar also opposed any special emphasis on the recruitment of women saying first that women could already apply at any school without discrimination and, then, "It's a well known fact in the medical profession that women are not as good an investment" because many of them quit to get married.

On March 14, the Coordinating Board issued a news release which cited Board Chairman Harry Provence's belief that "the best and quickest way for Texas to solve its shortage of physcians is to expand the medical schools it already has." Acknowledging that the unmistakable message of the Advisory Committee on Medical Education was that Texas needed more doctors and that every member of the Board endorsed that finding, the Coordinating Board "recommended that full funding of existing medical schools is the most rapid and efficient way to produce more physcians."

Following a hearing of House Bill 254 on March 11, the House Committee on Higher Education referred the bill to subcommittee where it was heard and amended on April 2 to include a medical school component in the Rio Grande Valley. The subcommittee returned it without recommendation to the full Committee on Higher Education, which heard the bill on April 16 and voted 8-0 to refer it to the House floor for approval.

A significant feature of the bill was that land and teaching hospitals for both components would be furnished at no expense to the state, which could never contribute funds for the construction, maintenance, or operation of teaching hospitals. The bill also specified that the school would require at least twenty-five per cent of the students admitted to "commit themselves to serve in rural and/or underserved urban areas of the state . . . for a period of at least five years after graduation . . . provided that such a requirement shall not be enforced against a student's will nor in violation of a student's constitutional rights."

On May 12, the bill passed its final reading in the House with a favorable vote of 109-29. The Fort Worth *Star-Telegram* carried a headline, "Meier says prospects good for medical school proposal," on May 22; and the Senate Affairs Committee voted 8-0 to refer the bill to the Senate floor for approval on May 29. But on May 30, Committee Chairman Bill Moore of Bryan refused to sign the bill. His parliamentary maneuver killed the proposal, which could not reach the Senate floor without his signature. Hailed as a wise legislator of heroic stature in some circles and castigated in others for his lack of manners and democracy, Moore defended his actions. The Dallas *Times Herald* of May 31 carried his statement that he was attempting to save Texas "the embarrassment of creating two medical schools with a hot check."[18]

The Legislature adjourned at midnight on June 2 with no further action on the bill, and an editorial in the Fort Worth *Star-Telegram* of June 4 pronounced the epitaph for TWU's proposed medical school: ". . . killed through a legislative technicality. . . . Hang the wishes of the whole. Hang the democratic process. Hang fair play. And, in this particular case, hang the dire need for more physicians in Texas—especially in rural areas."

On the TWU campus, however, there was no funeral. In fact, Guinn pledged to "redouble" the efforts for the school, finding, perhaps, slight consolation in the fact that the TWU campaign had helped focus attention on the needs of medically underserved areas of the state and that the Legislature had authorized medical schools to require at least twenty percent of their graduates to work four years in rural areas under the threat of stiff financial penalties if they did not meet their agreement.

In the *Lass-O* of June 4, Guinn expressed "surprise and disappointment" at the actions in Austin; but he renewed his pledge: "We intend with all honorable means at our disposal to get the school established and started at the earliest possible time." Guinn was not alone in his enthusiastic belief in the proposal. On October 30 the Fort Worth *Star-Telegram* reported the comments of Cecil Y. Ray, Jr., as representative of the support of many citizens: "I started working on this again the minute it failed."

On July 23 TWU Regents unanimously authorized the administration to proceed with "all appropriate efforts" to establish the school; and the *Lass-O* of August 28 quoted Board Chairman Marcella Perry, "This board heartily re-endorses the concept of the proposed medical school for TWU. . . . We want to pursue this proposal until it bears fruit." As concrete evidence of Regents' support, Fort Worth *Star-Telegram* contributing editor Jon McConal reported on October 26, "A $1 to $2 million cash gift for construction and start up expenses also has been firmly pledged by a member of the TWU board."

Preparing for renewed efforts before the Coordinating Board and the Legislature, TWU entered what Guinn called in the *Lass-O* of September 17, "an era of quiet planning." On other fronts, House Speaker Bill Clayton instructed a House Committee on Higher Education to examine a number of concerns, including the need for coordination and expansion of existing medical and dental schools and, some speculated, the feasibility of TWU's educating doctors.

On September 8, the Tarrant County Medical Society adopted a resolution supporting the Texas College of Osteopathic Medicine (TCOM) and calling for a moratorium on the building of *any* new medical schools until TCOM was fully funded (full enrollment was not expected until June, 1985). Speaking for the society, its president, Val Borum, declined to describe the vote either as "real close" or as "a substantial majority" in an interview with Fort Worth *Star-Telegram* writer Les Thomas on September 9. Borum insisted both that Fort Worth was not large enough for two medical schools and that starting a new medical school would cost from $100 million to $125 million. "You couldn't put up a real good medical library for $8 million," he said.

Nevertheless, Guinn, who admitted surprise but not disappointment at the move, was quoted in the *Star-Telegram* of September 10: "We are not going to reduce our efforts. . . . We will work harder than ever"; and Representative Doyle Willis predicted passage of the bill in the next Legislature, saying the medical society's opposition would not hamstring efforts.

Meanwhile, the Coordinating Board had declared a moratorium not just on medical proposals but on all proposals for new programs until April, 1976. In the *Lass-O* of September 17, 1975, Guinn reported, "People are busily working on it [the medical school proposal] all the time here and other places. . . . We're staying right on top of it. We have reasons for optimism."

Jon McConal described some of the efforts in the Fort Worth *Star-Telegram* of October 26. "The campaign," he said, ". . . is being conducted quietly, but there's no doubt about its intensity." There was also an intense campaign of opposition. McConal quoted Texas Medical Association president "Num" Barker: "We are not against Fort Worth. We are against the formation of any new medical school anywhere."

Barker saw the problem as one of doctor distribution rather than doctor shortage, but he agreed that additional money might need to be channeled through existing medical schools. Guinn, on the other hand, contended that the space required to train more doctors would cost the same whether

it was added to existing structures or started independently; and Willis predicted, "I believe if we don't provide doctors or give all Texans equal rights to medical facilities and the chance to be treated, there is a possibility the federal government may step in and take care of the matter. They've done that in education."

Throughout the fall and winter, Guinn and his associates and supporters worked all over the state to build their case and strengthen their position. Efforts came to a climax on March 10, 1976, when Governor Briscoe accompanied Mrs. Briscoe to the TWU campus in Denton where she addressed the TWU Woman's Day Colloquium. During a luncheon speech, after a tour of the campus, the Governor hoped that the Coordinating Board would "look with favor on establishing a TWU medical school." He added, "We are not turning out enough family practitioners to meet the needs of people today." In interviews after the speech, however, he again told reporters that he would be bound by the Coordinating Board's recommendations and speculated that any medical school in the Rio Grande Valley would operate through Pan American University. Guinn took the conditional support as a positive sign, but he would see neither victory nor another defeat in this battle, for within a month he suffered a stroke and died.

Throughout his tenure Guinn had directed major expansions of the University's physical facilities. His earliest additions had marked a new direction in the architecture of the campus; and the buildings of his last decade in office rose to give both TWU and the city of Denton a skyline which dramatically demonstrated the high spirits, the high principles, and the high ambitions of the man who headed the University for almost twenty-six years.

As work on the first tower dormitory, Stark Hall, neared completion in 1967, Guinn announced plans in March for a thirteen-story general purpose classroom and office building, a second tower dormitory, a student center, and a mall.[19] Plans also called for the completion of the basement (some thirteen thousand square feet) that had been left unfinished at the last expansion of the Library and for a $175,000 expansion of the Library Science Building.[20] By the fall, 1968—before these projects were all completed—Regents were discussing the need for an addition to the Administration Building as well; and by summer, 1969, Guinn announced the development of plans for an eight-thousand-square-foot enlargement of the building, saying, in the TWU bulletin of July 15, 1969, "We have outgrown this building. . . . We are going to try to bring it together." The two-story addition extended the building westward to accommodate all administrative offices except that of the president.

By summer, 1967, excavation for the thirteen-story Classroom and Faculty Office (CFO) Building was underway, and the University post office and book store were moved from Brackenridge Hall so that that building could be demolished to provide a site for the new Student Center.

The CFO Building included several small classrooms for twenty-four to forty-two students on the first floor and four large classrooms (for two hundred students each) equipped for instructional television and movie viewing on the second floor. In addition, the first floor included space for a reading clinic established by the College of Education. The remainder of the building provided approximately 125 offices for departmental faculty, administrators, and staff, with the thirteenth floor set aside for the regents, the president, and the president's staff. Odd-numbered floors offered small lounges and conference rooms, and a fourteenth floor provided space for storage and machinery.[21] Although the working name *Classroom and Faculty Office (CFO) Building* on the plans and contracts became the official name for the building when it was opened for occupancy May 1, 1969, students nicknamed it "The Ivory Tower."

In late fall, 1967, Regents awarded a $1.5 million construction contract to Busboom and Rauh of Dallas and authorized the sale of $1 million in revenue bonds which, with a $500,000 loan from the Department of Housing and Urban Development, would cover the cost of the new Student Center.[22] In contrast to the towers which were rising on the campus, the new Student Center had a low silhouette with only a basement plus two stories above ground. With walls mostly of glass shaded by a fourteen-foot overhang, the building included 5600 square feet of bookstore space,[23] 3600 square feet for a post office, 600 square feet for the three meeting rooms and a projection room, five offices for student officers, a lounge with lockers, tables, and other facilities for commuting students, and a beauty shop.

The main features of the second floor were a large enclosed lounge with a view of downtown Denton and a snack bar to serve some four hundred students. The floor also included a music library and listening rooms, a piano room, and some administrative offices. The main entrance, which offered access to both the first and second floors, faced the Old Gymnasium to the north; but entrances on the west and south sides provided access to the first floor as well.

Although officials expected completion of the center in twelve to fifteen months, bad weather, strikes, and other problems delayed occupancy until the fall of 1969. Students and alumnae welcomed the center. Alumna Ann Badolati Roznovsky wrote in the TWU bulletin of March 15, 1970, that students must find it pleasant to be able to get mail "without breaking their backs or knocking down a classmate"; and the bulletin added, "Any alumna who remembers whizzing through the rickety doors to the Pub, glancing at an empty mailbox, then grabbing a '500' to sip on the way to class will love it."[24]

At the same time they awarded the construction contract for the new Student Center, TWU Regents called for bids on a second highrise dormitory to the northwest of Stark Hall. Thus, when professor Harral Landry described Stark Hall at its dedication as a "modern, bold, and imaginative" demonstration that "TWU can be at the forefront of colleges and universities in America, at least in bricks and mortar," work was underway for a second tower that would be larger (twenty-four stories to house more than seven hundred students) and more expensive (approximately $3.5 million) than Stark Hall. It would, in fact, be taller than any other dormitory in the nation.

Alumnae began a successful movement to have the dorm named for the President of the University who would be ending almost twenty years of

The first nonresidential high-rise building on the campus was the Classroom and Faculty Office (CFO) Building.

Mary Eleanor Brackenridge Hall was demolished to make room for a new Student Center.

207

Reagan Houston Hall was named for a long-time member of the TWU Board of Regents.

The name of the Graduate Science Research Building specified its function.

service by the time the building was completed in the fall of 1969. The dormitory that had been named for Guinn when it opened in 1965 was renamed Reagan Houston Hall.[25]

The interior of the highrise Guinn Hall was similar to that of Stark with twenty apartments on the second and third floors reserved for graduate students, several floors reserved for freshmen, and all other floors available to sophomores, juniors, and seniors.[26] The building included 326 double rooms with private baths and fifteen single rooms arranged in five suites, each of which had a living room and a bath.

Construction of this newest and largest addition to the housing facilities of the Denton campus had barely begun before suggestions of even greater housing needs surfaced, however. The TWU bulletin of March 15, 1968, reported that existing dormitory facilities were ninety percent occupied and suggested that the lack of adequate housing might hinder future growth. In the fall of the same year, Mary Hufford Hall, the cooperative dormitory, became a part of the regular dormitory system. Although the residents took pride in their "home cooking," centralized meal service in Hubbard Hall became more economical; and quantity food service in Hufford ceased although the kitchen equipment remained for the use of residents. The Hufford Hall dining room was converted into an enlarged living room and lounge-study area. The change called for a $40 per semester increase in charges for living in the dorm, but Hufford remained the lowest priced residence hall on campus.

Within weeks after the dedication of the new John A. Guinn Hall, the TWU bulletin of March 15, 1970, reported, "Another tower dormitory may soar above the TWU landscape by 1972." The building proved unnecessary, however. Changing enrollment patterns—increased enrollment of graduate, commuter, and mature students—and changing student attitudes about the desirability of University-provided housing soon led to the availability of more than adequate dormitory space in Denton. By the fall of 1970 the oldest dormitories on the campus (Capps and Lowry Halls) had been retired.[27]

The Houston Center was operating at capacity, however, and by early spring, 1968, following receipt of a grant of $763,000 from the Department of Health, Education, and Welfare and a grant of $600,000 from Houston Endowment, Inc., construction was underway on a new six-story Mary Gibbs Jones Education Building. The College of Nursing and the Schools of Physical Therapy and Occupational Therapy, which would offer instruction in the Jones Building, contributed specifications for its extensive laboratory and classroom facilities.[28]

In late 1969 construction began on a $1.8 million eleven-story dormitory in Houston to house 258 students. Because of limited land availablity, both new buildings were planned to make possible the addition of floors when needed. Part of the new dormitory in Houston was occupied by the spring of 1971 even though it was not completed until later in the year; and the alumnae bulletin for the spring of 1971 reported, "A long-range plan in discussion is the building of another dorm for the Houston Center" (another dorm that has not been needed.)

On February 11, 1970, Governor Preston Smith, Lieutenant Governor Ben Barnes, State Senator Ralph Hall, and State Representative Walt Parker participated in dedication ceremonies for $9.5 million worth of new buildings on the Denton campus—the new highrise Guinn Hall and the CFO Tower, the new Student Center, the additions to the Library and the Library Science Building, and the Graduate Science Research Building.[29] Morning ceremonies consisted of three symposia—one in library science, one in biology and chemistry, and one in education—with the theme, "The Texas Woman's University's Modern Resources in Service to Texas and the Nation."

Following a luncheon in Hubbard Hall and dedication ceremonies in the Main Auditorium in the afternoon, the new buildings were open for tours. At the dedication Governor Smith reminded listeners in the standing room only crowd, "The facilities are merely symbolic of the human resources of this University that are even more impressive and are what we are really here to honor."

Lieutenant Governor Barnes challenged the audience, "For the first time, students have the rare opportunity, because of those who have gone before, to remove the world 'impossible' from their vocabularies" and predicted that the seventies would be "the most rewarding decade Texans or Americans have ever seen because of its women. They are ready to act, ready to lead."

Guinn expressed his confidence that the University was "headed in the right direction," adding "I'm proud that TWU is a vigorous part of higher education on the move." Indicative of the modern direction in which TWU was moving was the initiation of closed circuit color television service on the campus on the same day that the multimillion-dollar buildings were dedicated. The system was the first of its kind at a university in the North Texas area and possibly in the country.

The day was memorable, celebrating the largest increase ever in the physical plant of the University and receiving coverage by television crews from across the state. As usual, Agatha Exe viewed the proceedings from her special vantage point, writing in the TWU bulletin of March 15, 1970, "But the day was not left to the sameness of the usual dedicatory pomp. . . . Prominent in all activities were the students, TWU's finest advertisement." Nostalgia was not absent from her description either: "I am sure it was a fine day, but in all the clamor of praising the new, I felt sorry for the dignitaries who loved the new without ever having enjoyed the old. Who among them, I ask you, could truly appreciate the new research building not having dined in the cafeteria of the old home ec building that used to stand there? Or received hot cookies out the door of Gleason Cottage in one's way home from Dem School? Or galloped a spotted pony where the new dormitory now stands?"

Nostalgia, notwithstanding, TWU was committed to the future; and the rising towers on the Denton campus symbolized the upward reach of the University and its students. In late 1969 the University purchased three lots at the intersection of East College Street and Bell Avenue at a cost of $113,000 to serve as the location of the last high-rise instructional building to be built on the Denton campus.[30] In the early spring of 1970, with millions of dollars worth of construction recently completed, in progress, or planned, Regents approved a five-year extension of Guinn's contract. In the Alumnae Bulletin of the Fall of 1970, Guinn told an interviewer, "In my 20 years I don't recall any time that we weren't planning and growing and expanding," and there would be no such time during the remainder of his tenure.

The nine-story Multipurpose Classroom-Laboratory Building contained 114, 567 square feet, which included a four-hundred-seat auditorium plus office, classroom, laboratory, and clinic space. The first floor contained the auditorium, a dental hygiene clinic, and a nursing competency laboratory. Classrooms, offices, and a curriculum materials center for the College of Education were housed on the second through the fifth floors. The fifth floor also contained classroom and laboratory space for the School of Occupational Therapy which had office space on the sixth floor. The School of Physical Therapy occupied the seventh and eighth floors, and the eighth floor housed the speech and hearing clinic. The ninth floor contained space for the Institute for Mental and Physical Development. Texas Secretary of State Mark White delivered the dedicatory address for the building on November 7, 1973. Like the CFO Tower, the MCL Building

The Hubbard Hall oval became the only place on campus large enough to accommodate commencement. John A. Guinn and Nelda C. Stark Residence Halls rise in the background.

The Multipurpose Classroom-Laboratory Building added new high-rise instructional space.

A historical marker for Old Main was dedicated April 26, 1974.

The addition of six floors to Mary Gibbs Jones Hall at the TWU Houston Center (top) and a second floor for the academic building of the TWU Dallas Center doubled instructional space at both locations.

had, by the time of its dedication, acquired an unofficial title, "A New Tower of Learning."

Returning alumnae found their campus looking less and less as they remembered it, but students from every class shared the memory of the original building. And all who wished could join Stella Timberlake Kempster of the class of 1905 who reported in the TWU bulletin of July 15, 1969, that she always climbed the steps of the building when she returned to the campus "just for old times' sake." To assure the preservation of the building, the Past Presidents' Council of the TWU Alumnae Association sponsored the identification of "Old Main," as it came to be called, as a historical monument. The historical marker for the building was dedicated April 26, 1974, with U.S. Representative Ray Roberts delivering the dedicatory address. By the fall, renovation of the building was preparing it to house both research programs and the University's archives and historical collection.

Old space and new space in Denton, however, did not meet the needs in Houston and Dallas. In only three years, the programs in Houston had outgrown the original six floors of Mary Gibbs Jones Hall, and by the fall of 1973, Houston Endowment, Inc., had contributed $600,000 for the addition of six floors to the building. The new space would add multipurpose laboratories and graduate research areas which included metabolic laboratories, x-ray facilities, an instrumentation laboratory, and an animal storage area.[31] Almost simultaneously with the construction in Houston, the addition of a second story to the educational building at the Dallas Center doubled instructional space there, adding a two-hundred-seat auditorium and doubling the size of the library and learning resource areas.

In May, 1974, as Guinn approached the end of twenty-four years of service to the University, Regents approved a second new five-year contract for him and approved the sale of $9.47 million in state ad valorem tax bonds. As the additions in Dallas and Houston neared completion in the early spring of 1975, plans for a new building to contain administrative and faculty offices, meeting and conference rooms, and facilities for continuing education were announced. Although construction for the last of the highrise buildings, a $4 million, eighteen-story administration/conference tower, was begun in the fall of 1975, it would not be completed during Guinn's life. One other building, a small Undergraduate Science Laboratory Building just south of the Nutrition, Textiles, and Human Development Building, would also be begun on the Denton campus during Guinn's tenure as would the building for a new campus in Dallas near the Presbyterian Hospital;[32] but completion of all three would be the responsibility of Guinn's successor.

On March 27, as he waited backstage at TWU's Main Auditorium to crown the 1976 Redbud Queen, Guinn suffered a stroke. Rushed by ambulance to Westgate Hospital in Denton, he remained in the critical care unit there until his death on April 1.

[1]In explaining this and other changes in the alumnae bulletin for the fall of 1970, CGA President Annella Wright said, "We eliminated the honor code not because it was bad, but because, like the title *The University Woman,* it was being smirked at. We felt that honor should come from within the person and not because they were asked to sign a card."

[2]According to an informal poll conducted by the *Lass-O,* the majority of TWU students shared Pair's conservative views. The results of the poll published October 27 indicated that seventy-five percent of the seventy students polled considered themselves moderate on woman's liberation, and only two percent said they were "extremist"; but eighty-two percent said they believed in "equal opportunities for the sexes." Fifty-five percent of the students said they did not believe, "A woman's place is at home"; and twenty-five percent believed that her place was "where she wanted to be." Half of the students said that their views on women's liberation had remained the same since coming to TWU, and thirty-six percent said their views had been strengthened. Fifty-five percent of the students classified TWU as "conservative," and fifty-five percent said that they would go to a woman doctor if they had a choice between a man and a woman.

[3]The early performances involved at different times the YWCA and even the Faculty Club, which staged stunts related to financial needs and raising money in 1919. The tradition of freshman and sophomore presentations for the entertainment of the upper classes gave way in 1938 to competition among the four classes for a silver loving cup. Typically light in content, the stunts took a serious turn in the mid-fifties, "preaching sermons on social problems" according to Francis Emerson in the February 11, 1969, issue of the *Lass-O*; but when the freshmen won the cup in 1964 with a light presentation, the programs returned to their original focus on entertainment.

[4]Guinn was experienced in interuniversity agreements, having been elected first chairman of the Inter-University Council (IUC) formed in 1964 to further graduate education in the north central Texas area. Beginning with five member universities, the IUC had doubled its membership by 1969. Although the bylaws of the Federation permit membership by schools in Collin, Dallas, Denton, Ellis, Grayson, Hunt, Johnson, Kaufman, Rockwall, and Tarrant Counties, no other universities have elected membership.

[5]Students had been involved in social work field work since 1946.

[6]The baccalaureate and master's programs in therapeutic recreation are unique in Texas, and only six universities in the nation offer the Ph.D. in the field.

[7]The TWU bulletin of July 15, 1973, specified the areas of graduate study at the master's level which are, with few exceptions, still offered today: the Master of Arts in all areas in which bachelor's degrees may be obtained except journalism and physical therapy; the Master of Science in biology, chemistry, household arts and sciences, nursing, physics, and physical therapy; the Master of Science in Science Education in biology, chemistry, mathematics and physics; the Master of Education in education and communication disorders; the Master of Home Economics Education; the Master of Library Science; and the Master of Occupational Therapy.

[8]The existing college and schools continued to offer their established curricula. The new School of Health Care Services offered programs which led to the B.S. degree in dental hygiene, dietetics (beginning in the fall, 1973), medical record administration, and medical technology. It also offered programs which led to the M.S. degree in health care administration and in health sciences instruction.

[9]The policy was in compliance with Titles VII and VIII of the Public Health Service Act.

[10]Within three years (spring, 1975) students elected the first male president of the Campus Government Association. George Kydd, a junior occupational therapy major, was also the first black and the first non-residential student to be elected to the office; but he resigned his position before the fall, citing "inability to maintain particular eligibility requirements."

[11]Male students had attended a few graduate courses at TWU prior to this time through cooperative arrangements with institutions in the Federation of North Texas Area Universities; but they were enrolled in those institutions, not in TWU.

[12]The University General Divisions encompassed all undergraduate programs in the Colleges of Arts and Sciences; Education; Fine Arts; Health, Physical Education, and Recreation; and Household Arts and Sciences and in the School of Library Science.

[13]Newspapers termed the national shortage "acute," and some estimates placed the need for doctors in Texas at 2500 in 1973.

[14]Texas Medical Association records showed the average physician-population ratio in the U.S. to be 1:700 and the ratio in Texas to be 1:961. The Texas Rural Development Commission on Health reported the ratio of doctors to residents in rural Texas to be 1:1600.

[15]In explaining the reasons for the application Guinn pointed to TWU's broad range of doctoral studies in science, its nursing program (the largest in the United States), and the variety of already available allied health fields which usually had to be acquired after a medical school was begun. Guinn also pointed out to the Regents that a medical school had

Apathy in some areas did not diminish the excitement participants felt in winning the Stunts competition.

The student body came to include increasing numbers of "non-traditional" students.

been a planned part of the Institute of Health Sciences from its beginning (the Institute was the first in the state); and he concluded, "I have assiduously avoided, through the years, taking on things that weren't any of our business. . . . And I think this is very much a part of our institutional strength."

[16]Located on the north side of Fort Worth in the southeast quadrant of the intersection of Interstate Highway 35W and Loop 820, the land was contributed by the American Manufacturing Company of Texas (Edd Lott, General Manager), Sears, Roebuck and Co. (J. L. Oppel, General Manager of Sears operations in the Fort Worth area), and Woodbine Development Corporation (Ray L. Hunt, President).

[17]Data also showed that more than seventy percent of the M.D.s in Texas were concentrated in ten counties with a physician-population ratio of 1:725 whereas the remaining 244 counties had a ratio of 1:1464 and that the number of additional doctors in office-based practice in Texas had declined from 328 in 1969 to 52 in 1973. Projections showed the need for almost 4000 more M.D.s in Texas to bring the state's physician-population ratio to the national average.

[18]The original (1973) TWU proposal called for $9,859,000 for the construction of instructional, administrative, and support facilities with no funds for planning, for a site, or for clinical facilities. The estimate rose to $11,042,339 through adjustments for inflation in 1975 and doubled to approximately $22 million when the amended bill called for a second component in the Rio Grande Valley. Objections to the costs divided along two lines: (1) The state could not afford the new school (although the Conference Committee on Appropriations approved an increase of $24 million in state funds for the newly approved TCOM on May 28); (2) The requested amount was not enough to support a medical school properly (Planning alone for the Texas Tech Medical School, which opened August 21, 1972, had cost some $10 million).

[19]The mall has not become a reality.

[20]The two-story addition doubled the space available for Library Science instruction, providing space for a data processing laboratory, faculty offices, and other facilities. Both the Library Science addition and the finishing of the basement of the Library were completed by the end of January, 1969.

[21]Located between the Education Building (Old Main) and Stoddard Hall, facing Redbud Lane, the $1.7 million CFO Tower was financed by funds from the state ad valorem tax, passed in a constitutional amendment election in the fall of 1965, and from matching funds provided by the federal government under Title I of the Higher Education Act of 1965.

The main (first-floor) entrance of the building faced the proposed mall on Redbud Lane, across from the Arts and Sciences Building; and the entrance on the second floor opened to the east toward the Journalism Building.

[22]A group of Dallas firms bought the bonds at an interest rate of 5.614%. The interest rate on the loan was three percent.

[23]Although TWU and other state schools for many years provided textbooks on a rental basis, the practice was discontinued; and students were required to purchase their textbooks by the time the new center was built. The bookstore also provided a check-cashing service in place of the banking services the University offered for many years.

[24]Simultaneous with the construction of the new Student Center was the demolition of a landmark, Escues' College Store (the "C Store") across from the campus on Oakland Avenue. (A new Voertman Building, which housed a book store, gift shop, and other space, was constructed on the site. TWU purchased the Voertman Building and adjacent buildings in 1978.) The store, which had been operated by its owner R. B. Escue, Sr., from 1916 until it closed, delighted students with its round tables, its ice cream parlor chairs, and its wooden showcases full of home-made chocolate-covered peanuts, divinity, peanut brittle, and fudge. Sugar rationing, difficulty in obtaining special ingredients, and, according to Escue who made the candy, students' fear of "getting fat" put an end to the home-made candy in World War II; but the "C Store" remained an important part of campus life; and the Escue family contributed one of the original wooden showcases to the Alumnae Association.

[25]Reagan Houston, III, from San Antonio had been a member of the TWU Board of Regents throughout Guinn's years in office. He was Chairman of the Board in 1968.

[26]Reagan Houston Hall, often described as somewhat "motel-like," came to provide housing for some graduate students by the fall of 1974.

[27]The winter alumnae bulletin for 1973 offered a picture of the "typical Tessie" of 1972 based on information provided by registrar John Tompkins. She was 21 years old or older, married, and a resident of the Dallas metropolitan area. Of the 6259 students enrolled that fall 27.3% were graduate students. One student was only 15 years old, but 1519 students were at least 31 years old. Although 46.7% of the students lived within 100 miles of Denton, 9.9% came from states outside Texas (each of the 50 states was represented); and 3.2% represented 33 foreign countries, including brand new Bangladesh. The junior class with 978 students was the smallest class. The 1360 freshman comprised the largest class although almost as many (1350) students already held baccalaureate degrees.

[28]TWU Regent Reagan Houston, III, delivered the keynote address for the dedication of the Jones Building on March 16, 1970.

212

[29]The Graduate Science Research Building was completed in the fall of 1967.

[30]The $3.85 million building was financed by the sale of college revenue bonds at 6.445% interest. In the summer of 1971 the University received a federal grant of more than $2 million to be applied to the interest on the bonds, reducing the rate to 3%.

[31]C. R. Huppelsheuser of Fort Worth served as architect for the addition.

[32]In 1974, TWU completed an agreement with Presbyterian Hospital in Dallas which would allow one hundred TWU students in the health sciences to train at the hospital. The number of students would, according to the plan, reach four hundred in four years.

Moving Faster, Standing Closer

XII

Following Dr. Guinn's collapse on Saturday night, Regents turned immediately to the Dean of the TWU Graduate School, Mary Evelyn Blagg Huey, to serve as President pro tem of the University. Reports that Dr. Guinn was in "fair but stable" condition led some to believe that he would be able to return to work. A headline in the Denton *Record-Chronicle* of March 29, 1976, announced Dr. Huey's temporary appointment, "Huey Takes Guinn's Job At TWU," as if it were unthinkable that the job could belong to anyone besides the man who had held it for almost twenty-six years. Meeting with the faculty and staff on Monday morning, Dr. Huey told the assembly, "I look to you to move a little faster and stand a little closer because it's going to be business as usual at TWU."

A University official announced, "The staff will be running the show until Dr. Guinn comes back"; and when Dr. Huey met with the Campus Government Association on March 30, she promised, "I intend to maintain devotion to Dr. Guinn's basic purposes," noting that she anticipated his resumption of duties. President Guinn died, however, on April 1; and eight days later the Regents appointed Dr. Huey acting president. When she left the Graduate School, she told Associate Dean Phyllis Bridges, "I'll be right back." But Maggie Kennedy reported in the Dallas *Times Herald* on October 17, "Dr. Bridges is still waiting"; for the Regents elected Dr. Huey to be the seventh President of the University on August 19.

In her four months of service as acting president, a number of dreams begun under Dr. Guinn became realities. More than one thousand students received degrees at spring commencement; and Chairman of the TWU Board of Regents Marcella D. Perry received the University's fifth honorary doctorate, the LL.D. In the summer, accompanied by Professor Bethel M. Caster, Dr. Huey visited Tehran to complete an agreement for an academic and cultural exchange with Farah Pahlavi University, Iran's only university for women. Work on a new proposal for the medical school continued.

Making the presidency something besides "Guinn's Job" was not automatic; but even as acting president, Dr. Huey had noted that changes were inevitable. At spring commencement on May 15, she acknowledged the loss of a "great leader during this Diamond Jubilee year" and promised that the basics would continue in spite of some changing emphases. She promised an unchanged dedication to preparing graduates to fill the roles they chose for themselves and an expansion of the University as a

Alumna Mary Evelyn Blagg Huey was inaugurated the seventh President of TWU.

215

Marcella D. Perry, outstanding Houston businesswoman, received the fifth honorary doctorate awarded by TWU.

"wellspring of knowledge in the sciences, the liberal arts, the fine arts." In addition, she pledged, "We will continue and grow as a place of preparation for careers in the service, homemaking, and educating arts. We shall maintain TWU's place of leadership in preparation for the healing arts."

By the time of her selection as President, Dr. Huey was ready to make the job her own, noting in the TWU bulletin of August 15, 1976, "I will not be operating in anybody's shadow but in some important footsteps." Having been a student under President Hubbard and a member of the administrative staff under President Guinn, the new President could draw on the strengths of two great men who had together led the school in very different ways for more than two-thirds of its existence. In addition, she brought her own strengths and her own perceptions of the University, of what it had been, and of what it could be.

Living during her college years across the street from the campus in a house built by the first President of the College, being the daughter and sister of alumnae, attending the TSCW Demonstration School for kindergarten and first grade instruction, visiting frequently in the University printshop which was under her father's direction, enjoying association with the College's students from her third year, and earning two degrees from TSCW gave Dr. Huey a unique familiarity with the campus and a superlative feeling for and identification with its character. She had known the University twice as long at the beginning of her administration as either President Hubbard or President Guinn had known it at the end of theirs.

Students, alumnae, and faculty hailed her appointment. She shared with students and alumnae an intimate knowledge of and participation in the University's traditions. She had, as a student, contributed short stories and essays to the *Daedalian Quarterly,* played in the TSCW Symphony Orchestra, performed as soprano soloist with the TSCW Modern Choir, and graduated in 1942 with academic honors in each of her four years as a student of music and English.

She shared with the faculty the rigors of graduate study—having completed the Master of Arts degree in English literature at TSCW in 1943, a second Master of Arts degree in public administration at the University of Kentucky in 1947, and the Doctor of Philosophy degree in political science in 1954 at Duke University. She also shared with the faculty the discipline of scholarly research and writing—having published significant studies in public administration and political science—and the satisfaction of teaching—having served as instructor in English at TSCW from 1943 to 1945 and teaching government at North Texas State University from 1947 to 1951 and from 1954 to 1971.

Her academic career had also taken her to study at the University of Alabama, the University of Tennessee, and Harvard University. Research for her doctoral dissertation had carried her to the Library of Congress and to New York, Boston, Richmond, and Williamsburg.

In addition to her personal ties to the school and her academic accomplishments, Dr. Huey also brought administrative experience. Her participation in professional, civic, and governmental agencies had been extensive: a year's internship with the Tennessee Valley Authority, the directorship of the Bureau of Public Administration at the University of Mississippi, and five years of service as the Dean of the TWU Graduate School. Recognizing her accomplishments, TWU named her a distinguished alumna in 1974.

In an editorial on August 22, 1976, the Denton *Record-Chronicle* recognized her appointment as "another sign of progress on the TWU campus." Praising, Dr. Huey for her "love for the University . . . coupled with . . . savvy and understanding," the editor identified in the new President "a dedication to purpose, a deep compassion, and ad-

216

ministrative-academic credentials worthy of the president of any university."

As the University moved toward the completion of commitments made under Dr. Guinn, the new President began to declare her own goals. The *Lass-O* of September 9, 1976, included a statement of her belief that educators should teach values as well as communicate information to their students. The story by *Lass-O* editor Terry Parker also outlined Dr. Huey's interest in campus beautification, particularly in the restoration of the botanical gardens in Lowry Woods. The article included Dr. Huey's emphatic statement, "I want to change the image and the knowledge of Texas Woman's University. People have not heard of the University, and I intend to let the world know about us." To aid in these and other plans, the President's Council of TWU was formed both to raise money to help meet University needs not adequately financed through legislative appropriations and to offer support in an advisory capacity to the TWU President.

Among other goals identified by Dr. Huey in an interview with staff writer Maggie Kennedy for the Dallas *Times Herald* of October 17, 1976, were the building of a new library-media center, a renaissance of liberal and fine arts programs, and a possible restructuring of the curriculum to include fewer required courses in non-major areas. By November 12, Dr. Huey could report to the TWU chapter of the Texas Association of College Teachers (TACT) that search committees had been formed to seek chairmen, directors, and deans for components of the University which were without leaders, indicating that the new method of "peer selection" would be tried for a year or two. She also announced the development of plans for international and foreign studies and plans for improving relations between Denton and the TWU centers in Dallas and Houston.

Returning from the annual national convention of the American Association of State Colleges and Universities, Dr. Huey reported in the *Lass-O* of December 3, "I was both alarmed and reassured to discover that university presidents who have been in office 20-30 years have not found solutions to some of the problems I am trying to look at." Among the problems of state universities throughout the nation were funding, enrollment, curricula, and maintenance, none of which was a new problem for TWU and none of which lent itself to an easy solution.

Nevertheless, students, faculty, and alumnae shared widely the feeling expressed in a *Lass-O* editorial of September 10, 1976: "There is a sense of fresh air blowing through the University and its administration. The change in attitude felt is a good one." Enrollment continued to rise, reaching a new record of 8,739 for the fall (an 8.3 percent increase over the 1975 fall total) even though most schools in the area were experiencing modest rises of about 2.5 percent. The increase was less (3.6 percent) the following fall; but TWU still set a new record of 9,052. In the spring of 1978 TWU joined other universities throughout the country which were experiencing a loss of enrollment after many years of growth.

TWU also began, like other universities, to experience a significant change in the character of its student body. Registrar John Tompkins noted in a *Lass-O* article of April 29, 1977, that forty-four percent of TWU's students came from the Dallas-Fort Worth area, compared to twenty-two percent in the fall of 1968. Lysa Ausmus reported in the *Lass-O* of November 30, 1978, that twenty-seven percent of TWU's students during the current semester were thirty-one years of age or older and that the average age had risen from twenty in 1968 to twenty-seven in 1978. Nationwide, she reported, the number of college students at least thirty-five years old had risen thirty percent from 1972 to 1974.

Declining enrollments led to rumors in the spring of 1979 and even to a report in the Denton *Record-Chronicle* that TWU would be forced to reduce its faculty. Dr. Huey used both the Founders' Day celebration on February 16 and an interview in the *Lass-O* on February 20 to assure the faculty that no layoffs were in store, noting that the heavy graduate enrollment plus the strong sciences and health sciences enrollments would help secure adequate appropriations for the University through the formula funding system used by the Legislature. Regents, faculty, and staff concentrated major efforts on rebuilding the enrollment.

Declines in enrollment and changes in students brought challenges to a variety of long-established traditions. Complaints about parking, housing, and food at university campuses have been so widely voiced over so long a time that they seem almost traditions themselves. Expressing their dissatisfactions strongly, TWU students found new listerners willing to try to alleviate some of the problems. Sensitive to surveys, editorials in the *Lass-O,* and resolutions which demonstrated the desire of many undergraduate students to live off campus and in spite of low occupancy rates in the University's residence halls, Regents approved on November 2, 1978, a recommendation to allow junior and senior students to live off campus beginning the following spring. Unmarried students with fewer than sixty hours of credit would still be required to live on campus unless they lived with their parents or were more than twenty-one years old. The *Lass-O* editorial of November 7 urged students, "[We hope] this new degree of latitude will not result in a mad surge of students haplessly rushing to find an apartment. You have been put in an adult situation. Respond as an adult."

To improve food services, the University employed a consultant who studied both dining hall and snack bar facilities and recommended changes. To improve parking, the University purchased the Whitson and Voertman properties adjacent to the west edge of the campus on Oakland Avenue with plans to clear them for parking, and a large new parking lot was constructed on the southwest corner of the campus behind the Art Building.

Other student requests were newer to TWU students than to students at other universities. Following student petitions for the approval of national sororities on campus, Dr. Huey authorized, in January, 1978, establishment of a national panhellenic council for TWU. The *Lass-O* of January 27 reported that she noted in her recommendation to the Board of Regents that she made the recommendation "with some personal misgivings" and that she recognized that the action was "contrary to the tradition of all students being able to participate in all activities at TWU, regardless of their financial standing."

Another student demand resulted on October 24, 1977, in the adoption by the Student Government Association (SGA) of a resolution calling for permission to have and consume beer and wine in individual student's rooms on the campus. Shortly before Thanksgiving the following year the SGA adopted the following stronger resolution, reported in the *Lass-O* of November 30: "Be it resolved that the SGA Denton Campus, recommends the possession and consumption of alcoholic beverages be allowed in residence halls and at social activities registered with Student Life." Both the President and the Board of Regents rejected the requests.

A relatively small part of the University's energies, however, was spent in struggles for change. Traditional activities acquired an extra luster as the President supported them with her presence and participation. Stunts, Corn Huskin', Gold Rush, the Redbud Festival, and other traditional activities continued to incite feverish excitement among a limited number of students. In the 1977 Stunts, the senior class retired the stunt cup by winning its third consecutive competition, the first class since the class of 1967 to achieve such success.

President Huey became an enthusiastic participant in Gold Rush (shown here) and other campus activities and traditions.

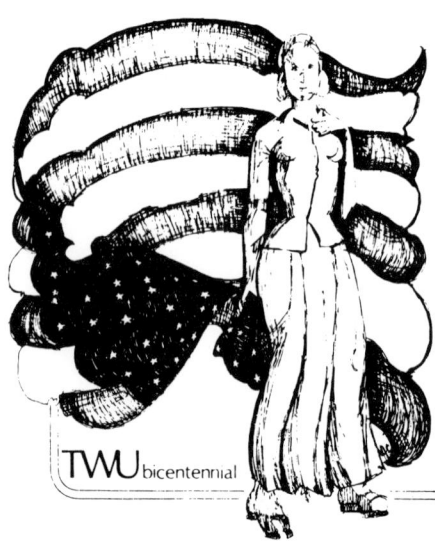

TWU joined the nation in celebrating the American bicentennial.

218

Along with strengthening traditions, Dr. Huey re-established and revitalized neglected traditions. On November 22, 1977, the University renewed its traditional Fall Convocation, which had ended in the early fifties. Following the academic processional with faculty in full regalia, Dr. John W. McFarland, Dean of the College of Education, convoked the assembly in a booming voice in the Main Auditorium and delivered the main address, "Potentialities of the University." In December, Dr. Jack K. Williams, Chancellor of the Texas A & M University System, addressed some four hundred fifty graduates in the first December graduation since 1956.[1] On February 24, 1978, delayed twice by ice storms, Founders' Day was celebrated on the Denton campus with a pancake buffet and the musical *Cinderella,* the first such celebration since the mid-fifties.

On April 25, 1979, the University held its first Honors Convocation in many years, recognizing 263 students and four distinguished alumnae for their outstanding accomplishments. History professor A. Elizabeth Taylor delivered the main address, "The Importance of Excellence," and was the surprised recipient of a Piper Professorship.

Mixed together with these revivals were a number of very special one-time occasions celebrating the nation's bicentennial, the University's Diamond Jubilee, and the inauguration of the new President. The week following President Guinn's death and funeral had been set aside, before his illness, for the celebration of the nation's bicentennial and the University proceeded with a full range of films, lectures, slide shows, and other commemorative activities. A highlight of the week was the appearance of "The Co-Respondents," a trio of women whose dramatic and musical presentations revealed women in literature, history, and politics.

Diamond Jubilee activities in the fall celebrated the seventy-fifth anniversary of the founding of the University with a week-long series of events highlighted by the appearance of soprano Leona Mitchell, pianist Ruth Slenczynska, and the Fort Worth Symphony Orchestra. Diamond Jubilee activities, with the theme "Marking a Trail," continued through the 1978-79 school year, which was the seventy-fifth anniversary of the beginning of classes at the University.

The celebration reached its peak in October, 1978, with a week-long series of activities which included film festivals, seminars, art exhibits, library tours, videotapes, addresses, open houses, receptions, and a wealth of other offerings. The focus of the week was the Diamond Jubilee Convocation on October 12. Dr. John R. Hubbard, President of the University of Southern California and son of TWU's fifth President, delivered the main address. Other key features of the convocation were the dedication of the Administration-Conference Tower and the awarding of the University's first Cornaro Award for excellence in teaching to Dr. Ethelyn C. Davis, professor of sociology and social work.[2]

Diamond Jubilee activities continued through the spring with a convocation at TWU's Dallas Center on February 26, featuring an address by President Huey.[3] On April 4, Chairman of the Board of Regents Marcella D. Perry addressed the Diamond Jubilee Convocation at the Houston Center.

In the midst of the jubilee activities came the inauguration of the seventh President of the University on April 15, 1977. Months of preparation by students, alumnae, faculty, and staff preceded the event, which served as a showcase for the widespread affection these groups shared for the new President and for a new sense of pride in the University. The inaugural committee, headed by Graduate School Dean Phyllis Bridges, organized and did the work of issuing invitations to hundreds of delegates, planning the convocation, greeting guests, and arranging the luncheon, reception, and inaugural gala.

Azam Kassirzadeh, an exchange student from the faculty of Farah Pahlavi University in Tehran, designed a new academic gown for the

Founders' Day celebrations were reinstituted in 1978. (Top) Alumnae Association President Laverne Collins Chatfield leads a candlelighting ceremony. (Bottom) the musical Cinderella *entertained guests at the traditional pancake supper.*

Graduate Dean Phyllis Bridges coordinated inaugual planning.

Azam Kassirzadeh designed the inaugural robe.

Norine Kitsinger designed a commemorative inaugural medallion.

President. Norine Kitsinger, sister of the President and TWU alumna, designed an inaugural medallion in gold, which was also issued as a commemorative medal in both bronze and silver. Textile science and clothing student Audrey Steele designed an inaugural ball gown, which was made for Dr. Huey by students in the department under the direction of Professor Bethel Caster.

Arthur E. (Bud) Green, assistant professor of art, designed and made the University's first mace. Describing his work in the *Lass-O* of February 4, Green explained, "The design of the TWU mace and the materials it is being made of were chosen to reflect the unique spirit and nature of the University for which it will serve as a symbol." Consisting of a staff of vermilion wood, banded by ivory, and topped with a sterling silver sphere with an encircling band of silver matched by a smaller sphere at the bottom, the mace effectively combined the traditional with the contemporary as did the medallion which depicted the original college building and the modern CFO Tower encircled by stars. The stars, Mrs. Kitsinger explained, represented the goals toward which the University should reach. Both the mace and the medallion captured the spirit of building toward the future on a solid past which would characterize Dr. Huey's administration.

The days before the inaugural, which was scheduled to coincide with alumnae homecoming activities, were full of floor scrubbing, grass trimming, flower planting, brass polishing, and sidewalk sweeping so that the University could present its best appearance for the new President and the hundreds of guests who arrived. The TWU Orchestra and Choir prepared the music for the convocation, and musicians and dancers practiced the entertainment for the gala. Lights burned late in the print shop as staff checked the last details of the special inaugural booklet. The day brought together the best efforts of people from all ranks of the University community in a celebration of the past, the present, and hopes for the future.

Dr. John H. Hallowell, James B. Duke Professor of Political Science at Duke University and director of Dr. Huey's doctoral dissertation, delivered the main address. Dr. Marcella D. Perry, Chairman of the TWU Board of Regents, invested Dr. Huey with the powers of her office, placing a symbolic gold chain and medallion around her neck. The orchestra played and the audience sang, "Hail! Alma Mater! Hail!" Contemporary students wondered at hearing alumnae sing the official alma mater which had not been sung for many years. The program included "To The Texas Woman's University" as well, for the song had been the unofficial school song for students of almost the last thirty years.[4]

In an open letter to the administration, faculty, staff, and students, dated September 2, 1977, Dr. Huey reported, "I am still writing thank-yous for the many lovely gifts and thoughtful deeds which came to me and to TWU on that occassion. . . . For this beautiful silver, and for your gifts of encouragement, friendship, support, and loyalty, I thank each and every one of you from by heart."[5]

An intensity of emotion and hard work characterized the inaugural activities to make them a unique experience, but life on the campus was not dull either before or after April 15, 1977. The Grand Concert of the All-Girl Orchestra Festival brought guest conductors Antonio Brico in April, 1976, and Fiora Contino in February, 1977. Other concerts included the 5 X 2 Dance Company in April, 1978; the Groupe Vocal de France in October, 1977; Melba Moore in November, 1977; and Texas Opera Theater performances of *Robinson Crusoe, Hansel and Gretel,* and *The Marriage of Figaro.* On February 9, 1979, "First Lady of Bach" Rosalyn Tureck dedicated the University's new Dowd harpsichord with an all-Bach concert in the MCLB Auditorium. On March 8, Edith Head appeared with a fashion show at a benefit dinner sponsored by Richard Brooks Fabrics of Dallas, Vogue-Butterick Patterns, and TWU to introduce the Southwest Institute of Design to some five hundred guests. A myriad of other visitors from the arts, the sciences, business, politics, and the health sciences brought an increased vitality to the campus.

The traffic was not all inward, however. In addition to signing the academic and cultural exchange agreement with Farah Pahlavi University, Dr. Huey effected subsequent agreements with Baiko-Jo Gaukin University in Japan and the University of Chihuahua in Mexico. Also, increasing numbers of professors were being invited to share the findings of their research at international conferences; and student groups were traveling internationally. In the fall of 1976, Janice McCaleb, doctoral student in dance, received a Fulbright-Hays grant to study in Denmark the following spring. The fifty-member Concert Choir toured Romania for two weeks in the summer of 1977, and the TWU Dance Repertory Theatre performed and taught master classes in Rio de Janeiro and Brazilia in July for the *Associacao dos Professores de Educacao Fisica* and for the Brazilian Ministry of Education.[6] Also during the summer, the University established a pilot program of studies abroad in cooperation with the American Institute for Foreign Study to complement a number of courses the University offered which included foreign travel. Seventy-eight students and six faculty members participated in the program in the summer of 1978.

Nearer to home, but still on a large scale, student athletes were also bringing recognition to TWU. In the spring of 1977, the track team won the Texas Association for Intercollegiate Athletics for Women (AIAW) championship for the ninth time in ten years. In the fall the softball team won the state softball championship. The following spring the team captured fourth place, the highest finish ever for a Texas team in the AIAW national tournament at the University of Nebraska at Omaha. Winning its second consecutive state tournament in the fall of 1978, the softball team completed the 1978-79 year with seventy-eight wins and six losses and won the Women's College World Series (the AIAW national tournament) in Omaha to be named National Women's Softball Champions.

A new emphasis on athletics strengthened the University's basketball, gymnastic, swimming, tennis, and volleyball teams; and individual students and teams regularly broke University records. In addition, individual students claimed national titles in a number of track and field competitions. An athletic banquet was instituted in the spring of 1978 to recognize the accomplishments of student athletes.

A.E. (Bud) Green designed and made the University's first mace.

Antonio Brico was one of several outstanding artists who visited the campus as a part of the Diamond Jubilee and inaugural celebrations.

Expanded athletic programs encouraged volleyball and other sports. Track and field continued to bring national recognition, and the softball team won the national championship in 1979.

As extracurricular opportunities grew at a rapid pace, curricular changes enriched the academic offerings of the University even though TWU, like universities throughout the state, experienced limits on curricular expansion imposed by the Coordinating Board, Texas College and University System. In spite of the Board's insistence on no new medical schools, TWU Regents, President Huey, and other members and friends of the TWU community continued the quest for a medical school for almost a year following Dr. Guinn's death.

The *Lass-O* of September 10, 1976, reported the submission to the Coordinating Board of a plan for a TWU medical school with two components. On October 8, the Texas House Committee on Higher Education endorsed the creation of new medical schools in Fort Worth, Tyler, and the Rio Grande Valley without designating a university to operate the schools. Shortly before the Coordinating Board was to consider the proposal on October 15, TWU requested a postponement and revised its proposal to include a medical school with a single component in the Rio Grande Valley.

The *Lass-O* of March 10, 1977, reported, "Med school plan axed by board" at its March 8 meeting. The article explained that the program development committee of the Coordinating Board voted against the TWU proposal 5-2 with one abstention on March 7; and the full Board voted the following day 10-2 to reject the proposal. Arguing that "The Board has applied as double standard on occasion," Tony Bonilla of Corpus Christi voted for the proposal as did Marshall Formby of Plainview; and President Huey reminded the Board that it had approved two new medical schools during the period since 1973 when TWU was first told, "No new medical schools."[7]

Without Coordinating Board approval, bills already introduced in the Legislature to establish the school were declared obsolete; and the Chairman of the TWU Board of Regents Marcella D. Perry declared in the *Lass-O* of March 23, "We'll try again," indicating that the University was just "waiting until the time is ripe."

While waiting on this issue, however, TWU directed its efforts to other areas of curricular improvement. New courses ranged from seminars on women in history and literature to courses in camping, advanced canoeing, and scuba diving, to business internships. By the fall of 1977, nine TWU students were participating in aerospace studies and leadership training (AFROTC) at North Texas State University through an agreement between that university and TWU.

TWU awarded its first Ph.D. degree in reading at the 1976 spring commencement, its first Bachelor of Social Work degrees in May, 1977, its first degrees in managerial dietetics at the 1978 spring commencement, and its first Master of Fine Arts degree at the 1980 spring commencement.

For nontraditional offerings, TWU initiated both cooperative education and continuing education courses. The first cooperative education coordinator was employed in the fall of 1977. The original emphasis on providing students practical experience in merchandising women's apparel quickly expanded to include the areas of art, business, and textile science and clothing. Other areas were added, and the University established the Southwest Institute of Design to provide students professional experience and direct contact with top professionals in every aspect of design. The Institute includes textile research and design, fashion illustration, interior design, home furnishings, journalism, photography, and merchandising and marketing.

Following the appointment of a Continuing Education Council in the fall of 1978, the University employed a director of continuing education in January, 1979, and offered a wide range of cummunity courses ranging from black and white photography and conversational Spanish to rifle shooting and backgammon during the spring semester. Almost two hundred residents of the community, aged ten to sixty-five, participated in the courses.

Other changes affecting the academic life of the University were the institution of the 4.0 system of grading beginning in the fall of 1977 and the reorganization of two of the colleges of the University in 1978. The College of Arts and Sciences and the College of Fine Arts were replaced by the College of Humanities and Fine Arts (Departments of Art, English and Speech, Foreign Languages, Journalism and Broadcasting, and Music and Drama) and the College of Natural and Social Sciences (Departments of Biology, Business and Economics, Chemistry, Communication Science, History and Government, Mathematics and Physics, and Sociology and Social Work).

A major change in the scheduling of classes was the initiation of the option for the four-day class week during the fall, 1979, in an attempt to help commuting students alleviate increasing transportation costs and to offer greater flexibility in scheduling by increasing the options for concentrated classes on the week-ends and at night for working students. The four-day week option was introduced into the summer schedule in 1980 as was the new summer pattern which allowed for eleven-week as well as five-and-one-half-week courses.

Students continue to "learn by doing." Physical therapy students increase their awareness of the needs of handicapped persons. Dance students dance. And ceramics students convert their imagination to sculptured forms.

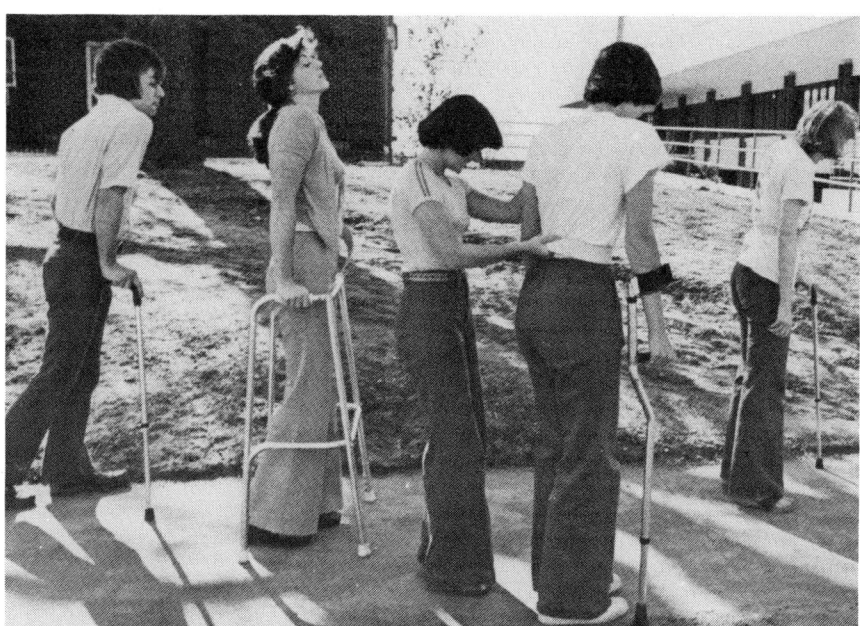

223

Accompanying academic and scheduling changes were major improvements in the physical plant of the University. As acting president, Dr. Huey had toured the campus to discover older residential units badly in need of refurbishing. She quickly ordered the repainting of Houston, Austin, Fitzgerald, Smith-Carroll, and Stoddard Halls along with new light fixtures and windowshades throughout and new carpeting in the hallways and living rooms. All student rooms in these halls were furnished with new pecan beds, chairs, and desks; and some lounges received new furniture. Although all the furnishings did not arrive until school had started in the 1976 fall semester, the new beds were installed and fix-up work was completed when the students returned in September.[8]

During the summer of 1976 the Houston Center, required major work after suffering more than $600,000 worth of damages during a flood on June 15. Water had accumulated in a service tunnel in an adjacent hospital, broken free, rushed into the dining room, and flooded it to near ceiling height before pouring into the basement parking area where it destroyed three university cars and damaged faculty automobiles. Both the kitchen and dining facilities and the lower areas of Jones Hall suffered extensive damage; and all electrical equipment—including elevators, air conditioners, and water distribution facilities—completely failed, requiring the evacuation of the residence hall and the interruption of classes. No persons were injured, however. Within five days classes had resumed, with students being transported by buses and station wagons between classes at the center and temporary living quarters at Rice University.

A federal grant made the emergency repairs possible; other repairs and rehabilitation funds came from the 65th Legislature, which met in 1977 and also appropriated funds for the renovation of the Nutrition, Textiles, and Human Development (NTHD) Building, the Music Building, and Old Main on the Denton campus. Appropriations of $708,741 for the NTHD Building, $801,500 for Old Main, and $523,600 for the Music Building made possible the installation of modern environmental systems, wiring, and plumbing, and limited decorative remodeling. The 66th Legislature appropriated $3.25 million in 1979 for rehabilitation of the Science Building and the Art Building on the Denton campus.

Along with the renovation came the construction or completion of buildings begun during the previous administration. The highrise Administration-Conference Tower (ACT) reached its full height of 232 feet and was topped out October 8, 1976. After a number of delays, occupancy

The latest high-rise building is the Administration-Conference Tower on the Denton campus.

of the building was effected in June, 1978; and the building was dedicated at the Diamond Jubilee Convocation the following fall.

Long hallways connect the building with the old Administration Building and with Hubbard Hall and extend eastward toward the Student Center. The halls provide lounge and meeting space for conferences and for students, and the hallway to Hubbard Hall includes work areas with computer terminals for students and faculty. The long second-floor extension includes offices for the University's information and computer services and a Digital Equipment Corporation System-20 (DEC 20) time-sharing computer. Floors three, five, and six are arranged for conferences and meetings held by groups from the University and from off campus. Floors seven through fourteen are administrative offices. The fifteenth floor holds the president's suite, and the sixteenth floor is set aside for the regents and for major University functions. The fourth and seventeenth floors house the mechanical equipment for the building—air conditioning and heating machinery, electrical equipment, and the works and West-minister chimes for the large clock that occupies each face of the tower at its top.

During the construction of the ACT Building, the University completed two smaller buildings, one on the Denton campus and one in Dallas. On October 6, 1977, TWU dedicated the new Classroom and Laboratory Building adjacent to Presbyterian Hospital at 8200 Walnut Hill Lane in North Dallas. Built at a cost of almost $2 million, the structure established a fourth campus for TWU, officially designated as the Institute of Health Sciences Building at Presbyterian Hospital of the TWU Dallas Center.

As the existing Inwood Center near Parkland Hospital reached its capacity of one thousand students, Presbyterian Hospital invited TWU to open a new center on a five-acre site which it agreed to lease to the University for ninety-nine years at a nominal rate. The Division of Nursing of the U.S. Department of Health, Education, and Welfare awarded a grant to finance seventy-five percent of the cost; and the Presbyterian Hospital Foundation covered the remainder of the cost through gifts.

Including a separate auditorium which accommodates 240 people, the three-story building contains 51,708 square feet to provide instructional space for four hundred students. Two floors were originally completed. The first floor includes classrooms for junior students, a competency lab, and a faculty lounge. The ground floor contains a classroom for seniors, an audio-visual laboratory, teachers' offices, and a library, reading room, and student lounge. Recessed into a wooded slope, the building is arranged so that a terrace overlooking a lake opens into the library.[9]

Two hundred fifteen students were assigned to the campus for the fall of 1977 when the building opened. Subsequent increases in enrollment there necessitated the completion of the third floor during the 1980 spring semester. This floor provides additional classroom, laboratory, and office space. Funds for its completion were provided by private donors and supporters of TWU.

On the Denton campus, the University dedicated a small Undergraduate Science Laboratory Building on January 26, 1978. Built immediately to the south of the NTHD Building, the simple rectangular structure contains two microbiology and two anatomy-physiology laboratories, each of which can accommodate twenty-four students at one time. Built at a cost of approximately $500,000 and containing some 9,650 square feet, the building serves approximately 350 undergraduate microbiology students and 650 to 700 undergraduate anatomy-physiology students per semester.

To guide future development of the Denton campus, the University commissioned the firm of Claudill, Rowlett, and Scott, Inc., to produce a ten-year master plan. Among the high priorities of the plan, which was

A second campus for the TWU Dallas Center opened in 1977 adjacent to the Presbyterian Hospital.

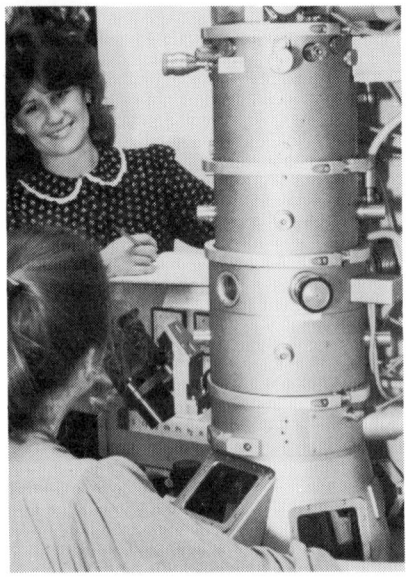

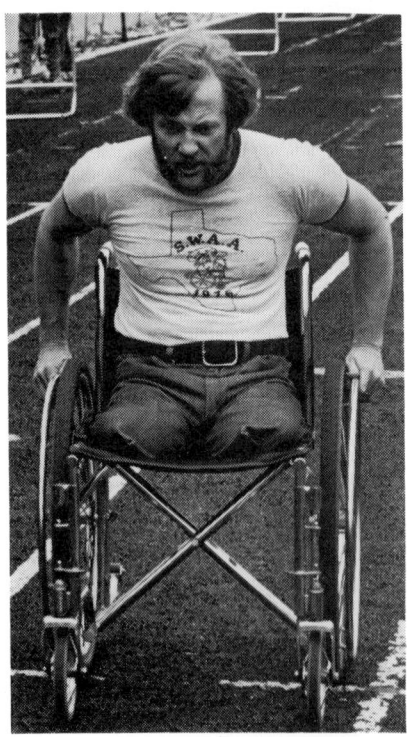

Diversity marks the modern campus. A golf course, an electron microscope, and facilities and activities for handicapped persons attract varied kinds of students and serve their needs.

unveiled in the fall of 1978, are the re-routing of Bell Avenue, which currently cuts through the campus, and the construction of a new library to be located near the eastern end of Dormitory Row and of a new activity center on the site of the Old SUB. The plan includes major provisions to beautify and unify the campus and make it comfortable and safe for student pedestrian traffic while providing adequate parking at convenient locations. Structures to be removed from the campus are the residence halls on Dormitory Row, which are no longer needed for residential use, and the old gymnasium. All plans are subject to the approval of the Coordinating Board and the receipt of legislative appropriations, but TWU Regents have adopted the plan as a guide.

Additions to the physical plant of the University which have been begun and completed during President Huey's administration are a golf club house and a large warehouse/service building, both of which are located in the southwest corner of the TWU Golf Course. O'Neil Ford, architect for the Little Chapel-in-the-Woods, has prepared a schematic design for the proposed library.

Inside the old and new and renovated buildings, new equipment has enhanced both instruction and the day-to-day operation of the University. New equipment added during the first four years of Dr. Huey's administration ranges from modern computerized offset printing equipment (a complete change from the letterpress system in use since the 1930s)[10] to a new five-rank, seven-stop mechanical action organ of the kind used by Bach; from a scanning electron microscope which allows the three-dimensional viewing of specimens to a new double harpsichord copied by William Dowd Company of Boston from an eighteenth-century French model.

Other improvements to the campus have ranged from the addition of four new lighted tennis courts to the removal of architectural barriers which hindered the movement of handicapped persons on campus and the addition of some one hundred new lights to add to both the safety and the beauty of the campus.

Because of plans for a new library building, the Library on the Denton campus has not experienced major growth or change in its physical facilities during Dr. Huey's administration. There has been a significant expansion of services and holdings, however. Computer connections with major data bases throughout the country offer bibliographic information quickly to students and faculty engaged in research. To complement the holdings of the TWU Library (more than 500,000 volumes in book form, 165,000 volumes on microfilm, and 3,000 periodical subscriptions), interlibrary loan agreements with a network of libraries throughout Texas make virtually unlimited materials available for research.

The new Woman's Collection is the largest of the Library's special collections. In addition to its cookbook and menu collection and its autographed copies of works by outstanding poets and novelists, the Woman's Collection contains five comprehensive microform collections—*The History of Women, The Gerritsen Collection of Women's History, Herstory,* the *Cornell University Collection of Women's Rights Pamphlets,* and the *Bibliography of American Women,* a microfilm list of some fifty thousand titles written by and about women between 1600 and 1900.

A second major collection was acquired during Dr. Huey's administration when the Organization of American States selected the TWU School of Library Science as the location for the Proyecto Leer Collection. The twenty-thousand-volume collection, which represents the best books available in Spanish and Spanish/English for children, is the primary resource for a future national research center on library materials for the Spanish speaking.

In addition to these special collections, TWU received legislative authorization signed by Governor William P. Clements in 1979 to create a Collection of the History of Texas Women. An integral part of the new collection will be the unique collection of gowns of the first ladies of Texas, which was gathered by the Texas Society of the Daughters of the American Revolution and donated to the University, and the collection of historical objects and archives of TWU which are now housed in Old Main.

The collection is characteristic of Dr. Huey's administration, which has been simultaneously a looking backward and a reaching forward. It was natural to pause and review the accomplishments of the University as it completed its first seventy-five years at the beginning of the administration of its seventh president. It was equally natural, although more difficult, to look to the future.

On January 30, 1979, having completed almost three years in the presidency and having guided TWU almost through the end of its seventy-fifth year of classes, President Huey addressed the TWU chapter of TACT, looking only briefly at the past before she outlined goals for the years which would lead to the University's centennial. Reaffirming her insistence upon maintaining the status of TWU as an institution primarily for women, she promised, "In the years ahead we will place emphasis on the recognition that TWU is a unique institution." Referring to rumors of consolidation with another institution, the President reminded listeners that such rumors had flourished since Bralley's administration. History shows, she said, "how long we have been able to resist our suitors."[12]

On her agenda for the future were the maintenance of the liberal arts as the center of preparation in all areas, the continued development of the physical facilities of the University—particularly the building of the new library as both the physical and the academic center of the campus—the development of increased flexibility in scheduling, the use of television in teaching, and a new emphasis on lifetime learning for all persons and on academic and extracurricular programs for older students.

The history of the next quarter century must now write itself, and TWU must make its place in that history. It seems most appropriate that the University enter the future as an aggregation of pioneers. Dr. Huey announced in her Founders' Day radio broadcast of February 11, 1979, that TWU had adopted the pioneer as the school symbol in response to requests from students, faculty, and alumnae. Reminding her audience, "TWU has always been a pioneering institution—leading the state and even the nation in developing new educational programs," the President promised, "Please know that we regard the pioneer not just as a symbol of past accomplishments but as a promise that we will continue always to seek new horizons."

Students plant redbud trees for future beauty.

The University's oldest and newest buildings stand in close proximity.

[1]The *Lass-O* of March 23, 1977, reported that the Faculty Council had voted to resurrect December commencements both as a convenience to graduates and as a means of accommodating commencement audiences which had outgrown the Hubbard Oval.

[2]The award was named to commemorate Maria Lucrezia Piscopia Cornaro, the first woman to receive a doctorate. TWU's Diamond Jubilee coincided with the three hundredth anniversary of her receipt of the degree from the University of Padua on June 25, 1678.

The University also established a second award during the Diamond Jubilee. The annual Texana Award, given ''in recognition of achievements contributing to the advancement of Texas,'' was first presented at the spring convocation on April 6, 1978. Jacqueline Donahue, editor-in-chief of *Fashion Showcase* received the first award.

[3]The convocation was the first to be held off the Denton campus.

[4]Mamie Walker, alumna and former professor of creative writing at the University, wrote the alma mater sometime before 1918. Jane Ward Poole, a 1946 graduate wrote ''To The Texas Woman's University'' as a class song for stunts.

[5]Members of the University community gave Dr. Huey a silver tea and coffee service to commemorate her inauguration.

[6]The dance group was only the second university dance group from the United States ever invited to perform for the Brazilian professional organizations.

[7]The Coordinating Board voted on this same day (March 8, 1977) to change Texas A&M's ''program of medicine'' to a full college.

[8]Students were pleased with the improvements and with the creation of the new recreation area on the second floor of the Student Center (They had earlier asked for basement space in the Old SUB). According to the *Lass-O* of September 22, ''Praise, suggestions and complaints

were voiced, but nobody didn't like the new student recreation area'' where students could play pool, foosball, and electronic games; listen to the juke box; and watch television.

[9]The F. W. and Bessie A. Dye Foundation provided a grant of $50,000 to purchase books and periodicals for the library which has been named the Dye Memorial Library. On October 1, 1978, in conjunction with the first of a series of Sunday afternoon musical recitals to be held at the campus, the University dedicated the library and a mural for the student lounge. The black and white acrylic montage, which includes scenes from the four campuses of TWU, was created by TWU graduate student Mara Smith.

[10]The modernization of the printing facilities made possible the reestablishment of the TWU Press which has since published two books. The first, *Trees, Prairies, and People,* is a hardbound history of the federal shelterbelt project, written by TWU Provost of the University General Divisions Wilmon H. Droze. Graduate student Velda Newcomer wrote the second book, *Texas' First Ladies,* a paperback guide to TWU's collection of gowns of the first ladies of Texas. The book is illustrated with both a line drawing and a color photograph of each of the gowns in the collection.

[11]The University's determined efforts to assist handicapped persons is reflected in numerous ways. An interdisciplinary program, called Creative Arts for the Handicapped, provides in-service training to assist teachers and other personnel in involving handicapped persons in art activities in schools and communities. Based in the Department of Physical Education, the program encompasses art, dance, drama, music, and the theater.

TWU received the Governor's Citation in 1979 as the Outstanding State Agency in the Employment of the Handicapped. Dr. Claudine J. Sherrill, Professor of Physical Education, simultaneously received the Governor's Citation as the Outstanding State Employee for her work in numerous projects designed to advance handicapped persons.

[12]A bill to merge the Texas Woman's University and North Texas State University was introduced in the Legislature in 1979 but died in committee.

Selected Bibliography *

Balkus, Mary Patricia. "History and Development of the Modern Dance Group of the Texas Woman's University from 1936 through 1965: Its Scope of Influence and Contributions to the Understanding and Appreciation of Dance as a Contemporary Art Form." M.A. thesis, Texas Woman's University, 1965.

Bates, Ed. F. *History and Reminiscences of Denton County.* Denton, Texas: McNitzky Printing Co., 1918.

Bellamy, Caroline Barbee. "A Study of the Significant Changes in the Growth and Development of the Texas State College for Women." M.A. thesis, Texas State College for Women (TWU), 1939.

Cornell, Charlotte. "Survey of Graduate Alumnae of the Texas State College for Women, 1904-1921." M.A. thesis, Texas State College for Women (TWU), 1941.

Holt, Mildred Pearce. "A History of the College of Industrial Arts." M.A. thesis, University of Texas at Austin, 1926.

Hubbard, Louis Herman. *Recollections of a Texas Educator.* Salado, Texas: n.p., 1964.

[James, Eleanor.] *A Summary History of the University, 1901-1961.* Denton: Texas Woman's University, 1961.

Lunday, Ella Ernestine. "The Biography of Francis Marion Bralley, LL.D." M.A. thesis, University of Texas at Austin, 1925.

[Taylor, A. Elizabeth.] *A Summary History of Texas Woman's University, 1901-1971.* Denton: Texas Woman's University, 1971.

White, Edmund Valentine. *Historical Record of the Texas State College for Women: The First Forty-five Years, 1903-1948.* Texas State College for Women Bulletin, no. 364, December 1, 1948.

_____. *Historical Sketch of the Texas State College for Women: The First Thirty-three Years, 1903-1936.* Texas State College for Women Bulletin, no. 217, November 15, 1936.

_____. *Lengthening Shadows or From Country School to College Campus: An Autobiography of E.V. White.* Denton, Texas: By the Author, n.d.

*Works listed here have proved valuable complements to the information gathered from a complete review of all official publications (catalogues and bulletins) of TWU since its beginning as the Girls Industrial College, from a thorough study of all issues of the TWU *Daily Lass-O* and all volumes of the *Daedalian,* and from a search of other archival and file materials generously made available through the TWU Library, the TWU Alumnae Association, individuals, and various administrative offices of the University. These sources, the heart of the study, are acknowledged in the text where appropriate.

Index

*illustration

*illustration   235

*illustration

236

science, 7, 8, 12, 20, 83*, 106, 107, 124, 125, 165
Science Building, 46, 80, 81*, 158, 224
Seagle, Oscar, 60, 67
Sebesta, Lou Ann, 176
Sehmann, Betty Jane, 105
Seiders, A. J., 6
senior houses, 48*, 50*, 72, 141, 159, 187
Shackleford Hall, 78
Shawn, Ted, 75
Shelton, Natalena, 161
Shepperd, John Ben, 134
Sherman, W. C., 197
Sherniavsky Trio, 60
Sherrill, Claudine J., 229
Sherrill, Joseph, 157
Shivers, Allan, 117, 132, 133, 156, 157
Shurtleff, Arthur A., 64
Simmons College, 127
Skinner, Cornelia Otis, 95
Sloan, Margaret, 193
Smith-Carroll Hall, 16, 26, 32, 49*, 77, 78*, 97, 117, 126, 145-6*, 150, 155, 159, 224
Smith College, 127
Smith, E. C., 9
Smith, Mrs. Gessner T., 6
Smith, Mara, 229
Smith, Preston, 208, 209
Smith, Tracey, 201
social work, see Sociology and Social Work
Sociology and Social Work, 56, 94, 107, 112, 124, 125, 142, 158, 159, 177, 197, 198, 199, 211, 222, 223
softball, 221, 222*
Solberg, Helen, 98
sororities, 59-60, 66, 143, 218
South, Gertrude, 67
Southern Methodist University, 99, 126
Southwest Institute of Design, 221, 223
Southwestern Baptist Theological Seminary, 126
Spalding, Albert, 60
Spann, Jo Ann, 161
Special Education, see Education
speech, see English and Speech, Music and Drama, Communication Sciences, or Journalism and Broadcasting
Spellman, Coreen, 98, 151, 154, 155
Sprague, Amelia B., 6
Stanley, Helen, 60
Stark, H. Lutcher, 134, 137, 172, 178, 182, 184, 186
Stark, Nelda Childers (Mrs. H. Lutcher), 134*, 137, 157, 172*, 178, 181, 182, 184, 186
Stark Hall, 181*, 182, 189, 206, 207, 208, 209*
Stark Laboratory for Human Nutrition Research, 137, 157-8
Stark, Ramona, 181*
Steele, Audrey, 220
Steinem, Gloria, 193*
Stephens, Maryann, 142
Stevenson, Coke, 123
Stoddard, Helen M., 2*, 3, 9, 16, 26, 85
Stoddard Hall, 16, 19, 20, 21, 22, 31, 32, 34, 45*, 48*, 59, 80*, 92, 155, 159, 160, 224

Stout, M.S., 9
Stovall, R.M., 202
Stover, B. J., 185
Stubbs, Mrs. Van Hook, 147
Student Center, 126, 183, 184, 206, 207*, 208, 228
student government, 50, 51, 65, 88, 92, 144, 190, 194, 211, 218
Student Union Building, 88, 92, 99, 113*, 119, 125, 149, 159, 182, 226
Stunts, 52, 53*, 59, 118, 144*, 174*, 184*, 195, 211*, 218, 228
Sullivan, Anne, 92
Swank, Arch B., 91, 150, 160
Switzer, Rebecca, 74

T
Tagore, Rabindramath, 60
Tarleton State University, 37
Tate, Sammy, 98
Taylor, A. Elizabeth, 219
Taylor, Joe, 202
telegraphy, 41, 56
Texana Award, 228
Texas A&M University, 1, 9, 24, 29, 34, 37, 40, 56, 57, 64, 93, 103, 120*, 121*, 127, 132, 157, 173, 174*, 201, 202
Texas Christian University, 51, 126
Texas College of Osteopathic Medicine, 203, 205
Texas Congress of Mothers, 42, 46
Texas Farmer's Congress, 21, 25
Texas Federation of Women's Clubs, 9, 12, 21, 24, 53, 85, 94, 97, 125, 147, 173
Texas Medical Center, 141, 168, 179, 182, 186
Texas Opera Theater, 221
Texas Tech University, 37, 157, 196
Texas Woman Suffrage Association, 59
Texas Woman's Press Association, 9
TWU Foundation, 131, 134*, 135, 147, 157, 159
TWU Research Institute, 150, 166*, 167*, 184*
textile science, see NTHD
Thomas, Rosser, 2*, 3, 9
Tolstoi, Ilya, 60
Tomkievicz, Shirley Abbott, 194
Tompkins, John, 217
track and field, 51, 196, 197*, 221, 222*
Trail, Mary Jane, 104
Trent, Robert, 161
Trinity University, 52
Tripp, Clarence A., 34
Tsiania, 60
Tuggle, Sarah Anderson, 94
Tureck, Rosalyn, 221
Turner, Mrs. E.P., 74
Turrentine Hall, 159
Tuttle, Mary Louise, 6, 12

U
Undergraduate Science Laboratory Building, 210, 225
uniforms, 25*, 26*, 27*, 60, 68*, 72*, 87-8*, 101, 186
United States Marine Band, 75
University of California, 25, 110

University of Chihuahua, 221
University General Divisions, 211
University of Kansas, 109
University of Oklahoma, 37, 121
University of Southern California, 110
University of Texas at Arlington, 37, 197
University of Texas at Austin, 9, 24, 29, 39, 40, 55, 69, 70, 74, 75, 109, 120, 121, 127, 132, 157, 185, 197
University of Texas at Dallas, 197
University of Washington, 109

V
Vassar College, 127
Vidas, Raoul, 72
vocational courses, 41, 55, 84
Vogue-Butterick Patterns, 221
Volk, Harold, 134*, 157
Vose, George P., 157, 158, 184

W
Wagner, Frances McDowell, 107*
Waldrop, Lenore, 2
Walker, Lucile Hill (Mrs. J. W.), 157
Walker, Mamie, 146, 228
Wallace, Mary Esther, 105, 126
Waln, Nora, 147
Ward, Ada, 72
Warde, Frederick, 17
Warren, Isabel, 82
Washington, George, 89
Watts, Hazel L., 105
Webb, Esther, 92
Webb, Walter Prescott, 95
Wellesley College, 64, 127
Werrenrath, Reinald, 60
Westcourt, Fred W., 88, 89, 151
West Texas State University, 55
WFAA, 85, 94, 125
Wham, George Sims, 157
Wheeler Hall, 78
White, E.V., 39, 40, 55, 63, 64, 65, 67, 69, 83
White, Mark, 209
White, William Allen, 67
White, W.T., 159
Paul Whiteman's Orchestra, 75
Whitten, Harriet V., 6, 35
Wiesemann, Carl, 125
Wiley, Autrey Nell, 95, 103
Willard Hall, 187
Williams, Blanche, 126
Williams, C. A., 9
Williams, Frank L., 186
Williams, Jack K., 219
Willis, Doyle, 203, 206
Wilmans, Edith Eunice Therrel, 123
Wilson, Lucy, 105
Wilson, R. J., 9
Wilson, Will, 168
Winston, Betty, 98
Winthrop College, 127
Witherspoon, C. F., 9
Woman's College of North Carolina, 127
Woman's Day Colloquium, 195, 206
Woman's Shakespeare Club of Denton, 3
Women's Army Auxiliary Corps, 124, 125*

*illustration
237

*illustration

MARKING A TRAIL IN A PATHLESS WILDERNESS, PRESSING FORWARD WITH UNSWERVING COURAGE, SHE MET EACH UNTRIED SITUATION WITH A RESOURCEFULNESS EQUAL TO THE NEED. WITH A GLAD HEART SHE BROUGHT TO HER FRONTIER FAMILY HER HOMELAND'S CULTURAL HERITAGE. WITH DELICATE SPIRITUAL SENSITIVENESS SHE ILLUMINED THE DULLNESS OF ROUTINE AND THE LONELINESS OF ISOLATION WITH BEAUTY AND WITH LIFE ABUNDANT. AND WITHAL SHE LIVED WITH CASUAL UNAWARENESS OF HER VALUE TO CIVILIZATION. SUCH WAS THE PIONEER WOMAN, THE UNSUNG SAINT OF THE NATION'S IMMORTALS.

JESSIE H. HUMPHRIES